新东方
NEW ORIENTAL

D0088690

TOEFL iBT
Vocabulary Classified 词汇
词以类记

■ 张红岩 编著

群言出版社

图书在版编目(CIP)数据

词以类记：TOEFL® iBT 词汇 / 张红岩编著. —北京：
群言出版社
ISBN 978-7-80080-634-6

Ⅰ. 词... Ⅱ. 张... Ⅲ. 英语—词汇—高等教育—
自学参考资料 Ⅳ. H313

中国版本图书馆 CIP 数据核字 (2006) 第 132519 号

责任编辑	周　雯	
封面设计	耿　辉	
出版发行	群言出版社	
地　　址	北京东城区东厂胡同北巷 1 号	
邮政编码	100006	
联系电话	65263345　65265404	
电子信箱	qunyancbs@dem-league. org. cn	
印　　刷	北京汇林印务有限公司	
经　　销	全国新华书店	
版　　次	2006 年 11 月第 1 版　2007 年 3 月第 3 次印刷	
开　　本	880×1230　　1/32	
印　　张	13. 25	
字　　数	347 千	
书　　号	ISBN 978-7-80080-634-6	
定　　价	35. 00 元	

新东方 NEW ORIENTAL 图书策划委员会

主任　俞敏洪

委员　（按姓氏笔划为序）

王　强　　王文山

包凡一　　仲晓红

汪海涛　　周成刚

徐小平　　钱永强

铁　岭　　窦中川

作者自介

　　自幼随父母拓荒于大兴安岭，长于辽西重镇兴城。求学乃率性而为，先后修习英语、计算机和工商管理三门工具，尝以五年青春韶华，挥洒新东方讲坛，弟子逾二十万，所著《TOEFL 词汇精选》，竟蒙数十万众青年才俊错爱。尝游学欧洲，亲历全球顶级 MBA 教育，蒙国际友人抬爱，破百年惯例，以华人身份当选法国高商（HEC）MBA 学生会主席，更深了解所谓欧洲主流社会，深悟英语实乃一工具，法国人多数掌握，而选择弃之不用。安能使国人有朝一日既可摒弃英语，又可屹立于世界民族之林，思前想后，唯有一解，先以高效方式征服英语，方可希冀某日凌驾其上，乃以语言巨人之态，屹立世界之东方。特盼读者以此为目的修习此书。

前　言

　　屈指算来，从最初踏上新东方TOEFL讲坛至今，十年时光，稍纵即逝。当年在新东方课堂上孜孜不倦的耕耘者，有的最终留学了，现在"海归"或"海待"了，而留守者也已经做到单位的中高层了。无论是教者还是学者，回首那段倾力学习TOEFL的日子，均感慨万千，回看人生奋斗的轨迹，徒生"人生漫长，关键处只有几步！"的感慨。留学是一个年轻人生命中的一件大事，它确实改变了很多人的人生轨迹。在我们国家日益向大国转变的今天，我们可以非常理性地预见，在祖国未来的发展中，将有相当多的具有海外留学或工作经验的人成为各行各业的领头人。只要留学这件事情是一个正确的选择，则帮助大家准备留学这件事情就值得我们付出宝贵的时光去做。

　　本书的出版，经过了作者再三的琢磨，作为一个以英语教育为价值体现的教育者，我希望通过这些经过岁月琢磨的文字，给正在经历者以深刻的启迪，让他们能够沿着成功者的足迹，顺利快速前行，这个心愿一部分表现为这本不断与时俱进的TOEFL词汇书，帮助大家通过TOEFL中最根本的词汇关；另一半表现为"新TOEFL作文实战技巧——《十天搞定TOEFL作文》"，以图帮助有一些写作基础的同学快速突破TOEFL中最难的写作关。

　　考试的形式决定考生学习的要点，从短期讲TOEFL iBT的考试方式增加了考生获得高分的难度，从长期讲对所有人却是一件好事。在巴黎高商（HEC）留学期间，我的班级里有200多名来自42个国家的中高层经理人，70％课程用英语授课，30％用法语授课，班上的中国学生的TOEFL和GMAT分数虽然都很高，课上主动发言者却很少，小组讨论礼让三先，小组报告最多写初稿，留待Native Speaker完善，类似情况，在欧美课堂中非常之多。导致这种情况主要有两个原因：一是我国大学阶段英语教育对学生学术性听力技能、实际口语交流和写作技能培养的匮乏造成了多数考生英语实际应用能力不高的局面；二是有些为考生提供考前培训的机构以考试为指向标。以往TOEFL口语是可选的，听力内容长期以单句或短对话为主要内容，听力和写作从不结合，这些考核方式最终决定了没有人会为考生切实提高他们在实际学习或工作中的交流能力负责任。TOEFL iBT的考核方式最终要求考生要切实提高听说读写的综合实力，并把听与写有机地结合，这对于考生未来胜任留学生活是一个很好的导向，对于培训师来说坚定了他们切实提高学生真实英语水平的决心。

针对TOEFL iBT的词汇书必将以下面的侧重点来适应最新的考试形式：

1、词汇学习需要兼顾听力、口语、写作多方面需求

因为听力部分加入了针对大段学术性讲座内容的考核，写作中增加了综合写作（Integrated Writing），所以不能再靠以往所谓的经验总结，比如听到"concert"就选"wonderful"，听到"movie"就选"awful"等技巧来解决。再也不可以按照课堂老师安排的人为分割来破坏语言学习本身的一致性和整合性。我们在学习词汇时，不只要培养看到一个词能够理解的能力，还要注重培养听到这些词汇后能够马上反应出其意义的能力，因此词汇书的配套音频显得比以往更加重要。

2、分类记忆词汇方法最适合TOEFL iBT词汇学习需要

对于听力中的short lecture来说，需要具备听懂各种可能的学科中的常用词汇的能力，学习和记忆这些词汇的最好方法是分学科集中完成，在按照字母顺序排列或随机组合次序排列的词汇书中，要实现这一点非常困难。这不是一个普通的词汇书编排问题，而是一个方法的问题。因为实现按学科分类编排词汇需要相当的时间和精力投入，并且从选择哪些学科、词汇到把它们归结到不同学科中去需要的是对TOEFL考试本身的深刻了解和像小区环卫工人一样的辛勤工作和可贵的务实精神。只有经过这样的工作，所出的产品才能够真正节省学习者宝贵的时间，提高效率，早日突破词汇关。

3、分类记忆词汇是适合成年人短期记忆大量词汇的重要方法

分类记忆单词不仅非常契合iBT考试的需要，还有助于快速、系统地记忆词汇。成年人记忆单词时的逻辑和分类意识是非常强的，有意识地利用这些特点来记忆单词是提高效率的关键。以往我针对词汇量较大的学生做过的调查表明，所有词汇量较高的学习者都是把词汇成串记忆或关联记忆的，他们大脑中词汇的

存储方式绝对不是点状的，而是网络化的，其中按学科分类和按意群分类是最主要的关联记忆方式。在已往的TOEFL授课中，学生在课上几乎要花30~50％的时间去记录成组的单词，但由于授课任务较重，讲师往往没有时间做系统归纳，所以课堂上讲师也只能针对部分词汇使用这种记忆法。

留学回国后我的大部分时间用来做针对中国学生英语教育与测试的研究，在经过对TOEFL iBT进行深入研究后，发现这种分学科、分意群记忆TOEFL词汇的意义非常重大。在经过近一年的准备后，将全部TOEFL词汇按照此思路编排的系统工程今天终于可以实现。

4、解决阅读中的词汇问题是本词汇书的一个主要任务，尤其是针对词汇题

附录中总结了截至iBT之前的经典TOEFL词汇题，总计400道，在学习中建议考生一定要系统做一遍，这部分题目的命中率很高，经验中，还没有一次TOEFL考试全部考核400题之外的词汇题。

附录一 提供了按照字母次序进行排列的顺序表，以便学习者查找。
附录二 阅读必备重要词组，包含对文章理解比较重要的和考核过的词组。
附录三 经典词汇400题，包含更新到iBT考试前的命中率较高的词汇题。

本书采用分学科、分意群的编排和记忆方法，与听力、阅读、写作三部分高度契合，是获得TOEFL iBT高分的重要手段。

本书对词汇的取舍、词义的选择建立在作者在新东方讲坛高强度授课中培养出的对TOEFL近20年来400多篇阅读文章的透彻把握之上，这些教学经验使作者敏感地体验到TOEFL核心词汇及其词义在近些年的逐步演化，词汇考核方法的变化和词汇考核重心的转移。 对词汇进行精选不仅需要非常熟悉目前的TOEFL考试，还需要深入研究大多数学习者目前词汇的掌握状况。

本书例句绝大多数摘选自《美国最佳例句词典》，这些例句能够提供独立的小语境帮助学习者深刻理解词义和用法。这就使单词学习成为一个相对独立的过程，避免了因为直接摘录TOEFL阅读文章的句子而让学习者在真题演习中产生"似曾相识"之感，进而影响了自我评测的客观性。

本书的编写过程，不仅受益于过去十年对TOEFL的大规模教学与研究的经验，也包含众多网友、已往的学生的智力贡献，在此表示深深感谢；感谢许寻、孙艳丽两位对本书的编辑工作做出的重要贡献；感谢新东方大愚文化传播有限

公司对我本人长期的支持和厚爱，这个做事一丝不苟的团队为英语图书出版事业树立了一个典范。

作为一个从事英语教学与研究的教育者和一个已经完成了留学生涯的过来者，我可以很负责任地告诉本书的学习者：本书所记载的词汇会是你留学生涯中应用最广泛的词汇，他们会出现在你要读到的课本中，你要参加的课堂讨论中，你要完成的毕业论文中。TOEFL词汇不同于应试技巧，后者在你的留学生活中不再有效。它也不同于GRE词汇，只在你今生今世考GRE时用得到。坦白地说，你在踏上留学征程前再也不会有机会这么认真地吸纳比TOEFL词汇更有用的词汇了。同时，TOEFL iBT考试的合理学习周期也决定了你只能采用背单词的方式迅速达到其词汇量的要求。明确了TOEFL词汇的意义和学习方法，你现在唯一需要做的就是：20~30天，学完此书中的词汇！

欢迎大家对本书提出宝贵的完善意见，敬请登陆作者个人网站(www.zhanghongyan.net)进行实时探讨，并获得可能的更新信息。

张红岩

利用本书记忆 TOEFL 词汇的方法

学习过程中请把握一些基本原则：

1. **少量多次**：正常情况是一天学习一课核心词汇，约 60 个词左右，这比较符合认知习惯，不可贪多；假如一天背单词的时间是两个小时，最好分成几次实现，如果能利用各种可能的时间记忆，效果更好。

2. **主次分明**：初记时每个单词都应仔细看一遍，即使是较熟悉的词汇也可能在 TOEFL 中考到它不常见的用法。在此基础上，标记出每课中较生疏的词汇，以便复习时重点记忆。

3. **学而时习**：开始背新一课前应复习以前背过的词汇，用卡片盖住本书右半部分，只看左面词汇做词义回想。如有以下情况更需要花一点时间，参照相关部分复习：阅读中或做题时遇见了曾背过的词汇，却忘了什么意思；一些比较接近的词汇经常在头脑中纠缠不清；背新单词时联想到了其他词汇，却一时想不起来具体的拼写。

4. **联想记忆**：同义词联想的思维模式是 TOEFL 考试要求的，学员每学一个新词，都要尽量想想是否学过它的同义词，它的同义词是哪些，切忌懒惰；将同类词汇一起记忆，比如背到"捕食者"(predator)时，你也应该联想到"被捕食者"(prey)。本书正是按照这种记忆规则来安排单词的顺序，因此只要认真遵循本书提供的记忆规律，必能事半功倍。

5. **背与练结合**：单词背到一定阶段，就应做一些附录中的精选词汇题，作为阶段成果检验，即便做得很差，也可以激励你。

6. **研习词根、词缀**：记忆一定数量的词根、词缀不仅可以加深理解记忆，还可以培养大家根据词根、词缀推测词义的能力。只要你花时间研读，就会有所收获。

7. **结合听力资料记忆**：已往的学习者反映，结合配套听力资料背单词可以实现最佳的记忆效果。其方法为：每天背完既定的单词后，利用一切空闲时间，比如在公交车上、睡前进行复习，听的时候要快速回想单词的汉语意思，努力做到在听到汉语朗读前或同时想起该单词的含义。

本书体例说明

本书共收录 4,200 个核心词汇,是 TOEFL 历次考试中的高频词汇,是理解 TOEFL 文章和解决 TOEFL iBT 听力长文章的必备基础。

1. 词语选择:收录历届 TOEFL 考试中的重要词汇。对于不影响理解的偏难词汇,不予收录,以减轻考生不必要的负担。

2. 音标选用:普遍使用美式音标,如"process"英音音标[ˈprəuses],而我们使用的是美音的 [ˈprɔses]。出现一词多音的,则分别列出,如:alternate *n*. [ˈɔːltənit] alternate *v*. [ˈɔːltəneit]。

3. 汉语释义:每个单词都列出它在 TOEFL 考试中常考到的词义和词性。

4. 同义词:TOEFL 阅读中考核词汇是以同义词替换的方式进行的,因此本书对于文章中可能以词汇题方式考核到的词汇均列出了同义词。这些同义词中有一部分是 TOEFL 考试已往考过的,还有一部分是扩充的。对于那些没有给出同义词的词汇,多数情况下只需要大家识记,今后在文章中见到时认识就可以了,一般不会考到。

5. 例句:含多个词义的重要词汇一般都配有一个或多个例句。仔细体会词汇在例句中的用法,对于阅读和写作均有益处。本书选用的例句部分来源于国外的优秀辞典,一部分来自作者的教学笔记。

目　录

❖ 现实 ❖

❖ 心理 ❖

❖ 行为 ❖

❖ 语言 ❖

❖ 属性 ❖

❖ 状态 ❖

iBT
TOEFL
按学科分类
Subjects

地理

insular [ˈinsjulə] *adj.* 海岛的 保守的

【记】insul(岛)＋ar

island [ˈailənd] *n.* 岛，岛屿，岛状物(孤立状态的物)，安全岛

【例】coral *island* *n.* 珊瑚岛；continental *island* 陆边岛

peninsula [piˈninsjulə] *n.* 半岛

【记】比较insular(海岛的)

islet [ˈailit] *n.* 小岛

marine [məˈriːn] *adj.* 海的(marine, deanic)；

海上的；近海的

【记】mari(海)＋ine

【例】Human beings are natural enemies of *marine* mammals.

maritime [ˈmæritaim] *adj.* 海的(marine, oceanic)；海上的；近海的

【记】mari(海)＋time

moist [moist] *adj.* 湿润的，多雨的(damp, humid)

ledge [ledʒ] *n.* 暗礁

【记】联想"l"加edge(边)

oasis [əuˈeisis] *n.* (沙漠中的)绿洲

【例】The travellers were saved when they finally found an *oasis*.

tide [taid] *n.* 潮汐

ebb [eb] *vi.* 退潮

【例】The water washed up on the shore, then slowly *ebbed* away.

continent [ˈkɔntinənt] *n.* 大陆

terrestrial [tiˈrestriəl] *adj.* 领土的

【例】*terrestrial* heat 地面干扰；*terrestrial* magnetism 地磁，地磁学

outskirt [ˈautskəːt] *n.* 外边，郊区(surrounding)

region [ˈriːdʒən] *n.* 地区，领域(zone, area, field, domain)

endemic [enˈdemik] *adj.* 地方的(native)

【例】This disease is *endemic* to the southerners, and will not spread in the cold north.

cosmopolitan [ˌkɔzməˈpɔlitən] *adj.* 全世界的(global)

【记】cosm(宇宙)＋oplitan

【例】The farmer was unused to the *cosmopolitan* ways of life in a large city.

subterrane [ˈsʌbtərein] *n.* 地下(underground)

subterranean [sʌbtəˈreiniən] *adj.* 地下的

cavern [ˈkævən] *n.* 大山洞，大洞穴

【记】比较cave(洞)

【例】Inside the *cavern* were the remnants of an ancient fire.

flaw [flɔ:] *n.* 裂隙

【例】The *flaw* in your theory is that you didn't account for gravity.

cleft [kleft] *n.* 裂缝(crevice)

crevice [ˈkrevis] *n.* 裂缝，破口(rift, slit)

【例】The rain came in through a *crevice* in the cabin wall.

gap [gæp] *n.* 裂口(opening)

【例】Generation *gap* lies between parents and children.

zone [zəun] *n.* 带(region, area)

【例】time *zone* 时区

equator [iˈkweitə] *n.* 赤道

【例】It is warmer near the *equator*.

longitude [ˈlɔndʒitju:d] *n.* 经度

【记】long(长)+itude→经度

altitude [ˈæltitju:d] *n.* (尤指海拔)高度，高处(海拔甚高的地方)

latitude [ˈlætitju:d] *n.* 纬度

【记】lati(阔)+tude→纬度

meridian [məˈridiən] *n.* 子午线，正午

subsidiary [səbˈsidjəri] *n.* 支流(branch)

【记】sub(下面)+sidi(坐)+ary→坐在下面辅助的

【例】He followed the *subsidiary* to trace its origin.

Antarctic [æntˈɑ:ktik] *adj.* 南极的，南极地带的

Antarctica [æntˈɑ:ktikə] *n.* 南极洲

Arctic [ˈɑ:ktik] *adj.* 北极的，北极区的 *n.* 北极，北极圈

coastland [ˈkəustlænd] *n.* 沿海岸地区

hemisphere [ˈhemisfiə] *n.* 半球

contour [ˈkɔntuə] *n.* 轮廓；海岸线(outline, profile)

【记】tour(旅行)

【例】The artist accentuated the model's *contours*.

geography [dʒiˈɔgrəfi] *n.* 地理学，地理

horizon [həˈraizn] *n.* 地平线

lowland [ˈləulənd, -ˈlænd] *n.* 低地，苏格兰低地 *adj.* 低地的

plain [plein] *n.* 平原，草原

strait [streit] *n.* 地峡，海峡

channel ['tʃænl] *n.* 海峡，水道，沟

valley ['væli] *n.* (山)谷，流域

volcano [vɔl'keinəu] *n.* 火山

plateau [plæ'təu] *n.* 高原

【记】plat(平)＋eau

basin ['beisn] *n.* 盆地

【例】The Amazon *basin* covers a vast amount of land.

navigation [ˌnævi'geiʃən] *n.* 航海

ranges [reindʒiz] *n.* 射程表尺数

salinity [sə'liniti] *n.* 盐分，盐度

sediment ['sedimənt] *n.* 沉淀物，沉积

elevation [ˌeli'veiʃən] *n.* 高地，正面图，海拔

formation [fɔː'meiʃən] *n.* 形成，构成

geothermy [dʒi'ɔθəmi] 地热

terrain ['terein] *n.* 地形

topography [tə'pɔgrəfi] *n.* 地形学

tropical ['trɔpikl] *adj.* 热带的

tropics ['trɔpiks] *n.* (天球的)回归线，热带

temperate ['tempərit] *adj.* (气候)温和的

【例】*temperate* latitudes 温带地区

Victory won't come to me unless I go to it.

—*Moore*

胜利不会向我走来，我必须自己走向胜利。

——穆尔

地 质

　　TOEFL 考试中地质学科文章一直是个难点，不妨从这里入手。

　　（请想象赵忠祥在"动物世界"里的配音，按其语调默读下面的文字。）在茫茫的 TOEFL 辞海中，地质学的内容占据了相当的比重。它的主体在于学术界流传已久的板块构造学说（plate tectonics）和大陆漂移学说（continental drift）。想要了解板块构造学说，我们需要先复习一下高中地理的一些常识：我们居住的星球，其外壳被称作 （crust），下面的一层被称作地幔，最中心的部分叫作地核（core）。由地壳（crust）和它下面比较硬的那部分地幔（mantle）构成了岩石圈（lithosphere）。板块构造学说的主体是板块（plate），板块之间的边界（boundaries）有两种：海中的山脊（mid-ocean ridge），潜沉区（subduction zone）。板块与板块之间有四种相对运动关系：收拢、汇聚（converge），分开（split apart），A 潜入到 B 的下方 （A dive under B），互相擦肩而过（slide past each other）。两个板块向相同方向收拢会产生碰撞，形成山脉（mountains）；两个板块向相反方向分离就在其中间产生了海洋（Oceans）。

vein	[vein] *n.* 矿脉	
pit	[pit] *n.* 坑，地坑(hole)	
borehole	['bɔːhəul] *n.* 钻孔	
pit	[pit] *n.* 煤矿	
quartz	[kwɔːts] *n.* 石英	
marble	['mɑːbl] *n.* 大理石	
gem	[dʒem] *n.* 宝石(jewel, precious stone)	
fieldstone	['fiːldstəun] *n.*(建筑用的)散石，大卵石	
emerald	['emərəld] *n.* 祖母绿，翡翠，绿宝石	
wiikite	['viːkait] 杂铌矿	
granite	['grænit] *n.* 花岗岩	
lead	[led] *n.* 铅	
limestone	['laimstəun] *n.* 石灰石	
lava	['lɑːvə] *n.* 熔岩，火山岩	
ruby	['ruːbi] *n.* 红宝石	
bonanza	[bə'nænzə] *n.* 富矿带	

【例】Winning the lottery was a *bonanza* for the Browns.

mineral	['minərəl] *n.* 矿物，矿石
ore	[ɔː] *n.* 矿石
vein	[vein] *n.* 静脉，血管(blood vessel)
sediment	['sedimənt] *n.* 沉淀物

【记】sedi=sit(坐)＋ment→沉下去的东西→沉淀物

fossil	['fɔsl] *n.* 化石
petrify	['petrifai] *vt.* 变为化石

【记】petr(石头)＋ify

【例】I was totally *petrified* with fear.

geology	[dʒi'ɔlədʒi] *n.* 地质学，地质概况
aluminum	[ə'ljuːminəm] *n.* 铝
core	[kɔː] *n.* 果核，中心，核心
crater	['kreitə] *n.* 弹坑
diamond	['daiəmənd] *n.* 钻石，菱形
glacial	['gleisjəl] *adj.* 冰的，冰状的，冰河的，冰河时代的

【例】*glacial* drift 冰碛；*glacial* epoch 冰川时期

glacier	['gleiʃə] *n.* 冰河，冰川

iceberg [ˈaisbəːg] *n.* 冰山

【记】ice(冰)＋berg(山)

plate [pleit] *n.* 盘子，金属板，图版，金银餐具

tremor [ˈtremə] *n.* 震动，颤动

earthquake [ˈəːθkweik] *n.* 地震

seism [ˈsaizəm] *n.* 地震

seismic [ˈsaizmik] *adj.* 地震的

【例】*seismic* wave 地震波，海震波，海啸波

seismology [saizˈmɔlədʒi] *n.* 地震学

magnitude [ˈmægnitjuːd] *n.* 震级

cataclysm [ˈkætəklizəm] *n.* 地震，灾难，大洪水

stratum [ˈstreitəm] *n.* 地层

mantle [ˈmæntl] *n.* 地幔

lithogenous [liθəuˈdʒenəs] *a.* 岩成的

lithosphere [ˈliθəˌsfiə] *n.* 岩石圈

layer [ˈleiə] *n.* 层，阶层

crust [krʌst] *n.* 地壳；硬外皮(shell)

【例】The *crust* of the pie was delicious.

fault [fɔːlt] *n.* 断层

【例】*fault* plane 断层面；*fault* zone 断层

magma [ˈmægmə] *n.* (有机物或矿物的)稀糊，岩浆

squirt [skwəːt] *v.* 喷出(spurt)

【例】Bishop named it Squirt because the drink seemed to "*squirt*" into your mouth like a freshly squeezed grapefruit.

erupt [iˈrʌpt] *vi.* 爆发(explode, burst out)

【例】We feared that the volcano would *erupt* again.

outburst [ˈautbəːst] *n.* (火山，感情等)爆发，喷出(surge, explosion)

eruption [iˈrʌpʃən] *n.* 爆发，火山灰

volcanic [vɔlˈkænik] *adj.* 火山的，像火山的

【例】*volcanic* island *n.* 火山；*volcanic* ash *n.* 火山灰；*volcanic* dust 火山尘

动 物 学

    TOEFL 动物类阅读文章涉猎的动物名称有一定范围，通常局限于一些属于脊椎门(vertebrate)的动物名，所以高中试验课上看到的草履虫之类的无脊椎动物(invertebrate)是很难有机会露脸的。如果按食性分，动物可以分为草食动物（herbivorous），肉食动物（carnivorous）和杂食动物（omnivorous）。如果按类别分，则考得较多的是哺乳动物（mammal），爬行动物（Reptile），如蜥蜴(lizard)，变色蜥蜴(chameleon)；两栖类动物(amphibian)没有代表动物专门考核，但作为一大类，同学们也要对该类单词表示基本的尊重。北美常见的啮齿目动物(rodent)是海狸(beaver)和河狸，TOEFL 文章主要讲它们在小溪里造水坝(dam)的丰功伟绩，以及人们对它们终生功过的褒贬不一。还有黑猩猩(chimpanzee)和树懒(sloth)，TOEFL 文章主要讲述它由于懒惰而不注重个人卫生 (personal hygiene)，以至于寄生虫(parasite)可以在其毛发间自由生长。值得一提的是树懒的懒散表现派生出一个形容词：slothful，其含义可想而知——懒散的。鸟类也是常考的对象，主要考查鸟类的迁徙(migration)，鸟类飞行的诀窍，鸟类寻找方向的本领等等。

gregarious [gre'gɛəriəs] *adj.* 群居的

【记】greg(群体)+arious→爱群体的

【例】My *gregarious* sister makes friends wherever she goes.

swarm [swɔ:m] *n.* (蜜蜂、蚂蚁等)群(throng, crowd, horde)

flock [flɔk] *n.* 羊群,(禽、畜等的)群

herd [hə:d] *n.* 兽群,牧群

mammal ['mæməl] *n.* 哺乳动物

【记】mamma(乳)+l

carnivore ['kɑ:nivɔ:] *n.* 食肉动物

carnivorous [kɑ:'nivərəs] *adj.* 食肉类的

appetite ['æpitait] *n.* 食欲

herbivorous [hə:'bivərəs] *adj.* 食草的

omnivorous [ɔm'nivərəs] *adj.* 杂食的,什么都吃的

predator ['predətə] *n.* 掠夺者,食肉动物

predatory ['predətəri] *adj.* 掠夺的,食肉的

prey [prei] *n.* 被掠食者,牺牲者

poikilotherm [pɔi'kiləuθə:m] *n.* 变温动物,冷血动物

rodent ['rəudənt] *n.* 啮齿动物

scavenger ['skævindʒə] *n.* 清道夫,食腐动物

microbe ['maikrəub] *n.* 微生物,细菌

reptile ['reptail] *n.* 爬虫动物

homotherm ['həuməθə:m] *n.* 恒温动物

primate ['praimit] *n.* 灵长类的动物

primates ['praimits] *n.* 灵长类

mollusk ['mɔləsk] *n.* 软体动物

coelenterate [si'lentəreit] *n.* 腔肠动物

vertebrate ['və:tibrit] *n.* 脊椎动物

invertebrate [in'və:tibrit] *n.* 无脊椎动物

finch [fintʃ] *n.* 鸣禽

【记】fin(尾翅)+ch

【例】This kind of birdseed is perfect for all kinds of *finches*.

bird [bə:d] *n.* 鸟

fowl [faul] *n.* 鸡;家禽(chicken;poultry)

monster ['mɔnstə] *n.* 怪物,巨兽(demon)

hordes [ˈhɔːds] *n.* 昆虫群

insect [ˈinsekt] *n.* 昆虫

worm [wəːm] *n.* 虫，蠕虫

beast [biːst] *n.* 兽，畜牲

aquatic [əˈkwætik] *adj.* 水的，水上的，水生的，
水栖的

amphibian [æmˈfibiən] *adj.* 两栖类的，水陆两用的

migrate [maiˈgreit, ˈmaigreit] *vi.* (鸟类的)迁徙

【例】Some birds *migrate* to find warmer weather.

graze [greiz] *v.* 放牧

【例】This field will *graze* 30 head of cattle.

gasp [gɑːsp] *v.* 气喘，喘息(breathe, gulp)

【例】The terrible scene made me *gasp*.

peck [pek] *v.* 啄，啄起(bite, nibble)

【例】Woodpeckers *pecked* wood for a pest.

trot [trɔt] *vi./n.* (马)小跑，慢跑(jog)

【例】The horses *trotted* along the road.

dormant [ˈdɔːmənt] *adj.* 休眠的(inactive)

【记】dorm(睡眠)＋ant

【例】The *dormant* volcano has not erupted for two hundred years.

offspring [ˈɔːfspriŋ] *n.* 子孙，后代(descendant)

spawn [spɔːn] *n./v.* 产卵(generate, produce)

pregnant [ˈpregnənt] *adj.* 怀孕的，孕育的

hatch [hætʃ] *v.* 孵出，孵(卵)(incubate, breed, emerge from the egg)

【例】Don't count your chickens before they are *hatched*.

breed [briːd] *v.* (使)繁殖，教养，抚养

【例】Many animals *breed* in the spring.

domesticate [dəˈmestikeit] *vt.* 驯养，教化(tame)

【例】No one has ever been able to *domesticate* the African elephant.

fertilize [ˈfəːtilaiz] *vt.* 使受精

regeneration [riˌdʒenəˈreiʃən] *n.* 再生，重建

reproduce [ˌriːprəˈdjuːs] *v.* 繁殖，再生

【例】Birds *reproduce* by laying eggs.

squeak [skwiːk] *vi.* (老鼠或物体)吱吱

【例】Rats *squeak* while flies buzz. It is quite a house.

chirp [tʃəːp] *vi.* 喳喳(虫和鸟的叫声)

【例】The injured bird did not move or *chirp*.

hibernate [ˈhaibəneit] *v.* 冬眠

【例】Polar bear can *hibernate* for a long time.

camouflage [ˈkæməflɑːʒ] *v./n.* 伪装

【例】They *camouflaged* their hatred with professions of friendship.

extinction [iksˈtiŋkʃən] *n.* 灭绝

monogamous [mɔˈnɔgəməs] *adj.* 单配的，一雌一雄的

polyandrous [ˌpɔliˈændrəs] *adj.* 一雌多雄(配合)的

nest [nest] *n.* 巢，窝

niche [nitʃ] *n.* 小生态环境

pest [pest] *n.* 有害物

habitat [ˈhæbitæt] *n.* （动植物的）生活环境，产地，栖息地，居留地，自生地，聚集处

rhinoceros [raiˈnɔsərəs] *n.* 犀牛

chimpanzee [ˈtʃimpənˈziː] *n.* 非洲的小人猿，黑猩猩

baboon [bəˈbuːn] *n.* 狒狒

gorilla [gəˈrilə] *n.* 大猩猩

lizard [ˈlizəd] *n.* 蜥蜴

moth [mɔθ] *n.* 蛾，蛀虫

canary [kəˈnɛəri] *n.* 金丝雀，淡黄色

caterpillar [ˈkætəpilə] *n.* 毛虫

dinosaur [ˈdainəsɔː] *n.* 恐龙

chameleon [kəˈmiːljən] *n.* 变色龙

larva [ˈlɑːvə] *n.* 幼虫

bat [bæt, bɑːt] *n.* 蝙蝠，球棒

family [ˈfæmili] *n.* 科

class [klɑːs] *n.* 纲

suborder [ˈsʌbˌɔːdə] *n.* 亚目

order [ˈɔːdə] *n.* 目

genus [ˈdʒiːnəs] *n.* 种，类

antenna [ænˈtenə] *n.* 触须

tentacle	[ˈtentəkl] n. (动物)触须、触角,(植物)腺毛
brain	[brein] n. 脑,头脑

【例】Tom has no *brain* at calculus.

spleen	[spliːn] n. 脾脏
hide	[haid] n. 兽皮(skin)
spine	[spain] n. 脊骨(backbone)
spineless	[ˈspainlis] adj. 无脊椎的
toe	[təu] n. 脚趾
bill	[bil] n. 鸟嘴
beak	[biːk] n. 鸟嘴,喙
fuzzy	[ˈfʌzi] adj. 有绒毛的,绒毛状的(frizzy, downy)
head	[hed] n. 头
hump	[hʌmp] n. 驼峰
scale	[skeil] n. 鳞片
wing	[wiŋ] n. 翅,翅膀,翼
fluffy	[ˈflʌfi] adj. 绒毛的

【记】fluff(绒毛)+y

【例】Newly hatched chickens are like *fluffy* balls.

carnal	[ˈkɑːnl] adj. 肉体的(corporeal)

【记】carn(肉)+al

nervous	[ˈnəːvəs] adj. 神经的

【记】nerv(神经)+ous

fat	[fæt] n. 脂肪,肥肉
grease	[griːs] n. 动物脂,脂肪
greasy	[ˈgriːzi] adj. 多脂的;油脂的(oily)

【例】To keep you fit, keep away from *greasy* food.

turtle	[ˈtəːtl] n. 海龟
beaver	[ˈbiːvə] n. 海狸(毛皮)
jellyfish	[ˈdʒelifiʃ] n. 水母

【记】jelly(胶冻,果冻)+fish(鱼)

starfish	[ˈstɑːfiʃ] n. 海星
whale	[weil, hw-] n. 鲸
porpoise	[ˈpɔːpəs] n. 海豚,小鲸
dolphin	[ˈdɔlfin] n. 海豚

prawn	[prɔːn]	n. 对虾，明虾，大虾
shrimp	[ʃrimp]	n. 小虾
lobster	[ˈlɔbstə]	n. 龙虾
sponge	[spʌndʒ]	n. 海绵，海绵体，海绵状物
plankton	[ˈplæŋkt(ə)n]	n. 浮游生物
oyster	[ˈɔistə]	n. 牡蛎，蚝
clam	[klæm]	n. 蛤
coral	[ˈkɔrəl]	n. 珊瑚，珊瑚虫
crab	[kræb]	n. 螃蟹，类似螃蟹的动物

You will never have what you like until you learn to like what you have.　　　　　　　—*Goethe*

欲得到你喜欢的东西，应先学会喜欢你已有的东西。

　　　　　　　　　　　　—歌德

法　　律

penal ['pi:nl] *adj.* 受刑罚的，刑事的
【记】pen(惩罚)+al

illicit [i'lisit] *adj.* 违法的(unlawful, illegal)

unruly [ʌn'ru:li] *adj.* 不守法的(disorderly)
【记】un(不)+rul(e)(法)+y

illegitimate [ˌili'dʒitimit] *adj.* 非法的；私生的(illegal)
【记】il(不)+legitim(合法)+ate→不合法的
【例】A special commission tried to reduce the number of *illegitimate* births in the country.

default [di'fɔ:lt] *n.* 不履行责任(nonfulfilment)，缺乏 *v.* 不履行；拖欠
【记】de(犯)+fault(错误)→拖(债)
【例】If they can't raise the money to pay the debt, they will have to *default*.

violate ['vaiəleit] *v.* 违犯，违背，侵犯(break, offend)
【例】These findings appear to *violate* the laws of physics.

violation [ˌvaiə'leiʃən] *n.* 违犯
【例】If you get one more traffic *violation*, your driver's license will be revoked.

infringe [in'frindʒ] *v.* 侵犯(encroach, intrude)；违反
【例】Your book *infringes* on my copy right.

bound [baund] *adj.* 负有义务的
【例】The employees are not *bound* to keep working at the factory after work.

compulsory [kəm'pʌlsəri] *adj.* 义务的；必修的(obligatory, mandatory, required)
【记】com+puls(推，冲)+ory
【例】The use of seat belts is *compulsory* in many states; failure to wear them may result in fines. / A composition class is *compulsory* for all college students.

oblige [ə'blaidʒ] *vt.* 强迫(force)
【例】I was *obliged* to finish the work by the end of this week.

obligatory [əb'ligətəri] *adj.* 义务的；必须的(compulsory, necessary)
【记】oblig(强迫)+atory→必须的
【例】Wearing seat belts while driving is *obligatory* in most states.

responsible [ris'pɔnsəbl] *adj.* 有责任的

domineering [ˌdɔmi'niəriŋ] *adj.* 专权的(tyrannical, dictatorial)

【记】domin(统治)＋eering→统治者的→盛气凌人的

【例】The *domineering* father made every decision in his children's lives.

mandatory ['mændətəri] *adj.* 命令的；强制的(obligatory, compulsory)

【例】Many colleges have *mandatory* foreign language requirement.

licensed ['laisnst] *adj.* 被许可的(permissive)

【记】licen(允许)＋sed

heirship ['ɛəʃip] *n.* 继承权

jurisdiction [ˌdʒuəris'dikʃən] *n.* 司法权

【记】juris(法律)＋dict(说，命令)＋ion→法律上命令→司法权

arbitration [ˌɑːbi'treiʃən] *n.* 调停，仲裁

【记】arbi(判断，裁决)＋tration→进行裁决

【例】The matter was sent into *arbitration* to avoid the costs of a court trial.

fine [fain] *n.* 罚金

【例】The *fine* for overtime parking is outrageously high.

confiscate ['kɔnfiskeit] *vt.* 没收，充公(seize)

【记】con＋fisc(钱，财)＋ate

【例】The police *confiscated* the stolen goods.

convict [kən'vikt] *vt.* 判罪；证明(penalize; prove)

【记】con＋vict(征服)→(征服)罪犯→判罪

【例】The defendant was *convicted* of murder.

verdict ['vəːdikt] *n.* 判决(decision, judgment)

judgment ['dʒʌdʒmənt] *n.* 判决

【记】judg(判断)＋ment

indemnity [in'demniti] *n.* 赔偿

【记】in(不)＋demn(损坏)＋ity→使不再坏→赔偿

imprisonment [im'priznmənt] *n.* 监禁

invalidate [in'vælideit] *vt.* 使作废(nullify)

【例】The making of false statements could result in the *invalidation* of the contract.

imprisonment [im'prizənmənt] *n.* 关押

captivity [kæp'tiviti] *n.* 囚禁，拘留

【例】Zoo animals are kept in *captivity*.

trial ['traiəl] *n.* 审判(hearing, inquisition)

【例】The scandal put the president on *trial*.

detain [diˈtein] *vt.* 拘留；阻止

【记】de＋tain(拿，抓)→拘留

【例】Please do not *detain* me; I am in a hurry.

extenuate [eksˈtenjueit] *vt.* 使(罪过等)显得轻微(diminish, lessen)

【记】ex＋tenu(细薄)＋ate→使轻微

【例】"Your money cannot help to *extenuate* your crime,"said the judge.

saddle [ˈsædl] *vt.* 使负担(burden, load)

【例】The landowner *saddled* his tenants with heavy taxes.

court [kɔːt] *n.* 法庭(bar)

【例】I have to go to *court* today to give evidence in a trial.

bar [baː] *n.* 法院(court)

authorize [ˈɔːθəraiz] *vt.* 授权(empower, permit)

【例】A visa *authorizes* a person to enter and leave a country.

empower [imˈpauə] *vt.* 授权；使能够

【记】em＋power(权力)→获得权力

【例】The owner *empowered* Jane to hire new employees for the store.

plea [pliː] *n.* 恳求(appeal)

oath [əuθ] *n.* 誓言；誓约；宣誓(oath, pledge, promise)

pledge [pledʒ] *n.* 誓言 *vt.* 使发誓(promise, vow)

plaintiff [ˈpleintif] *n.* 原告

【记】plain(哀诉)＋tiff

plead [pliːd] *v.* 抗辩；恳求(argue, protest; beg)

【例】"Let me out, please." The prisoner *pleaded* to the jail keeper, but in vain.

flee [fliː] *v.* 逃跑，逃离(escape)

【例】When the rain began, we *fled* for cover.

defend [diˈfend] *vt.* 辩护

【例】Mary *defended* her actions when she was accused of cheating.

proscribe [prəuˈskraib] *vt.* 禁止(ban, forbid, forestall)

【记】pro(前)＋scribe(写)→写在前面→禁止

【例】The sale of opium is *proscribed* by law.

forbid [fəˈbid] *vt.* 禁止(prohibit, prevent)

【记】for(前)＋bid(出价)→预先出价→阻止(别人)

【例】Chewing gum in class was *forbidden*.

abstinence ［'æbstinəns］ *n.* 禁戒；节制

【例】*Abstinence* from fatty foods and smoking can probably lengthen your life.

abstain ［əb'stein］ *vi.* 戒绝

【记】abs(不)＋tain(拿住)→不拿住→放弃

【例】Because my cholesterol is high, my doctor told me to *abstain* from eating fat.

ban ［bæn］ *n.* 禁令 *vt.* 禁止(prohibit, forbid)

【例】The principal announced a *ban* on guns at the school.

veto ［'vi:təu］ *n.* 否决，否决权(rejection) *vt.* 否决，禁止(negate)

【记】比较vote(投票)

【例】As a member of the management board, I have the right to *veto*.

revise ［ri'vaiz］ *vt.* 修订(amend, emend, edit)

【记】re(再)＋vise(看)→重新审查

【例】The student *revised* his paper carefully, following the professor's suggestions.

verify ［'verifai］ *vt.* 验证(confirm, substantiate)

【例】Your signature here will *verify* that you understand the terms of the agreement. / The ambassador *verified* the report before he called the State Department.

deserve ［di'zə:v］ *vt.* 应得

【例】After six years in colleges, I think I *deserve* a good job.

stipulate ［'stipjuleit］ *vt.* 约定，规定(set, specify)

【例】The workers'contract *stipulated* that they couldn't smoke on the job.

testify ［'testifai］ *vt.* 证明，证实；作证(give evidence, verify)

【例】Her tears *testified* her grief.

testimony ［'testiməni］ *n.* 证言(evidence, affirmation)

justify ［'dʒʌstifai］ *vt.* 证明…是正当的(defend, vindicate)

【记】just(公正的)＋ify

【例】How can you *justify* what you did yesterday?

substantiate ［səbs'tænʃieit］ *vt.* 证实(corroborate, verify)

【例】Evidences *substantiated* that he was the murderer.

confirm ［kən'fə:m］ *vt.* 证实，确认(substantiate, verify)

【记】con＋firm(坚实的)

【例】Please *confirm* our reservations at the restaurant.

affirm [ə'fə:m] *vt.* 证实(assert)

【记】af(一再)＋firm(肯定)→断言

assure [ə'ʃuə] *vt.* 使确信,向…保证(gurantee, pledge)

【记】as＋sure(确信)

【例】The doctor *assured* the patient that everything would be all right.

evidence ['evidəns] *n.* 证据;证人

follow ['fɔ:ləu] *v.* 跟随,遵循(abide by, obey)

【例】If you disregard the doctor's orders, a relapse will *follow*.

observe [əb'zə:v] *vt.* 遵守(follow)

【记】TOEFL常考词义为"遵守"

【例】All participants of the contest have to *observe* the rules.

observance [əb'zə:vəns] *n.* 遵守

abide [ə'baid] *vi.* 遵守(adhere, observe)

【记】abide by(遵守)

【例】He will *abide* by his promise if he gives it.

accuse [ə'kju:z] *vt.* 控告;归咎(charge)

【例】I *accused* John of hitting my dog.

accusation [,ækju'zeiʃə] *n.* 控告

【例】Anne objected to the untrue *accusations*.

complaint [kəm'pleint] *n.* 控告;诉苦

【例】The boss had a *complaint* about Bill's tardiness.

impeach [im'pi:tʃ] *vt.* 弹劾;控告(accuse)

【记】im(进入)＋peach(告发)

【例】The Congress has the right to *impeach* a president.

indictment [in'daitmənt] *n.* 起诉(charge, accusation)

【记】in＋dict(言,说)＋ment→说出缘由→起诉

incriminate [in'krimineit] *vt.* 控告(accuse);使负罪

【记】in(进入)＋crimin(罪行)＋ate→使负罪

【例】He was *incriminated* of murder.

prosecute ['prɔsikju:t] *v.* 起诉;检举(accuse, charge)

【例】Trespassers will be *prosecuted*.

denounce [di'nauns] *vt.* 告发

【记】de(坏)＋nounce(讲话)→讲坏话→告发

【例】Jane loudly *denounces* anyone who litters.

lawsuit ['lɔ:su:t] *n.* 诉讼

【记】law(法律)＋suit(诉讼)

query ['kwiəri] *n.* 质问，问题 *v.* 询问(inquiry)

【例】He couldn't bear his wife's daily *queries* about where he had been and he demanded a divorce.

interrogate [in'terəgeit] *vt.* 审问；询问

【记】inter(中间)＋rog(问)＋ate→审问

【例】The police *interrogated* Sally about the robbery.

impunity [im'pju:niti] *n.* 免罚(let-off)

【记】im(不)＋pun(罚)＋ity

【例】You can not do this with *impunity*.

exempt [ig'zempt] *vt.* 免除(prevent, immune) *adj.* 被免除的(excused)

【例】The teacher *exempted* the smartest students from taking the quiz.

condone [kən'dəun] *vt.* 宽恕，赦免(forgive, pardon)

【例】"I will not *condone* cheating," the teacher said.

liberate ['libəreit] *vt.* 释放(discharge, release)

【记】liber(自由)＋ate→使···自由，解放

【例】I *liberated* the rabbit from its cage.

remit [ri'mit] *vt.* 赦免

【记】re(再)＋mit(送)→再送出去→汇款

【例】"*Remit* my sins," he prayed.

release [ri'li:s] *n.* 释放，让渡，豁免

absolve [əb'zɔlv] *vt.* 赦免；解除(责任等)(free, emancipate)

【记】ab＋solve(解决)→解除责任→赦免

【例】The dying man asked the priest to *absolve* him of his sins. / Mary was *absolved* from further responsibility on the project.

acquit [ə'kwit] *vt.* 宣告无罪(exonerate, vindicate)

【记】ac＋quit(免除)→开释

【例】The court *acquitted* Max of all charges.

abolish [ə'bɔliʃ] *vt.* 废除，取消(abandon, annul, terminate)

【记】abolis(消失)＋h→废除

【例】If I were the king, I would *abolish* taxes.

term [tə:m] *n.* 条款

【例】Knowing more technical *terms* gives a translator more advantages.

clause [klɔ:z] *n.* 条款

【例】The sentence had too many *clauses* in it.

bill [bil] *n.* 法案

【例】The proposed *bill* would limit government officials' terms.

constitution [ˌkɔnstiˈtjuːʃən] *n.* 宪法

decree [diˈkriː] *n.* 法令，规定（regulation, order）*v.* 颁布

【例】No one dared ignore the owner's firm *decree*.

legislate [ˈledʒisleit] *vi.* 立法（make law）

【记】legis(法律)＋late(放)→放出法律→立法

【例】It is impossible to *legislate* for every contingency.

legislation [ˌledʒisˈleiʃən] *n.* 立法，法律的制定（或通过）

legalize [ˈliːɡəlaiz] *vt.* 合法化，法律认可（authorize, legitimate）

【例】Some peole in China want to *legalize* the possession of guns.

prescribe [prisˈkraib] *v.* 指示，规定（dictate）

【例】The law *prescribes* what should be done.

set [set] *vt.* 规定

【例】The boss *set* the first day of each month as the rest day.

credential [kriˈdenʃəl] *n.* 凭证（reference, certificate）

【记】cred(相信)＋ential

standard [ˈstændəd] *n.* 标准，规格（criteria）*adj.* 标准的（regular）

enact [iˈnækt] *vt.* 制定（法律）（impersonate）

【记】en＋act(扮演)

【例】Congress *enacted* the new crime bill.

You are not in charge of the universe; you are in charge of yourself.

—Bennett

你并不掌管整个宇宙，但你得掌管你自己。

——贝内特

化　学

hackneyed [ˈhæknid] *adj.* 陈腐的(mouldy, stale)

【记】参考hack(陈腐的), Internet用语hacker(黑客)

【例】The old professor's *hackneyed* style of coaching arouses complaints from among students.

caustic [ˈkɔːstik] *adj.* 腐蚀性的(abrasive, corrosive)

erosion [iˈrəuʒən] *n.* 腐蚀

【例】*Erosion* of the soil made the farmer's land less valuable.

erode [iˈrəud] *vt.* 蚀，腐蚀(corrode, wear away)

【例】A constant stream of water *eroded* the rock mountain.

stale [steil] *adj.* 陈腐的(smelly, musty, flat)

【例】The *stale* bread was dry and hard.

rot [rɔt] *v.* 腐烂(perish, decay)

【例】The body of the dead wolf began to *rot*.

rotten [ˈrɔtn] *adj.* 腐烂的(decaying, decomposed)

【例】The *rotten* fruit smelled horrible.

decay [diˈkei] *v.* (使)腐败(rot, decompose)

【例】Sugar can cause tooth to *decay*.

corrode [kəˈrəud] *v.* 腐蚀(erode, eat away)

【记】比较erode(腐蚀)

【例】Battery acid *corroded* the inside of the camera.

decomposition [ˌdiːkɔmpəˈziʃən] *n.* 分解，腐烂

rust [rʌst] *v.* 生锈，氧化(oxidize)*n.* 铁锈

【例】An iron plow would get *rusted* under wet weather. /If you leave your metal tools outside in the rain, they will *rust*.

silica [ˈsilikə] *n.* 硅土

limestone [ˈlaimstəun] *n.* 石灰石

crystal [ˈkristl] *n.* 水晶，晶体

【例】Salt *crystals* can be found in every home.

gasoline [ˌgæsəˈliːn] *n.* 汽油

methane [ˈmeθein] *n.* 甲烷，沼气

hydrocarbon [ˈhaidrəuˈkɑːbən] *n.* 碳氢化合物

petroleum [piˈtrəuliəm] *n.* 石油

【例】*petroleum* products 石油产品，成品油

plastic [ˈplæstik, plɑːstik] *n.* 塑胶，可塑体，塑料制品

intermediary [ˌintəˈmiːdjəri] *n.* 媒介物；居间者(mediator)

【记】inter(中间)＋medi(中间)＋ary→媒介物

【例】I always play *intermediary* when my sisters quarrel with each other.

catalysis [kəˈtælisis] *n.* 催化作用

catalyst [ˈkætəlist] *n.* 催化剂

adhesive [ədˈhiːsiv] *n.* 粘合剂 *adj.* 胶粘；粘着性的

scorch [skɔːtʃ] *vt.* 使褪色(discolor)

【例】Do not leave the iron on that delicate fabric or the heat will *scorch* it.

bleach [bliːtʃ] *vt.* 去色，漂白(blanch, whiten) *n.* 漂白剂

【例】You can remove some stains from white shirts with a little *bleach*.

tint [tint] *vt.* 上色，染色 *n.* 上色，色彩(tinge；hue)

【例】At dawn, the sky *tints* with green and pink.

dye [dai] *n.* 颜料 *v.* 染色(pigment)

【例】I asked the hairdresser to *dye* my hair blond.

chemistry [ˈkemistri] *n.* 化学

biochemistry [ˌbaiəuˈkemistri] *n.* 生物化学

【记】bio(生物)＋chemistry(化学)

hydronic [haiˈdrɔnik] *adj.* 液体循环加热(或冷却)的

alchemy [ˈælkimi] *n.* 炼金术，魔力

artificial [ˌɑːtiˈfiʃəl] *adj.* 人造的，假的，非原产地的

ion [ˈaiən] *n.* 离子

molecule [ˈmɔlikjuːl, ˈməu-] *n.* 分子，些微

solubility [ˌsɔljuˈbiliti] *n.* 溶度，溶性，可解决性，可解释性，溶解性

solution [səˈljuːʃən] *n.* 解答，解决办法，溶解，溶液，解决方案

solvent [ˈsɔlvənt] *adj.* 溶解的，有偿付能力的，有溶解力 *n.* 溶媒，溶剂

dissolve [diˈzɔlv] *v.* 溶解，解散

【例】Water *dissolves* salt as heat *dissolves* ice.

element [ˈelimənt] *n.* 元素

【例】Water is made of the *elements*: oxygen and hydrogen.

impurity [imˈpjuəriti] *n.* 杂质

blend [blend] *v./n.* 混和(combine, mix)

【例】The room's decoration was a good *blend* of traditional and modern pieces. / The artist *blended* painting with etching.

compound [ˈkɔmpaund] *n.* 混合物，化合物

substance ['sʌbstəns] *n.* 物质，实质

particle ['pɑːtikl] *n.* 颗粒，微粒

【记】比较article（文章）

explosive [iks'pləusiv] *adj.* 爆炸的 *n.* 炸药

【例】Dynamite is highly *explosive*.

blast [blɑːst] *n.* 爆破

【例】The leaves were lifted into the air by a sudden *blast* of wind.

explode [iks'pləud] *v.* (使)爆炸（blast）

【例】The red balloon *exploded* when I popped it with a pin.

burning ['bəːniŋ] *adj.* 燃烧的

kindle ['kindl] *vt.* 燃起（ignite, inflame）

【记】比较candle（蜡烛）

【例】Her cruelty *kindled* hatred in my heart.

sear [siə] *vt.* 烧灼

【例】The hot iron *seared* the trousers.

ignite [ig'nait] *vt.* 使燃着（inflame, kindle）

【例】A smoldering cigarette *ignited* the newspapers.

action ['ækʃən] *n.* 作用

combination [ˌkɔmbi'neiʃən] *n.* 化合；组合

【例】The safe *combination* of the two chemicals required a complicated chemical process.

neutralize ['njuːtrəlaiz] *v.* 中和（counteract）

【例】Alkalis *neutralize* acids.

polymerization [ˌpɔlimərai'zeiʃən] *n.* 聚合

functional ['fʌŋkʃənl] *adj.* 起作用的（useful）

【例】My bike is not luxurious, but still *functional*.

synthetic [sin'θetik] *adj.* 综合的；合成的（artificial, man-made）

carbon ['kɑːbən] *n.* 碳

copper ['kɔpə] *n.* 铜

lead [led] *n.* 铅

Mercury ['məːkjuri] *n.* 水星；[罗马神话]墨丘利神（众神的信使）

nickel ['nikl] *n.* 镍，镍币

platinum ['plætinəm] *n.* 白金，铂

silver ['silvə] *n.* 银，银子

sodium	['səudjəm, -diəm]	n. 钠
tin	[tin]	n. 锡，马口铁
zinc	[ziŋk]	n. 锌
calcium	['kælsiəm]	n. 钙(元素符号Ca)
helium	['hiːljəm, -liəm]	n. 氦(化学元素，符号为He)
silicon	['silikən]	n. 硅，硅元素
ammonia	['æməunjə]	n. 氨，氨水
sulfur	['sʌlfə]	n. 硫磺，硫黄
iodine	['aiədiːn;(US)'aiədain]	n. 碘，碘酒
nitrogen	['naitrədʒən]	n. 氮
oxygen	['ɔksidʒən]	n. 氧气

【记】oxy(氧)＋gen; 如 oxyacid(含氧酸), oxyhydrogen(氧氢混合气)

【例】*Oxygen* and Nitrogen constitute the main part of the air.

We must accept finite disappointment, but we must never lose infinite hope.　　　　　*—Martin Luther King, Jr.*

我们必须接受失望,因为它是有限的,但千万不可失去希望,因为它是无穷的。

　　　　　　　　　　　　　　——马丁·路德·金

环 境

noxious [ˈnɔkʃəs] *adj.* 有害的；有毒的(poisonous, toxic)

【记】nox(毒)+ious

pollute [pəˈluːt] *vt.* 污染(contaminate, defile)

pollutant [pəˈluːtənt] *n.* 污染物质

【例】Rivers in the neighbourhood were *polluted* by the chemical wastes from the factories.

pollution [pəˈluːʃen] *n.* 污染，玷污

【例】air *pollution* 空气污染；noise *pollution* 噪音污染；soil *pollution* 土壤污染；water *pollution* 水质污染

contaminate [kənˈtæmineit] *vt.* 污染(defile, pollute)

【例】The Department of Resources notified the town council that the water supply was *contaminated*.

waste [weist] *n.* 废物

【例】solid *waste* 固体废物

sewage [ˈsjuː(ː)idʒ] *n.* 下水道，污水

fume [ˈfjuːm] *n.* (浓烈或难闻的)烟，气体

habitat [ˈhæbitæt] *n.* (动、植物的)生活环境，居留地(home, environment)

【例】The polar region is the *habitat* of polar bear.

balance [ˈbæləns] *n./v.* 平衡(equilibrium)

【例】I lost my *balance* and fell.

ecosystem [iːkəˈsistəm] *n.* 生态系统

fauna [ˈfɔːnə] *n.* 动物群，动物区系

decibel [ˈdesibel] *n.* 分贝

ozonosphere [ˌəuˈzəunəsfiə] *n.* 臭氧层

Always aim for achievement and forget about success.

—Helen Hayes

永远要争取做出成就，别多考虑成功。

——海伦

教　育

didactic [diˈdæktik] *adj.* 教诲的，说教的（instructive）

【例】He started to know the real meaning of life from a *didactic* speech given by a celebrity.

leading [ˈliːdiŋ] *adj.* 指导的

sermon [ˈsəːmən] *n.* 说教（speech）

initiate [iˈniʃieit] *vt.* 启蒙

instill [inˈstil] *vt.* 灌输（infuse, impart）

【记】in(进入)＋still(滴)→灌输

【例】Courtesy must be *instilled* in childhood.

instruct [inˈstrʌkt] *vt.* 教

【例】She *instructed* me in the use of the telephone.

enlighten [inˈlaitn] *vt.* 启发，开导；启蒙（edify, illuminate）

【记】en＋light(光)＋en

【例】The speaker *enlightened* the students about the dangers of drinking.

edify [ˈedifai] *vt.* 陶冶，教化（enlighten, teach）

【例】A trip to the art museum *edified* the tourists and helped them understand the local culture better.

lead [liːd] *vt.* 引导

【例】The path *led* them to a cave.

direct [diˈrekt] *vt.* 引导（instruct）

【例】The receptionist's job is to *direct* people to the correct office.

conduct [kənˈdʌkt] *vt.* 引导（lead）

【例】The students are *conducted* to do the experiment.

curriculum [kəˈrikjuləm] *n.* 课程

discipline [ˈdisiplin] *n.* 学科

We cannot always build the future for our youth , but we can build our youth for the future. —Roosevelt

我们不能总是为我们的青年造就美好未来，但我们能够为未来造就我们的青年一代。 ——罗斯福

经　济

toll	[təul]	*n.* 费(fee, charge)
precious	['preʃəs]	*adj.* 宝贵的，珍贵的(valuable)
prosperous	['prɔspərəs]	*adj.* 繁荣的(thriving, flourishing)
prosperity	[prɔ'speriti]	*n.* 繁荣(well-being)

【例】The *prosperity* of the society promises a rapid economic growth.

rich	[ritʃ]	*adj.* 肥沃的(fertile)
rare	[rɛə]	*adj.* 稀罕的，珍贵的(scarce, uncommon)
asset	['æset]	*n.* 财产，财富(possessions, property)

【例】The President's greatest *asset* was his reputation for honesty.

fortune	['fɔːtʃən]	*n.* 财富(wealth)
opulence	['ɔpjuləns]	*n.* 财富；富裕(wealth; affluence)

【记】opul(财富)＋ence

finance	['fainæns]	*n.* 财政 *vt.* 资助(sponsor, subsidize)

capital 【记】比较fiance(未婚夫)；fiancee(未婚妻)

【例】Joe *financed* his girlfriend to study abroad, but she never came back.

economic	[ˌekə'nɔmik]	*adj.* 经济的

【例】The newspaper featured an article about the nation's *economic* future.

indigent	['indidʒənt]	*adj.* 贫穷的(needy, poor)

【记】indi(内部)＋gent(缺乏)

depression	[di'preʃən]	*n.* 萧条(recession)

【例】Many people lost their fortune during the Great *Depression*.

penury	['penjuri]	*n.* 贫穷(destitution)

【记】penur(缺少)＋y

bidding	['bidiŋ]	*n.* 投标

【例】The *bidding* was higher than expected.

drawback	['drɔːbæk]	*n.* 退款
exponent	[eks'pəunənt]	*n.* 指数(index, indicator)

【记】另一个意思是"支持者"，比较 opponent(反对者)

lease	[liːs]	*n./v.* 出租(lend, loan)

【记】联想"l"加ease(安心的)

【例】The owner *leased* his spare houses to make a fortune.

redress	[ri'dres]	*n.* 补偿(rectify, remedy)
compensation	[ˌkɔmpen'seiʃən]	*n.* 补偿，赔偿

【例】Max received his *compensation* in stock rather than cash.

deficit ['defisit] *n.* 赤字

【记】de(坏)+fic(做)+it

【例】The government tried to avoid a budget *deficit*.

levy ['levi] *n.* 课税 *v.* 征收(collect, charge)

【例】The Empire *levied* heavy taxes upon its colonies.

ration ['ræʃən] *n.* 定量，配给量(share, allowance) *v.* 配给，分发(allocate, share)

rebate ['riːbeit] *n.* 返回款；折扣(refund, repayment)

【记】比较debate(争论)

【例】The government uses tax *rebate* as a means to attract investment on this line.

merchandise ['məːtʃəndaiz] *n.* 商品(commodities, goods)

【记】比较merchant(商人)

commerce ['kɔməːs] *n.* 商业

【记】注意和commence(开始)的区别

【例】*Commerce* flourished between the two friendly countries.

enterprise ['entəpraiz] *n.* 事业，企业

【例】The new *enterprise* will require additional staff and equipment.

currency ['kʌrənsi] *n.* 通货；通用；市价(money, exchange)

【例】We exchanged our *currency* at a bank in the airport.

inventory ['invəntəri] *n.* 物品清单；库存品

quota ['kwəutə] *n.* 限额，定额(portion, share)

tariff ['tærif] *n.* 关税，关税表

inflation [in'fleiʃən] *n.* 通货膨胀

deal [diːl] *v.* 交易(handle)

【例】Do you *deal* with Smith, the butcher?

yen [jen] *n.* 日元

cause [kɔːz] *n.* 事业(career)

【例】The boy took pride in being a successor in the revolutionary *cause*.

consume [kəm'sjuːm] *vt.* 消费，消耗(spend)

【记】con+sum(结束)+e→全部结束→用光

【例】Americans *consume* a huge amount of sugar each year.

disburse [dis'bəːs] *vt.* 支付，支出；分配(distribute)

【记】dis+burse(钱包)

【例】On payday, the manager *disburses* our pay.

acting [ˈæktiŋ] *adj.* 代理的 (substitutive)
【记】act(行动)+ing→代替执行的→代理的

inertia [iˈnəːʃə] *n.* 惯性，惯量

discount [ˈdiskaunt] *n./vt.* (打)折扣 (reduction)
【例】Mary gets an employee *discount* at the department store.

audit [ˈɔːdit] *n./vt.* 审查；查账 (censor)
【例】The *audit* of the man's estate revealed unpaid taxes.

shipment [ˈʃipmənt] *n.* 装船，出货

surplus [ˈsəːplʌs] *n.* 过剩，剩余(物资) *adj.* 过剩的 (extra, excess)
【记】比较plus(加)
【例】The farmer's *surplus* grain was stored in silos.

residue [ˈrezidjuː] *n.* 残余 (remains, leftover, remnant)

account [əˈkaunt] *n.* 户头；账目
【例】I have an *account* with the Midland Bank.

bankruptcy [ˈbæŋkrʌptsi] *n.* 破产
【记】bank(银行)+rupt(断)+cy
【例】Sue couldn't pay her debts, so she declared *bankruptcy*.

savings [ˈseiviŋz] *n.* 储蓄

collateral [kɔˈlætərəl] *n.* 抵押品
【例】The Smiths used valuable jewelry as *collateral* for their loan.

bill [bil] *n.* 钞票；账单

check [tʃek] *n.* 支票

coin [kɔin] *n.* 铸币

depreciate [diˈpriːʃieit] *v.* 贬值
【记】de(坏)+preci(价值)+ate
【例】The US dollar has *depreciated* against the Japanese Yen.

merge [məːdʒ] *v.* 合并 (combine, amalgamate)
【例】The two companies are going to *merge* by the end of the year.

reimburse [ˌriːimˈbəːs] *vt.* 偿还 (pay back, refund)
【记】re(重新)+im=in(进入)+burse(钱包)→偿还
【例】You should *reimburse* the taxi fee those strangers paid to get you to hospital.

garner [ˈgɑːnə] *vt.* 储存 (store)
【例】People began to *garner* food to prepare for the war.

underestimate [ˌʌndəˈestimeit] *vt.* 低估 (undervalue)

【例】The width of the nation has long been *underestimated* before the recent investigation.

exchange [iks'tʃeindʒ] *vt.* 兑换；交换（barter）

【例】They *exchange* their labor for room and board.

assess [ə'ses] *vt.* 估计（estimate, evaluate）

【例】It took a while to *assess* the damage from the tornado.

consolidate [kən'sɔlideit] *vt.* 合并（merge）

【记】con＋solid(固体的，结实的)＋ate

【例】The two schools were *consolidated* to reduce costs.

loan [ləun] *n.* 贷款 *vt.* 借（lend）

【例】Many colleges provide *loans* to students.

refund [ri:'fʌnd] *vt.* 退还，偿还（repay, pay back）

【记】re(重新)＋fund(钱)→重新还回钱→退还

【例】I will *refund* you the full of your fare.

utility [ju:'tiliti] *n.* 效用（function, usefulness）

selection [si'lekʃən] *n.* 选择（choice）

【记】select(选择)＋ion

option ['ɔpʃən] *n.* 选择，取舍（choice, alternative）

economics [,ekə'nɔmiks] *n.* 经济（学）

【例】A committee was formed to study the *economics* of closing some military bases.

output ['autput] *n.* 产量，输出量（turnout, yield）

【记】来自put out(生产)

goods [gudz] *n.* 货物（merchandise, commodity）

opportunity [,ɔpə'tju:niti] *n.* 机会（chance）

【例】*Opportunities* favor those with prepared minds.

benefit ['benifit] *n.* 利益（profit, interest）

【例】Volunteer work *benefits* society.

contract ['kɔntrækt] *n.* 契约（agreement）

lottery ['lɔtəri] *n.* 奖券；抽奖

【例】"Marriage is just a *lottery*. Don't believe in love."said the old man.

transaction [træn'zækʃən] *n.* 交易（business, trade, deal）

【记】trans(交换)＋action(活动)→交易

budget ['bʌdʒit] *n.* 预算 *v.* 做预算

【例】The department's *budget* did not include money for electricity. We've budgeted $1,000 for advertising.

patronage ['peitrənidʒ] *n.* 赞助，资助

【记】patron(赞助人)＋age

choose [tʃuːz] *vt.* 选择(select, pick)

【例】You can *choose* the classes you want to take.

choice [tʃɔis] *n.* 选择(selection)

barter ['bɑːtə] *n./vt.* 易货(trade, exchange)

【例】Before currency came into use, people used the *barter* system, exchanging goods directly for goods.

purchase ['pəːtʃəs] *n./vt.* 购买(buy)

deposit [di'pɔzit] *v.* 放置，存款(place, lay) *n.* 押金

【记】比较draw(取款)

【例】Tom *deposited* his luggage in the hotel.

commission [kə'miʃən] *n.* 佣金

【例】Our agents in other areas usually get a 3-5% *commission*.

ransom ['rænsəm] *n.* 赔偿金(payment, redemption)

toll [təul] *v.* 鸣(钟)(ring, strike)

【例】For whom does the bell *toll*?

charge [tʃɑːdʒ] *n.* 费用 *v.* 收费

【例】There is no *charge* for window-shopping.

bond [bɔnd] *n.* 公债

【例】An inverse relationship exists between the price of a *bond* and the interest rate.

custom ['kʌstəm] *n.* 进口税

bonus ['bəunəs] *n.* 红利；奖金(award, gift)

【例】At the end of the year, the employees all received cash *bonuses*.

interest ['intrist] *n.* 利息

means [miːnz] *n.* 钱(money)

【例】You ought to live within your *means*.

debt [det] *n.* 债务(liability)

【例】Bill is working very hard to get out of *debt*.

fund [fʌnd] *n.* 资金，基金(money) *vt.* 投资

revenue ['revinjuː] *n.* 收入 (income, returns, earnings)

军　事

confidential [ˌkɔnfiˈdenʃəl] *adj.* 机密的
【记】confident＋ial→相信的人才知道→机密的
【例】That matter is so *confidential* that it must not be discussed outside this office.

clandestine [klænˈdestin] *adj.* 秘密的(secret, covert)
【记】分割记忆clan(宗派)＋destine(注定)
【例】Some angry peasants had a *clandestine* plan to overthrow the leader.

cipher [ˈsaifə] *n.* 暗号；密码(code)
【记】比较记忆decipher(解码)
【例】Spies intercepted the *cipher* but could not decode it.

dissimulate [diˈsimjuleit] *vt.* 假装，掩饰(disguise, dissemble)
【记】比较simulate(模仿)
【例】The soldiers *dissimulated* themselves by wearing white garments in the snow.

disarm [disˈɑːm] *vt.* 缴械；消除(敌意)
【记】dis(不再)＋arm=army(军队)
【例】The security guard *disarmed* the robber.

disarming [disˈɑːmiŋ] *adj.* 消除敌意的(relieving, soothing)
【例】The spy's *disarming* nature earned other people's trust.

scout [skaut] *v.* 侦察
【例】She *scouts* for a professional basketball team.

fort [fɔːt] *n.* 要塞，堡垒

fortress [ˈfɔːtris] *n.* 堡垒，要塞
【例】Soldiers attacked the enemy's *fortress*.

hatchet [ˈhætʃit] *n.* 短柄斧

dagger [ˈdægə] *n.* 短剑
【例】The nobleman wore an ornate *dagger* at his hip.

armor [ˈɑːmə] *n.* 装甲，武器
【例】A turtle has a soft body, but it also has the *armor* of a hard shell to protect it.

corps [kɔː] *n.* 军团，兵团
【例】Susan worked for the Peace *Corps* for two years in Central America.

armament [ˈɑːməmənt] *n.* 兵力，军力(arms, munitions)

【记】arma(军队)＋ment

【例】*Armament* is thought to be a protection against aggression.

enlist [in'list] *vt.* 征召，招募(enroll)

【记】en＋list(列入名单)

【例】I *enlisted* Mary and Bill to help decorate the party room.

recruit [ri'kru:t] *vt.* 征兵，征募(enlist, enroll)

【例】He was *recruited* into the army.

array [ə'rei] *n.* 队列，排列(order, display)

【例】The colorful *array* of candy made the children's eyes bulge.

squad [skwɔd] *n.* 小队；班

raid [reid] *n./v.* 袭击(attack, foray)

【例】Air *raids* involved in the war destroyed many families.

charge [tʃɑ:dʒ] *v.* 猛攻(attack)

【例】Our soldiers *charged* the enemy.

encroach [in'krəutʃ] *vi.* 蚕食，侵占(intrude, trespass)

【记】比较crochet(钩)

【例】The reporter *encroached* on my privacy.

despoil [dis'pɔil] *vt.* 夺取

【例】The region is *despoiled* of its scenic beauty by unchecked development.

invade [in'veid] *vt.* 侵入，侵略，侵犯(intrude, agress)

【例】Before they could attack they needed to decide upon the plan about how they could *invade* the country.

assault [ə'sɔ:lt] *vt.* 袭击 *n.* 攻击(attack, assail)

【例】Mike very unwisely *assaulted* a police officer.

exterminate [eks'tə:mineit] *vt.* 消灭(eradicate, eliminate)

【记】ex＋termin(范围)＋ate→清除出范围→消灭

【例】The landlord *exterminated* the rats in the cellar.

extinguish [iks'tiŋgwiʃ] *vt.* 消灭(exterminate)

【例】John *extinguished* the campfire with water.

absorb [əb'zɔ:b] *vt.* 并吞

【记】ab＋sorb(吸)

【例】Large nations should *absorb* smaller ones.

onset ['ɔnset] *n.* 攻击(attack)

【记】来自set on(攻击)

【例】 The *onset* of arthritis stopped the old lady from doing needlework.

repulse [ri'pʌls] *vt.* 击退(repel)

【记】 re(反)+pulse(推)→排斥

【例】 Tom *repulsed* the attacker by punching him in the stomach.

expedition [ˌekspi'diʃən] *n.* 远征(exploration)

【记】 ex+ped(脚)+ition→脚出动→远征

【例】 The explorers started on a year-long *expedition* down the Nile.

siege [siːdʒ] *n./vt.* 围困,围攻(besiege, encircle)

【例】 During the enemy's *siege*, no one could leave or enter the city.

envelop [in'veləp] *vt.* 包围(besiege, enclose)

【例】 Accompanying the darkness, a stillness *envelops* the city.

beset [bi'set] *vt.* 包围(besiege, surround)

【例】 The small town was *beset* by enemy troops.

besiege [bi'siːdʒ] *vt.* 围(enclose)

【记】 be+siege(围攻)

【例】 The speaker was *besieged* with questions.

morale [mə'rɑːl] *n.* 民心;士气

【记】 比较moral(道德)

【例】 With no food and water, the soldiers are in low *morale*.

mandate ['mændeit] *n.* 命令;要求(command)

【记】 mand(命令)+ate

tactics ['tæktiks] *n.* 战术

【记】 tact(机智)+ics

naval ['neivl] *adj.* 海军的

【记】 比较navy(海军)

military ['militəri] *adj.* 军事的,军用的

考古学

archeology [ˌɑːkiˈɔlədʒi] *n.* 考古学

invaluable [inˈvæljuəbl] *adj.* 无价的(valuable, precious)

【记】invaluable=valuable(有价值的);比较 valueless(无价值的)

unearth [ʌnˈəːθ] *vt.* 发掘,发现(uncover, exhume)

【记】un+earth(土地)→弄开土→挖掘

【例】A recent excavation *unearthed* a pottery of Ming dynasty.

scoop [skuːp] *vt.* 汲取;挖掘(dig, pick)

【例】He used his bare hands to *scoop* up water from the river.

exhume [igˈzuːm] *vt.* 掘出(excavate, dig)

【记】ex(出)+hume(土)→出土→掘出

【例】The coroner *exhumed* the body in order to perform tests regarding the cause of death.

excavate [ˈekskəveit] *vt.* 挖掘(dig, delve)

【记】ex+cav(洞)+ate→挖出洞→挖掘

【例】They *excavated* a huge hole for the foundation of the building.

excavation [ˌekskəˈveiʃən] *n.* 挖掘,发掘;挖掘成的洞;出土文物

Neolithic [niːəuˈliθik] *adj.* 新石器时代的

Mesolithic [ˌmesəuˈliθik, ˌmez-] *n.* 中石器时代(旧石器时代与新石器时代之间的时代)

Paleolithic [ˌpæliəuˈliθik] *adj.* 旧石器时代的

origin [ˈɔridʒin] *n.* 起源,由来

chronological [ˌkrɔnəˈlɔdʒikl] *adj.* 按年代顺序的

【例】This article describes events in a *chronological* order.

archaic [ɑːˈkeiik] *adj.* 古的(old)

【记】arch(古)+aic

【例】The *archaic* ship was just like the ones used centuries earlier.

ascend [əˈsend] *v.* 追溯

【例】His ancestors *ascend* to the 15th century.

originate [əˈridʒineit] *vi.* 发源于(initiate, start)

【例】The compass *originated* from China.

primitive [ˈprimitiv] *adj.* 原始的,最初的(crude, original, primordial)

remnant [ˈremnənt] *n.* 残余;遗迹(remains, leftover, vestige)

【例】No *remnants* of the settlement of Roanoke, Virginia were found by the next group of colonists.

porcelain	['pɔːsəlin] *n.* 瓷器(china)
antique	[æn'tiːk] *n.* 古物，古董
antiquity	[æn'tikwiti] *n.* 古代，古老，古代的遗物
skull	[skʌl] *n.* 头脑；头骨
artifact	['ɑːtifækt] *n.* 人造物品

The tragedy of life is not so much what men suffer, but what they miss. ——*Carlyle*

生活的悲剧不在于人们受到多少苦，而在于人们错过了什么。

——卡莱尔

农 业

prolific [prə'lifik] *adj.* 多产的(productive)

【例】The *prolific* author published over 80 novels.

rich [ritʃ] *adj.* 富有的(wealthy)

fertile ['fə:tail] *adj.* 肥沃的；多产的(fruitful; rich)

【记】fert=fer(带来)+ile→能带来粮食→肥沃的

【例】The very *fertile* couple had six children in eight years.

harvest ['hɑ:vist] *n./v.* 收获(glean, gather)

【例】It's already autumn, a time to *harvest*.

agriculture ['æɡrikʌltʃə] *n.* 农业，农艺，农学

agricultural [ˌæɡri'kʌltʃərəl] *adj.* 农业的，农艺的

aquaculture ['ækwəˌkʌltʃə] *n.* 水产业

arable ['ærəbl] *adj.* 适于耕种的(farmable, fruitful)

【记】ara(耕种)+ble

indigenous [in'didʒinəs] *adj.* 土产的，当地的

【记】indi(内部)+gen(产生)+ous→内部产生→土产的

【例】The *indigenous* people of the area know which plants are safe to eat and which are poisonous.

fertilizer ['fə:tilaizə] *n.* 肥料

【记】来自fertilize(施肥)

husbandry ['hʌzbəndri] *n.* 耕种；管理(farming management)

【记】husband(丈夫)+ry→丈夫负责→耕种

【例】He studied animal *husbandry* in college.

graze [ɡreiz] *v.* 吃草(feed)

【例】This field will *graze* 30 head of cattle.

cultivate ['kʌltiveit] *vt.* 耕种；培养(till; foster, train)

【记】cult(培养)+ivate

【例】The botanist *cultivated* tropical flowers.

cultivation [ˌkʌlti'veiʃən] *n.* 耕种；培养

【例】Max's natural skills at painting only needed *cultivation*.

manure [mə'njuə] *vt.* 施肥(fertilizer, dung)

【例】The farmers *manured* the fields in the spring.

horticulture ['hɔ:tikʌltʃə] *n.* 园艺

hydroponics ['haidrəu'pɔniks] *n.* 水耕法，水栽培

insecticide [in'sektisaid] *n.* 杀虫剂

irrigate [ˈirigeit] vt. 灌溉，修水利

【例】They *irrigated* the land in order to increase the produce.

pesticide [ˈpestisaid] n. 杀虫剂

ridge [ridʒ] v. 起皱，成脊状延伸，翻土作垄

【例】The land *ridges* toward the south.

silt [silt] n. 淤泥，残渣，煤粉，泥沙

tractor [ˈtræktə] n. 拖拉机

squash [skwɔʃ] n. 南瓜

cotton [ˈkɔtn] n. 棉花，棉线

garlic [ˈgɑːlik] n. 大蒜，蒜头

eggplant [ˈegplɑːnt] n. 茄子

fodder [ˈfɔdə] n. 饲料，草料

hay [hei] n. 干草

haystack [ˈheistæk] n. 干草堆

vegetable [ˈvedʒitəbl] n. 蔬菜，植物 adj. 蔬菜的，植物的

weed [wiːd] n. 野草，杂草 v. 除草，铲除

【例】Ofen *weeding* the garden will do good to the flowers.

sorghum [ˈsɔːgəm] n. 高粱属的植物

livestock [ˈlaivstɔk] n. 家畜，牲畜

poultry [ˈpəultri] n. 家禽

buffalo [ˈbʌfələu] n. (印度，非洲等的)水牛

cattle [ˈkætl] n. 牛，家养牲畜

fowl [faul] n. 家禽，禽，禽肉

sow [səu] v. 播种，散布，使密布 [sau] n. 大母猪

【例】As you *sow*, so will you reap.

conservatory [kənˈsɔːvətəri] n. 温室(greenhouse)

【例】Like flowers in the *conservatory*, children are very fragile.

barn [bɑːn] n. 谷仓，畜棚，畜舍

cowshed [ˈkauʃed] n. 牛棚，牛舍

granary [ˈgrænəri] n. 谷仓

greenhouse [ˈgriːnhaus] n. 温室，花房

seedbed [ˈsiːdbed] n. 苗床

sheepfold [ˈʃiːpfəuld] n. 羊圈

orchard [ˈɔːtʃəd] n. 果园，果园里的全部果树

pasture	['pɑːstʃə] *n.*	牧地，草原，牧场
pigpen	['pigpen] *n.*	猪舍，猪舍似的地方
pigsty	['pigstai] *n.*	猪舍，脏房子
plantation	[plæn'teiʃən] *n.*	耕地，种植园，大农场，森林，人造林
ranch	[ræntʃ] *n.*	大农场 *v.* 经营牧场
trough	['trɔːf] *n.*	槽，水槽，饲料槽，木钵

All that you do, do with your might; things done by halves are never done right.　　　　　　　　　　—*Sloddard*
做一切事情都应尽力而为,不可半途而废。

——斯托达德

気象

balmy [ˈbɑːmi] *adj.* 温和的(refreshing, mild, temperate, moderate)
【记】balm(香气)+y

humid [ˈhjuːmid] *adj.* 潮湿的(damp, moist)
【例】The *humid* weather made everyone sticky and uncomfortable.

humidity [hjuːˈmiditi] *n.* 潮湿(moisture)
【记】humid(湿)+ity→潮湿

damp [dæmp] *adj.* 潮湿的,有湿气的(wet, moist)
【例】Tony wiped the counter with a *damp* rag.

dank [dæŋk] *adj.* 阴湿的(damp, clammy)
【例】Our cellar is *dank* and dark.

moisture [ˈmɔistʃə] *n.* 潮湿,湿气

saturate [ˈsætʃəreit] *v.* 使饱和,浸透,使充满
【例】Don't forget to *satuatate* the meat in the mixture of oil and herbs.

drought [draut] *n.* 干旱(aridity, dry period, prolonged lack of rain)
【例】The lawns turned brown and the trees lost their leaves during the *drought*.

arid [ˈærid] *adj.* 干旱的(barren, infertile, dry)
【例】The desert is an *arid* place.

chilly [ˈtʃili] *adj.* 寒冷的
【例】It is a bit *chilly* outside today.

chill [tʃil] *n.* 寒冷 *vt.* 使变冷
【例】A freezing draft gave everyone in the room a *chill*.

frigid [ˈfridʒid] *adj.* 严寒的(icy, freezing); 冷淡的
【记】frig(寒冷)+id
【例】The Eskimos are used to *frigid* weather.

serene [səˈriːn] *adj.* 晴朗的
【例】In the countryside people can enjoy *serene* skies and clean air.

tepid [ˈtepid] *adj.* 微温的(lukewarm, warm)
【例】The coffee that was hot fifteen minutes ago is now *tepid*.

gale [geil] *n.* 大风(storm, tempest)

hurricane [ˈhʌrikein] *n.* 飓风
【记】twister 龙卷风, tornado 龙卷风

atmosphere [ˈætməsfiə] *n.* 气氛;大气层
【例】The Smith's favorite restaurant has a friendly, relaxed *atmosphere*.

climate [ˈklaimit] *n.* 气候,气氛(weather, atmosphere)

【例】The *climate* in this part of the country is very mild.

barometer　[bə'rɔmitə] *n.* 气压计(indicator)

【记】baro(压力)＋meter

【例】A *barometer* is useful in predicting the weather.

breeze　[briːz] *n.* 微风

blast　[blɑːst] *n.* 一阵(风)(gust, blow)

【例】The leaves were lifted into the air by a sudden *blast* of wind.

whirlwind　['(h)wəːlwind] *n.* 旋风

typhoon　[tai'fuːn] *n.* 台风

tornado　[tɔː'neidəu] *n.* 旋风，龙卷风，大雷雨

meteorology　[ˌmiːtjə'rɔlədʒi] *n.* 气象学，气象状态

troposphere　['trɔpəusfiə] *n.* 对流层

current　['kʌrənt] *n.* 气流

funnel　['fʌnəl] *n.* 漏斗云

smog　[smɔg] *n.* 烟雾

fog　[fɔg] *n.* 雾，烟雾，尘雾

【记】比较frog(青蛙)

precipitate　[pri'sipiteit] *v.* 凝结(形成雨、雪)

【记】pre(提前)＋cipit(落下)＋ate→降下

【例】It's supposed to *precipitate* today, so bring an umbrella.

precipitation　[priˌsipi'teiʃən] *n.* 降水

drizzle　['drizl] *v.* 下细雨(rain, sprinkle)

【例】Today it *drizzled* and was cold.

blizzard　['blizəd] *n.* 大风雪

dew　[djuː] *n.* 露，露水般的东西

downpour　['daunpɔː(r)] *n.* 倾盆大雨

droplet　['drɔplit] *n.* 小滴

frost　[frɔst, frɔːst] *n.* 霜，霜冻，严寒 *v.* 结霜

【例】The cold has *frosted* the windows.

vapor　['veipə] *n.* 水汽，水蒸气

tempest　['tempist] *n.* 暴风雨

shower　['ʃauə] *n.* 阵雨；淋浴

hail　[heil] *n.* 冰雹

condense　[kən'dens] *v.* (使)浓缩，精简

【例】Steam *condenses* to water when it touches a cold surface.

crystal ['krıstl] *adj.* 结晶状的

Our greatest glory consists not in never falling but in rising every time we fall. —*Goldsmith*

我们最值得自豪的不在于从不跌倒，而在于每次跌倒之后都爬起来。

——戈德史密斯

人类学

juvenile [ˈdʒuːvinail] *adj.* 青少年的（adolescent, young）

【记】juven（年青）＋ile

【例】The clerk directed Jane and her mother to the *juvenile* clothing section of the store.

adult [əˈdʌlt] *n.* 成人 *adj.* 成人的，成熟的（mature）

human [ˈhjuːmən] *adj.* 人类的，人性的

【例】Being angry at something that is unfair is very *human*.

anthropology [ˌænθrəˈpɔlədʒi] *n.* 人类学

tribe [traib] *n.* 部落，部族

ethnic [ˈeθnik] *adj.* 种族的（racial, national）

【记】ethn（种族）＋ic

【例】The chef prepared many *ethnic* dishes.

ethnology [ˌeθˈnɔlədʒi] *n.* 人种学，人类文化学

minority [maiˈnɔriti] *n.* 少数；少数民族

【记】minor（小，少）＋ity→少的状态→少数

descent [diˈsent] *n.* 血统（ancestry）

hybrid [ˈhaibrid] *n.* 杂种；混血儿

intelligence [inˈtelidʒəns] *n.* 智力

【记】intel（中间）＋lig（选择）＋ence→从中选出好的智力

intellectual [ˌintiˈlektʃuəl] *adj.* 智力的

【记】intellect（智力）＋ual

aboriginal [ˌæbəˈridʒənəl] *n.* 土著 *adj.* 土著的，原来的（native）

【记】ab＋original（原版的，原来的）

ancestor [ˈænsistə] *n.* 祖先，祖宗

forerunner [ˈfɔːˌrʌnə] *n.* 先驱，祖先（ancestor, predecessor）

【记】fore（前）＋runner（奔跑者）→先驱

hominid [ˈhɔminid] *n.* 原始人类

cranial [ˈkreinjəl] *adj.* 头盖的，头盖形的

人　物

场景:新东方课堂(人数约 800)

REDROCK：在 TOEFL 人物文章中,讲得最多的是什么人?

众生齐答:"女人!"

我必须承认他们是正确的,在讲述人物的文章中,有一个特殊的现象是:在曾经考过的 30 多个人物中,只有两位男性——发明电灯的 Edison 和发明润滑器的 McCoy。

TOEFL 阅读中出现的女性无论从事何种职业,她们在有生之年大多被认为是性情孤僻(eccentric)、性格独特(unique)、多愁善感(sentimental)等等。而到离世之后(posthumously)却获得了人们普遍的认可(acclaimed),她们很快与杰出(preeminent)为伍,变得家喻户晓(household),每次讲到这里我都替她们深深遗憾,如果 Emily Dickinson 们能活到现在该多好啊! 她们不仅能看到自己的抒情诗(lyrics)终被列为经典馆藏起来,而且她们也会看到 ETS 关注的大多是她们平生不愿意上"对话"节目的那一部分,而不是她们的艺术或文学成就。很显然, ETS 没有歧视她们。在研究美国女权主义(feminism)起源的一篇文章中,数位杰出而不知名的女性被一一列出,这是何等的荣耀啊!

counsel	[ˈkaunsəl] *n.* 律师

crew [kruː] *n.* 船员

【例】The *crew* rowed the boat up and down the river.

aviator [ˈeivieitə] *n.* 飞行家(pilot)

【例】The navy *aviator* had been trained for many years.

playwright [ˈpleirait] *n.* 剧作家

【记】play(戏剧)＋wright(作家)

operator [ˈɔpəreitə] *n.* 接线员

clergy [ˈkləːdʒi] *n.* 神职人员

【例】Bill and his wife are both members of the *clergy*.

auditor [ˈɔːditə] *n.* 审计员；旁听者

【记】audi(听)＋or

athlete [ˈæθliːt] *n.* 运动员

satirist [ˈsætirist] *n.* 讽刺作家

sculptor [ˈskʌlptə(r)] *n.* 雕刻家

mathematician [ˌmæθiməˈtiʃən] *n.* 数学家

astronaut [ˈæstrənɔːt] *n.* 太空人，宇航员

astronomer [əˈstrɔnəmə(r)] *n.* 天文学家

spaceman [ˈspeismən] *n.* 太空船上的飞行员，宇宙人

botanist [ˈbɔtənist] *n.* 植物学家

choreographer [ˌkɔriˈɔgrəfə(r)] *n.* 舞蹈设计师

scout [skaut] *n.* 侦察员；童子军

【例】He is a responsible *scout* with keen observation.

geographer [dʒiˈɔgrəfə] *n.* 地理学者

geologist [dʒiˈɔlədʒist] *n.* 地质学者

educator [ˈedjuːkeitə(r)] *n.* 教育家

faculty [ˈfækəlti] *n.* 全体教员

treasurer [ˈtreʒərə] *n.* 司库，财务员，出纳员

archeologist [ˌɑːkiˈɔlədʒist] *n.* 考古学家

paleoanthropologist [ˌpæliəuˌænθərəˈpɔlədʒist] *n.* 古人类学家

pilot [ˈpailət] *n.* 飞行员，领航员，引水员

meteorologist [ˌmiːtjəˈrɔlədʒist] *n.* 气象学者

anthropologist [ˌænθrəˈpɔlədʒist] *n.* 人类学者，人类学家

artist [ˈɑːtist] *n.* 艺术家，画家

imagist ['imədʒist] *n.* 意象派诗人

inventor [in'ventə(r)] *n.* 发明家

mechanic [mi'kænik] *n.* 技工,机修工,机械师

biographer [bai'ɔgrəfə] *n.* 传记作者

censor ['sensə] *n.* 检查员 *vt.* 检查

【例】The dictator *censored* news of the war.

physician [fi'ziʃən] *n.* 医师(doctor)

hermit ['hə:mit] *n.* 隐居者

【例】The *hermit* lived in a tiny cottage in the woods.

recluse ['reklu:s] *n.* 隐士(hermit)

【记】re(重新)+cluse(close关闭)→隐居

ecologist [i'kɔlədʒist] *n.* 生态学者 *ecologist*

critic ['kritik] *n.* 批评家,评论家,吹毛求疵者

philanthropist [fi'lænθrəpist] *n.* 慈善家

attorney [ə'tə:ni] *n.* 代理人,辩护律师(lawyer)

【例】Bob hired an *attorney* to get a patent for his invention.

congressman ['kɔŋgresmən] *n.* 国会议员

【例】Five *congressmen* spoke in favor of the amendment.

connoisseur [ˌkɔni'sə:] *n.* 鉴赏家,行家

【记】con+nois(知道)+seur→懂行的人

【例】The art *connoisseur* thought the exhibit was distasteful.

entrepreneur [ˌɔntrəprə'nə:] *n.* 企业家;主办人

principal ['prinsəpl] *n.* 校长(head, headmaster)

staff [stɑ:f] *n.* 全体人员或职员

commander [kə'mɑ:ndə] *n.* 司令官,指挥员

【例】The soldiers stood at attention while their *commander* inspected them.

commentator ['kɔmenteitə] *n.* 注释者,评论家

【例】The sports *commentator* had his own radio program.

attendant [ə'tendənt] *n.* 侍者,护理人员(waiter)

【例】The queen's *attendants* went everywhere with her.

trapper ['træpə] *n.* 设陷阱捕兽者

orator [ˈɔːrətə] *n.* 演讲者（speaker）

idiot [ˈidiət] *n.* 白痴，傻子

【记】idio（个人）＋t→特殊的个人→白痴

idiocy [ˈidiəsi] *n.* 白痴

【记】来自idiot

moron [ˈmɔːrɔn] *n.* 低能儿，白痴（idiot）

【记】moro（笨）＋n

illiterate [iˈlitərit] *n.* 文盲（uneducated）

【记】il（不）＋literate（识字的）

proxy [ˈprɔksi] *n.* 代理人（deputy）

【例】I'm acting as a *proxy* for the president while he's on vacation.

deputy [ˈdepjuti] *n.* 代理人（representative）

【例】The head of the company could not be there in person, so he sent his *deputy*.

proprietor [prəˈpraiətə] *n.* 所有者，经营者

consumer [kənˈsjuːmə] *n.* 顾客，消费者（customer）

employer [imˈplɔiə] *n.* 雇用者，雇主

【例】I asked my *employer* for a raise.

employee [ˌemplɔiˈiː] *n.* 雇员

【例】The factory *employees* must arrive by 7:30 a.m..

debtor [ˈdetə] *n.* 债务人

【例】I don't borrow money because my parents told me never to be a *debtor*.

arbitrator [ˈɑːbitreitə] *n.* 仲裁者（mediator, arbiter）

【例】The disputing parties agreed to accept the decision of the *arbitrator*.

superintendent [ˌsjuːpərinˈtendənt] *n.* 主管，负责人，指挥者（supervisor, manager）

【记】super（上面）＋intendent（监督）

apprentice [əˈprentis] *n.* 学徒（disciple）

tenant [ˈtenənt] *n.* 租户，房客（occupant, inhabitant）

miser [ˈmaizə] *n.* 守财奴，吝啬鬼

donor [ˈdəunə] *n.* 捐助者（contributor）

【例】The hospital asked for blood *donors*.

personnel [ˌpəːsəˈnel] *n.* 人员，职员

【记】person(人)＋nel

benefactor [ˈbenifæktə] n. 恩人，捐助人

【记】bene(好)＋fact(做)＋or→做好事的人

【例】The generous *benefactor* remained anonymous.

mortal [ˈmɔːtl] n. 凡人(human)

【记】mort(死)＋al

【例】All *mortals*, however outstanding, are to die one day.

company [ˈkʌmpəni] n. 伙伴

【例】You would not have been robbed if you had taken me as your *company*.

audience [ˈɔːdjəns] n. 观众(spectator)

【例】The *audience* loved the opera and gave it a standing ovation.

recipient [riˈsipiənt] n. 接受者(receiver, payee)

exponent [eksˈpəunənt] n. 解释者(interpreter, expositor)

【记】另一个意思是"支持者"，比较opponent(反对者)

【例】The senator is a staunch *exponent* of civil rights.

resident [ˈrezidənt] n. 居民(inhabitant, occupant)

【例】The population of *resident* bacteria in a clean square centimeter on human skin exceeds a million.

inhabitant [inˈhæbitənt] n. 居民，住户(resident, occupant)

【记】inhabit＋ant

bachelor [ˈbætʃələ] n. 单身汉(unmarried man)；学士

idol [ˈaidl] n. 偶像

novice [ˈnɔvis] n. 新信徒；生手(beginner, tyro, layman)

【记】nov(新)＋ice(表示人)

believer [biˈliːvə] n. 信徒(faithful)

【记】来自believe(相信)

【例】The faithful *believers* always went to church.

cult [kʌlt] n. 崇拜者

【例】The *cult* leader believed he was the son of God.

fanatic [fəˈnætik] n. 盲信者

【记】fan(迷)＋atic→着迷的人→盲信者

adherent [ədˈhiərənt] n. 信奉者(supporter)

【记】adhere(粘着)＋ent→坚持的人

【例】The political party's loyal *adherents* contributed a lot of money.

faithful ['feiθful] *n.* 信徒

【记】faith(忠诚)＋ful

【例】In Amish tribe, the *faithful* are not allowed to own auto-mobiles.

disciple [di 'saipl] *n.* 门徒(apprentice)

【例】Jesus had twelve *disciples*.

champion ['tʃæmpjən] *n.* 冠军

【例】Liu Xiang is the famous athlete who won the 28th Athen Olympic Games men's 110m hurdles *champion*..

assassin [ə 'sæsin] *n.* 刺客

【例】The spy was a trained *assassin*.

bandit ['bændit] *n.* 强盗(robber, pirate)

【例】The *bandit* tried to hide from the sheriff.

burglar ['bəːglə] *n.* 夜盗，窃贼

【例】Bill thought he heard a *burglar* downstairs, but it was only the dog.

barbarian [bɑː 'bɛəriən] *n.* 野蛮人

【记】barbar(愚昧)＋ian(人)

【例】Bob's manners are worse than a *barbarian's*.

exile ['ekzail] *n.* 被流放者

【例】The king was *exiled* when his expire was taken over.

rebel ['rebl] *n.* 背叛者(traitor)

【例】He is the perfect recruit for fascist movements: a *rebel* not a revolutionary, contemptuous yet envious of the rich and involved with them.

addict ['ædikt] *n.* 沉溺于…者(indulger, surrender)

【例】John is an *addict* when it comes to cigarettes.

egoist ['iːgəuist] *n.* 自我主义者

【记】ego(我)＋ist

eyewitness ['aiwitnis] *n.* 目击者(spectator)

【记】eye(眼睛)＋witness(证人)

【例】An *eyewitness* to the crime testified against the suspect.

spectator ['spekteitə] *n.* 旁观者；观众(viewer, audience)

【记】sepct(看)＋ator(人)

spouse [spaus] *n.* 配偶(partner, mate)

couple ['kʌpl] *n.* 一对(夫妇)(pair)

beneficiary [ˌbeni 'fiʃəri] *n.* 受益者

【例】The museum was the *beneficiary* of Mary's generosity.

inferior [inˈfiəriə] *n.* 下级，晚辈

【记】infer(低)＋ior；比较superior(上级)

【例】You can't talk like you are God even if he is your *inferior*.

zealot [ˈzelət] *n.* 热心者(fanatic, bigot)

precursor [pri(ː)ˈkəːsə] *n.* 先驱

avant-garde [ˌævɔnˈɡɑːd] *n.* 先锋派，前卫

alumni [əˈljuːmnai] *n.* 男毕业生，男校友

skeptic [ˈskeptik] *n.* 怀疑者

malcontent [ˈmælkəntent] *n.* 不平者，不满者

【记】mal(坏)＋content(满意的)

foe [fəu] *n.* 敌人(enemy, adversary)

opponent [əˈpəunənt] *n.* 敌人；对手(enemy; rival)

rival [ˈraivəl] *n.* 对手 *v.* 竞争

【例】Edison is a genius who can't be *rivaled* by ordinary mortals though advancedly educated.

celebrity [siˈlebriti] *n.* 名人(person of note)

【例】The unknown actress became a *celeberity* when her first film was released.

figurehead [ˈfiɡəhed] *n.* 名义领袖

【记】figuar(形象)＋head(头，首领)

veteran [ˈvetərən] *n.* 老兵，老手(ex-serviceman, old soldier)

traitor [ˈtreitə] *n.* 叛徒，卖国贼(betrayer)

advocate [ˈædvəkit] *n.* 辩护者；拥护者

【记】ad＋voc(说)＋ate

【例】She is an *advocate* of equal pay for men and women.

feminist [ˈfeminist] *n.* 男女平等主义者，女权扩张论者

humanitarian [hju(ː)ˌmæniˈtɛəriən] *n.* 人道主义者

throng [θrɔːŋ] *n.* 群众(crowd, swarm)

【例】The noisy *throng* of teenagers jammed the hall to hear the rock concert.

civilian [siˈviljən] *n.* 平民 *adj.* 平民的

【例】The *civilians* watched the soldiers marching in the parade.

monarch [ˈmɔnək] *n.* 君主，最高统治者

【记】mon(单个)＋arch(统治者)→君主

conservative [kənˈsəːvətiv] *n.* 保守的人 *adj.* 保守的

【例】A *conservative* estimate of the cost to repair the car is ＄100.

envoy [ˈenvɔi] *n.* 使者，公使

【例】The *envoy* traveled regularly to foreign countries.

aristocrat [əˈristəkræt] *n.* 贵族(blue blood)

【记】aristo(最好)＋crat(统治者)

gentry [ˈdʒentri] *n.* 贵族

autocrat [ˈɔːtəkræt] *n.* 独裁者(dictator)

【记】auto(自己)＋crat(统治者)→独裁者

【例】The *autocrat* ruled the country unjustly.

delegate [ˈdeligit] *n.* 代表(deputy, representative)

【记】de(加强)＋leg(法律)＋ate→加强法律之人→代表

democrat [ˈdeməkræt] *n.* 民主党人

independent [indiˈpendənt] *n.* 中立派，无党派者

candidate [ˈkændidit] *n.* 候选人

【例】The reporter asked the *candidate* some tough questions.

Our destiny offers not the cup of despair, but the chalice of opportunity. —*Nixon*

命运给予我们的不是失望之酒，而是机会之杯。

——尼克松

社会学

urban ['ə:bən] *adj.* 城市的（municipal, metropolitan）

rustic ['rʌstik] *adj.* 乡村的（rural, unsophisticated）

【记】rust（乡村）+ic

community [kə'mju:niti] *n.* 社区；社会；公社

【记】commune（公共的）+ity→公共状态→社会，社区

【例】There are seven churches in our *community*.

metropolitan [metrə'pɒlit(ə)n] *adj.* 首都的，主要都市的，大城市的

exotic [ig'zɒtik] *adj.* 外来的；有异国风味的（unusual, foreign）

【记】exo（外面）+tic→外来的

【例】Susan and Bill love to eat spicy and *exotic* food.

conventional [kən'venʃənl] *adj.* 传统的，习俗的（traditional, customary）

【例】Mary thought marriage and family was too *conventional* so she joined the army.

convention [kən'venʃən] *n.* 传统

【例】Chinese people have the *convention* of shaking hands.

patriarchal [ˌpeitri'ɑːkəl] *adj.* 家长的，族长的

institutionalize [ˌinsti'tjuːʃənəlaiz] *v.* 使制度化或习俗化

【例】One question that is raised is how to *institutionalize* our scholarship disciplines.

clan [klæn] *n.* 部落，氏族，宗族，党派

status ['stætəs] *n.* 地位（position, rank）

【例】The *status* of colonial women had been well studied.

taboo [tə'buː] *n./vt.* 禁忌；禁止（ban, prohibition）

【例】Four-letter words are *taboo* words to these ladies.

ethics ['eθiks] *n.* 伦理学

【记】eth=ethn（种族）+ics→种族规范→伦理学

genteel [dʒen'tiːl] *adj.* 上流社会的（well-bred, courteous）

【记】比较gentle（温柔）

marital ['mæritl] *adj.* 婚姻的（wedded, conjugal）

【记】比较marriage（结婚）

polygamous [pɒ'ligəməs] *adj.* 一夫多妻的，一妻多夫的

household ['haushəuld] *n.* 一家人，家庭，家族

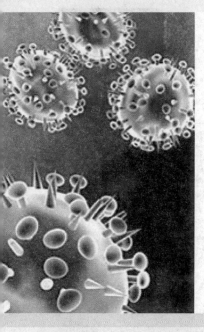

生物学

parasite ['pærəsait] *n.* 寄生虫；寄生植物

【记】para(旁边)+site(坐)→坐在旁边的→寄生虫

parasitic [ˌpærə'sitik] *adj.* 寄生的

mimicry ['mimikri] *n.* 模仿；拟态(camouflage)

【记】mimic(模枋)+ry

【例】The stick caterpillar's vivid *mimicry* enlarged its chances of survival.

symbiosis [simbai'əusis] *n.* 共生(现象)，合作(或互利，互依)关系

symbiotic [ˌsimbai'ɔtik] *adj.* 共生的

creature ['kri:tʃə] *n.* 生物

organism ['ɔ:gənizəm] *n.* 生物，有机物

【记】organ(器官)+ism

strain [strein] *n.* (动物、昆虫等的)种；血统

species ['spi:ʃiz] *n.* 物种

vital ['vaitl] *adj.* 活的，活体的

ripe [raip] *adj.* 成熟的(mature, ready)

【例】We describe plants as "*ripe*", and animals as "mature".

evolve [i'vɔlv] *v.* (使)进化；(使)发展(develop, grow)

【例】Modern turtles *evolved* from a very large, prehistoric species of turtle.

evolutionary [ˌevə'lu:ʃənəri] *adj.* 进化的

Darwinism ['dɑ:winizəm] *n.* 达尔文学说，进化论

extinct [iks'tiŋkt] *adj.* 灭绝的

【记】ex+tinct(促使)→促使出去→灭绝

extinction [iks'tiŋkʃən] *n.* 灭绝

【例】What caused the *extinction* of dinosaurs?

breed [bri:d] *vt.* 养育，繁殖(raise) *n.* 品种(species, strain)

【例】The housewife has been *breeding* chickens for years.

reproduction [ˌri:prə'dʌkʃən] *n.* 繁殖(multiplication)；复制品

【记】re(重新)+production(生产)→复制

【例】Don't get yourself cheated. The vase is only a *reproduction*.

proliferate [prəu'lifəreit] *v.* 繁衍(multiply, increase)

【记】pro(前)+lifer(后代)+ate→增殖，激增

【例】Autumn is the best season for crab to *proliferate*.

propagate ['prɔpəgeit] *vt.* 繁殖(multiply, proliferate)；传播

【例】Missionaries went far afield to *propagate* their faith.

subsist [səb'sist] *vi.* 生存(live, survive)

【例】The poor farmer's family *subsisted* on potatoes.

exist [igˈzist] *vi.* 生存(survive)

【例】We wish our love will *exist* forever.

posterity [pɔsˈteriti] *n.* 后代(offspring, descendant)

【记】post(后)+erity

fermentation [ˌfəːmenˈteiʃn] *n.* 发酵

【记】ferm=ferv(热)+entation→热而发酵

【例】During *fermentation*, yeast emits a distinctive smell.

respiration [ˌrespəˈreiʃən] *n.* 呼吸(breathing)

【记】re(反复)+spir(呼吸)+ation

stodgy [ˈstɔdʒi] *adj.* 难消化的

secrete [siˈkriːt] *vt.* 分泌(discharge, release)

【例】The stomach begins to *secrete* a certain type of enzyme when food reaches it.

secretion [siˈkriːʃən] *n.* 分泌(物)

assimilate [əˈsimileit] *vt.* 吸收(absorb, integrate, incorporate)

【记】as+simil(相同)+ate→使相同→同化, 吸收

【例】I have not quite *assimilated* the new rules so I sometimes violate them by mistake.

immune [iˈmjuːn] *adj.* 免除的; 免疫的(unaffected, unsusceptible)

【记】im(没有)+mune(责任)→没有责任→免除的

【例】I had the mumps when I was six, so now I am *immune*.

immunity [iˈmjuːniti] *n.* 免疫性

metabolism [meˈtæbəlizəm] *n.* 新陈代谢

【记】meta(变化)+bolism→产生变化→新陈代谢

【例】Lazy people with slow *metabolism* tend to gain weight.

morphology [mɔːˈfɔlədʒi] *n.* 形态学

microscope [ˈmaikrəskəup] *n.* 显微镜

calorie [ˈkæləri] *n.* 卡路里

carbohydrate [ˈkɑːbəuˈhaidreit] *n.* 碳水化合物, 醣类

glucose [ˈgluːkəus] *n.* 葡萄糖

protein [ˈprəutiːn] *n.* 蛋白质 *adj.* 蛋白质的

organ [ˈɔːgən] *n.* 器官

数　学

　　TOEFL 的数学类文章展现下列主题：

　　数学是人类的一项本能（instinct），假如一个小孩子出生后就被遗弃（deserted）到一个荒岛（isolated island），七八年后把他或她接回来放到小学一二年级，数学上没有任何问题啊。

　　这当然是一个狂野并惨无人道的假想试验，但证明了人们计数的能力是本能。

　　人们的计数系统是如何发展起来的呢？

　　人们最早先是在数羊的时候发现需要十进制（decimal system）来解决问题，用双手的十个指头来数羊当然容易理解，多了就无法计算了，某些种族估计也使用了脚趾头，就有了二十进制，再多就采用打结的方式记录，小结太多也不够用，大结就代表十，小结就代表一了。

　　TOEFL 文章对古代数学水平非常艳美，总是慨叹啊呀古人真厉害啊，在没有纸张等介质（medium）的情况下就算出了圆周率，估计祖冲之老先生在天有灵，对外夷的崇拜一定感到很无聊的。

rank ［ræŋk］ *v.* 排序，排行 *n.* 等级

【例】He *ranked* first in the class. / The railroad novel was not treated as the first-*rank* novel.

discrete ［dis'kriːt］ *adj.* 不连续的；离散的（separate）

【例】A computer can perform millions of *discrete* functions per second.

symmetry ［'simitri］ *n.* 对称（性），匀称（balance, harmony）

【记】sym（共同）＋metry（测量）→两边测量一样→对称

sequence ［'siːkwəns］ *n.* 序列（procession, progression）

【记】sequ（跟随）＋ence→跟随着→序列

dual ［'djuːəl］ *adj.* 二重的；两层的（double; twofold）

【例】This stove has *dual* ovens, so you can bake bread and roast meat at the same time.

induction ［in'dʌkʃən］ *n.* 感应，感应现象；归纳

inference ［'infərəns］ *n.* 推论

circular ［'səːkjulə］ *adj.* 循环的，圆的（circuitous, roundabout）

【记】circul（绕圈）＋ar

【例】The carpenter used a special saw to cut a *circular* hole.

circulate ［'səːkjuleit］ *v.* (使)循环

【例】The rumor *circulated* through the office.

circulation ［ˌsəːkju'leiʃən］ *n.* 循环

【例】A tight ring cut off *circulation* to my finger.

probability ［ˌprɔbə'biliti］ *n.* 可能性，或然性，概率

qualitative ［'kwɔlitətiv］ *adj.* 性质上的，定性的

dispersion ［dis'pəːʒən］ *n.* 离差，差量

vertical ［'vəːtikl］ *adj.* 垂直的（perpendicular, upright）

plumb ［plʌm］ *adj.* 垂直的（straight, vertical）

upright ［'ʌprait］ *adj./adv.* 垂直的(地)，笔直的(地)（vertical, upstanding）

【记】up(上)＋right(正的)

【例】An empty sack cannot stand *upright*.

cubic ［'kjuːbik］ *adj.* 立方体的

circuitous ［sə'kjuːitəs］ *adj.* 迂回的（indirect, roundabout）

【记】circuit（绕圈）＋ous

【例】You could tell Mary was evading our question when she gave a *circuitous* response.

facet ['fæsit] *n.* 平面

【例】The stonecutter decided to improve the rough diamond by providing it with several *facets*.

sphere [sfiə] *n.* 球体（ball, globe）

【例】The earth is usually represented by a *sphere*.

loop [lu:p] *n.* 圈，环，环孔（circle, ring）

triangle ['traiæŋgl] *n.* 三角形

circumference [sə'kʌmfərəns] *n.* 圆周

【记】circum(绕圈)＋ference

【例】The *circumference* of the round table is five feet.

cone [kəun] *n.* 圆锥

【例】The top of a *cone* comes to a sharp point.

caliber ['kælibə] *n.* 口径

diameter [dai'æmitə] *n.* 直径

【记】dia(对)＋meter(量)→量到对面的线→直径

figure ['figə] *n.* 图形，形状（design, shape）

circle ['sə:kl] *n.* 圆周，圆形物，派系，循环

cube [kju:b] *n.* 立方体，立方

column ['kɔləm] *n.* 圆柱，柱壮物

angle ['æŋgl] *n.* 角，角落

area ['ɛəriə] *n.* 范围，区域，面积，地区，空地

ellipse [i'lips] *n.* 椭圆，椭圆形

diagram ['daiəgræm] *n.* 图表（sketch, drawing）

【记】dia(交叉)＋gram(画图)→交叉画图

【例】A good *diagram* helped me assemble the bike.

polygon ['pɔligən] *n.* 多角形，多边形

intersect [ˌintə'sekt] *vi.* 相交（cross, meet）

【记】inter(中间)＋sect(切，割)→从中间相切→相交

【例】These two fences *intersect* at the creek.

radius ['reidjəs] *n.* 半径

rectangle ['rektæŋgl] *n.* 长方形，矩形

square [skwɛə] *n.* 正方形，广场，平方，直角尺

parallel ['pærəlel] *vt.* 与…平行 *adj.* 平行的

【记】para(旁边)＋llel→旁边的→平行的

【例】His paintings *parallels* that of Qi Baishi.

deduction [di'dʌkʃən] n. 扣除，扣除之量；推论，演绎法

degree [di'griː] n. 度数，度，程度

geometry [dʒi'ɔmətri] n. 几何学

【记】geo(地)＋metry→测量地面→几何学

mathematics [ˌmæθə'mætiks] n. 数学

arithmetic [ə'riθmətik] n. 算术

【记】arithm(数学)＋etic

【例】*Arithmetic* is a basic school subject.

statistics [stə'tistiks] n. 统计学；统计表

even ['iːvən] adj. 平的；偶数的

【记】比较odd(奇数)

【例】The children skated on the sidewalk's *even* surface.

decimal ['desiml] adj. 十进制的 n. 小数

【记】decim(十分之一)＋al

【例】The metric system is a *decimal* system.

ratio ['reiʃiəu] n. 比率(proportion, rate)

【例】The *ratio* of men to women is 3 to 1.

estimate ['estimeit] vt. 估计(gauge, compute)

【例】I *estimate* that Tom will be promoted to department manager.

calculate ['kælkjuleit] vt. 计算，估计(count)；计划

【例】Mary *calculated* her monthly expenses.

enumerate [i'njuːməreit] vt. 枚举；计数(count; numerate)

【记】e(出)＋numer(数字)＋ate→按数列出→列举

【例】Sam can *enumerate* all the presidents of the United States.

evaluate [i'væljueit] vt. 评价，估计(estimate, assess)

【记】e＋valu(价值)＋ate

【例】The assessor *evaluated* the plot of land before Anne sold it.

variant ['vɛəriənt] n. 变量(variable)

【记】vari(变化)＋ant

variable ['vɛəriəbl] n. 变量

abacus ['æbəkəs] n. 算盘

aggregate ['ægrigeit] n. 合计，总计；集合体

sum [sʌm] n. 总数，和；金额；算术题

calculation [ˌkælkju'leiʃən] n. 计算，考虑

calculator ['kælkjuleitə] n. 计算机，计算器

calculus [ˈkælkjuləs] n. 微积分学

digit [ˈdidʒit] n. 阿拉伯数字；手指或足趾；一指宽（约四分之三英寸）

function [ˈfʌŋkʃən] n. 函数

subtract [səbˈtrækt] vt. 减去（deduct）

【例】If you *subtract* 2 from 6, you get 4.

addition [əˈdiʃən] n. 加法

minus [ˈmainəs] adj. 负的，减的 prep. 减去 n. 负数

multiply [ˈmʌltiplai] v. 乘，增加

multiplication [ˌmʌltipliˈkeiʃən] n. 乘法，增加

【例】*multiplication* table 乘法表

numeral [ˈnjuːmərəl] n. 数字

percentage [pəˈsentidʒ] n. 百分数，百分率，百分比

plus [plʌs] prep. 加上 adj. 正的，加的

equation [iˈkweiʃən] n. 等式

【例】1＋2＝3 is a simple *equation*.

quarter [ˈkwɔːtə] n. 四分之一

【例】A *quarter* of a century would be 25 years.

fraction [ˈfrækʃən] n. 分数

【记】fract（碎裂）＋ion

divide [diˈvaid] vt. 分割；除

【例】The woman's estate was *divided* among her children.

Not ignorance, but the ignorance of ignorance, is the death of knowledge.　　　　　　　　　　　—*Whitehead*

不是无知本身，而是对无知的无知，才是知识的死亡。

——怀特海德

SUN
MERCURY
VENUS
EARTH
MARS
JUPITER
SATURN
URANUS
NEPTUNE
PLUTO
OTHER

天　文

　　据说在 80 年代的美国大学校园里，帅哥都用这样的话打动美眉："Consider the darkness of outer space(想想外层空间的黑暗吧……)。"这句话足以证明掌握一定的天文学知识是何等重要！在 TOEFL 文章中，天文学文章占据了相当的比重，而且被认为是较难的文章(尽管实际上并非如此)。所有复杂深奥的天文学理论，比如大爆炸(big bang)、黑洞理论(black whole)都不会在 TOEFL 文章中出现，因为宇宙的起源和终结并不是 ETS 关注的主题。TOEFL 文章讲述的只是一些基本的天文学(astronomy)现象，或者某一类天体(celestial body/ heavenly body)。这些文章从宇宙（cosmos/universe）这一大概念出发，讲到其中有无数星系(galaxy)，星系中有无数颗恒星(star, 偶尔也用小写的 sun)，围绕恒星轨道(orbit)运行的是行星(planet)，围绕行星运行的是卫星(satellite)，围绕卫星(如月亮)运行的是人造卫星(man-made satellite)，另外还有一些不规则的天体，如大星云(nebulae)、小星云 / 小行星(asteroid)、流星(meteor)等，流星落到地上被称为陨石(meteorite)。人类发射到太空的一些卫星在老化或失去联系后，就成为太空垃圾(space debris)。

celestial [səˈlestʃəl] *adj.* 天上的，天体的；神圣的（astronomical, heavenly）

【记】celes(天)+tial

【例】The book showed a map of the *celestial* realms.

universe [ˈjuːnivəːs] *n.* 宇宙（cosmos）

universal [ˌjuːniˈvəːsl] *adj.* 宇宙的

orbit [ˈɔːbit] *n.* 轨道（track, path）

【例】Our planet is in *orbit* around the sun.

comet [ˈkɔmit] *n.* 彗星

galaxy [ˈgæləksi] *n.* 星系；银河

constellation [ˌkɔnstəˈleiʃən] *n.* 星座

【记】con+stell(星星)+ation

asteroid [ˈæstərɔid] *n.* 小游星，小行星

planet [ˈplænit] *n.* 行星

chondrite [ˈkɔndrait] *n.* 球粒状陨石

cluster [ˈklʌstə] *n.* 星团

meteor [ˈmiːtjə] *n.* 流星；大气现象

【例】*meteor* shower 流星雨

dwarf [dwɔːf] *n.* 白矮星

star [staː] *n.* 星，恒星

stellar [ˈstelə] *adj.* 恒星的

cosmos [ˈkɔzmɔs] 宇宙

cosmic [ˈkɔzmik] *adj.* 宇宙的

【例】*cosmic* radiation 宇宙辐射；*cosmic* rays 宇宙射线

cosmology [kɔzˈmɔlədʒi] *n.* 宇宙哲学，宇宙论

nebula [ˈnebjulə] *n.* 星云，云翳

quasar [ˈkweisaː] *n.* 恒星状球体，类星体

space [speis] *n.* 空间

planeroid [ˈplænərɔid] *n.* 位面

intergalactic [ˌintəgəˈlæktik] *adj.* 银河间的

interplanetary [ˌintə(ː)ˈplænitəri] *adj.* 行星间的，太阳系内的

interstellar [ˈintə(ː)ˈstelə] *adj.* 星际的

corona [kəˈrəunə] *n.* 日冕

chromosphere [ˈkrəuməsfiə] *n.* 色球

solar ['səulə] *adj.* 太阳的

【例】*solar* system 太阳系；*solar* corona 日冕；*solar* eclipse 日食；*solar* radiation 太阳辐射

photosphere ['fəutəusfiə] *n.* 光球

pseudoscience [(p)sjuː'daisaiəns] *n.* 假科学，伪科学

astronomy [əs'trɔnəmi] *n.* 天文学

【记】astro(星星)＋nomy(学科)→研究星星的学科

astronomical [æstrə'nɔmik(ə)l] *adj.* 天文学的；庞大无法估计的 *n.* 天文

【例】*astronomical* observatory 天文台

astrology [ə'strɔlədʒi] *n.* 占星术，占星学(以观测天象来预卜人间事务的一种方术)

astrophysics [æstrəu'fiziks] *n.* 天体物理学

Jupiter ['dʒuːpitə] *n.* 木星

lunar ['luːnə] *adj.* 月的，月亮的

Mars [mɑːz] *n.* 火星；战神

mercury ['məːkjuri] *n.* 水银，汞

Earth [əːθ] *n.* 地球

Uranus ['juːərənəs] *n.* 天王星

Venus ['viːnəs] *n.* 金星

Pluto ['pluːtəu] *n.* 冥王星；阴间之神

Neptune ['neptjuːn] *n.* 海王星

Saturn ['sætə(ː)n] *n.* 土星

emission [i'miʃən] *n.* (光、热等的)散发，发射，喷射

infinite ['infinit] *adj.* 无穷的，无限的，无数的，极大的

interferometer [ˌintəfiə'rɔmitə] *n.* 干涉仪

radiation [ˌreidi'eiʃən] *n.* 发散，辐射；放射物

revolve [ri'vɔlv] *v.* (使)旋转

【例】Their troubles *revolve* around money management.

land [lænd] *vt.* 着陆，降落

【例】The plane finally *landed* itself safely on the ground.

spaceship ['speisʃip] *n.* 太空船(space shuttle)

spacecraft ['speiskrɑːft] *n.* 太空船

telescope ['teliskəup] *n.* 望远镜

物　理

compatible [kəmˈpætəbl] *adj.* 兼容的（harmonious, congruous）

【例】Is this software *compatible* with my computer?

boundary [ˈbaundəri] *n.* 边界（border, limit）

【例】A fence marked the *boundary* of the woods.

boundless [ˈbaundlis] *adj.* 无限的（vast, limitless）

endless [ˈendlis] *adj.* 无止境的（everlasting）

【例】The long and boring drive seemed *endless*.

cohesive [kəuˈhiːsiv] *adj.* 有凝聚力的

horizontal [ˌhɔriˈzɔntl] *adj.* 水平的

bulk [bʌlk] *n.* 容积

【例】The *bulk* of this oil tank is about 500 tons.

brim [brim] *n.* （杯、碗的）边（margin, edge, rim）

【例】A bird perched on the *brim* of the flowerpot.

edge [edʒ] *n.* 边（rim, margin）

【例】John is at the *edge* of death.

rim [rim] *n.* 边缘（edge, border）

【例】The horse finally came to a halt on the very *rim* of the cliff.

brink [briŋk] *n.* 边缘（margin, edge, rim）

【例】A fence was built along the *brink* of the cliff to prevent accidents.

constituent [kənˈstitjuənt] *n.* 成分（component）

dimension [diˈmenʃən] *n.* 尺度；（数）维（size, proportion）

【例】He drew a house in three-*dimension*.

elasticity [ˌelæsˈtisiti] *n.* 弹性

cohesion [kəuˈhiːʒən] *n.* 附着（力），结合，凝聚力

【例】Since Bob's paper had no *cohesion* and merely listed facts, he received a failing grade.

mechanics [miˈkæniks] *n.* 力学

pressure [ˈpreʃə] *n.* 压力

【记】press(压)＋ure

【例】He feels the *pressure* soon after he takes up the job.

gravity [ˈgræviti] *n.* 引力

【记】grav(重)＋ity

impetus [ˈimpitəs] *n.* 推动力（urge, momentum）

【记】im(进入)＋pet(追求)＋us→追求力→推动力

【例】His longing for another kind of life is a major *impetus* for his hard working.

release [ri'li:s] *n./vt.* 释放（give off, discharge, dismiss, emit）

【例】Thousands of balloons were *released* at the opening ceremony.

decelerate [di:'seləreit] *v.* （使）减速（decrease the speed of）

【记】反义词 accelerate（加速）

【例】Many countries are seeking measures to *decelerate* the arms buildup.

precipitate [pri'sipiteit] *v.* 向下投掷

【记】pre(提前)＋cipit(落下)＋ate→降下

【例】The finest bridge of the city broke and *precipitated* five travelers into the river below.

expedite ['ekspidait] *vt.* 加速（speed up, hasten）

【记】ex＋ped(脚)＋ite→脚跨出去→加速

【例】The person I talked to on the phone promised to *expedite* the shipment of the book I ordered.

quiver ['kwivə] *vt.* 振动，颤抖（shiver, tremble）

【例】The dog *quivered* in the rain.

jar [dʒɑ:] *vt.* 震动

【例】Her announcement really *jarred* me. I was shocked!

vibration [vai'breiʃən] *n.* 震动

discharge [dis'tʃɑ:dʒ] *v.* 释放（let out, release, liberate）

【例】The patient was *discharged* from the hospital after complete recovery.

shrink [ʃriŋk] *vi.* 收缩（contract, compress, dwindle）

【例】Because my shirt had *shrunk*, I gave it to my younger cousin.

diffuse [di'fju:z] *vt.* 传播，扩散（scatter, spread）

【记】di(分开)＋fuse(流)→分流→散播

【例】The winds *diffused* the smoke throughout the neighborhood.

emit [i'mit] *vt.* 发出，放射（discharge, give off）

【例】All the cars that *emit* poisonous gas have been called back.

transpire [træn'spaiə] *vt.* 发散；排出（exhale, send out）

【例】It was *transpired* that the king was already dead.

constitute ['kɔnstitju:t] *vt.* 构成，组成（form, compose, make up）

【例】Not telling the whole truth *constitutes* lying.

eject [i'dʒekt] *vt.* 喷出；逐出（emit; ejaculate）

【记】e(出)＋ject(扔)→扔出→喷出

【例】The machine *ejected* finished parts faster than we could count them.

radiate ['reidieit] *vt.* 射出（emit, give off）

【例】Heat *radiated* from the stove.

molecule ['mɔlikjuːl] *n.* 分子

【记】mole("摩尔")＋cule("小"的后缀)

ion ['aiən] *n.* 离子

electron [i'lektrɔn] *n.* 电子

neutron ['njuːtrɔn] *n.* 中子

nucleus ['njuːkliəs] *n.* 核子

proton ['prəutɔn] *n.* 质子

atom ['ætəm] *n.* 原子

【例】An *atom* is made up of protons, neutrons and one or more electrons.

nuclear ['njuːkliə] *adj.* 原子的

physics ['fiziks] *n.* 物理学

fusion ['fjuːʒən] *n.* 熔合

thermometer [θə'mɔmitə] *n.* 温度计

【记】thermo (热) ＋meter

temperature ['tempəritʃə] *n.* 温度

thaw [θɔː] *v.* (使)溶化,(使)融解（melt, defrost）

【例】Last week it was so warm that the frozen pond *thawed*.

centigrade ['sentigreid] *adj.* 摄氏的

【记】centi(百)＋grade(级，度)

【例】*Centigrade* scale is used in most countries except the United States.

clot [klɔt] *n./v.* (使)凝块（gelatinize, congeal）

【例】Blood had begun to *clot* around the gaping wound.

sublimate ['sʌblimeit] *vt.* 使升华（elevate, refine）

【记】sublime(崇高的)＋ate

【例】Water are *sublimated* from the gaseous to the solid state without becoming a liquid.

distillation [ˌdisti'leiʃən] *n.* 蒸馏

【记】de＋still(水滴)＋ation

【例】*Distillation* is used to produce very pure water.

chaos [ˈkeiɔs] *n.* 混乱(disorder)

【例】*Chaos* broke out when the fire alarm went off.

clutter [ˈklʌtə] *n.* 混乱 *vt.* 使混乱(litter, disarray)

【例】My office is filled with useless *clutter*.

equilibrium [ˌiːkwiˈlibriəm] *n.* 平衡状态(balance)

【例】The gymnast has perfect *equilibrium*.

density [ˈdensiti] *n.* 密度

【例】The population *density* is very high in Hong Kong.

liquid [ˈlikwid] *n.* 液体

【例】The three phases of matter are solid, *liquid* and gas.

dilute [daiˈljuːt] *vt.* 稀释；冲淡(thin, weaken)

【记】di(分开)＋lute(冲)→冲开→冲淡

【例】As the ice melted, it *diluted* my drink.

dehydrate [diːˈhaidreit] *vt.* (使)脱水(dry)

【记】de(去除)＋hydrate(水合物)

【例】Her body had *dehydrated* dangerously with the heat.

declivity [diˈkliviti] *n.* 下倾的斜面

【记】de＋cliv(倾斜)＋ity

foam [fəum] *n.* 泡沫(bubble, froth)

ventilation [ˌventiˈleiʃən] *n.* 通风(airing, air circulation)

evaporate [iˈvæpəreit] *v.* 蒸发(vaporize)

【记】e＋vapor(蒸汽)＋ate

【例】The rubbing alcohol *evaporated* as soon as the nurse dabbed it on the patient's arm.

evaporation [iˌvæpəˈreiʃən] *n.* 蒸发(作用)

thermodynamics [ˈθəːməudaiˈnæmiks] *n.* 热力学

friction [ˈfrikʃən] *n.* 摩擦

【例】The wheel has been expired due to *friction*.

attrition [əˈtriʃən] *n.* 磨损(wear and tear)

chafe [tʃeif] *vt.* 擦热(rub, scrape)

【例】Coarse fabric will *chafe* your skin.

resonance [ˈrezənəns] *n.* 回声，反响

【记】re(反复)＋son(声音)＋ance→回声

– 87 –

【例】The opera singer's voice has very good *resonance*.

echo	[ˈekəu]	n. 回声, 回音, 回波
ultrasonics	[ˌʌltrəˈsɔniks]	n. 超音波学
sonar	[ˈsəunɑː]	n. 声纳, 声波定位仪
accoustic	[əˈkuːstik]	adj. 音响的
band	[bænd]	n. 波段(stripe)
charge	[tʃɑːdʒ]	n. 电荷 v. 充电(fill, replenish)
electricity	[ilekˈtrisiti]	n. 电流, 电, 电学

【例】static *electricity* n. 静电

electromagnet	[ilektrəuˈmægnit]	n. 电磁石
electromagnetism	[ilektrəuˈmægnitiz(ə)m]	n. 电磁, 电磁学
electronic	[ilekˈtrɔnik]	adj. 电子的

【例】*electronic* component 电子元件

electronics	[ilekˈtrɔniks]	n. 电子学
amplifier	[ˈæmpliˌfaiə]	n. [电工]扩音器, 放大器
battery	[ˈbætəri]	n. 电池

【例】dry *battery* 干电池

chip	[tʃip]	n. 芯片
conductor	[kənˈdʌktə]	n. 导体
insulator	[ˈinsjuleitə]	n. 绝缘体, 绝热器
magnet	[ˈmægnit]	n. 磁体, 磁铁
magnetism	[ˈmægnitizəm]	n. 磁, 磁力, 吸引力, 磁学
semiconductor	[ˈsemikənˈdʌktə]	n. 半导体
transistor	[trænˈzistə]	n. 晶体管
ultraviolet	[ˌʌltrəˈvaiəlit]	adj. 紫外线的, 紫外的 n. 紫外线辐射
microwave	[ˈmaikrəuweiv]	n. 微波(波长为1毫米至30厘米的高频电磁波)
mechanics	[miˈkæniks]	n. (用作单数)机械学、力学; (用作复数)技巧, 结构
gravitation	[ˌgræviˈteiʃən]	n. 地心吸力, 引力作用
oscillation	[ˌɔsiˈleiʃən]	n. 摆动, 振动
statics	[ˈstætiks]	n. 静力学
relativity	[ˌreləˈtiviti]	n. 相对性, 相关性, 相对论
velocity	[viˈlɔsiti]	n. 速度, 速率
dynamics	[daiˈnæmiks]	n. 动力学
force	[fɔːs]	n. 力

current [ˈkʌrənt] n. (液体、气体的)流

【例】direct current 直流电；alternating current 交流电

accelerate [ækˈseləreit] vt. 加速 vi. 增速，进行(expedite, speed)

【记】ac＋celer(速度)＋ate→加速

【例】The car accelerated as it went downhill.

acceleration [ækˌseləˈreiʃən] n. 加速度

transparent [trænsˈpærənt] adj. 透明的(clear, limpid)

【例】The sunset shined through the transparent glass.

opaque [əuˈpeik] n. 不透明物 adj. 不透明的，不传热的

translucent [trænzˈljuːsnt] adj. 半透明的，透明的

optical [ˈɔptikəl] adj. 眼的，视力的，光学的

【例】optical fiber 光纤

optics [ˈɔptiks] n. 光学

ray [rei] n. 光线

【例】Gamma rays 伽马射线；infrared rays 红外线；X rays X射线

spectrum [ˈspektrəm] n. 光，光谱，型谱，频谱

wavelength [ˈweivleŋθ] n. 波长

magnifier [ˈmægnifaiə] n. 放大镜，放大器

lens [lenz] n. 透镜，镜头

Man cannot discover new oceans unless he has courage to lose sight of the shore.　　　　　—Gide

人只有鼓起勇气，告别海岸，才能发现新的海洋。

——纪德

医　学

　　医学的起源更是不堪回首，原本是一些炼丹术士（alchemist）为了获得长生不老的灵药（elixir）逐渐积累了医学知识，当年他们连"萃取"这种试验都做过，当然，现代科学已经证明他们当年用以炼丹的物质（matter）是铅（lead）的某种化合物，是有毒的（poisonous），会引起铅中毒（lead poisoning）。基于此，炼丹术（alchemy）也成了伪科学（pseudo-science）的代名词。

　　早期医学发展缓慢的原因：

　　1、本身特性，系统性差（not systematic）；

　　2、炼丹术（alchemy）发展的秘传性（esoteric nature），限制了早期医学知识的传播。

contagious [kən'teidʒəs] *adj.* 传染的（catching, infectious）

【记】con＋tag(接触)＋ious

【例】Cancer is not *contagious*, so you shouldn't be afraid to touch someone with cancer.

catching ['kætʃiŋ] *adj.* 传染的（contagious, infectious）；迷人的

【记】catch(抓)＋ing→心被抓住→迷人的

【例】Mary is quite *catching* on campus.

infect [in'fekt] *vt.* 传染，感染（spread, affect）

【记】in(进入)＋fect(做)→做进去→传染进去

【例】The new disease will be sure to *infect* the population.

infectious [in'fekʃəs] *adj.* 传染的，感染性的（contagious）

【记】infect(传染)＋ious

contract ['kɔntrækt] *vt.* 感染（infect）

【例】She *contracted* a serious illness.

acute [ə'kju:t] *adj.* 急性的

【例】Severe *Acute* Respiratory Syndrome (SARS) is taking it toll on China's tour industry.

feverish ['fi:vəriʃ] *adj.* 发烧的

【记】fever(发烧)＋ish

【例】Your forehead feels very hot. Are you *feverish*?

invalid ['invælid] *adj.* 有病的

morbid ['mɔ:bid] *adj.* 病态的，不健康的（sick, diseased）

【记】morb(病)＋id→疾病的

【例】The patient has a *morbid* imagination that made his illness worse.

numb [nʌm] *adj.* 麻木的（senseless, dead）

unconscious [ʌn'kɔnʃəs] *adj.* 失去知觉的；不察觉的

fragile ['frædʒail] *adj.* 体质弱的

【记】frag(碎)＋ile→易碎的

【例】He's feeling a bit *fragile* after last night's party.

susceptible [sə'septəbl] *adj.* 易受感染的（vulnerable, exposed）

【记】sus(下面)＋cept(接受)＋ible→接受的→受感染的

【例】Infants and the elderly are more *susceptible* to illness than other people.

malady ['mælədi] *n.* 疾病

【记】mal(坏)＋ady→坏的东西→疾病

corpse [kɔ:ps] *n.* 尸体

【例】The mortician dressed and made up the *corpse*.

gash [gæʃ] *n.* 深的切口

【记】比较gush(喷涌而出)

【例】The doctor stitched up the *gash* on Anne's arm.

symptom ['simptəm] *n.* 症状，征候，征兆(sign, indication)

【例】One *symptom* of the disease is a high fever.

fracture ['fræktʃə] *n./v.* 骨折(crack)

【记】fract(碎裂)+ure→断的状态→骨折

bleed [bli:d] *v.* 流血

【例】Your cut will *bleed* if you pick the scab.

tingle ['tiŋgl] *vi.* 刺痛

【例】The uncertainty of national events made his blood *tingle*.

recur [ri'kə:] *vi.* 复发，重来(repeat, return)

【例】Really scared by SARS, the world is frightened at the news that it is *recurring* this spring.

relapse [ri'læps] *vi.* 复发；回复(recur)

【记】re(重新)+lapse(错误)→再犯错误→复发

【例】Her disease *relapsed* once she returned to her home.

bruise [bru:z] *vt.* 打伤 *n.* 瘀伤

【例】Mary got a *bruise* where she bumped against the table.

fester ['festə] *vt.* 使化脓(decay)

【例】It's lucky that the wound did not *fester*.

intoxicate [in'tɔksikeit] *vt.* 使中毒

【记】in(进入)+toxic(毒)+ate→进入毒→使中毒

【例】He was *intoxicated* by many awards he received and ceased his step toward the peak of his career.

survive [sə'vaiv] *vt.* 幸免于… *vi.* 活下来(outlive, remain)

【例】Those who *survived* rebuilt the city.

diagnose ['daiəgnəuz] *vt.* 诊断，分析(analyze)

【例】A pathologist *diagnosed* the fatal virus.

diagnosis [,daiəg'nəusis] *n.* 诊断

【记】dia(穿过)+gnos(知道)+is→穿过(身体)知道→诊断

inject [in'dʒekt] *vt.* 注射；注入(infuse)
【记】in(进)＋ject(扔)→扔进去→注射
【例】The dog fell on the ground after being *injected*.

heal [hiːl] *v.* 治愈,(使)和解 *n.* 痊愈(cure, recover)
【例】The wound soon *healed* under the care of the nurse.

remedy ['remidi] *n.* 治疗法，药物 *vt.* 治疗(cure, rectify)
【例】The doctor tried all means to *remedy* the beloved man.

treatment ['triːtmənt] *n.* 治疗

prescription [pris'kripʃən] *n.* 药方

dissect [dai'sekt] *vt.* 解剖
【记】dis＋sect(部分)→去除部分→解剖
【例】Bill *dissected* a small shark in anatomy class.

sterile ['sterail] *adj.* 消过毒的(sanitary)

clinic ['klinik] *n.* 门诊所

anatomy [ə'nætəmi] *n.* 剖析；解剖学

healthful ['helθful] *adj.* 有益健康的(wholesome)

condition [kən'diʃən] *n.* 健康情形(circumstance)
【例】My shoes are in bad *condition* and need to be replaced.

hygiene ['haidʒiːn] *n.* 卫生(sanitation)
【例】The dentist instructed his patients on dental *hygiene*.

sanitation [sæni'teiʃən] *n.* 卫生；卫生设施

physical ['fizikəl] *adj.* 身体的；物质的

sustenance ['sʌstənəns] *n.* 营养物
【例】For *sustenance*, the vegetarian ate fruits, nuts, and vegetables.

malnourished [mæl'nʌriʃt] *adj.* 营养失调的，营养不良的

nutrition [njuː'triʃən] *n.* 营养；营养学

mental ['mentl] *adj.* 精神的，智力的

spiritual ['spiritjuəl] *adj.* 心灵的

subject ['sʌbdʒikt] *n.* 试验对象

艺 术

picturesque [ˌpɪktʃəˈresk] *adj.* 如画般的，生动的（vivid）

【记】picture(图画)＋sque

【例】City dwellers would sometimes long for a *picturesque* and serene rural life.

vivid [ˈvivid] *adj.* 生动的（lively, active）

【例】David's *vivid* description seems to bring the students to the real battle field.

sculpture [ˈskʌlptʃə] *n.* 雕塑品（carving, engraving）

【例】*Sculpture* is the art of shaping solid materials.

statue [ˈstætju] *n.* 雕像

draw [drɔː] *v.* 画

gallery [ˈɡæləri] *n.* 画廊

portrait [ˈpɔːtrit] *n.* 肖像，画像；描写

impressionism [imˈpreʃənizm] *n.* 印象派

portray [pɔːˈtrei] *vt.* 绘制（delineate, depict）

【例】His work *portrays* the beautiful view of his hometown.

mold [məuld] *vt.* 塑造（shape）

【例】The sculptor *molded* the clay into a flowerpot.

embroider [imˈbrɔidə] *vt.* 绣花

【记】em＋broider(刺绣)

【例】Susan *embroidered* the edges of all her pillowcases.

tragedy [ˈtrædʒidi] *n.* 悲剧

opera [ˈɔpərə] *n.* 歌剧

【记】通过创作(operate)而来

enact [iˈnækt] *vt.* 扮演（impersonate）

【记】en＋act(扮演)

【例】Children like to *enact* the part of the parent.

pose [pəuz] *vt.* 构成；(使)摆好姿势（frame, constitute）

【例】The forced marriage from his parents *posed* a big distress in his entire life.

rehearse [riˈhəːs] *vt.* 预演，排练（prepare, try out）

【例】*Rehearse* yourself before you take a real test.

prelude [ˈpreljuːd] *n.* 序幕（preface）

【记】pre(先)＋lude(玩，演奏)→先演奏→序曲

character ['kæriktə] *n.* 角色

【例】That actress plays my favorite *character* on a television show.

role [rəul] *n.* 角色(part)

design [di'zain] *n.* 设计，图案 *v.* 设计(pattern)

【记】de＋sign(标出)→设计

【例】Everyone agreed that Jane had made a great *design* for the building.

profile ['prəufail] *n.* 外形，轮廓 (outline, contour, sketch)

【记】pro(前)＋file(线条)→前面的线条→轮廓

renaissance ['renəzɑ:ns] *n.* 文艺复兴

【记】re(重新)＋naiss(出生)＋ance→新生

conjure ['kʌndʒə] *vt.* 用魔术做成(或变出)

【例】I don't know how I'll *conjure* up the money, but I'll pay rent tomorrow.

aesthetic [i:s'θetik] *adj.* 审美的，美学的(artistic)

【记】a＋esthe(感觉)＋tic→对美有感觉的→美学的

【例】I added an *aesthetic* touch to the living room with silk flowers.

romantic [rə'mæntik] *adj.* 传奇式的，浪漫的

The horizon of life is broadened chiefly by the enlargement of the heart. —Black

生活的地平线是随着心灵的开阔而变得宽广的。

——布莱克

音　乐

euphonious [juːˈfəʊnjəs] *adj.* 悦耳的（sweet）

【记】eu（好）＋phon（声音）＋ious→悦耳的

【例】Her praise is surely a *euphonious* song to me.

harsh [hɑːʃ] *adj.* 刺耳的（hoarse, unpleasant）

【例】The *harsh* words by Tom annoyed Mike.

jazz [dʒæz] *n.* 爵士乐

movement [ˈmuːvmənt] *n.* 乐章

note [nəut] *n.* 音符

score [skɔː, skɔə] *n.* 乐谱

instrument [ˈinstrumənt] *n.* 乐器

【例】Flute, piano and violin are all musical *instruments*.

lyric [ˈlirik] *n.* 抒情诗

conservatory [kənˈsɔːvətəri] *n.* 音乐学校

【例】Twenty students were accepted to the music *conservatory* this year.

episode [ˈepisəud] *n.* 插曲（interlude）

【例】The long lecture I got from my boss was one *episode* that I did not want to undergo a second time.

orchestra [ˈɔːkistrə] *n.* 管弦乐队（band, ensemble）

chorus [ˈkɔːrəs] *n.* 合唱团（choir, ensemble）

【例】A *chorus* accompanied the orchestra.

concert [ˈkɔnsət] *n.* 音乐会

【例】The pianist will give a *concert* at the high school.

band [bænd] *n.* 乐队

record [ˈrekɔːd] *n.* 档案，唱片

【例】The famous singer is expecting to release his second *record*.

record [riˈkɔːd] *v.* 记录，录音（register）

【例】The book *recorded* Diana's life honestly.

percussion [pəˈkʌʃn] *n.* 打击乐器；震荡

【记】per（全部）＋cuss（震动）＋ion→震荡

string [striŋ] *n.* 弦乐

wind [waind] *n.* 管乐

语言学

implicit [im'plisit] *adj.* 含蓄的

【记】im(进入)+plic(重叠)+it→重叠状态→含蓄的

concise [kən'sais] *adj.* 简明的(succinct, terse)

【记】con+cise(切)→切掉多余的→简明的

【例】The winner of the award gave a short and *concise* acceptance speech.

succinct [sək'siŋkt] *adj.* 简明的，简洁的(terse, concise)

fluent ['fluːənt] *adj.* 流利的，流畅的(fluid, smooth)

【记】flu(流动)+ent→流利的

【例】Before you go travelling in America, make sure you speak *fluent* spoken English.

cogent ['kəudʒənt] *adj.* 强有力的；有说服力的(convincing; compelling)

【例】The defense attorney's *cogent* argument was persuasive.

persuasive [pə'sweisiv] *adj.* 有说服力的

【记】动词persuade(说服)

【例】The *persuasive* saleswoman sold me a used car.

character ['kæriktə] *n.* 文字

【例】I wish this book was written in bigger *characters*.

glossary ['glɔsəri] *n.* 词汇表

【记】gloss(舌头，语言)+ary→词汇表

dialect ['daiəlekt] *n.* 方言，土语(vernacular, jargon)

【记】dia+lect(说)→方言

【例】John's Southern *dialect* is hard for me to understand.

clause [klɔːz] *n.* 分句

【例】The sentence had too many *clauses* in it.

linguistics [liŋ'gwistiks] *n.* 语言学

【记】lingu(语言)+istics(学科后缀)→语言学

phonetics [fəu'netiks] *n.* 语音学

【记】phone(声音)+tics→语音学

tense [tens] *n.* 时态

version ['vəːʒən] *n.* 说法；版本(description, account)

genre ['ʒɑːŋr] *n.* 体裁；风格(style; manner)

【记】通常指文学等类型

【例】His six String Quartets is the most important works in the *genre* since Beethoven's.

tag ['tæg] *n.* 附加语；标签(label, tab)

slogan ['sləugən] *n.* 口号；标语(motto)

【例】Each candidate needs a clever *slogan* to attract the attention of the voters.

lyric ['lirik] *n.* 歌词

verse [vəːs] *n.* 诗，韵文

fiction ['fikʃən] *n.* 小说

【记】fict(做)＋ion→做出的故事→小说

byword ['baiwəːd] *n.* 谚语(adage)

fable ['feibl] *n.* 寓言，传说(allegory)

【例】Many *fables* were first told by an old Greek story-teller named Aesop.

term [təːm] *n.* 术语(expression)

【例】Knowing more technical *terms* gives a translator more advantages.

maxim ['mæksim] *n.* 格言；箴言(proverb, motto)

【记】比较maximum(最大值)；minimum(最小值)

satire ['sætaiə] *n.* 讽刺文学

【例】The political *satire* was censored by the government.

farce [fɑːs] *n.* 闹剧

adage ['ædidʒ] *n.* 格言，谚语(proverb)

【例】Isn't there an old *adage* that a stitch in time saves nine?

synopsis [si'nɔːpsis] *n.* 大纲，梗概(outline, summary)

【例】The history professor gave a *synopsis* of the events leading to World War I.

compile [kəm'pail] *vt.* 收集；编纂(collect, put together)

【记】com＋pile(堆)→有序地堆→编

【例】The scientists *compiled* a great amount of data to help develop their theory.

entitle [in'taitl] *vt.* 题目为

【例】My favorite poem is *entitled* "Summer Rain".

emend [i'mend] *vt.* 修订(amend, improve)

【记】e＋mend(修补)→修订

【例】John had spent a whole day *emending* a faulty text.

paraphrase ['pærəfreiz] *vt.* 意译；改写(rewrite)

【记】para(旁边)＋phrase(词句)→在旁边用不同的词写→改写

【例】Would you please *paraphrase* the speech in colloquial English?

adapt [ə'dæpt] *v.* 改编（revise, amend）

adaptable [ə'dæptəbl] *adj.* 可修改的（flexible, pliant）

adaptation [ˌædæp'teiʃən] *n.* 改写；修改

【例】The movie was an *adaptation* of a classic novel.

excerpt ['eksə:pt] *n.* 摘录（selection, extract）

【例】The actor auditioned by performing an *excerpt* from the play.

abstract [æb'strækt] *vt.* 摘要，提炼

【记】abs＋tract(拉)→从原文中拉出来→摘要

abstraction [æb'strækʃən] *n.* 摘要

【例】By looking at what happened in many similar cases, we were able to create an *abstraction* that also covered other instances.

abridge [ə'bridʒ] *vt.* 缩短，删节（shorten, condense, abbreviate）

【记】a＋bridge→桥使路程变短→弄短→删节

【例】The rights of citizens must not be *abridged*.

coin [kɔin] *vt.* 创造（create, fashion, invent）

【例】The advertising company *coined* a new word to name the new product.

It never will rain roses. When we want to have more roses we must plant trees.
　　　　　　　　　　　　　　　　　　　　　　—*G.Eliot*
天上永远不会掉下玫瑰来，如果想要更多的玫瑰，必须自己种植。
　　　　　　　　　　　　　　　　　　　　—— 艾略特

政　治

factious ['fækʃəs] *adj.* 党派的（tribal）

【记】faction（党派）的形容词

partisan ['pɑːtizæn] *adj.* 党派的，派系感强的

【例】Her *partisan* speech angered the opposing party.

board [bɔːd] *n.* 委员会

Senate ['senit] *n.* 参议院，上院

Congress ['kɔŋgres] *n.* （代表）大会；（美国等国的）国会，议会

diplomatic [ˌdiplə'mætik] *adj.* 外交的；有策略的（tactful）

【例】She is always *diplomatic* when she deals with angry students.

diplomacy [di'pləuməsi] *n.* 外交；策略（tact）

【例】The clerk spoke with *diplomacy* to the angry customer.

confederate [kən'fedərit] *n.* 同盟（partner, company）

【例】The gangster and his *confederates* were arrested.

league [liːg] *n.* 同盟，联盟；联合会

affiliate [ə'filieit] *v.* 加盟，入会（associate, ally）

【例】She *affiliates* herself with a new law firm.

unconventional [ˌʌnkən'venʃənl] *adj.* 自由的

dictatorial [ˌdiktə'tɔːriəl] *adj.* 独裁的，专断的（tyrannical）

【记】dictat（说，命令）＋orial→独裁的

domestic [də'mestik] *adj.* 国内的；家庭的

【例】The police called the fight between the husband and wife a *domestic* matter.

potent ['pəutənt] *adj.* 强有力的；有全权的（cogent, powerful）

【记】poten（力量）＋t→强有力的

【例】His *potent* speech impressed all the people present.

authoritative [ɔː'θɔriteitiv] *adj.* 权威性的，官方的

【例】Make sure you ask an *authoritative* source for directions.

influential [ˌinflu'enʃəl] *adj.* 有影响的；有权势的（powerful）

centralized ['sentrəlaizd] *adj.* 集中的，中央集权的

authority [ɔː'θɔriti] *n.* 权威

【例】The teacher gave her assistant the *authority* to grade papers.

privilege ['privilidʒ] *n.* 特权（prerogative）

【记】privi（个人）＋lege（法律）→个人的法律→特权

democracy [di'mɔkrəsi] *n.* 民主

【记】demo(人民)+cracy(统治)→人民统治的→民主

【例】People must participate in their government if a *democracy* is to work.

petition [pə'tiʃən] *n.* 请愿 *vt.* 向…请愿

【记】pet(寻求)+ition→请愿

domain [dəu'mein] *n.* 领土，领域(field, region)

territory ['teritəri] *n.* 领土，版图，地域

nationality [ˌnæʃə'næliti] *n.* 国籍

【记】nation(国家)+ality→国籍

kingdom ['kiŋdəm] *n.* 王国(realm)

【记】king(国王)+dom(地域)→国王统治的地域→王国

realm [relm] *n.* 王国；领域(field, domain)

regimen ['redʒimen] *n.* 政权

【记】regi(统治)+men(人)→政权

sovereignty ['sɔvrənti] *n.* 主权

autonomy [ɔː'tɔnəmi] *n.* 自治权(independence)

【记】auto(自己)+nomy(统治)→自己统治→自治权

【例】The nation's *autonomy* was compromised by the treaty.

commission [kə'miʃən] *n.* 委员会

【例】The president appointed a *commission* to study poverty.

committee [kə'miti] *n.* 委员会，委员

【例】The *committee* planned the club's budget for next year.

election [i'lekʃən] *n.* 选举

【记】elect(选择)+ion→选举

【例】How many people voted in the last *election*?

ballot ['bælət] *n.* 选票(vote, poll)

ideology [aidi'ɔlədʒi] *n.* 意识形态

【记】ideo(意识)+ology(学科)→意识形态

parade [pə'reid] *n.* 游行(procession, march)

govern ['gʌvən] *v.* 决定；支配；控制(determine; control)

【例】The evil dictator *governed* unfairly.

confer [kən'fəː] *v.* 协商

【记】con(共同)+fer→共同带来观点→协商

【例】I *conferred* with my friends about what we should eat for dinner.

entitle [in'taitl] *vt.* 给…权利

【例】Every citizen is *entitled* to equal protection under the law.

exploit ['eksplɔit] *vt.* 剥削;开发(explore)

【记】ex+ploit(重叠)→从重叠中拿出→开发

【例】The company *exploited* the workers by falsely promising them pay raises.

maneuver [mə'nuːvə] *vt.* 调遣 *n.* 策略(move, step, tactic)

【记】man(手)+euver(劳动)→用手劳动→操纵

【例】At the last moment, the basketball player made a clever *maneuver* that allowed a goal to be made.

reform [ri'fɔːm] *vt./n.* 改革,革新(regenerate)

【记】re(再次)+form(形状)→再改形→改革

【例】The *reform* and open policy has brought us Chinese people a rich and colourful life.

inspect [in'spekt] *vt.* 检查(examine, survey);视察

【记】in(内)+spect(看)→看里面→检查

【例】The general *inspected* the troops.

emigrate ['emigreit] *v.* 移民

【记】e(出)+migr(移)+ate→移出→移民

【例】Mary *emigrated* from Germany to France during World War I.

immigrate ['imigreit] *vt.* 移居入境

【记】im(进)+migr(移)+ate→移进

【例】Britain *immigrated* many colonists to the New World.

exile ['ekzail] *vt.* 流放(banish, deport) *n.* 放逐

【例】The king was *exiled* when his expire was taken over.

enslave [in'sleiv] *vt.* 奴役

【记】en+slave(奴隶)→奴役

【例】The addict was *enslaved* by drugs.

hustle ['hʌsl] *vt.* 驱赶(hurry, hasten)

【例】To make more money, the restaurant owner *hustled* customers in and out quickly.

impel [im'pel] *vt.* 驱使(compel, urge)

【记】im(进入)+pel(推动)→驱使

【例】He was *impelled* by a strong passion to save the diseased boy.

oust [aust] *vt.* 驱逐(dismiss, throw out)

【例】He was *ousted* from his position as chairman.

banish ['bæniʃ] *vt.* 驱逐出境(exile, expel)

【例】The naughty child was *banished* to his room until dinner.

deport [di'pɔːt] *vt.* 驱逐出境, 放逐

enable [i'neibl] *vt.* 使能够(make possible, allow, help)

【例】An unexpected inheritance *enabled* me to buy a house.

reign [rein] *vt.* 统治(govern, rule)

【例】The old king has been *reigning* the nation for 30 years.

dominate ['dɔmineit] *vt.* 统治, 支配, 控制(control)

【记】domin(统治)+ate→统治

【例】The older brother *dominated* his younger siblings.

abdicate ['æbdikeit] *vt.* 放弃权力(abandon)

【记】ab+dic(说话, 命令)+ate→不再命令→放弃权力

【例】King Edward *abdicated* in 1936.

administer [əd'ministə] *vt.* 管理(govern, supervise)

【记】ad+minister(部长)→做部长→管理

【例】The personnel director *administers* the attendance policy.

administration [əd,minis'treiʃən] *n.* 行政(management)

【记】administer(执行)+ation

【例】Lisa is involved in *administration* at the company she works for.

institute ['institjuːt] *vt.* 建立(establish, set up, start)

【例】The village *instituted* a welfare system on their own.

amendment [ə'mendmənt] *n.* 改善, 改正

colonize ['kɔlənaiz] *vt.* 拓殖, 殖民

【例】Britain *colonized* many parts of Africa.

check [tʃek] *n./v.* 检查(examine; inspect)

【例】Raising interest rate is commonly used as a tool to *check* inflation.

monarchy ['mɔnəki] *n.* 君主政体, 君主政治, 君主国

republican [ri'pʌblikən] *adj.* 共和国的, 共和政体的, 共和主义的, 有关共和的

anarchism ['ænəkiz(ə)m] *n.* 无政府主义

doctrine ['dɔktrin] *n.* 主义(principle)

immigrant ['imigrənt] *adj.* (从外国)移来的，移民的，移居的

municipal [mju(:)'nisipəl] *adj.* 市政的，市立的，地方性的，地方自治的

strike [straik] *n.* 罢工(work stoppage)

【例】In France, going on *strike* is frequently being utilised by the union in fighting for the workers' interest, which strikes the nation's economy heavily.

scandal ['skændl] *n.* 丑闻(disgrace, defamation)

【例】The president's *scandal* was soon publicized and exaggerated.

vote [vəut] *n.* 投票，选票

welfare ['welfɛə] *n.* 福利；安宁，幸福

Ideas are like the stars—we never reach them, but like mariners, we chart our course by them. —C. Schur

理想就像是星星——我们永远无法到达，但是我们像水手一样，用它们指引航程。 ——舒尔茨

植物学

shrub [ʃrʌb] *n.* 灌木丛(bush)

laurel ['lɔːrəl] *n.* 月桂树

prairie ['preəri] *n.* 大草原，牧场，<美方>林间小空地

sequoia [si'kwɔiə] *n.* 美洲杉

herb [həːb] *n.* 药草，香草

plant [plɑːnt] *n.* 植物，庄稼

fern [fəːn] *n.* 蕨类植物

orchid ['ɔːkid] *n.* 兰，兰花；淡紫色

rosette [rəu'zet] *n.* 玫瑰形饰物，圆花饰

germinate ['dʒəːmineit] *v.* 发芽(sprout)

【记】germ(幼芽)＋inate→发芽

【例】After the seeds *germinated*, I transplanted them to a larger pot.

sprout [spraut] *v.* 萌芽，长出(bud, burgeon, germinate)

【例】The plants *sprouted* from the ground a week after I planted them.

timber ['timbə] *n.* 木材，木料(lumber, wood)

【记】比较timbre(音色)

cluster ['klʌstə] *n.* 丛，束(bunch) *v.* 丛生；聚集(concentrate)

【例】A *cluster* of strawberries grew in the field.

bunch [bʌntʃ] *n.* 串，束

bark [bɑːk] *n.* 树皮

twig [twig] *n.* 小树枝(small branch)

【记】比较wig(假发)

【例】Some insects will mime a *twig* when in danger.

bough [bau] *n.* 大树枝，主枝

branch [brɑːntʃ] *n.* 枝，分枝

stem [stem] *n.* 茎，干；词干

stalk [stɔːk] *n.* 茎，柄，梗，秆

trunk [trʌnk] *n.* 干线；树干

leafstalk ['liːfs'tɔːlk] *n.* 叶柄

leaflet ['liːflit] *n.* 小叶；传单

bud [bʌd] *n.* 芽 *v.* 发芽

【例】The trees *budded* in early April.

flower ['flauə] *n.* 花，开花的植物

foliage ['fəuliidʒ] *n.* 树叶；植物

petal ［'petl］*n.* 花瓣

cell ［sel］*n.* 单元；细胞

tissue ［'tisju:］*n.* 组织

【例】The *tissues* of the body constitute the organ.

husk ［hʌsk］*n.* (果类或谷物的)外壳(通常用复数)，皮

pollen ［'pɔlin］*n.* 花粉 *vt.* 传授花粉给…

root ［ru:t］*n.* 根，根部

log ［lɔg］*n.* 圆木(wood, timber)

【例】If you roll my *log*, I will roll yours. We help each other.

flora ［'flɔ:rə］*n.* 植物界

【记】flor(花草)＋a→植物界

botany ［'bɔtəni］*n.* 植物学

【记】botan(草)＋y→植物学

【例】Mary liked plants so much that she decided to study *botany* at the university.

botanical ［bə'tænik(ə)l］*adj.* 植物学的 *n.* 植物性药材

crossbreed ［'krɔsbri:d］*n.* 杂种 *v.* 异种交配，培育杂种，(使)杂交

necrosis ［ne'krəusis］*n.* 坏疽，骨疽

peel ［pi:l］*v.* 剥，削，剥落

【例】Her sunburned skin began to *peel*.

photosynthesis ［ˌfəutəu'sinθəsis］*n.* 光合作用

pollinate ［'pɔlineit］*vt.* 对…授粉

【例】Many crops require bees to *pollinate* them.

pollination ［pɔli'neiʃən］*n.* 授粉

seeds ［si:dz］*n.* 雏形；种子形

shell ［ʃel］*vt.* 去壳；脱落

【例】The chef was *shelling* oysters.

shoot ［ʃu:t］*vi.* 发出，发芽

【例】Rose bushes *shoot* again after being cut back.

starch ［stɑ:tʃ］*n.* 淀粉

vitamin ［'vaitəmin］*n.* 维他命，维生素

luxuriant ［lʌg'ʒuəriənt］*adj.* 多产的

【记】luxur(丰富)＋iant→多产的

自　然

natural [ˈnætʃərəl] *adj.* 自然的

scenic [ˈsiːnik] *adj.* 风景优美的(picturesque)

scenery [ˈsiːnəri] *n.* 景色

spectacle [ˈspektəkl] *n.* 奇观,景象(sight, scene)

shade [ʃeid] *n.* 荫

jungle [ˈdʒʌŋgl] *n.* 丛林

meadow [ˈmedəu] *n.* 草地,牧场

shrub [ʃrʌb] *n.* 灌木,灌木丛

lawn [lɔːn] *n.* 草地,草坪,草场

summit [ˈsʌmit] *n.* 山顶(peak, top, apex)

【例】The climbers placed their country's flag at the mountain's *summit*.

gorge [gɔːdʒ] *n.* 峡谷(ravine, canyon)

【例】I stood on the edge of the cliff and threw a rock into the *gorge*.

puddle [ˈpʌdl] *n.* 小水洼

creek [kriːk] *n.* 小湾;小溪(brook)

canyon [ˈkænjən] *n.* <美>峡谷,溪谷

spring [spriŋ] *n.* 泉水

trickle [ˈtrikl] *vi.* 滴,淌 *n.* 滴;细流(dribble, drip)

【例】The water *trickled* over the edge of the basin.

crystal [ˈkristl] *adj.* 清澈的 *n.* 水晶;结晶

【例】Salt *crystals* can be found in every home.

limpid [ˈlimpid] *adj.* 清澈的(transparent, clear)

luxuriant [lʌgˈʒuəriənt] *adj.* 繁茂的(lush, abundant)

【记】luxur(丰富)+iant→繁茂的

Have no fear of perfection—you'll never reach it.

—*S.Dali*

不要为十全十美担心——你永远也做不到十全十美。

——达里

宗　教

blessed [blesd] *adj.* 受祝福的

【例】We are surely *blessed* because we escaped the fire.

invocation [ˌinvəuˈkeiʃən] *n.* 祈祷(plea, prayer)

pious [ˈpaiəs] *adj.* 虔诚的(loyal, faithful)

【例】Those *pious* faithfuls are not allowed to take photos of themselves.

devout [diˈvaut] *adj.* 虔诚的(pious, religious)

【例】The *devout* worshiper attended church each week.

cult [kʌlt] *n.* 崇拜(常用于修饰另一个名词)

【例】The *cult* leader believed he was the son of God.

consecrate [ˈkɔnsikreit] *vt.* 奉为神圣；奉献(dedicate, devote)

【记】比较sacred(神圣的)

【例】The priest *consecrated* the water in the baptismal basin.

creed [kriːd] *n.* 信仰，信条(belief, faith)

【例】The newspaper prints its *creed* on the front page every day.

doomed [duːmd] *adj.* 命定的，注定失败的

【例】The marriage was *doomed* from the beginning.

destine [ˈdestin] *vt.* 命运注定

【例】Lisa is *destined* for the presidency.

destiny [ˈdestini] *n.* 命运(fate)

【例】I didn't plan for my future, instead I left it to *destiny*.

fatalism [ˈfeitəlizəm] *n.* 宿命论

【记】fat=fate(命运)＋alism→宿命论

sacred [ˈseikrid] *adj.* 上帝的；神圣的(holy, heavenly)

【例】In maternal tribes, *sacred* things were kept by the elderest woman.

Christian [ˈkristʃən] *n.* 基督教徒 *adj.* 基督教的

【例】The *Christian* religion in Europe and the Americas is divided into Protestant, Catholic, and a few other varieties.

doctrine [ˈdɔktrin] *n.* 教义(dogma)

【例】How are the *doctrines* of the two churches different?

dogma [ˈdɔgmə] *n.* 教义，教条(belief, view)

【例】Tom rejected the *dogma* of his church and joined another.

rite [rait] *n.* 宗教仪式(ritual, procedure, ceremony)

religion [riˈlidʒən] *n.* 宗教

deity [ˈdiːiti] *n.* 神(god)

oracle [ˈɔːrəkl] *n.* 神谕

【记】ora(嘴)+cle→神的嘴巴

atheism [ˈeiθiizəm] *n.* 无神论

【记】a(无)+the(神)+ism→无神论

【例】Anne's *atheism* contrasted with her friend's strong religious beliefs.

heresy [ˈherəsi] *n.* 异端；邪说

【记】here(异)+sy→异端

immerse [iˈməːs] *vt.* 给…施洗礼(indulge)

【记】im(进)+merse(沉)→沉进去→沉浸→给…施洗礼

【例】I *immersed* myself in the hot bath and relaxed.

invoke [inˈvəuk] *vt.* 恳求，祈求(beg, pray)

【记】in+voke(喊)→恳求

【例】I *invoked* their forgiveness.

enchant [inˈtʃɑːnt] *vt.* 施魔法于(enthrall, fascinate)

【记】en+chant(歌曲)→施魔曲→施魔法于

【例】The witch *enchanted* the handsome knight, turning him into a frog.

preach [priːtʃ] *vt.* 说教，布道；鼓吹(advocate, advise)

【记】联想reach(到达)

【例】He *preached* tolerance and peaceful coexistence.

exodus [ˈeksədəs] *n.* 大批离去

【例】The refugees made an *exodus* to a safe place.

Great men are rarely isolated mountain peaks; they are the summits of ranges.
　　　　　　　　　　　　　　　　　　　　　—Higginson
伟人很少是突兀的山，他们是众山中的最高峰。
　　　　　　　　　　　　　　　　　　　── 希金森

连 线 题

左列单词在右列中有一个或多个同义词,请画线连接。

(一)

	Advise
administer	advocate
doctrine	banish
exile	burgeon
kingdom	bush
limpid	deport
parade	dogma
preach	dribble
shrub	drip
sprout	germinate
trickle	govern
	march
	procession
	realm
	supervise
	transparent

(二)

	cogent
adaptable	contour
concise	flexible
enact	impersonate
episode	interlude
euphonious	outline
factious	pliant
paraphrase	powerful
picturesque	register
potent	rewrite
profile	sketch
record	succinct
	sweet
	terse
	tribal
	vivid

(三)

	affect
	bubble
accelerate	diseased
charge	everlasting
diffuse	expedite
endless	fill
foam	froth
hygiene	outlive
infect	remain
morbid	replenish
sterile	sanitary
survive	sanitation
	scatter
	sick
	speed
	spread
	spread

(四)

	astronomical
attrition	camouflage
celestial	cosmos
diagram	cross
discrete	deduct
intersect	discharge
mimicry	drawing
ratio	heavenly
secrete	proportion
subtract	rate
universe	release
	separate
	sketch
	wear and tear

（一）

administer	govern
administer	supervise
doctrine	dogma
exile	banish
exile	deport
kingdom	realm
limpid	dribble
parade	drip
parade	transparent
preach	procession
preach	march
shrub	advocate
sprout	advise
sprout	bush
trickle	burgeon
trickle	germinate

（二）

adaptable	flexible
adaptable	pliant
concise	succinct
concise	terse
enact	impersonate
episode	interlude
euphonious	register
factious	sweet
paraphrase	rewrite
picturesque	vivid
potent	tribal
potent	cogent
profile	powerful
profile	outline
profile	contour
record	sketch

（三）

accelerate	expedite
accelerate	speed
charge	fill
charge	replenish
diffuse	scatter
diffuse	spread
endless	everlasting
foam	bubble
foam	froth
hygiene	sanitation
infect	spread
infect	affect
morbid	sick
morbid	diseased
sterile	sanitary
survive	outlive
survive	remain

（四）

attrition	wear and tear
celestial	astronomical
celestial	heavenly
diagram	sketch
diagram	drawing
discrete	separate
intersect	cross
mimicry	camouflage
ratio	proportion
ratio	rate
secrete	discharge
secrete	release
subtract	deduct
universe	cosmos

连 线 题

左列单词在右列中有一个或多个同义词,请画线连接。

(五)

addict

bandit

exotic

aboriginal

juvenile

proxy

recipient

recluse

ripe

illiterate

adolescent
deputy
foreign
hermit
indulger
mature
native
payee
pirate
ready
receiver
robber
surrender
uneducated
unusual

(六)

clandestine

consolidate

discount

humid

invade

originate

porcelain

prolific

raid

agress
attack
china
covert
damp
foray
initiate
intrude
merge
moist
productive
reduction
secret

(七)

benefit

bonus

didactic

dye

fortune

noxious

output

prosperous

rust

utility

award
flourishing
function
gift
instructive
interest
oxidize
pigment
poisonous
thriving
toxic
turnout
usefulness
wealth
yield

(八)

affirm

authorize

credential

incriminate

licensed

offspring

query

spine

stale

standard

accuse
assert
backbone
certificate
criteria
descendant
empower
flat
inquiry
musty
permissive
permit
reference
regular
smelly

连线题答案

（五）

addict	indulger
addict	surrender
bandit	robber
bandit	pirate
exotic	foreign
exotic	unusual
aboriginal	native
juvenile	adolescent
proxy	deputy
recipient	receiver
recipient	payee
recluse	hermit
ripe	mature
ripe	ready
illiterate	uneducated

（六）

clandestine	covert
clandestine	secret
consolidate	merge
discount	reduction
humid	moist
humid	damp
invade	intrude
originate	initiate
porcelain	china
prolific	productive
raid	agress
raid	attack
raid	foray

（七）

benefit	interest
bonus	award
bonus	gift
didactic	instructive
dye	pigment
fortune	wealth
noxious	poisonous
noxious	toxic
output	turnout
output	yield
prosperous	thriving
prosperous	flourishing
rust	oxidize
utility	function
utility	usefulness

（八）

affirm	assert
authorize	empower
authorize	permit
credential	reference
credential	certificate
incriminate	accuse
licensed	permissive
offspring	descendant
query	inquiry
spine	backbone
stale	smelly
stale	musty
stale	flat
standard	criteria
standard	regular

填 空 题

请将恰当的词填入横线内。

1. Lobsters and dolphins are kinds of _____ animals.

2. A _____ is a person who has travelled widely and feels at home everywhere.

3. The thick steam in the bathroom had made the walls _____.

4. Earth on this world we lived is divided into seven _____.

5. The _____ of the Atlantic coast of America is very irregular.

6. In Tibet, the people live at a very high _____.

7. They cut a _____ from the river to bring water to the field.

8. They went a hike and over the _____ the sun was rising

9. Clouds are _____ of tiny drops of water in the sky.

10. It is reported by radio that the _____ of yesterday accounted for five deaths.

11. Coke and Pepsi and Sprite come in an _____ can.

12. The Northern _____ is the part of the world north of the equator, and the Southern Hemisphere is south of the equator.

13. The chickens _____ this morning.

14. The most effective agent in the _____ of species is the pressure of other species.

15. Darwin's theory of evolution illustrates the process of natural _____.

16. Sharks are considered as the most ferocious _____ in nature.

17. Most animals go into _____ in winter.

18. An animal capable of living both on land and in water is called _____.

19. Tigers are _____; cattle are not.

20. Attendance at the meeting is _____.

21. He behaved badly with _____ as he knew the teacher was weak.

22. They were in _____ for a week for their crime.

23. They had no strong testimony that could _____ the defendant.

24. The government has the power to gratify or change the _____ when they feel necessary.

25. This _____ dress material does not crush.

26. The liquid _____ when somebody dropped a match in it accidentally.

27. Many different kinds of junk food have _____ flavoring.

28. A _____ is made up of atoms.

29. Heat _____ the candle into a pool of wax in a few minutes.

30. _____ consists of two or more substances or elements.

31. Most people, especially girls wear sunglasses to prevent ultraviolet _____ from hurting their eyes.

32. The process of deforestation caused a severe land _____.

33. The Amazon _____ covers more than a billion acres of SouthAmerica.

34. In the past decade, many cultural relics have been threatened by _____.

35. Morality may be _____ into their minds.

36. Young students are advised to read _____ books to improve their mind.

37. In recent years, _____ growth in China has been soared.

38. At the airport the _____ officers searched his case.

39. It seems our little establishment has finally been deemed worthy of the bank's _____.

40. The rich man was asked to pay a high _____ for his daughter who was taken away by criminals.

41. Independent accountants should _____ the company annually to check out the questionable tax incomes.

42. According to the law, a young man should _____ when he is 18.

43. The police _____ the criminals.

44. We will never allow anybody to _____ upon China's territorial integrity and sovereignty.

45. The project was _____ with difficulties.

46. The _____ is a fake.

47. The Stone Age was divided into the old Paleolithic period and the New _____ period.

48. There is still not a clear conclusion about the _____ of human being.

49. Sometimes, unarable land can be turned into _____ land by digging new irrigation canals and wells.

50. It seems that the biggest difference between farming and animal _____ lies in their symbols—houses and tents.

51. The _____ area in this table is underestimated and must be further verified.

52. If the _____ land of Earth runs out, food production will soon be unable to meet the need of the whole population.

53. _____ refers to the art of cultivating fruits, vegetables, flowers etc.

54. The _____ flung their motor boat upon the rocks.

55. The winter _____ has killed several of our new young plants in the garden.

56. The science that deals with the phenomena of the weather and weather conditions is called _____.

57. The problem of _____ delinquency presented itself for the attention from the whole society.

58. If we say someone is _____, we mean he can express himself in a very intelligent manner.

59. The alchemists were the _____ of the scientists of today.

60. The people _____ their power to the Congress.

61. We beat our _____ at football.

62. Every four year, many _____ attempt to become the president of the United States.

63. The _____ of the hole was the mouse.

64. My friend, Crawley, has always been a _____ supporter of the Progressive Party.

65. He's _____ to a craftsman.

66. He was forced to leave his country and has been an _____ for five years.

67. She is expecting a _____ church wedding.

68. In ancient China, women had to accept the _____ marriages.

69. The immune system can develop long-term _____ to some diseases.

70. _____ is a close ecological relationship between the individuals of two (or more) different species.

71. We found more children at the circus than we could _____.

72. The railway line runs _____ with/to the highway.

73. There are two types of integral in _____, the indefinite and the definite.

74. The sun, the stars, and the moon are _____ bodies.

75. China released the news that it would launch another spaceship as its fourth unmannned space capsule _____ the earth.

76. A practitioner of _____ is called an astrologer or, less often, an astrologist.

77. This alloy is formed by the _____ of two types of metal.

78. The pool of water on the playground _____ in the sun.

79. Some kinds of bacteria can only be visible through a powerful _____.

80. This pocket calculator needs two dry _____.

81. The force exerted by a magnetic field is known as _____.

82. The Pop is the _____ leader of many Christians.

83. Colds are _____ , and so are some eye diseases.

84. I got a cold and felt _____ all night.

85. In the interests of _____, please do not smoke in this shop.

86. The doctor wrote me a _____ for medicine for my cough.

87. Children in Africa are suffering from severe _____ because of the lack of food.

88. She _____ into unconsciousness again and was sent to the hospital.

89. My hometown is a _____ fishing village in the bay.

90. New York city has many art _____ among which some are world famous.

91. She plays a flute in the _____.

92. The church _____ performed very well today.

93. The election was a _____, for it was fixed.

94. Phonetics, syntactics are two branches of _____.

95. The novel and short story are different _____.

96. Britain _____ many colonists to the New World.

97. He was inclined to _____; he hated system and organization and uniformity.

98. China government has granted _____ to the national minorities.

99. You are not _____ to unemployment benfit if you have never worked.

100. _____ leaves were used by the ancient Greeks and Romans as an emblem of victory or honor.

101. Most forms of _____ processed by green plants release oxygen as a byproduct.

102. Seeds will not _____ without water.

103. _____ forests covered the hillside.

104. One can hardly forget the _____ splendours of the Roky Mountain.

105. Temples, mosques, churches and synagogues are all _____ buildings.

106. The witch lived in a palace in an _____ wood.

1. marine	28. molecule	55. frost	82. spiritual
2. cosmopolitan	29. dissolved	56. meteorology	83. infectious
3. moist	30. Compound	57. juvenile	84. feverish
4. continents	31. radiation	58. intellectual	85. hygiene
5. contour	32. erosion	59. forerunners	86. prescription
6. altitude	33. rain forest	60. delegate	87. malnutrition
7. channel	34. acid rain	61. opponents	88. relapsed
8. horizon	35. instilled	62. candidates	89. picturesque
9. formation	36. edifying	63. inhabitant	90. galleries
10. earthquake	37. economic	64. fanatic	91. orchestra
11. aluminum	38. custom	65. apprenticed	92. chorus
12. hemisphere	39. patronage	66. exile	93. farce
13. hatched	40. ransom	67. conventional	94. linguistics
14. extinction	41. audit	68. polygamous	95. genres
15. selection	42. enlist	69. immunity	96. immigrated
16. predator	43. disarmed	70. symbiosis	97. anarchism
17. hibernation	44. encroach	71. enumerate	98. autonomy
18. amphibian	45. beset	72. parallel	99. entitled
19. carnivores	46. antique	73. calculus	100. laurel
20. mandatory	47. neolithic	74. celestial	101. photosynthesis
21. impunity	48. origin	75. orbits	102. germinate
22. captivity	49. arable	76. astrology	103. Luxuriant
23. incriminated	50. husbandry	77. fusion	104. scenic
24. constitution	51. cultivated	78. evaporated	105. sacred
25. synthetic	52. fertile	79. microscope	106. enchanted
26. ignited	53. horticulture	80. batteries	
27. artificial	54. hurricane	81. magnetism	

品　质

记忆小贴士：表象记忆法

　　心理学研究表明，与自己有关的事物记得最牢。看看下面表示品质的单词，想想你身边哪些人符合这些单词描绘的特征。

卑 鄙

despicable ['despikəbl] *adj.* 可鄙的(detestable, contemptible)

【例】That *despicable* child trampled my flowers.

contemptible [kən'temptəbl] *adj.* 可鄙的(mean, despicable)

【例】Tom's rude behavior is *contemptible*.

ignominious [ˌignə'miniəs] *adj.* 可耻的；不光彩的(disgraceful, humiliating)

【记】ig(不)＋nomin(名字)＋ious→不好的名字→不光彩的

menial ['miːnjəl] *adj.* 奴仆的；卑贱的(humble, mean)

scornful ['skɔːnful] *adj.* 轻蔑的(disdainful, contemptuous)

filthy ['filθi] *adj.* 污秽的；卑鄙的(dirty; squalid)

【记】filth(脏)＋y→污秽的

【例】Dave spent two hours cleaning his *filthy* kitchen.

shameless ['ʃeimlis] *adj.* 无耻的

【例】The *shameless* couple caressed each other on the bus.

disrespectful [ˌdisris'pektful] *adj.* 无礼的，轻视的

【例】Heckling is *disrespectful* to the person who is trying to talk.

discrimination [disˌkrimi'neiʃən] *n.* 歧视(prejudice)

【记】dis＋crimin(罪行)＋ation

【例】Different groups of people in many countries of the world face *discrimination*.

contemn [kən'tem] *vt.* 蔑视(disdain, scorn)

【例】I *contemn* your pompous delicacies.

belittle [bi'litl] *vt.* 轻视(depreciate, despise)

【记】be＋litter(小)→小看→轻视

【例】The reporter's comments *belittled* the candidate.

disdain [dis'dein] *vt.* 轻视，不屑(despise, scorn) *n.* 轻蔑

【记】dis(不)＋dain=deign(俯就)→不俯就

【例】He *disdains* any wasting behavior.

despise [dis'paiz] *vt.* 轻视，蔑视(belittle, disdain, contemn)

【记】de(坏)＋spi(看)＋se→蔑视

【例】Mary *despised* her rude and unschooled neighbors.

mean [miːn] *adj.* 卑鄙的(inferior)

【例】He played such a *mean* trick on me that I no longer treated him as my friend.

笨 拙

awkward [ˈɔːkwəd] *adj.* 笨拙的，尴尬的（clumsy, inept）
【例】The growing teenager went through an *awkward* stage.

clumsy [ˈklʌmzi] *adj.* 笨拙的；愚笨的（awkward）
【例】The *clumsy* waiter dropped my dinner on the floor.

inert [iˈnəːt] *adj.* 不活泼的（immobile, inactive）；迟钝的
【记】in(不)＋ert(动)→迟钝的

blunt [blʌnt] *adj.* 迟钝的 *v.* 使变钝
【例】The knife was too *blunt* to cut through the tough meat.

torpid [ˈtɔːpid] *adj.* 迟钝的；不活泼的（lethargic, sluggish）
【例】The giant panda, after lunch, seems *torpid* and reluctant to entertain the spectators.

silly [ˈsili] *adj.* 傻的，糊涂的

idiotic [idiˈɔtik] *adj.* 愚蠢的

fatuous [ˈfætjuəs] *adj.* 愚昧的（foolish, stupid, indolent）
【记】fatu(笨)＋ous→愚昧的

hoax [həuks] *n. / vt.* 愚弄(trick, prank)
【记】比较coax(哄骗)
【例】April Fools' Day is a popular time to play *hoaxes*.

草 率

curt [kəːt] *adj.* 简短的，草率的(abrupt, blunt)
【例】Our waiter was so *curt* that we almost walked out.

reckless [ˈreklis] *adj.* 鲁莽的(rash)
【记】reck(顾虑)＋less→没有顾虑→鲁莽的
【例】The *reckless* driver drove above the speed limit.

impudent [ˈimpjudənt] *adj.* 鲁莽的(rude, rash)
【记】im(不)＋pud(谦虚，小心)＋ent→不小心的→鲁莽的

rashly [ˈræʃli] *adv.* 鲁莽地，匆忙地
【记】rash(匆忙的)＋ly→匆忙地
【例】The student *rashly* decided to take the exam.

imprudent [im'pru:dənt] *adj.* 轻率的，不谨慎的（rash）

【记】im(不)+prudent(小心的)→轻率的

【例】It is *imprudent* to accept a date with a stranger.

blunt [blʌnt] *adj.* 直率的，粗鲁的

【例】John Wayre was a *blunt* talker and straight shooter.

聪 颖

intelligent [in'telidʒənt] *adj.* 聪明的（ingenious, wise）

smart [smɑ:t] *adj.* 聪明的，敏捷的（clever, intelligent）

versatile ['və:sətail] *adj.* 多才多艺的（many-sided, talented, all-around）

【例】The *versatile* worker was assigned to many different jobs.

astute [əs'tju:t] *adj.* 机敏的，狡猾的（shrewd, canny）

【例】The boss appreciated Mary's *astute* observations about how to improve the company's image.

shrewd [ʃru:d] *adj.* 精明的（clever, smart）

【例】The *shrewd* business owner made large profits.

sensible ['sensəbl] *adj.* 理智的（wise, rational）

【记】sens(感觉)+ible→理智的

【例】His *sensible* decision greatly promoted our enterprise.

sane [sein] *adj.* 理智的；健全的（sensible, reasonable）

【例】The nation's economy will only improve under *sane* policy.

flexible ['fleksəbl] *adj.* 灵活的，变通的（agile）

【记】flex(弯曲)+ible→易弯曲的→灵活的

【例】Jane easily bent the *flexible* wire into a loop.

exquisite ['ekskwizit] *adj.* 灵敏的

【例】The artists have an *exquisite* sense of color.

expeditious [,ekspi'diʃəs] *adj.* 敏捷的；迅速的（prompt; speedy）

nimble ['nimbl] *adj.* 轻快的；灵敏的（agile, brisk）

【记】比较nim(偷窃)

knowledgeable ['nɔlidʒəbl] *adj.* 有见识的

capable ['keipəbl] *adj.* 有能力的

【例】The very *capable* caterer fed everyone well at the party.

tact ［tækt］*n.* 老练；机智（diplomacy, thoughtfulness）

sharpen ［ˈʃɑːpn］*vt.* 使敏锐

【例】You need to *sharpen* your eyes in doing experiments.

adroit ［əˈdrɔit］*adj.* 机巧的（skillful, adept, deft）

【记】a＋droit（灵巧）→机巧的

【例】The elderly man couldn't walk, but he was still *adroit* with his hands.

acute ［əˈkjuːt］*adj.* 敏锐的（sharp）

【例】Dogs have very *acute* hearing.

acumen ［ˈækjuːmen］*n.* 敏锐（acuteness）

【记】acu（尖端）＋men→敏锐

【例】Bill has a lot of business *acumen* and earns a high salary.

粗 野

gauche ［gəuʃ］*adj.* 笨拙的；粗鲁的（awkward, clumsy, unapt）

【例】People laugh at Forrest Gump's *gauche* behavior at the White House.

rough ［rʌf］*adj.* 粗暴的（rude）

【例】The boy who lost his parents ran with a *rough* crowd.

rugged ［ˈrʌgid］*adj.* 粗俗的（coarse, rough）

coarse ［kɔːs］*adj.* 粗糙的，粗野的（rough, crude）

【例】Bill's *coarse* manners were becoming quite offensive.

rustic ［ˈrʌstik］*adj.* 粗俗的

【记】rust（乡村）＋ic→粗俗的

grumpy ［ˈgrʌmpi］*adj.* 坏脾气的，性情暴躁的（ill-tempered）

brutal ［ˈbruːtl］*adj.* 野蛮的

【例】The *brutal* beast tore the deer to pieces.

胆 小

spineless ['spainlis] *adj.* 没骨气的（weak, feeble）

timid ['timid] *adj.* 胆怯的，羞怯的
【例】The *timid* student was afraid to talk to his teacher.

bashful ['bæʃful] *adj.* 害羞的，胆小的（coy, shy, timid）
【记】bash(羞)＋ful→害羞的
【例】The *bashful* child hid behind his mother.

shy [ʃai] *adj.* 害羞的；胆小的（coy, timid）

和 蔼

pitiful ['pitiful] *adj.* 慈悲的
【记】名词pity(可怜)

genial ['dʒiːnjəl] *adj.* 和蔼的（kindly, good-natured）
【记】gen(产生)＋ial→产生(感情)的→和蔼的

modest ['mɔdist] *adj.* 谦虚的；适度的（humble, unassuming）
【记】mod(方式)＋est→做事有规矩→礼貌的

benign [bi'nain] *adj.* 亲切的，良好的（kind, benevolent）
【例】The poor farmer had a *benign* manner.

facile ['fæsil] *adj.* 轻而易举的（easy, effortless）；随和的
【记】fac(做)＋ile→能做得出的→轻而易举的
【例】I'm bored at work because my boss only gives me *facile* work as signments.

merciful ['məːsiful] *adj.* 仁慈的，宽大的
【记】名词mercy(仁慈)

humane [hjuː'mein] *adj.* 仁慈的，亲切的（sympathetic, kind）
【记】human(人)＋e→有人情味的→仁慈的

ductile ['dʌktail] *adj.* 柔软的；驯良的（plastic; malleable）

frank [fræŋk] *adj.* 坦白的，直率的（direct, honest）
【例】Be *frank* with your friends, or you will have no true friendship.

outspoken [aut'spəukən] *adj.* 坦率直言的(forthright, straight-forward)
【记】来自speak out(说出)

moderate ['mɔdərit] *adj.* 温和的；适度的(average, reasonable)
【记】moder=mod(方式)＋ate→方式正确→适度的

meek [miːk] *adj.* 温顺的(docile, submissive)；柔和的

tractable ['træktəbl] *adj.* 易驾驭的；温顺的(obedient)
【记】tract(拉)＋able→能拉得动的→易驾驭的
【例】Being *tractable* and loyal are essential qualities the owners ask for their slaves.

facetious [fə'siːʃəs] *adj.* 幽默的，滑稽的(amusing, jesting)
【例】Don't be offended; it was just a *facetious* remark.

humorous ['hjuːmərəs] *adj.* 幽默的

sociable ['səuʃəbl] *adj.* 友善的，好交际的(gregarious, friendly)
【例】Because Mary is *sociable*, she introduced herself to everyone at the party.

courteous ['kəːtjəs] *adj.* 有礼貌的；谦恭的(polite, gracious)
【例】The *courteous* child always says "please" and "thank you".

gracious ['greiʃəs] *adj.* 有礼貌的；仁慈的(affable)
【记】grac(优雅，讲究礼仪)＋ious→有礼貌的
【例】I thanked Jane for her *gracious* hospitality.

gregarious [gre'gɛəriəs] *adj.* 合群的(social, sociable)
【记】greg(群体)＋arious→爱群体的
【例】My *gregarious* sister makes friends wherever she goes.

gentility [dʒen'tiliti] *n.* 有教养；文雅
【例】These young ladies brought up with *gentility* showed great elegance in their behavior.

affable ['æfəbl] *adj.* 和蔼可亲的(genial, benevolent)
【记】af＋fable(说，讲)→可以说话的→和蔼的
【例】Mary is quite *affable* and is always invited to parties.

狡 猾

crooked ['krukid] *adj.* 狡诈的(bent, twisted)
【记】crook(弯曲)＋ed→拐弯抹角的→狡诈的

sly	[slai] *adj.* 狡猾的

【例】The *sly* spy managed to trap those loyal people.

cunning	[ˈkʌniŋ] *adj.* 狡猾的(sly, tricky)

【例】The successful owner had developed a *cunning* business sense.

designing	[diˈzainiŋ] *adj.* 狡猾的；蓄意的(cunning)

【例】The *designing* employee intended to get a promotion somehow.

节 俭

frugal	[ˈfruːɡəl] *adj.* 节约的(thrifty, economical)
economize	[iˈkɔnəmaiz] *vi.* 节俭(save, cut costs)

【例】When they bought a house, the family had to *economize* to pay their mortgage.

economical	[ˌiːkəˈnɔmikəl] *adj.* 节约的，经济的(thrifty)

【例】Purchasing clothing that will only be worn once is not very *economical*.

canny	[ˈkæni] *adj.* 精明的；节俭的(shrewd, cunning)
stoically	[ˈstəuikli] *adv.* 淡泊地(impassively)
austerity	[ɔsˈterəti] *n.* 节俭

【例】*Austerity* is the chosen lifestyle of a monk.

thrift	[θrift] *n.* 节约(economy, frugality)

谨 慎

conservative	[kənˈsəːvətiv] *adj.* 保守的(modest; cautious)

【例】A *conservative* estimate of the cost to repair the car is ＄100.

composed	[kəmˈpəuzd] *adj.* 沉着的

【记】比较pose(姿态)

composure	[kəmˈpəuʒə] *n.* 镇静(calmness, self-control)

【例】The irate customer lost his *composure* and yelled at the clerk.

prudent	[ˈpruːdənt] *adj.* 谨慎的(cautious)

【记】prud(小心)＋ent→谨慎的

vigilant	[ˈvidʒilənt] *adj.* 警惕着的，清醒的(watchful, alert)

【例】The president's *vigilant* bodyguard immediately noticed the man with a gun.

hardheaded [hɑːdˈhedid] *adj.* 冷静的

【记】hard(硬的)+head(想法)+ed

sober [ˈsəubə] *adj.* 清醒的

【例】The drunk man is totally another one when *sober*.

discreet [disˈkriːt] *adj.* 慎重的，谨慎的（prudent, cautious）

【例】You can tell Jane anything; she is very *discreet*.

discretion [disˈkreʃən] *n.* 慎重（caution, prudence）

【例】The decorator showed no *discretion* in her purchases for our new house, everything costing too much money.

circumspect [ˈsəːkəmspekt] *adj.* 慎重的，小心的（prudent, cautious）

【记】circum(绕圈)+spect(看)→四处看→小心的

【例】Never very *circumspect* in expressing his views, Bill annoyed almost everyone at the party.

cautious [ˈkɔːʃəs] *adj.* 小心的，谨慎的

【例】Be *cautious* when you approach strangers.

meticulously [məˈtikjuləsli] *adv.* 很仔细地（carefully, scrupulously）

【记】metic(害怕)+ulously→害怕出错地→细心地

【例】The editor kept on checking spelling mistakes *meticulously*.

sanity [ˈsæniti] *n.* 神志清楚（saneness, rationality）

懒 惰

sluggish [ˈslʌgiʃ] *adj.* 怠惰的（lethargic, listless, slow）

【例】The snake was *sluggish* because of the cold weather.

indolent [ˈindələnt] *adj.* 懒惰的（lazy, slothful）

inertia [iˈnəːʃjə] *n.* 惯性；惰性（laziness, indolence）

slug [slʌg] *n.* 慢吞吞的人（或物）

sloth [sləuθ] *n.* 怠惰，懒惰

slothful [ˈsləuθful] *adj.* 偷懒的

强 壮

stout [staut] *adj.* 健壮的（strong, sturdy）

【例】The athlete boasts his *stout* figure.

firm [fə:m] *adj.* 坚挺的；结实的（hard）

【例】Bob lifts weights everyday, so his muscles are very *firm*.

stocky ['stɔki] *adj.* 结实的，粗短的（sturdy）

【例】Many Eskimos are short and *stocky*.

robust [rəu'bʌst] *adj.* 强壮的（strong, sturdy）

【记】也就是谐音"乐百氏"

【例】If you want to be healthy and *robust*, you need to exercise yourself routinely.

hardy ['hɑːdi] *adj.* 强壮的（tough, rugged）；耐劳的

【例】Those *hardy* and stocky Eskimos have been living in this frozen world for centuries.

lusty ['lʌsti] *adj.* 强壮的；有精神的（vigorous, energetic）

【记】lust（光亮）＋y→人满面红光→有精神的

stiff [stif] *adj.* 硬的，僵直的

奢 侈

prodigal ['prɔdigəl] *adj.* 浪费的（extravagant, wasteful）

improvident [im'prɔvidənt] *adj.* 浪费的（thriftless, wasteful）

【记】im（无）＋provident（前瞻性的）

lavish ['læviʃ] *adj.* 浪费的，奢侈的（wasteful）

【记】lav（洗）＋ish→冲掉→浪费的

【例】My neighbors spoiled their children with *lavish* gifts.

luxurious [lʌg'ʒuəriəs] *adj.* 奢侈的（expensive, costly）

extravagant [iks'trævəgənt] *adj.* 奢侈的，浪费的（wasteful）

【记】extra＋vag（走）＋ant→游走外面的世界→奢侈的

【例】The accountant warned the owner against *extravagant* purchases.

squander ['skwɔndə] *vt.* 浪费（dissipate, waste）

【例】He was not at all shameful when *squandering* his family fortune on gambling.

flamboyant [flæm'bɔiənt] *adj.* 华丽的，浮夸的（dazzling, showy）

熟 练

deft [deft] *adj.* 灵巧的，熟练的（skillful, adroit）

【例】The pianist's *deft* fingers were delightful to watch.

adept [ə'dept] *adj.* 擅长的(adroit, apt)

【例】Mary is very *adept* at tuning pianos.

skillful ['skilful] *adj.* 熟练的(adroit)

【例】Lisa is *skillful* at repairing lamps.

experienced [iks'piəriənst] *adj.* 有经验的

【记】比较experience(经验)

【例】An *experienced* babysitter will not panic in an emergency situation.

stunt [stʌnt] *n.* 惊人的技艺(trick, feat)

【例】In the film he had to drive a car into the sea, and do other hair-raising *stunts*.

craft [kræft] *n.* 手艺(workmanship)

【记】craftsman(手艺人)

facility [fə'siliti] *n.* 熟练(proficiency);(复数)工具

【例】To write well, you need to have *facility* of language.

familiarize [fə'miljəraiz] *vt.* 熟悉

【记】familiar(熟悉的)+ize(动词词尾)→熟悉

【例】It is important to *familiarize* yourself with a foreign langugae nowadays.

accomplished [ə'kɔmpliʃt] *adj.* 熟练的(experienced, skillful)

【例】Bill is the most *accomplished* musician I have ever known.

素 质

aptitude ['æptitjuːd] *n.* 才能(talent, knack)

【记】apti(能力)+tude→才能

【例】I have no musical *aptitude* and I can't even sing a simple tune.

vigor ['vigə] *n.* 精力(energy, enthusiasm)

caliber ['kælibə] *n.* 品质(quality, capacity, ability, talent)

【例】Students are suggested to bring with them tea of high *caliber*.

quality ['kwɔliti] *n.* 品质(trait, calibre)

temperament ['tempərəmənt] *n.* 气质,性情(disposition, nature)

【记】tempera(脾气)+ment→性情

stamina ['stæminə] *n.* 体力,精力(endurance)

【例】Wrestling tests one's agility and *stamina*.

talent [ˈtælənt] *n.* 天才；才能；人才(gift, aptitude, knack)

confidence [ˈkɔnfidəns] *n.* 信心

【记】con＋fid(相信)＋ence→信心

【例】The patient had *confidence* in her surgeon's skills.

disposition [dispəˈziʃən] *n.* 性情(temperament, nature)

【例】The happy clerk had a pleasant *disposition*.

mass [mæs] *n.* 质量

ability [əˈbiliti] *n.* 能力(capability)

versatile [ˈvəːsətail] *adj.* 通用的，万能的，多才多艺的，多面手的

power [ˈpauə] *n.* 能力，力量

贪婪

avid [ˈævid] *adj.* 贪婪的(greedy)

ravenous [ˈrævinəs] *adj.* 贪婪的

rapacious [rəˈpeiʃəs] *adj.* 贪婪的(avaricious, covetous)

【记】rap(抓，夺)＋acious→贪婪的

greedy [ˈgriːdi] *adj.* 贪婪的(voracious, insatiable)

covetous [ˈkʌvitəs] *adj.* 贪心的(desirous, avaricious)

【记】动词covet(贪心)

avarice [ˈævəris] *n.* 贪婪(greed, lust)

【记】参考avid(渴望的)

【例】*Avarice* has caused the downfall of many people.

avaricious [ˌævəˈriʃəs] *adj.* 贪婪的，贪心的(greedy)

【例】Bill is so *avaricious* that he donates nothing to charity.

acquisitive [əˈkwizitiv] *adj.* 贪得无厌的(covetous, greedy)

【记】ac＋quisit(得到)＋ive→一再要得到→贪婪的

【例】Jane has an *acquisitive* nature and will probably want a new car just like yours.

严酷

exacting [igˈzæktiŋ] *adj.* 费力的，严格的(demanding, rigorous)

【记】比较exact(一丝不差的)

【例】Jane is very *exacting* in her work.

ascetic [əˈsetik] *adj.* 苦行的（austere, rigorous, strict）

grim [grim] *adj.* 冷酷的（cruel, merciless）

【例】Each day, the chance for peace became more *grim*.

relentless [riˈlentlis] *adj.* 无情的（merciless, ruthless）

【记】relent(怜悯的)＋less→无怜悯的

【例】The *relentless* bully beat Jimmy up.

ruthless [ˈruːθlis] *adj.* 无情的，冷酷的（merciless, pitiless）

【例】The *ruthless* tyrant caused the deaths of millions of people.

rigid [ˈridʒid] *adj.* 严格的，僵化的（strict, fixed）

【例】Their *rigid* notion of true womanhood had been restricting women's life for centuries.

stern [stəːn] *adj.* 严格的；僵化的（harsh, hard, strict）

【例】The museum guard gave us a *stern* warning not to touch the paintings.

stringent [ˈstrindʒənt] *adj.* 严格的；迫切的（strict, rigid）

【例】Our company has a *stringent* policy against smoking.

scrupulous [ˈskruːpjuləs] *adj.* 严谨的，讲究的（prudent, meticulous）

【例】The secretary is *scrupulous* about her dress.

drastic [ˈdræstik] *adj.* 严厉的（severe）

【例】The principal felt that the cheater's punishment should be *drastic*. / The emergency called for *drastic* measure.

harsh [haːʃ] *adj.* 严厉的（severe）

【例】The judge gave the criminal a *harsh* sentence.

rigor [ˈrigə] *n.* 严格，严厉（rigidity, hardship）

【例】Those homeless children had to face the *rigors* of life by themselves.

rigorous [ˈrigərəs] *adj.* 严厉的，严峻的（strict, rigid）

【记】rig(严厉的)＋orous→严厉的

【例】The trainings soldiers received were *rigorous*.

serious [ˈsiəriəs] *adj.* 严肃的

【例】*Serious* arts are becoming more and more popular among consideration.

severe [siˈviə] *adj.* 严重的，严肃的（grave, grievous）

austerity [ɔsˈterəti] *n.* 严峻

【记】au＋ster(冷)＋ity→冷冰冰→严峻

【例】War was followed by many years of *austerity*.

ordeal [ɔːˈdiːl] *n.* 严酷的考验(difficult experience, trial)

勇 敢

bold [bəuld] *adj.* 大胆的(daring, brave)

【例】The *bold* employee insisted on better working conditions.

daring [ˈdɛəriŋ] *adj.* 大胆的, 勇敢的(bold, audacious)

【记】比较dare(胆敢)

【例】A *daring* firefighter pulled the child from the fire.

undaunted [ʌnˈdɔːntid] *adj.* 无畏的, 勇敢的(intrepid, fearless)

dauntless [ˈdɔːntlis] *adj.* 勇敢的

【记】daunt(害怕)+less→不害怕的→勇敢的

【例】The *dauntless* pilot flew through the rough storms.

valiant [ˈvæljənt] *adj.* 英勇的(courageous, dauntless, intrepid)

【例】The *valiant* soldier was given a medal.

gallant [ˈgælənt] *adj.* 英勇的(courageous, heroic)

【记】gall(胆)+ant→有胆的→英勇的

【例】Mary and Jane gave their *gallant* waiter a generous tip.

intrepid [inˈtrepid] *adj.* 勇敢的(fearless, dauntless)

【记】in(不)+trepid(害怕)→勇敢的

【例】The *intrepid* explorers reached the South Pole.

valor [ˈvælə] *n.* 勇气(bravery, courage)

【记】val(强大)+or

【例】The terminally ill patient showed great *valor* in the last months of his life.

自 私

flighty [ˈflaiti] *adj.* 不负责任的; 轻浮的(fickle, capricious)

【记】flight(飞)+y→轻浮的

【例】It's unwise to ask a *flighty* person to make such a serious decision.

skimpy [ˈskimpi] *adj.* 吝啬的

stingy [ˈstindʒi] *adj.* 吝啬的(miserly, ungenerous)

miserly [ˈmaizəli] *adj.* 吝啬的(stingy)

snobbish [ˈsnɔbiʃ] *adj.* 势利的，谄上欺下的

【记】snob(势利)＋bish→势利的

【例】My *snobbish* coworker thinks she is the most important employee in the company.

selfish [ˈselfiʃ] *adj.* 自私的

Carve your name on hearts and not on marbles.

— *J.Addison*

把你的姓名刻在人们的心上，而不是刻在大理石上。

——爱迪生

连 线 题

左列单词在右列中有一个或多个同义词,请画线连接。

(一)

	bravery
avaricious	calibre
	calmness
composure	cautious
craft	courage
economical	greedy
miserly	harsh
prudent	self-control
quality	stingy
	strict
robust	sturdy
stern	thrifty
valor	trait
	workmanship

(二)

acumen	acuteness
benign	agile
	benevolent
despicable	brash
discrimination	contemptible
filthy	detestable
impudent	prejudice
nimble	ragged
reckless	rash
rough	squalid
versatile	talented

（一）

avaricious	greedy
composure	calmness
composure	self-control
craft	workmanship
economical	thrifty
miserly	stingy
prudent	cautious
quality	trait
quality	calibre
robust	sturdy
stern	harsh
stern	strict
valor	bravery
valor	courage

（二）

acumen	acuteness
benign	benevolent
despicable	detestable
despicable	contemptible
discrimination	prejudice
filthy	squalid
impudent	brash
nimble	agile
reckless	rash
rough	ragged
versatile	talented

填 空 题

将恰当的词填入横线处

1. We _____ all cowards and flatterers.

2. The opera was marred by an _____ aria.

3. He made an _____ decision.

4. He is a _____ musician.

5. There are many _____ professors in our university.

6. The _____ work of the student disappointed his teacher.

7. The _____ girl flushed when she heard the words.

8. The _____ millionaire donate much money to the village.

9. To be _____, I am very busy these days.

10. The _____ fox cheated the wolf with its sweet words.

11. _____ is a virtue of Chinese people.

12. The deer is _____ all day long.

13. He had throughout been almost worryingly _____ in his business formalities.

14. No leaders like _____ workers.

15. To be _____, we need more nutrition.

16. We are shocked at the _____ furniture.

17. He is an _____ worker in our factory.

18. _____ is more important than quantity.

19. Everyone should have _____ in himself.

20. The _____ merchant was finally punished by himself.

21. He suffered _____ persecution for years.

22. The _____ soldiers defeated the enemy.

23. The _____ landlord placed heavy burden on the farmers.

填空题答案

1. despise	7. shy	13. meticulous	19. confidence
2. awkward	8. merciful	14. indolent	20. avaricious
3. intelligent	9. frank	15. robust	21. relentless
4. versatile	10. cunning	16. luxurious	22. intrepid
5. knowledgeable	11. Thrift	17. experienced	23. miserly
6. coarse	12. vigilant	18. Quality	

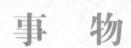

事　物

记忆小贴士：挂钩记忆法

将一组熟悉的地点，房间摆设等与要记的东西之间挂钩，主要利用视觉表象，以地点位置作为以后的提取线索。

食 品

cabbage	['kæbidʒ] *n.* 甘蓝，卷心菜	
carrot	['kærət] *n.* 胡萝卜	
celery	['seləri] *n.* 旱芹，芹菜	
cereal	['siəriəl] *n.* 谷类食品，谷类	
corn	[kɔːn] *n.* <美>玉米，<英>谷物，五谷	
cucumber	['kjuːkʌmbə] *n.* 黄瓜	
grain	[grein] *n.* 谷物，谷类，谷粒，细粒，颗粒，粮食	
leek	[liːk] *n.* 韭	
lettuce	['letis] *n.* 莴苣，生菜	
millet	['milit] *n.* 稷，粟	
mustard	['mʌstəd] *n.* 芥菜，芥末	
oats	[əuts] *n.* 燕麦，燕麦片	
onion	['ʌnjən] *n.* 洋葱	
pea	[piː] *n.* 豌豆	
peanut	['piːnʌt] *n.* 花生	
pepper	['pepə] *n.* 胡椒粉	
potato	[pə'teitəu] *n.* 马铃薯	
pumpkin	['pʌmpkin] *n.* 南瓜	
radish	['rædiʃ] *n.* 萝卜	
rice	[rais] *n.* 稻，米	
rye	[rai] *n.* 裸麦，黑麦	
sesame	['sesəmi] *n.* 芝麻	

soybean	['sɔibiːn] *n.* 大豆
spinach	['spinidʒ;(US)'spinitʃ] *n.* 菠菜
tomato	[tə'mɑːtəu, tə'meitəu] *n.* 番茄，西红柿
wheat	[wiːt, hw-] *n.* 小麦；小麦色
edible	['edibl] *adj.* 可食的(eatable, comestible)

【记】ed(吃)＋ible

【例】The cake was garnished with *edible* decorations.

bland	[blænd] *adj.* (食物等)无刺激性的(mild, gentle)

【例】Mary added spices to the *bland* dishes.

seasoning	['siːzniŋ] *n.* 调味品，佐料(flavoring, spice)

condiment [ˈkɔndimənt] *n.* 调味品
【例】The only *condiments* I like on my hamburger are ketchup and mustard.

butter [ˈbʌtə] *n.* 奶油

chop [tʃɔp] *n.* 排骨

cuisine [kwiˈziːn] *n.* 烹调
【例】The restaurant served *cuisine* from Thailand.

dessert [diˈzəːt] *n.* 甜点
【例】*Dessert* is the last course of a meal.

beverage [ˈbevəridʒ] *n.* 饮料
【记】bever(喝)＋age
【例】What sort of *beverages* should we serve at the party?

diet [ˈdaiət] *n.* 饮食，食物 *v.* 节食
【例】Pizza was the staple of the college students' *diet*.

nutriment [ˈnjuːtrimənt] *n.* 营养品

nibble [ˈnibl] *vt.* 细咬；细食(bite; eat)
【记】nib(小)＋ble
【例】The fish were *nibbling* at the bait.

imbibe [imˈbaib] *vt.* 饮(absorb, assimilate)
【记】im(进入)＋bibe(喝)
【例】Grandpa *imbibed* a bit of wine each night.

scoop [skuːp] *n.* 勺子 *v.* 舀
【例】He used his bare hands to *scoop* up water from the river.

barley [ˈbɑːli] *n.* 大麦

beet [biːt] *n.* 甜菜，甜菜根

broccoli [ˈbrɔkəli] *n.* 椰菜

本 质

indigenous [inˈdidʒinəs] *adj.* 固有的(aboriginal, native)
【记】indi(内部)＋gen(产生)＋ous→内部产生→土产的
【例】The *indigenous* people of the area know which plants are safe to eat and which are poisonous.

intrinsic [inˈtrinzik] *adj.* 本质的(substantive)；本身的
【例】Paying careful attention and responding quickly are *intrinsic* parts

of good driving.

radical ['rædikl] *adj.* 根本的

【例】The American Revolution is not a *radical* one, but a gradual evolution.

radically ['rædikəli] *adv.* 根本上（basically）

rudimentary ['ruːdimentəri] *adj.* 根本的，低级的（undeveloped, elementary, primitive, unsophisticated）

【记】rudi(无知的)＋ment＋ary→无知的→最初的

【例】I took a *rudimentary* cooking class in high school.

inherent [in'hiərənt] *adj.* 固有的（innate, intrinsic）

【记】in(里面)＋her(连)＋ent→天生(与身体内)连着→天赋的

inherently [in'hiərentli] *adv.* 天性地，固有地（intrisically, fundamentally, basically）

objective [ɔb'dʒektiv] *adj.* 客观的

【记】object(客观)＋ive

internal [in'təːnl] *adj.* 内在的（inside, interior）

【记】比较external(外在的)

incisive [in'saisiv] *adj.* 深刻的（profound）

【例】His *incisive* criticism gave us a thorough understanding of Dicksen's writings.

substantive ['sʌbstəntiv] *adj.* 实质性的（actual）

【例】An accident is just the appearance; a malicious murder is actually *substantive*.

innate [i'neit] *adj.* 天生的（inborn, inherent）

【记】in(进)＋nate(生)→与出生一起来→天生的

【例】The singer had an *innate* talent for music.

inborn ['inbɔːn] *adj.* 天生的（innate）

【记】in(内)＋born(出生)→与生俱来的

【例】Man's ability to compute is far from *inborn*; you have to acquire after birth.

instinctive [in'stiŋktiv] *adj.* 天生的，本能的（impulsive, spontaneous）

【记】instinct(本能)＋ive

crude [kruːd] *adj.* 未提炼的；生的（raw, unpolished, unprocessed）

spontaneous [spɔn'teiniəs] *adj.* 自发的；本能的（impulsive, involuntary）

【记】spont(自然)＋aneous→自然的→自发的

【例】There was the *spontaneous* applause at the end of Mary's speech.

interior [inˈtiəriə] *n.* 内部(inside, inner)

【记】比较exterior(外部)

【例】The building's *interior* needed to be repaired.

attribute [ˈætribjuːt] *n.* 性质(characteristic, quality, trait)

【例】As a great leader, generosity is his first *attribute*.

abstruse [æbˈstruːs] *adj.* 深奥的(complicated, profound)

【记】abs+trus(走)+e→走不进去的→难懂的

比较概念

comparative [kəmˈpærətiv] *adj.* 比较的

【例】Bill is a *comparative* stranger in town. He has just moved here.

comparable [ˈkɔmpərəbl] *adj.* 可比的；类似的(similar)

【例】I suggested two *comparable* solutions to the problem.

similar [ˈsimilə] *adj.* 相似的，类似的(comparable)

dissimilar [diˈsimilə] *adj.* 不相似的，不同的(different)

【记】dis+similar(相似的)

【例】Your children are so *dissimilar*; it is hard to believe they are related.

subordinate [səˈbɔːdinit] *adj.* 次要的，附属的(inferior, secondary)

【记】sub(下面)+ordin(顺序)+ate→下面的顺序→附属的

【例】Pleasure should be *subordinate* to duty.

monotonous [məˈnɔtənəs] *adj.* 单调的(boring, dull)

【记】mono(单个)+ton(声音)+ous

typical [ˈtipikəl] *adj.* 典型的，代表性的(ordinary)

【例】My aunt just moved to Beijing; she is not a *typical* Beijing local.

invert [inˈvəːt] *vt.* 倒转(overturn, reverse)

【例】I *inverted* the glasses so the water would drain out of them.

inverse [inˈvəːs] *adj.* 反的(contrary, opposite)

【记】in(反)+verse(转)→反转的→相反的

preferable [ˈprefərəbl] *adj.* 更好的

【记】prefer(喜欢)+able

【例】A *preferable* option is to store the food in a refrigerator rather than throw it away.

approximate [əˈprɔksimit] *adj.* 近似的(proximate)

【记】ap＋proxim(接近)＋ate→接近的，近似的

【例】What is the *approximate* travel time from your house to your job?

coordinate [kəuˈɔːdinit] *adj.* 同等的，并列的(equal, juxtaposed)

【例】John only speaks to those who are *coodinate* with him in ranks.

homogeneous [ˌhɔməˈdʒiːnjəs] *adj.* 同类的；相似的(uniform, same)

【记】homo(同)＋gen(产生)＋ous→产生相同的

【例】The population of the small town was *homogeneous,* mostly merchants and laborers.

identical [aiˈdentikl] *adj.* 同一的(tantamount, same)

【记】iden(相同)＋tical

【例】Bill and John have *identical* briefcases, and sometimes Bill picks up John's briefcase by mistake.

peerless [ˈpiəlis] *adj.* 无与伦比的(matchless, unparalleled)

【记】peer(同等)＋less→无相提并论者→无与伦比的

equal [ˈiːkwəl] *adj.* 相等的，同样的(equivalent)

【记】equ(平)＋al

【例】Put an *equal* amount of sugar into both bowls.

equate [iˈkweit] *vt.* 使相等，视为同等

【例】It's a mistake to *equate* wealth with happiness.

equivalent [iˈkwivələnt] *adj.* 相等的 *n.* 等同品(counterpart, match)

【例】Both of them expressed their agreement with *equivalent* statements. / I lost the necklace borrowed from Jenny, and I didn't have any *equivalent* to return to her.

intermediate [ˌintəˈmiːdiət] *adj.* 中级的

neutral [ˈnjuːtrəl] *adj.* 中性的；中立的(nonaligned)

【记】neutr(中)＋al

backward [ˈbækwəd] *adj./adv.* 退步的；相反的

【记】back(背，后)＋ward(方向)

【例】The senator's *backward* views were very uneducated.

relatively [ˈrelətivli] *adv.* 相关地，相对地(comparatively)

【例】The SMART car has an engine *relatively* powerful to its weight.

shade [ʃeid] *n.* 差别（difference）

【例】If you want to write well, frequently distinguish the fine *shades* between words.

reproduction [ˌriːprə'dʌkʃən] *n.* 复制品（copy）

【记】re(重新)＋production(生产)→复制

【例】Don't get yourself cheated; the vase is only a *reproduction*.

inferior [in'fiəriə] *n.* 次品 *adj.* 自卑的，劣等的

【记】infer(低)＋ior; 比较superior(高级的)

【例】No *inferior* products should be allowed to pass.

sample ['sæmpl] *n.* 范例，样品（specimen）

medium ['miːdiəm] *n.* 媒介; 中间 *adj.* 中等的

【记】medi(中间)＋um→中间物，媒介

counterpart ['kauntəpɑːt] *n.* 相对物; 极相似之物（equivalent, correspondent）

【例】In London, the *counterpart* of the New York subway is called the "tube".

midst [midst] *n.* 中间 *prep.* 在…之间（during, undergoing）

contrast ['kɔntræst] *n.* 对比（着重于相异处）

【例】Today's rain is a sharp *contrast* to yesterday's sunshine.

compare [kəm'peə] *vt.* 比较（着重于相似处）; 比喻

【例】If you *compare* this book with that one, you will find that one is larger. / Bob *compared* Mary's messy hair to a bird's nest.

copy ['kɔpi] *vt.* 复制，模仿（imitate）

【例】Bill *copied* the original article for his personal use.

imitate ['imiteit] *vt.* 模仿（copy, mimic）

【例】Anne *imitated* the famous artist's style in her own paintings.

resemble [ri'zembl] *vt.* 像，类似

【例】Mary *resembles* her mother in many ways.

affinity [ə'finiti] *n.* 类似处（similarity）

【记】af(一再)＋fin(范围)＋ity→一再能进入别人的范围→亲密

【例】There is a close *affinity* between apes and monkeys.

范　围

exception [ik'sepʃən] *n.* 例外

【记】ex＋cept(拿)＋ion→拿出去→例外

【例】Everyone passed the math test, with the *exception* of Tom.

exceptional [ik'sepʃənl] *adj.* 例外的

【例】The *exceptional* tennis player won the championship.

relieved [ri'li:vd] *adj.* 免除的(exempted)

【记】名词relief(宽慰)

extra ['ekstrə] *adj.* 额外的(additional, surplus)

extraneous [eks'treiniəs] *adj.* 无关的(irrelevant, unrelated);外来的

【记】extra(外)+neous

【例】The editor cut the *extraneous* material from the first chapter.

irrelevant [i'relivənt] *adj.* 离题的;无关的(impertinent, extraneous)

【记】ir(无)+relevant(有关的)

【例】Bob's comments about religion were *irrelevant* to our discussion about politics.

exclude [iks'klu:d] *vt.* 把…排除在外(rule out)

【记】ex+clude(关闭)→关出去→排除在外

【例】Please don't *exclude* grains from your diet.

exclusive [iks'klu:siv] *adj.* 排外的;独占的(prohibitive; restrictive)

【例】The CNN covered this moving story *exclusively*.

exclusion [iks'klu:ʒən] *n.* 除外(omission)

【例】The contract covers everything with no *exclusions* stated.

unconventional [ˌʌnkən'venʃənl] *adj.* 破例的

external [eks'tə:nl] *adj.* 外部的(exterior)

【例】The crab's *external* shell must be removed before you eat the meat inside.

impertinent [im'pə:tinənt] *adj.* 无关的(unrelated)

【例】Don't talk anything *impertinent* to the main issue.

besides [bi'saidz] *adv.* 除了(还有)

【例】*Besides* hot dogs, we had potato salad.

scope [skəup] *n.* 范围;余地(range, extent)

【例】There is not much *scope* for imagination in his tedious job.

span [spæn] *n.* 跨度 *vt.* 跨越(cover, reach across)

content ['kɔntent] *n.* 内容(matter)

save [seiv] *prep.* 除了(except)

【例】For money, the selfish gangster would kill anyone *save* himself.

deviate ['di:vieit] *v.* 出轨;离题(deflect, diverge)

【记】de＋via(路)＋te→离正路→出轨

【例】I do not like to *deviate* from the set schedule.

digress [dai'gres] *vi.* 离开本题(deviate, turn away)

【记】di(偏离)＋gress(走)→走偏离→离题

【例】Mary *digressed* and forgot what she was originally talking about.

embrace [im'breis] *vt.* 包含, 拥抱(hug, cuddle)

【例】Computer software develops like this: the new version should *embrace* the former ones. / The students tearfully *embraced* each other on their last day of school.

cover ['kʌvə] *vt.* 包括

【例】His lecture *covers* all aspects of that language.

comprise [kəm'praiz] *vt.* 包括(constitute, contain, consist of, be made up of)

【例】The committee *comprises* seven persons.

bias ['baiəs] *vt.* 使…偏离

【例】The government used newspapers and the radio to *bias* the opinions of the people.

deflect [di'flekt] *vt.* 使偏离(divert, deviate)

【记】de(偏离)＋flect(做)→偏斜

【例】The ball hit a wall and was *deflected* from its course.

embody [em'bɔdi] *vt.* 体现; 包含(include, incorporate)

【记】em＋body(身体, 主体)

【例】The monitor *embodied* his idea in a short speech.

accommodate [ə'kɔmədeit] *vt.* 容纳(contain, load)

【例】This elevator *accommodates* twelve people.

preclude [pri'klu:d] *vt.* 排除; 防止(prevent, prohibit)

【记】pre(提前)＋clude(关闭)→防止

【例】Modesty *precludes* me from accepting the honor.

方 法

forthright ['fɔ:θrait] *adj.* 直接的(frank, direct)

【例】The brave soldiers marched *forthright* with a knowledge that there would not be any enemy ahead.

shortcut ['ʃɔ:tkʌt] *n.* 捷径(direct route)

tip [tip] *n.* 窍门（cleverness）

【例】He learned a lot of *tips* on cooking through the book.

means [mi:nz] *n.* 手段，方法（way）

【例】Try every *means* to achieve the ends.

via [ˈvaiə] *prep.* 经过，经由（by way of）

【例】She started her self-study *via* radio.

direct [daiˈrekt] *adj.* 直接的（straightforward）

access [ˈækses] *n.* 通路，入门（outlet）

【记】ac＋cess(走)→走过去→通道

【例】The strikers blocked the *access* to the factory.

光

faint [feint] *adj.* 模糊的

【例】I stayed up until I saw *faint* rays of light from the rising sun.

gloom [glu:m] *n.* 黑暗

gloomy [ˈglu:mi] *adj.* 暗的（dark, dim）

【例】It's looking *gloomy* outside. You'd better take an umbrella.

luminous [ˈlu:minəs] *adj.* 发光的；光亮的（glowing; bright）

【记】lumin(光)＋ous

【例】The astronomer gazed at the *luminous* star.

illuminate [iˈlju:mineit] *vt.* 照明，照亮

【记】il(一再)＋lumin(光明)＋ate→给予光明→照亮

【例】Could you please *illuminate* your theory with a little more explanation? / Cleverly-made attacks can often serve to *illuminate* important differences between candidates, as well as entertain the voters.

dingy [ˈdindʒi] *adj.* 昏暗的

dim [dim] *adj.* 昏暗的；朦胧的（faint, vague）

【例】Mike's eyes adjusted to the *dim* room.

obscure [əbˈskjuə] *adj.* 模糊的（unclear）

【记】ob(离开)＋scure(跑)→跑开→模糊的

【例】Alchemists made these symbols purposely *obscure*. They don't want people to know all this.

vague ［veiɡ］ *adj.* 模糊的，含糊的（imprecise, elementary, obscure, ambiguous）

【例】Tom evaded Jane's question by giving her a *vague* answer.

dusky ［'dʌski］ *adj.* 微暗的，肤色黑的（dim, dark）

【例】The *dusky* light makes the old house look horrible.

extinct ［iks'tiŋkt］ *adj.* 熄灭的

【记】ex＋tinct（促使）→促使出去→灭绝

glaring ［'ɡlɛəriŋ］ *adj.* 耀眼的（dazzling）

【记】参考glare（瞪）

dazzling ［'dæzliŋ］ *adj.* 耀眼的

【例】The *dazzling* dress looked stunning on the mannequin.

dismal ［'dizml］ *adj.* 阴暗的

【例】Mary cried during the *dismal* movie.

glossy ［'ɡlɔsi］ *adj.* 有光泽的（smooth, lustrous）

【例】I polished the silver until it was *glossy* again.

luster ［'lʌstə］ *n.* 光彩；光泽（brightness, distinction, radiance）

【记】lust（光亮）＋er

glaze ［'ɡleiz］ *v.*（使）光滑

【例】Sue *glazed* the pottery and waited for it to dry.

flare ［'flɛə］ *v.* 闪耀（glare, shine）

【记】比较flame（火焰）

【例】A match *flares* in the darkness.

burnish ［'bə:niʃ］ *vt.* 磨光，使光滑（polish）

【例】The craftsman *burnished* the brass plates until they glowed.

flicker ［'flikə］ *vt.* 闪烁（flutter, waver）

【例】The candle *flickered* in the wind.

brighten ［'braitn］ *vt.* 使发光

【记】bright（光亮）＋en

【例】A little furniture polish will *brighten* that old table.

gleam ［ɡli:m］ *vt.* 使闪光；闪烁（glimmer; flash）

【例】It shone with gold and *gleamed* with ivory.

extinguish ［iks'tiŋwiʃ］ *vt.* 熄灭

【例】John *extinguished* the campfire with water.

ablaze ［ə'bleiz］ *adj.* 闪耀的（gleaming, glowing）

【记】a（加强）＋blaze（火焰）→闪耀的

twinkle [ˈtwiŋkl] v. 闪烁，闪耀，(使)闪光

【例】The stars *twinkled* in the sky.

科　学

tentative [ˈtentətiv] adj. 试验性的(trial)

【记】tent=test(测试)＋ative

【例】*Tentative* measures have been taken to settle these refugees.

mechanical [miˈkænikl] adj. 机械的

exact [igˈzækt] adj. 精确的，严格的(accurate, precise)

【例】By asking the student to repeat the *exact* words he had just said, the teacher proved himself an exact person.

theoretical [θiəˈretikəl] adj. 理论的(academic)

precise [priˈsais] adj. 周密的，精确的(accurate, exact)

trial [ˈtraiəl] adj. 实验性的

specimen [ˈspesimən] n. 标本，样品(sample, instance)

symbol [ˈsimbl] n. 符号(emblem, token)

symbolic [simˈbɔlik] adj. 象征的，符号的

precision [priˈsiʒən] n. 精确，精密度(accuracy, exactness)

doctrine [ˈdɔktrin] n. 学说(theory)

【例】How are the *doctrines* of the two churches different?

threshold [ˈθreʃəuld] n. 阈值；门槛(doorsill)

expertise [ˌekspəˈtiːz] n. 专门知识(know-how, special skill)

【记】expert(专家)＋ise→专家的知识

【例】Do you have the *expertise* required to tune the piano?

institute [ˈinstitjuːt] n.(研究)所

invent [inˈvent] v. 发明(create, originate)

【例】The inventor wanted to *invent* something that no one had thought of before.

dissect [diˈsekt] vt. 详细研究(analyze)

【例】Bill *dissected* a small shark in anatomy class.

contrive [kənˈtraiv] vt. 发明(invent)

【例】A group of scientists *contrived* a new synthetic plastic.

launch [lɔːntʃ] vt. 发射，投射(send off)；推出

【例】My company *launch*ed a new insurance plan.

devise [di'vaiz] *vt.* 计划；发明(create, invent)

【例】The student *devised* an excuse to skip class without being caught.

gauge [geidʒ] *vt.* 精确计量(calculate, measure)

【例】Tom *gauged* the distance to the river to be about a mile.

accurate ['ækjurit] *adj.* 准确的，正确的(exact, correct)

【例】Your statements about the cost of the house were not *accurate*.

scale [skeil] *n.* 规模；尺度；天平

【例】I'll be glad when I tip the *scales* at a few pounds less.

逻 辑

logical ['lɔdʒikl] *adj.* 合逻辑的(reasonable)

therefore ['ðεəfɔː] *adv.* 因此(thus, consequently, in result)

hence [hens] *adv.* 因此，从此(as a result)

framework ['freimwəːk] *n.* 构架，框架(structure, skeleton)

hypothesis [hai'pɔθəsis] *n.* 假设(assumption)

【记】hypo(下，次)+thesis(论点)→次论点→非正式论点→假设

assumption [ə'sʌmpʃən] *n.* 假设(supposition; hypothesis)

【例】a valid *assumption*

presume [pri'zuːm] *vt.* 假定，假设(suppose, imagine, assume)

【例】We cannot *presume* the existence of life on other planets.

presumption [pri'zʌmpʃən] *n.* 推定；猜想(assumption, presupposition)

clue [kluː] *n.* 线索(information)

【例】The police found a *clue* which will help them catch the robber.

generalize ['dʒenərəlaiz] *v.* 归纳，概括(summarize, outline)

【例】He *generalized* from the president's speech that the nation is not going to involve in the war.

incur [in'kəː] *vt.* 承担；遭遇；招致(arouse, provoke)

【记】in(进入)+cur(跑)→跑进来→招致

【例】His arrogant attitude has *incurred* many people's discontent.

suppose [sə'pəuz] *vt.* 假想，推测(think, speculate, imagine)

【例】Scientists *supposed* that large dinosaurs lived in swamps.

premise ['premis] *vt.* 提出前提 *n.* 前提(assumption, hypothesis)

【例】We must act on the *premise* that the worst can happen.

infer [inˈfəː] *vt.* 推知(deduce, imply)

【记】in(进入)+fer→带进(意义)→推断

【例】We can *infer* that his motive in publishing the diary was less than honorable.

demonstrate [ˈdemənstreit] *vt.* 演示；论证

【例】The mechanic *demonstrated* how to change the car's oil.

时 间

due [djuː] *adj.* 到期的；预定的,约定的

【例】This bill was *due* two weeks ago, but I forgot to pay it. / Their plane is *due* in 15 minutes.

cursory [ˈkəːsəri] *adj.* 仓促的(hurried)

【记】curs(跑)+ory

【例】The reviewer gave a *cursory* report about the uninteresting book.

perennial [pəˈrenjəl] *adj.* 长久的,永远的(permanent, long-lasting, year-round)

【记】per(全部)+enn(年)+ial

chronic [ˈkrɔnik] *adj.* 长期的；慢性的(recurring, periodic)

【记】chron(时间)+ic→长时间的

【例】Mike said a *chronic* disease troubled John in his whole life.

lasting [ˈlɑːstiŋ] *adj.* 持久的(enduring, long-term, continuing)

【记】last(持久)+ing

everlasting [ˌevəˈlɑːstiŋ] *adj.* 永恒的,持久的

hasty [ˈheisti] *adj.* 匆忙的(rushed)

transitory [ˈtrænzitəri] *adj.* 短暂的(temporary, momentary)

【记】trans(交换)+it(走)+ory→交换走,你走他来→短暂的

transient [ˈtrænziənt] *adj.* 短暂的；过路的(temporary, short-term)

【例】He made a *transient* stay at the hotel.

obsolete [ˌɔbsəˈliːt] *adj.* 过时的,偶然的(disused, outmoded)

【记】ob(不)+solete(使用)→过时的

【例】This new computer rendered my old one *obsolete*.

extemporaneous [eksˌtempəˈreinjəs] *adj.* 即席的(impromptu, improvised)

【记】ex+tempor(时间)+aneous→在安排时间之外→即席的

【例】I gave an *extemporaneous* lecture because the invited speaker was late.

urgent [ˈəːdʒənt] *adj.* 紧急的，迫切的（imperative）

【例】It is *urgent* that food and clothing be sent to the refugees.

pressing [ˈpresiŋ] *adj.* 紧迫的（urgent）

immediate [iˈmiːdiət] *adj.* 立即的（instant）

【记】im(无)+medi(中间)+ate→无中间休息→立刻的

forthright [ˈfɔːθrait] *adj.* 立即的

【例】The critic gave the *forthright* criticism to the director of the film.

offhand [ɔfˈhænd] *adj.* 临时的

【例】I gave an *offhand* guess that it's about three o'clock.

temporal [ˈtempərəl] *adj.* 一时的；暂时的（transient, momentary）

【记】tempor(时间)+al

temporary [ˈtempərəri] *adj.* 临时的（momentary, make-do）

contemporary [kənˈtempərəri] *adj.* 当代的，同时代的

impromptu [imˈprɔmptjuː] *adj.* 临时的；即兴的（extempore, improvised）

【记】im(不)+promptu(时间)→不在时间表内→临时的

【例】The pianist gave an *impromptu* performance at the party.

occasional [əˈkeiʒənəl] *adj.* 临时的；偶然的

【例】The silence was broken by an *occasional* scream.

punctual [ˈpʌŋktʃuəl] *adj.* 守时的

【记】punct(点)+ual→卡着点的→守时的

【例】Mary is *punctual*; she would never be late for an appointment.

instantaneous [ˌinstənˈteiniəs] *adj.* 瞬间的，即刻的（ephemeral）

【记】instant(马上)+aneous→瞬间

subsequent [ˈsʌbsikwənt] *adj.* 随后的，后来的（following, later）

【记】sub(下面)+sequent(随着的)

【例】*Subsequent* events proved the man to be right.

current [ˈkʌrənt] *adj.* 现今的（present）

【例】Recent reports will give the most *current* news about the accident. / He reads the newspaper every day to know the *current* events.

concurrent [kənˈkʌrənt] *adj.* 同时发生的（simultaneous）

【记】con+current(发生)→同时发生

【例】There were several *concurrent* attempts to climb the mountain.

extant [ˈekstænt] *adj.* 现存的（existing）

nocturnal [nɔkˈtəːnl] *adj.* 夜间的（nighttime, nightly）

【记】noct(夜)＋urnal；比较diurnal(白天的)

【例】An owl is an *nocturnal* bird, while a sparrow is diurnal.

former ['fɔ:mə] *adj.* 以前的(ago, previous)

【例】My *former* students still kept in touch with me through e-mails.

formerly ['fɔ:məli] *adv.* 从前，原来(previously)

previous ['pri:viəs] *adj.* 以前的(preceding, foregoing)

【记】pre(预先)＋vious

previously ['pri:viəsli] *adv.* 先前，以前(earlier, formerly)

eternal [i'tə:nl] *adj.* 永恒的(everlasting, perpetual)

【例】The bride and groom pledged their *eternal* love to each other.

permanent ['pə:mənənt] *adj.* 永久的(constant, continuous)

【例】Anne took a *permanent* position with the law firm.

abiding [ə'baidiŋ] *adj.* 永久的，永恒的(enduring, lasting)

dated ['deitid] *adj.* 有年头的，陈旧的

【记】date(时间，日子)＋d

【例】The *dated* movie was still quite entertaining.

overdue [ˌəuvə'dju:] *adj.* 逾期的(tardy, late)

【记】over(过)＋due(到期)→逾期

tentative ['tentətiv] *adj.* 暂时的(temporary)

【例】*Tentative* measures have been taken to settle these refugees.

beforehand [bi'fɔ:hænd] *adv.* 事先地(in advance)

【例】Please make a reservation at the restaurant *beforehand* so we don't have to wait.

simultaneously [ˌsiml'teiniəsli] *adv.* 同时地(at the same time, concurrently)

【例】The two balls, big and little, hit the ground *simultaneously*.

recently ['ri:sntli] *adv.* 最近地(lately, currently)

lately ['leitli] *adv.* 最近

duration [djuə'reiʃən] *n.* 持续时间，为期(length)

epoch ['epək] *n.* 纪元；时代(age, era)

interlude ['intəlu:d] *n.* 间隔；插曲(interval; episode)

【记】inter(在…中间)＋lude(玩)→在中间玩→中间休息

era ['iərə] *n.* 时代，时期(period, age)

schedule ['skedʒul] *n.* 时间表；计划表(calendar, timetable)

juncture ['dʒʌŋktʃə] *n.* 时刻

session ['seʃən] *n.* 一段时间；一次

【例】A very dehydrated man can not drink too much water at one *session*, or he will get himself killed through water intoxication.

elapse [i'læps] *vi.* (时间)消逝(go by, pass)

【记】e(出)+lapse(滑)→滑出去→时光流去

【例】Time *elapsed* slowly while I waited for the bus.

concur [kən'kəː] *vi.* 同时发生

【例】After hearing my point, Bill *concurred* with me.

improvise ['imprəvaiz] *vt.* 即席而作(extemporize)

【记】im(不)+pro(前)+vise(看)→没有预先看过→即席而作

【例】The actors *improvised* a scene based on an audience's suggestion.

synchronize ['siŋkrənaiz] *vt.* 同时发生(concur)

【记】syn(共同)+chron(时间)+ize→同时

【例】They *synchronized* their steps.

abruptly [ə'brʌptli] *adv.* 突然地,唐突地(suddenly)

水相关动作

itinerant [ai'tinərənt] *adj.* 巡回的(travelling);流动的

【记】itiner(走)+ant→走来走去的→巡回的

【例】The *itinerant* preacher has been travelling around Europe for decades.

flow [fləu] *n.* 流程,流动(circulation) *v.* 流动(travel)

influx ['inflʌks] *n.* 流入;灌输

【记】in(进入)+flux(流入)→涌入

spray [sprei] *n./v.* 喷雾(sprinkle, shower)

【例】John *sprayed* insecticide on the plants.

drift [drift] *n./v.* 漂流(move aimlessly)

【例】The piece of wood was *drifting* down the river.

fluctuate ['flʌktʃueit] *v.* 波动(waver, alternate, move up and down)

【记】fluct=flu(流动)+uate

【例】The stock prices *fluctuated* wildly.

splash [splæʃ] *v.* 溅,泼(sprinkle)

【例】The *splashing* turbulence when glaciers broke into the ocean constitutes a spectacle.

dip [dip] *v.* 浸，蘸，沾（immerse in）

【例】She *dipped* her finger into the liquid and tasted it.

spurt [spə:t] *v.* 喷出，涌出（burst, squirt）

【例】The sea cucumber can *spurt* out its internal organ when in seeds.

spout [spaut] *v.* 喷出，涌出（gush, spurt）

【例】Blood *spouted* out from the wound.

meander [mi'ændə] *v.* 蜿蜒而流（wind, zigzag）

【例】The river *meanders* through the mountain to the east.

gush [gʌʃ] *vi.* 涌出（effuse）

【例】Blood *gushed* out from his deep cut.

immerse [i'mə:s] *vt.* 沉浸

【记】im（进）＋merse（沉）→沉进去→沉浸

【例】I *immersed* myself in the hot bath and relaxed.

overflow [ˌəuvə'fləu] *vt.* 从⋯中溢出（surplus, excess）

【记】over（过）＋flow（流）→流出

【例】The lake *overflowed* till all the villages in the neighbourhood were awash.

infuse [in'fju:z] *vt.* 灌输（imbue, instill）；浸渍

【记】in（进入）＋fuse（流）→注入

【例】The leader's speech *infused* new energy into the workers.

submerge [səb'mə:dʒ] *vt.* 浸没，淹没；*vi.* 潜水

【记】sub（下面）＋merge（沉）→沉到下面→淹没

【例】I *submerged* my head in the water completely. / The submaine *submerged* to avoid enemy ships.

imbue [im'bju:] *vt.* 浸染；灌输（permeate）

【例】The child was *imbued* with heroism since his father was a retired war hero.

saturate ['sætʃəreit] *vt.* 浸透（soak, imbue）

【例】His shoes were *saturated* after the rain.

exude [ig'zju:d] *vt.* 渗出；流出（discharge）

【记】ex＋(s)ude（出汗）→渗出

【例】The runner *exuded* sweat.

permeate ['pə:mieit] *vt.* 渗透；透过（penetrate, pervade）

【记】per(全部)＋mea(通过)＋te→渗透

【例】Nasty water from the flood *permeated* our carpeting.

dampen ['dæmpən] *vt.* 使潮湿，给…泼冷水（wet）

【例】*Dampen* a cloth for your forehead to make your headache go away.

/ I don't want to *dampen* your enthusiasm, but take it easy!

moisten ['mɔisn] *vt.* 使湿润

【例】The dew *moistened* the meadows.

物　体

article ['ɑ:tikl] *n.* 物品

【例】*article* reserves 物品储存

craft [kræft] *n.* 船(单复数相同)（vessel）

【记】craftsman(手艺人)

【例】*Craft* of all kinds come to this seaport.

vessel ['vesl] *n.* 器皿，导管，船（ship）

girdle ['gə:dl] *n.* 带状物；带，腰带（waistband）

【记】gird(束腰)＋le

canvas ['kænvəs] *n.* 帆布

【例】The tent was made of waterproof *canvas*.

stick [stik] *n.* 棍，棒

【例】a walking *sticky*

souvenir ['su:vəniə] *n.* 纪念品（reminder）

【例】The couple bought a *souvenir* of their honeymoon in Florida.

board [bɔ:d] *n.* 木板

screen [skri:n] *n.* 屏幕

【例】Security guards formed a *screen* around the President.

container [kən'teinə] *n.* 容器（receptacle, vessel）

【例】The perfume was in a beautiful glass *container*.

entity ['entiti] *n.* 实体

【例】Your company and my company are separate business *entities*.

spur [spə:] *n.* 踢马刺

leash [li:ʃ] *n.* 牵狗的皮带；控制

【例】I managed to hold my anger in *leash*.

strip [strip] *n.* 条，带

【例】a *strip* of paper; *strips* of beef

band [bænd] *n.* 条；带(stripe)

hinge [hindʒ] *n.* 铰链(joint, pivot)

ledge [ledʒ] *n.* 突出物；壁架

【记】联想"1"加edge(边)

bulk [bʌlk] *n.* 物体

【例】Dave placed his great *bulk* on the tiny chair, and it broke.

varnish ['vɑ:niʃ] *n.* 油漆(gloss, polish)

tug [tʌg] *n.* 拖船

效 果

null [nʌl] *adj.* 无效的(invalid, void)

valid ['vælid] *adj.* 有效的(soundly based, acceptable)

【例】A traveler's passport is *valid* within 6 months.

invalid ['invælid] *adj.* 无效的(void)

【记】in(不)＋valid(有效的)

effect [i'fekt] *n.* 效果；印象(result; impression)

【记】ef(出)＋fect(做)→做出来→生效，效果

【例】What will the *effect* be on the twins if they are separated?

effective [i'fektiv] *adj.* 有效的；有影响的(valid; resultful)

【记】effect(效果)＋ive

【例】The *effective* politician cut waste from the budget.

efficient [i'fiʃənt] *adj.* 有效率的(effective, competent)

【记】ef(出)＋fic(做)＋ient→能做出事来→有效率的

【例】The financial analyst found *efficient* ways for the company to save money.

outcome ['autkʌm] *n.* 后果；成果(result, consequence)

【记】来自come out(结果是)

impotence ['impətəns] *n.* 无效

【记】im(无)＋potence(能力)→无能

原 因

gratuitous ［grə'tjuitəs］ *adj.* 无理由的

【例】Her *gratuitous* performance is not expected by the producer.

source ［sɔːs］ *n.* 来源，源头（beginning, origin）

account ［ə'kaunt］ *n.* 原因

【例】On no *account* can we ignore the value of knowledge.

reason ［'riːzn］ *n.* 原因 *v.* 推论（deduce）

sake ［seik］ *n.* 缘故，原因（reason）

【例】He would do anything for money's *sake*.

cause ［kɔːz］ *vt.* 导致 *n.* 原因（reason）

【例】The heavy rain was the *cause* of the flood.

impute ［im'pjuːt］ *vt.* 归咎于（ascribe, attribute）

【记】比较put（放，归于）

【例】I *impute* his failure to laziness.

attribute ［ə'tribjuːt］ *vt.* 归因于（accredit, ascribe）

【例】The discovery of electricity is *attributed* to Benjamin Franklin.

整体与局部

superficial ［ˌsjuːpə'fiʃəl］ *adj.* 表面的，肤浅的（seeming, apparent）

【记】super（上面）＋fic（做）＋ial→表面的

【例】Susan prefers deep thinkers to people who are *superficial*.

partial ［'pɑːʃəl］ *adj.* 部分的（fractional, part）

【记】part（部分）＋ial

partially ［'pɑːʃəli］ *adv.* 部分地

overall ［'əuvərɔːl］ *adj.* 全部的，全面的（general）

integral ［'intigrəl］ *adj.* 组成的；整的（complete, full）

【记】integr（完整）＋al

integrate ［'intigreit］ *vt.* 使结合，使并入（combine, join）

【例】Quality training was *integrated* into your basic courses through newcomers.

integrity ［in'tegriti］ *n.* 完整性（congruity）

seemingly ［'siːmiŋli］ *adv.* 表面上，似乎（apparently）

【例】The *seemingly* occasional accident is actually purposely designed.

portion [ˈpɔːʃən] *n.* 一部分（part, fraction）

【例】Mary decorated her *portion* of the office.

proportion [prəˈpɔːʃən] *n.* 比例；部分（percentage, ration）

【记】比较portion（部分）

segment [ˈsegmənt] *n.* 部分；片段（part, section, portion, sector）

【例】The Cultural Revolution in fact affected every *segment* of the nation.

facet [ˈfæsit] *n.* 方面（aspect）

【例】The teacher carefully explained each *facet* of the theory.

aspect [ˈæspekt] *n.* 方面（facet）

【记】a＋spect（看）→看上去的样子→外观

【例】I asked my lawyer to explain the legal *aspects* of the problem.

juncture [ˈdʒʌŋktʃə] *n.* 结合点（junction, joining）

junction [ˈdʒʌŋkʃən] *n.* 连接，汇合处

【记】junct（连接）＋ion

【例】We meet at the *junction* of U. S. and Canada.

fraction [ˈfrækʃən] *n.* 片断（part, bit）

【记】fract（碎裂）＋ion

respect [risˈpekt] *n.* 着眼点，方面（aspect）

【例】David is an excellent teacher in all *respects*.

component [kəmˈpəunənt] *n.* 组成部分（constituent, ingredient）

【例】An essay question is one *component* of the test.

system [ˈsistəm] *n.* 系统，体系

Better to light one candle than to curse the darkness.

— *Strong*

与其诅咒黑暗，不如燃起蜡烛。

——斯特郎

连 线 题

左列单词在右列中有一个或多个同义词,请画线连接。

(一)

integrity	aspect
facet	congruity
reason	deduce
effective	imbue
container	move aimlessly
girdle	receptacle
craft	resultful
overflow	surplus
infuse	valid
drift	vessel
	waistband

(二)

doctrine	circulation
flow	emblem
formerly	extempore
imprompty	extemporize
improvise	momentary
logical	permanent
overdue	previously
perennial	reasonable
symbol	tardy
temporary	theory

(三)

direct	absorb
edible	brightness
exclusion	cleverness
identical	comestible
imbibe	comparable
incisive	exempted
invert	impertinent
irrelevant	nonaligned
luster	omission
neutral	overturn
relieved	profound
similar	radiance
tip	reverse
	straightforward
	tantamount

连线题答案

（一）

integrity	congruity
facet	aspect
reason	deduce
effective	valid
effective	resultful
container	receptacle
girdle	waistband
craft	vessel
overflow	surplus
infuse	imbue
drift	move aimlessly

（二）

doctrine	theory
flow	circulation
formerly	previously
imprompty	extempore
improvise	extemporize
logical	reasonable
overdue	tardy
perennial	permanent
symbol	emblem
temporary	momentary

（三）

direct	straightforward
edible	comestible
exclusion	omission
identical	tantamount
imbibe	absorb
incisive	profound
invert	overturn
invert	reverse
irrelevant	impertinent
luster	brightness
luster	radiance
neutral	nonaligned
relieved	exempted
similar	comparable
tip	cleverness

现　实

记忆小贴士：联想记忆法

　　"联想是钓钩，在茫茫的艺海中，它能准确地钓住你所识记的事物。"联想越丰富，越多彩，记忆的艺术也就越高超。

犯 罪

deceit [di'siːt] *n.* 欺骗，欺诈(cheat, fraud)

【例】No one trusts John because they know of his *deceit*.

deceitful [di'siːtful] *adj.* 欺骗的(sly, dishonest)

【例】The *deceitful* merchant's store was closed by the government.

deceive [di'siːv] *vt.* 欺骗，行骗

【例】Mary *deceived* the interviewer about her past experience.

deceptive [di'septiv] *adj.* 虚伪的，骗人的(deceitful, misleading.)

【例】Many customers were angered by the *deceptive* ads.

gangster ['gæŋstə] *n.* 暴徒，歹徒(mobster, hoodlum)

fraud [frɔːd] *n.* 欺骗(fault, deception)

【例】Never try to get money by *fraud*.

fraudulent ['frɔːdʒələnt] *adj.* 欺诈的，不诚实的(deceitful, dishonest)

homicide ['hɔmisaid] *n.* 杀人(slaughter)

theft [θeft] *n.* 偷窃(stealing)

pilferage ['pilfəridʒ] *n.* 偷窃(stealing)

【记】pilfer(偷)＋age

counterfeit ['kauntəfit] *n.* 赝品 *adj.* 伪造的，假冒的(fake, sham)

【例】This *counterfeit* money is obviously an imitation.

conspire [kən'spaiə] *vi.* 阴谋，密谋(intrigue, plot)

【例】The bank tellers *conspired* to rob the bank.

conspiracy [kən'spirəsi] *n.* 阴谋(plot)

【例】The police officer uncovered a *conspiracy* to assassinate the President.

sin [sin] *n.* 罪过，过失

brew [bruː] *v.* 酿造；图谋(ferment, plot)

【例】We could tell by the clouds that a storm was *brewing*.

beguile [bi'gail] *vi.* 欺骗(deceive)

【记】be＋guile(欺诈)

【例】He *beguiled* the voters with his good looks.

despoil [dis'pɔil] *vt.* 抢劫(rob)

【例】The region is *despoiled* of its scenic beauty by unchecked development.

forge [fɔːdʒ] *vt.* 伪造(feign, fabricate)

【例】The gangsters think the best way they could get money is to *forge* them in their own factory.

assassinate [əˈsæsineit] *vt.* 暗杀，行刺

【例】A horrible war began when the terrorist *assassinated* a government official.

kidnap [ˈkidnæp] *vt.* 绑架（abduct）

【记】kid（小孩）＋nap（睡）→（小孩睡时被）绑架

【例】Two businessmen have been *kidnapped*.

embezzle [emˈbezl] *vt.* 盗用（公款；公物）（misappropriate）

【例】Two employees planned to *embezzle* a million dollars over a period of years.

extort [eksˈtɔːt] *vt.* 勒索，强索（extract, squeeze）

【记】ex＋tort（扭）→扭出来→强索

【例】A blackmailer *extorted* thousands of dollars from the millionaire.

blackmail [ˈblækmeil] *vt.* 勒索

【记】black（黑）＋mail（信）

【例】The gangsters who knew of Bill's past crimes tried to *blackmail* him.

delude [diˈluːd] *vt.* 欺骗，迷惑（beguile, deceive, hoax）

【记】de（坏）＋lude（玩）→使坏→欺骗

【例】That playboy often *deludes* his girl with empty promises.

defraud [diˈfrɔːd] *vt.* 欺诈（deceive, beguile, cheat）

【记】de＋fraud（欺诈）

【例】The tax accountant *defrauded* the government.

fabricate [ˈfæbrikeit] *vt.* 伪造（forge, coin）

【记】fabric（结构）＋ate→使出现结构→伪造

【例】Jane *fabricated* the story that she was late because she was caught in traffic.

purge [pəːdʒ] *vt.* 洗涤（罪等）

【记】比较pure（纯的）

【例】The old tycoon did a lot of good deeds to *purge* away his sins.

belie [biˈlai] *vt.* 掩饰（conceal, cover up）

【记】be＋lie（谎言）

【例】He spoke roughly in order to *belie* his air

of gentility.

trap [træp] *vt.* 诱捕，陷害 *n.* 陷阱(entrap)

【例】The general was *trapped* and sentenced to death.

accomplice [əˈkɔmplis] *n.* 从犯(accessory)

【记】ac＋com(共同)＋plic(做)＋e→一起干→同谋

【例】Bill and his *accomplice* Max were arrested last week.

abduct [æbˈdʌkt] *vt.* 绑架，诱拐(kidnap)

【记】ab＋duct(引导)→把人带走→绑架

【例】The police think the boy has been *abducted*.

福 气

convenient [kənˈviːnjənt] *adj.* 便利的，方便的

【例】Tom picked a *convenient* time to come for a visit.

grateful [ˈgreitful] *adj.* 感谢的(thankful)

【记】grate(高兴)＋ful(多)

【例】He can't help being *grateful* for his parents who brought him up in the war.

gratitude [ˈgrætitjuːd] *n.* 感谢，感激

【记】grat(满意)＋itude

auspicious [ɔːsˈpiʃəs] *adj.* 吉兆的，幸运的(promising, favorable)

【例】Spring is an *auspicious* time to begin new activities.

cozy [ˈkəuzi] *adj.* 舒适的(comfortable, snug)

【例】Sitting in front of a fire on a snowy day is quite *cozy*.

fortunate [ˈfɔːtʃənit] *adj.* 幸运的(lucky)

【记】fortun(e)(财富)＋ate→发财→幸运的

readily [ˈredili] *adv.* 容易地(easily, quickly)

boon [buːn] *n.* 恩惠(blessing, benefit)

【例】Having a parent who is a teacher is a real *boon* to the kids.

bonanza [bəˈnænzə] *n.* 幸运

【例】Winning the lottery was a *bonanza* for the Browns.

blessing [ˈblesiŋ] *n.* 祝福

【例】Mary gave a *blessing* before dinner.

thrive [θraiv] *vi.* 繁荣，旺盛(flourish, do well on)

【例】The wild deer that *throve* here are no more visible due to deforestation.

工具使用

furrow [ˈfʌrəu] *vt.* 犁，耕，弄绉
【例】The farmers *furrow* the soil before seeding.

instrument [ˈinstrumənt] *n.* 工具
【例】Flute, piano and violin are all musical *instruments*.

implement [ˈimplimənt] *n.* 工具(device, instrument, facility)

tool [tuːl] *n.* 工具，用具(instrument)

shaft [ʃæft] *n.* 轴，柄(handle, pole)

pump [pʌmp] *n.* 水泵 *v.* 抽，吸(drive)

snap [snæp] *v.* (使)猛然断裂(break)
【例】My shoelace *snapped* when I pulled it too tightly.

squeeze [skwiːz] *v.* 挤(cram, press)
【例】Anne *squeezed* the oranges to make orange juice.

prune [pruːn] *v.* 剪修(shear, trim)
【例】He is *pruning* the branches of the tree in the garden.

glaze [ˈgleiz] *v.* 上釉 *n.* 釉
【例】Sue *glazed* the pottery and waited for it to dry.

tug [tʌg] *v.* 拖，牵引(pull, haul)
【例】The child *tugged* at my hand to make me go with her.

fix [fiks] *v.* 修理(repair)
【例】You've forgotten to *fix* that shelf.

maintain [meinˈtein] *vt.* 维修(repair)

extract [iksˈtrækt] *vt.* 拔出，榨取(remove)
【例】The research team undertakes the responsibility to *extract* samples from the sediments.

flay [flei] *vt.* 剥…的皮
【例】He *flayed* a dead dog.

flush [flʌʃ] *vt.* 冲洗(flow, pour)
【记】比较blush(脸红)
【例】*Flush* the toilet after you use it.

clinch [klintʃ] *vt.* 钉牢，揪住
【例】Barca shut out Milan to *clinch* final

place.

gild [gild] *vt.* 镀金

【例】She was *gilding* the lily by attaching something unnecessary to the new car.

scratch [skrætʃ] *vt.* 刮擦 *n.* 划痕(rub)

【例】The cat *scratched* the piano leg with its claws.

clip [klip] *vt.* 夹住,修剪(cut, shear) *n.* 夹子,钳子

【例】Mary *clipped* a few roses off from the bushes.

clamp [klæmp] *vt.* 夹

【例】I glued and *clamped* the broken plate.

hew [hjuː] *vt.* 砍,伐;削(cut, chop)

【例】They *hewed* a path through the underbrush.

rap [ræp] *vt.* 敲击(tap, knock)

【例】The angry man *rapped* the table with his fist.

cleanse [klenz] *vt.* 使清洁(clean, purify)

【例】The nurse *cleansed* the wound before sewing it up.

rend [rend] *vt.* 撕开(tear);揪扯

【例】The cruel enemies *rent* the child away from his mother.

cram [kræm] *vt.* 填塞

【例】I *crammed* as many clothes as I could into the suitcase.

smear [smiə] *vt.* 涂

【例】The politician was *smeared* by his opponent's accusations.

efface [i'feis] *vt.* 涂抹(obliterate)

【例】Weathering has *effaced* the inscription on the tombstone so that people cannot read it.

remove [ri'muːv] *vt.* 移动,搬开;脱掉

【记】re(再次)+move(动)→移动

【例】Please *remove* the dishes from the table.

forge [fɔːdʒ] *vt.* 铸造(make)

【例】*forge* coins

tow [təu] *vt./n.* 拖引,牵引(pull, haul)

【例】The idea to *tow* icebergs to arid regions seemed impractical at first.

incise [in'saiz] *vt.* 切割,切开(cut)

【例】The carpenter *incised* the tablet with chisels.

chop [tʃɔp] *vt.* 砍(cut, hew)

【例】Anne *chopped* the logs in two with an axe.

harrow ['hærəu] *vt.* 耙掘

【例】He *harrowed* the land every day.

pick [pik] *v.* 摘，掘，凿，挖，挑选

【例】The lawyer *picked* the testimony apart.

shovel [ʃʌvl] *n.* 铲，铁铲 *v.* 铲

sickle ['sikl] *n.* 镰刀

spade [speid] *n.* 铲，铁锹 *v.* 铲

bore [bɔː] *v.* 钻孔

工 作

hectic ['hektik] *adj.* 忙碌的(busy)

【记】hect(许多)＋ic→许多事要做→紧张兴奋的

【例】Being a sales manager, Tom is always so *hectic* that his wife can only see him once a week.

officially [ə'fiʃəli] *adv.* 职务上；正式地(formally)

【例】He was *officially* appointed Chairman of the committee.

entry ['entri] *n.* 登记；入口

【例】There is a back *entry* into the house.

role [rəul] *n.* 任务

log [lɔg] *n.* 日志(journal)

draft [drɑːft] *n.* 草案 *v.* 起草，设计(formulate, draw up)

sketch [sketʃ] *n.* 草图(drawing, chart) *v.* 勾画(compose, outline)

【例】He *sketched* out a plan for his inferiors to execute.

assumption [ə'sʌmpʃən] *n.* 就职

【例】The vice president's *assumption* of the presidency occurred as the president died.

drudgery ['drʌdʒəri] *n.* 苦差事(tedium)

chore [tʃɔː] *n.* 零工，杂务

【例】Doing laundry at the laundromat is a real *chore*.

undertaking [ˌʌndə'teikiŋ] *n.* 任务，工作(endeavor, enterprise)

task [tɑːsk] *n.* 任务，作业(chore, duty, job)

career [kə'riə] *n.* 生涯，职业(profession, pursuit, vocation)

【例】Bill trained for years for his *career*.

audition [ɔːˈdiʃən] *n.* 试听；面试

【记】audi(听)＋ion

【例】Jane did so well at her *audition* that she was cast in the movie.

vocation [vəuˈkeiʃən] *n.* 职业，行业（occupation, profession）

charge [tʃɑːdʒ] *n.* 职责

【例】You are in *charge* of making the salad.

major [ˈmeidʒə] *n.* 专业

resign [riˈzain] *n./v.* 辞职（give up）

【例】Being so depressed, he *resigned* from a board of directors.

solicit [səˈlisit] *v.* 拉客

【例】Bob was almost arrested for *soliciting* in an apartment building.

register [ˈredʒistə] *vt.* 登记（enroll, enlist）

【例】It is for the historian to discover and *register* what actually happened.

inaugurate [iˈnɔːgjureit] *vt.* 开始（commence, initiate）；使就职

【记】in(进入)＋augur(开始)＋ate

【例】He will be *inaugurated* as president in January.

promote [prəˈməut] *vt.* 升职；促进

【记】pro(前)＋mote(动)→促进

【例】You're so happy. Are you *promoted*? / The go-between tried to *promote* relationship between the boy and the girl.

officeholding [ˈɔfisˌhəuldiŋ] *n.* 任职

供 给

provide [prəˈvaid] *vt.* 提供（supply, furnish, give）

【例】She *provides* for her family by working in a hospital.

provision [prəˈviʒən] *n.* 供应（supply, furnishing）

accommodate [əˈkɔmədeit] *vt.* 供给住宿

【例】This hotel can *accommodate* 600 guests.

furnish [ˈfɜːniʃ] *vt.* 供应，供给（equip, supply, provide）

【例】The room was *furnished* with the simplest essentials, a bed, a chair, and a table.

render [ˈrendə] *vt.* 提供（provide）

【例】The passengers are not satisfied with the service *rendered* by the driver.

关　系

incompatible [ˌinkəm'pætəbl] *adj.* 不兼容的(inconsistent, incongruous)

【记】in(不)＋compatible(和谐的，融合的)

congruity [kɔŋ'gruːiti] *n.* 一致，协调

【记】con＋gru=agree(同意)＋ity

incongruity [ˌinkɔŋ'gruːiti] *n.* 不和谐(之物)

incongruous [in'kɔŋgruəs] *adj.* 不协调的(inconsistent)

【记】in(不)＋congruous(和谐的)

【例】It is *incongruous* to insert a dogfood ads into such a serious political report.

respective [ri'spektiv] *adj.* 分别的，各自的(individual)

【例】The applicants received *respective* interviews.

close [kləuz] *adj.* 亲密的 *adv.* 紧密地

【例】Lily is a *close* friend of my brother.

mutual ['mjuːtjuəl] *adj.* 相互的；共同的(reciprocal; joint)

【记】mut(变化)＋ual→你变我也变→相互的

【例】We signed the contract based on *mutual* benefit.

concerted [kən'səːtid] *adj.* 协定的；协调的(unisonous)

【例】The team made a *concerted* effort to win the game.

fraternal [frə'təːnl] *adj.* 兄弟的，兄弟般的；友爱的(brotherly; cordial)

【记】fratern(兄弟)＋al

【例】They fought side by side, and developed *fraternal* love to each other.

dependent [di'pendənt] *adj.* 依靠的，依赖的

congenial [kən'dʒiːnjəl] *adj.* 意气相投的(compatible, agreeable, pleasant, pleasing)

【例】The Smiths are very *congenial* and accepting of others.

relevant ['reləvənt] *adj.* 有关的；贴切的(related, pertinent)

【例】What you say is not *relevant* with the matter in hand.

bond [bɔnd] *n.* 联结，联系(tie, link)

【例】Glue acted as a strong *bond* between the layers of cardboard.

complement ['kɔmplimənt] *n.* 补足物 *vt.* 补足

【记】比较complete(完整的)

complementary [ˌkɔmpli'mentəri] *adj.* 补充的(supplementary, subsidiary)

【例】The green sweater is *complementary* to Bill's trousers.

discord ['diskɔːd] *n.* 不和谐(disharmony, disagreement)

【记】dis＋cord（和谐）

【例】The modern symphony was filled with *discord* and strange rhythms.

association [əˌsəuʃiˈeiʃən] *n.* 关联（relationship）

【例】The dog made an *association* between hearing a bell and receiving food.

associate [əˈsəuʃieit] *v.* 联合（unite, combine）*n.* 伙伴（partner）

【例】I do not *associate* with people who use vulgar language.

cooperation [kəuˌɔpəˈreiʃən] *n.* 合作

【记】co＋operation（操作）→一起做→合作

【例】Without everyone's *cooperation*, we will fail.

fusion [ˈfjuːʒən] *n.* 联合（association）

intimate [ˈintimit] *adj.* 亲密的 *vt.* 暗示

【例】"*Intimate* friend" was usually used as written form of "close friend", which is more popular in oral English.

intimacy [ˈintiməsi] *n.* 熟悉；亲近（proximity）

【记】intim（内部）＋acy→内部的→熟悉

substitute [ˈsʌbstitjuːt] *n.* 替代品 *v.* 替代（replacement; replace）

【例】Fantasies are more than *substitutes* for unpleasant reality.

consensus [kənˈsensəs] *n.* 一致（unanimity）

【例】The school board could not reach a *consensus* on the curriculum.

concurrence [kənˈkʌrəns] *n.* 一致

impact [ˈimpækt] *n.* 影响，作用（collision, force）*v.* 对…发生影响

【例】The Cultural Revolution greatly *impacted* many Chinese families.

link [liŋk] *n./v.* 链接（connect）

proximity [prɔkˈsimiti] *n.* 接近，邻近（nearness）

【记】proxim（接近）＋ity

【例】He look around the *proximity* for his lost dog.

band [bænd] *v.* 联合，结合（form, group）

【例】We must *band* ourselves against natural calamities despite the disputes on the working plan.

collaborate [kəˈlæbəreit] *vi.* 合作（cooperate, work together）

【记】col（共同）＋labor（劳动）+ate→共同劳动→合作

【例】The prisoners *collaborated* to plan the escape.

hinge [hindʒ] *vi.* 依…而定（depend, rely）

【例】This plan *hinges* on her approval.

replenish [ri'pleniʃ] *vt.* 补充(fill up, refill)

【记】re(重新)＋plen=plenty(多)＋ish→重新变多→补充

【例】The music will *replenish* my weary soul.

supplant [sə'plænt] *vt.* 排挤；取代(replace)

【例】The ambitious duke plotted to *supplant* the king.

implicate ['implikeit] *vt.* 牵连(involve)

【例】The mayor was *implicated* in the murder.

displace [dis'pleis] *vt.* 取代(replace; substitute)

【记】dis＋place(位置)→取代(位置)

【例】My computer has *displaced* my old typewriter.

supersede [ˌsjuːpə'siːd] *vt.* 替代(replace, substitute)

【记】super(上面)＋sede(坐)→坐上→替代

【例】The use of robots will someday *supersede* manual labor.

correlate ['kɔrileit] *vt.* 相关联(associate, relate)

【记】cor＋relate(关联)

【例】The scientist could not *correlate* the data with his hypothesis.

grant [grɑːnt] *vt.* 赠予(award, give)

【例】He was *granted* a pension.

subsidiary [səb'sidjəri] *adj.* 辅助的；附属的(supplementary)

【记】sub(下面)＋sidi(坐)＋ary→坐在下面辅助的

【例】The corporation has many *subsidiarg* companies.

affinity [ə'finiti] *n.* 密切关系(liking)

【记】af(一再)＋fin(范围)＋ity→一再能进别人范围→亲密

【例】There is a close *affinity* between apes and monkeys. / Mary's *affinity* for classical music accounts for her large collection of recordings.

fitting ['fitiŋ] *adj.* 适合的,相称的

【记】fit(合适)＋ting

【例】It is a *fitting* gesture to offer a reward to someone who returns something you have lost.

sway [swei] *v.* 影响(persuade)

【例】His speech *swayed* the voters.

affect [ə'fekt] *vt.* 影响,感动(influence, impress)

【记】af(使)＋fect(做)→使人做→影响

【例】Did the blunder *affect* your promotion?

derivative [di'rivətiv] *n.* 派生的事物

patronage ['pætrənidʒ] *n.* 保护人的身份，保护，赞助，光顾

unionization [juːnjənai'zeiʃən] *n.* 联合，结合

建 筑

haven ['heivn] *n.* 港口；避难所(shelter, refuge)

【记】比较heaven(天堂，天空)

refuge ['refjuːdʒ] *n.* 避难所(shelter, protection)

【记】re(回)＋fuge(逃)→逃回去的(地方)→避难所

depot ['diːpəu] *n.* 仓库 *vt.* 把…存放在仓库里(house, contain)

auditorium [ɔːdi'tɔːriəm] *n.* 大礼堂

【记】audi(听)+t+orium(名词字尾，表示场所、地点)

【例】The new *auditorium* had velvet seats.

vault [vɔːlt] *n.* 拱形圆屋顶；地窖

block [blɔk] *n.* 街区

【例】We know all the neighbors on our *block*.

stall [stɔːl] *n.* 厩；摊位(stable, barn)

dormitory ['dɔːmitəri] *n.* 宿舍

【例】The prison *dormitory* is heavily guarded.

tower ['tauə] *n.* 塔 *v.* 屹立，高耸

【例】The skyscraper *towered* among the city.

dwelling ['dweliŋ] *n.* 住所(residence, shelter, accommodation)

【例】A dormitory is the typical *dwelling* of a college student.

forge [fɔːdʒ] *n.* 铁匠铺

canopy ['kænəpi] *n.* 天篷，遮篷

困 难

laborious [lə'bɔːriəs] *adj.* 费力的，艰难的(arduous, painstaking)

【记】labor(劳动)＋ious(的)→劳动的，苦的

【例】Anne received a raise for her *laborious* efforts.

precipitous [pri'sipitəs] *adj.* 陡峭的，急躁的(sheer, extremely steep)

devious ['diːvjəs] *adj.* 曲折的(circuitous)

【例】The teacher gave us a *devious* explanation at first which confused us for a long time.

arduous [ˈɑːdjuəs] *adj.* 险峻的，困难的（difficult, strenuous, laborious, back-breaking）

【记】ardu(高，险)＋ous

【例】The preparation for GRE is as long and as *arduous* work for a normal undergraduate.

strenuous [ˈstrenjuəs] *adj.* 辛苦的（energetic, laborious）

【例】It is really a *strenuous* job to get well prepared for a GRE test.

plight [plait] *n.* (恶劣的)情势，困境（predicament, dilemma）

【例】I cried when I heard of the refugees' *plight*.

strait [streit] *n.* 困难

painstaking [ˈpeinzteikiŋ] *n.* 辛劳 *adj.* 劳苦的（careful, scrupulous）

【记】pains(痛苦)＋taking(花，费)→付出痛苦的→劳苦的

dilemma [diˈlemə] *n.* 左右为难，困境

【例】I have the *dilemma* of choosing a new car or a new computer.

flounder [ˈflaundə] *vi.* 挣扎

【记】另一个意思是"比目鱼"

【例】The economy in southeast Asian continues to *flounder*.

embarrass [emˈbærəs] *vt.* 使困窘

【例】Anne's older brother tried to *embarrass* her in front of her friends.

流 行

fashionable [ˈfæʃənəbl] *adj.* 流行的，时髦的（popular）

【记】fashion(时髦)＋able

prevail [priˈveil] *vi.* 流行，盛行（dominate）

prevalent [ˈprevələnt] *adj.* 普遍的，流行的（prevailing, widespread, popular）

tide [taid] *n.* 潮流

vogue [vəug] *n.* 流行（fashion）

novelty [ˈnɒvəlti] *n.* 新颖；新奇的事物（newness, unusualness）

【记】novel(新)＋ty

名 誉

gorgeous [ˈgɔːdʒəs] *adj.* 极好的
【记】参考gorge(峡谷)
【例】The flower appears a *gorgeous* shape under the sun.

outstanding [aut ˈstændiŋ] *adj.* 杰出的
【记】来自stand out(醒目，突出)

obscure [əbˈskjuə] *adj.* 无名气的(unknown, inconspicuous)
【例】Jude, the *obscure*, was not treated as a celebrity in the banquet.

immortal [iˈmɔːtl] *adj.* 不朽的(undying, everlasting)
【记】im(不)＋mort(死)＋al

notorious [nəuˈtɔːriəs] *adj.* 臭名昭著的(infamous)
【记】not(知道)＋orious(多)→臭名昭著的
【例】Bill is a *notorious* loudmouth.

infamous [ˈinfəməs] *adj.* 臭名昭著的(notorious, disgraceful)
【记】in(不)＋famous(著名的)
【例】My teacher is *infamous* for giving a great bulk of assignments.

legendary [ˈledʒəndəri] *adj.* 传奇的(renowned, famed)
【记】legend(传奇)＋ary

glorious [ˈglɔːriəs] *adj.* 光荣的

illustrious [iˈlʌstriəs] *adj.* 辉煌的；著名的(famous, distinguished)
【记】il(一再)＋lustr(光)＋ious→一再光明→辉煌的

eminent [ˈeminənt] *adj.* 杰出的(outstanding, distinguished)
【记】e(出)＋min(伸)＋ent→伸出的→突出的
【例】The *eminent* poet won numerous awards.

deferential [ˌdefəˈrenʃəl] *adj.* 充满敬意的(respectful, dutiful)
【例】A teacher should not act too *deferential* to the students.

exemplary [igˈzempləri] *adj.* 模范的，典范的
【例】The principal rewarded Susan for her *exemplary* performance in school.

matchless [ˈmætʃlis] *adj.* 无与伦比的(unbeatable, incomparable)
【记】match(相配的)＋less

excel [ikˈsel] *v.* 优秀，胜过他人(superior, surpass, exceed)
【例】Being a leader does not mean you should *excel* in everything; your talent lies in being able to manage the right persons.

excellent ['eksələnt] *adj.* 优秀的，杰出的（outstanding, preeminent）

compliment ['kɔmplimənt]（praise, commend）*vt.* 赞美，祝贺

【例】The artist received many *compliments* on her paintings.

complimentary [ˌkɔmpli'mentəri] *adj.* 赞美的（praising）

【例】The professor rarely makes *complimentary* remarks to students.

renowned [ri'naund] *adj.* 知名的（acclaimed, distinguished, famous）

【记】re(重新)＋nown(名字)＋ed→名字一再出现→知名的

laudable ['lɔːdəbl] *adj.* 值得赞美的（praiseworthy, commendable）

supreme [sjuː'priːm] *adj.* 至高的（highest, greatest）

【例】The *supreme* ruler ordered the execution of his enemies.

celebrate ['selibreit] *vt.* 赞扬，表扬（praise）

【例】The names of many heroes are *celebrated* by the poets.

celebrated ['selibreitid] *adj.* 著名的（distinguished, famous）

notable ['nəutəbl] *adj.* 著名的，显要的（distinguished, celebrated）

【记】not(知道)＋able→大家都知道的→著名的

【例】One of our most *notable* poets won a Nobel Prize.

noted ['nəutid] *adj.* 著名的，知名的（distinguished, celebrated）

exceptional [ik'sepʃənl] *adj.* 卓越的（extraordinary）

【例】The *exceptional* tennis player won the championship.

preeminent [priː'eminənt] *adj.* 卓越的（prominent, outstanding）

【记】pre(前)＋eminent(突出的)→向前突出→杰出的

prominent ['prɔminənt] *adj.* 卓越的，突出的（conspicuous, protruding）

【记】pro(前)＋minent(伸)→突出的

【例】The *prominent* politician made an appeal to end the war.

dignify ['dignifai] *vt.* 使尊荣，使显贵（ennoble, elevate）

【例】The president *dignified* the gathering by giving a short speech.

dignified ['dignifaid] *adj.* 尊严的；高贵的（noble）

【例】Bob gave a *dignified* response to the insult.

dignity ['digniti] *n.* 尊严

【例】The black robes of a judge give a look of *dignity*.

lofty ['lɔfti] *adj.* 高尚的

【记】loft(阁楼，顶楼)＋y

【例】He has *lofty* ideals about life.

odor ['əudə] *n.* 名声（fame）

【例】The scholar's doctrine is not currently in good *odor*.

credit ['kredit] *n.* 信誉（trust, credence）

【例】I could not get a loan from the bank because my *credit* was bad.

feat [fi:t] *n.* 功绩，壮举（achievement, accomplishment）

homage ['hɔmidʒ] *n.* 敬意（respect, reverence）

【记】hom(人)＋age→把对方当人看

deference ['defərəns] *n.* 敬意

【记】defer(服从，敬意)＋ence

【例】Mary's *deference* to her parents' wishes was expected.

virtue ['və:tju:] *n.* 美德（morality, goodness）

prestige [pres'ti:ʒ] *n.* 威望，声望（fame, reputation）

【例】Our mayor's *prestige* is known throughout the state.

grandeur ['grændʒə] *n.* 庄严，伟大（magnificence）

reverence ['revərəns] *n.* 尊敬（respect, veneration）

awe [ɔ:] *n./vt.* 敬畏（reverence, veneration; dread）

【例】I am always in *awe* of people who can cook well.

esteem [is'ti:m] *n./vt.* 尊敬（respect）

【例】I have a great deal of *esteem* for my parents.

commend [kə'mend] *v.* 赞扬（praise）

【记】com＋mend(相信)→都信→赞扬

【例】The teacher *commends* him upon his good manner.

exalt [ig'zɔ:lt] *vt.* 称赞；提升（extol, laud; promote）

【记】ex＋alt(高)→使高出→赞扬

【例】The campaign manager's speech *exalted* the candidates.

exalted [ig'zɔ:ltid] *adj.* 尊贵的（noble）

【例】The *exalted* prince entered the hall and everyone stood up.

venerate ['venəreit] *vt.* 敬拜，崇拜（respect, revere）

【例】He was *venerated* as a god.

embalm [em'ba:m] *vt.* 使不朽

【例】Ancient Egyptians used oils and natural substances to *embalm* the dead.

tarnish ['ta:niʃ] *vt.* 使晦暗，败坏（名誉）（darken, lose luster）

【例】The firm's good name was badly *tarnished* by the scandal.

extol [iks'təul] *vt.* 颂扬（exalt）

【记】ex＋tol(举)→推举出→颂扬

【例】Movie critics *extolled* the young performer's acting debut.

laud [lɔːd] *vt.* 赞美（compliment, praise）

【记】比较laurel（桂冠，月桂树）

【例】They *lauded* the virtues of the old man.

revere [riˈviə] *vt.* 尊敬（respect, worship）

【例】The political leader was *revered* by the people of his country.

admirable [ˈædmərəbl] *adj.* 可敬的，极好的（redoubted, wonderful）

【例】The child's honesty was *admirable*.

disreputable [disˈrepjutəbl] *adj.* 声名狼藉的（notorious）

【记】dis＋reputable（有声望的）

【例】The newspaper reported about the senator's *disreputable* conduct.

classic [ˈklæsik] *adj.* 第一流的

respect [risˈpekt] *n./vt.* 尊重，敬重（admire, esteem, honor）

【例】My parents think that the contemporary young people have no *respect* for authority.

adore [əˈdɔː] *vt.* 敬爱，极喜爱（admire, love, esteem）

【记】ad＋ore（讲话）→说好听的话

【例】Grandpa *adored* Grandma from the day they first met.

admire [ədˈmaiə] *vt.* 钦佩（respect）；赞美，夸奖

【记】ad（一再）＋mire（高兴）→一再让人惊喜

【例】I have always *admired* my mother's charm.

advocate [ˈædvəkeit] *vt.* 拥护（hold, maintain）

【例】The social activist *advocated* change.

气 氛

hilarious [həˈlɛəriəs] *adj.* 热闹的

sullen [ˈsʌlən] *adj.* 阴沉的（moody, bad-tempered）

hilarity [həˈlæriti] *n.* 欢闹

aura [ˈɔːrə] *n.* 气氛（atmosphere, mood）

社会活动

formal [ˈfɔːməl] *adj.* 正式的；礼仪上的

【记】informal(非正式的)

session ['seʃən] *n.* 会议(meeting)

【例】The traitors went into secret *session* before insurgence.

conference ['kɔnfərəns] *n.* 会议，讨论会

【例】Anne had a *conference* with her son's teacher to discuss his progress.

reception [ri'sepʃən] *n.* 接待；招待会

etiquette ['etiket] *n.* 礼节

【记】e＋tiquette=ticket(票)→凭票入场→礼仪

【例】I consulted a book of *etiquette* before I attended the formal dance.

decorum [di'kɔːrəm] *n.* 礼仪(ceremony)

【记】decor(美)＋um

【例】Tom found the *decorum* at the banquet to be formal and tedious.

banquet ['bæŋkwit] *n.* 宴会，盛会(feast)

【例】Mary served us a *banquet* that was fit for a king.

bidding ['bidiŋ] *n.* 邀请

ceremony ['serɪˌməni] *n.* 仪式

【例】The wedding *ceremony* took place in a garden.

ceremonial [ˌseri'məunjəl] *n./adj.* 仪式；正式的

ceremonious [ˌseri'məunjəs] *adj.* 隆重的；正式的，恭敬的(formal, solemn)

【例】The symphony conductor took a *ceremonious* bow.

unveil [ʌn'veil] *v.* 开幕

【记】un(不)＋veil(罩面纱)→揭开

【例】Anne *unveiled* her painting at the opening of the art exhibit.

celebrate ['selibreit] *vi.* 庆祝

【例】We *celebrated* the New Year with a dance party.

entertain [ˌentə'tein] *vt.* 招待；娱乐(amuse)

【例】Dave is fun to be around. He always finds ways to *entertain* us.

身体动作

glaring ['glɛəriŋ] *adj.* 瞪眼的

【记】参考glare(瞪)

grip [grip] *n.* 紧握(grasp, clasp)

posture ['pɔstʃə] *n.* 人体的姿势(pose, bearing)

grasp ［ɡræsp］ *n./v.* 抓紧

【例】*Grasp* the rope with both hands.

jerk ［dʒə:k］ *n./v.* 急拉；抽搐

【例】I felt a *jerk* when Bill hit the car brakes.

chuckle ［ˈtʃʌkl］ *n./vi.* 咯咯的（地）笑

【例】The comedian couldn't get even a *chuckle* out of the audience.

flip ［flip］ *v.* 翻滚（overturn）；（用手指）弹，投

【例】The car ran off the road and *flipped* over in the ditch./ They *flipped* a coin to decide who would go first.

stagger ［ˈstæɡə］ *v.*（使）蹒跚

【例】The wounded man *staggered* along.

trudge ［trʌdʒ］ *v.* 跋涉，吃力地走（plod, trek）

【例】The soldiers *trudged* through the thick mud.

fasten ［ˈfɑ:sn］ *v.* 扣牢，抓住（affix, attach）

【例】In Europe even passengers sitting on the back seats need to *fasten* their seat belts.

hurl ［hə:l］ *v.* 猛投；猛冲（throw, fling）

【例】He *hurled* the brick through the window.

face ［feis］ *v.* 面对（confront）

【例】The audience *faced* the speaker.

leap ［li:p］ *v.* 跳跃（jump）

【记】hop 单脚跳, skip 跨步跳, jump 双脚跳, leap 飞跃（多用于比喻义中的跳）

【例】The dog *leapt* over the fence.

bow ［bau］ *v.* 弯腰，屈服

【例】Bill *bowed* to his parents' wishes and went to law school.

blink ［blink］ *v.* 眨眼（wink）

【例】Every time we take John's picture, he *blinks*.

erect ［iˈrekt］ *v.* 直立（straight）

【记】e＋rect（立，竖）

【例】He could *erect* a tent in 10 minutes.

trample ［ˈtræmpl］ *v./n.* 践踏，蹂躏（tread, crush）

【记】tramp（踩踏）＋le

【例】The neighbor's dog *trampled* my tulips.

tremble ['trembl] *vi.* 发抖；摇晃(shake, shiver)

【例】I *tremble* at the very thought of it.

glide [glaid] *vi.* 滑动；溜走

【例】The tip of the pen *glided* across the sheet of paper.

depart [di'pɑːt] *vi.* 离开，出发(leave, set off)

【记】de+part(离开)

【例】What time does the train *depart*?

slump [slʌmp] *vi.* 猛然落下(drop, lapse)

【例】He *slumped* down to the floor in a faint.

gaze [geiz] *vi.* 凝视(stare)

【例】It is impolite to *gaze* at a stranger's face.

creep [kriːp] *vi.* 爬，蹑手蹑脚(crawl, move slowly)

【例】We *crept* upstairs so as not to wake the baby.

limp [limp] *vi.* 蹒跚；瘸着走

【记】比较limb(四肢)

【例】He *limped* off the football field.

sigh [sai] *vi./n.* 叹息

【例】"I wish I had finished this work," she said with a *sigh*.

recoil [ri'kɔil] *vi./n.* 后退，退缩(retreat, withdraw)

【例】The little girl *recoiled* at seeing the dead cat.

uphold [ʌp'həuld] *vt.* 举起；支撑(support, sustain)

【记】来自hold up(举起)

【例】The soldier *upheld* the flag proudly.

grab [græb] *vt.* 攫取，抓住(snatch, rob)

【例】The poor boy *grabbed* his chance to become a millionaire.

stride [straid] *vt.* 跨越(step, pace)

【例】He *strode* angrily into the classroom.

thrust [θrʌst] *vt.* 力推(push, shove)

【例】We *thrust* our way through the mass of people.

gnaw [nɔː] *vt.* 啃(bite)

【例】She *gnawed* anxiously at her fingernails.

spew [spjuː] *vt.* 呕吐(eject, gush)

【例】She *spewed* up the entire meal.

dab [dæb] *vt.* 轻拍

【例】Don't press it, just *dab* it gently.

plunge [plʌndʒ] *v.* 投入（dive, sink）

【例】We *plunged* into the icy mountain lake.

dart [dɑːt] *vt.* 投掷（hurl, throw）

【例】She *darted* an angry look at him.

shove [ʃʌv] *vt.* 推挤（push, jostle）

【例】*Shove* over, friend, and make room for me.

drag [dræg] *vt.* 拖动（tow）

【例】Billy *dragged* the toy duck behind him.

haul [hɔːl] *vt.* 拖曳；拖运（drag, transport, pull）

【例】They *hauled* the boat up onto the shore.

shake [ʃeik] *vt.* 摇；震动

【例】She was *shaking* with laughter.

jolt [dʒəult] *vt.* 摇动（shake, jar）

【例】The coach stops and starts *jolting* the passengers.

embrace [im'breis] *vt.* 拥抱（hug, cuddle）

【例】The students tearfully *embraced* each other on their last day of school.

heave [hiːv] *vt.* 用力举起；拖（lift, fling）

【记】参考heaven（天空）去掉"n"

【例】He *heaved* the box of books onto the table.

slap [slæp] *vt.* 掌击，拍（clap, blow）

【例】He *slapped* her for what she has done.

clutch [klʌtʃ] *vt.* 抓住　*vi.* 掌握，攫（grab, grip）

【例】The crying child *clutched* her father around the neck.

flush [flʌʃ] *n./v.* 脸红

【记】比较blush（脸红）

【例】He *flushed* with anger.

sprawl [sprɔːl] *v.* 伸开手脚（stretch）

【记】比较crawl（爬）

【例】He found her *sprawled* out in front of a comfortable chair asleep.

sway [swei] *v.* 摇摆

【例】She *swayed* her body in time with the music.

spring [spriŋ] *v.* 跳跃

【例】The waiting tiger *sprang* at his prey.

footbeat ['futbiːt] *n.* 跺脚

生 产

industrial [in'dʌstriəl] *adj.* 工业的

practical ['præktikl] *adj.* 实践的；实用的（pragmatic）

instrument ['instrumənt] *n.* 仪器（device）

【例】Flute, piano and violin are all musical *instruments*.

instrumental [ˌinstru'mentl] *adj.* 仪器的，器械的

textile ['tekstail] *adj.* 纺织的 *n.* 纺织品（fabric, fiber, cloth）

【记】text(编织)＋ile

outfit ['autfit] *n.* 装备；用具（equipment）

【记】来自 fit out(装备)

【例】The *outfit* for a cowboy identified him.

mine [main] *n./v.* 采矿

gear [giə] *n.* 齿轮

fixture ['fikstʃə] *n.* 固定设备（apparatus, appliance, device）

monitor ['mɔnitə] *v.* 监视，监听

【记】另一个词义是"班长"

【例】The president can *monitor* the whole campus through advanced computer system.

device [di'vais] *n.* 器械，装置；设计（equipment; scheme, ploy）

【例】Dave bought a special *device* to peel potatoes.

equipment [i'kwipmənt] *n.* 设备（facility, fixture）

cement [si'ment] *n.* 水泥，黏合物 *vt.* 接合（stick, bond）

【例】Custom was the *cement* of society in early days.

pivot ['pivət] *n.* 轴（axis, axle）

axis ['æksis] *n.* 轴（shaft）

【例】The earth spins on its *axis*.

release [ri'liːs] *n./vt.* 发行

【例】The republisher *released* 500 new books last year.

load [ləud] *n.* 负荷 *v.* 装载（burden）

behave [bi'heiv] *v.* 运转

【例】My car has been *behaving* well since it was repaired.

erect [i'rekt] *v.* 建设（build, set up, establish）

【记】e＋rect(立，竖)

【例】Within the past decade, there were many skyscrapers *erected* in this city.

raise [reiz] *vt.* 养殖(breed)

【例】He *raised* horses.

manipulate [mə'nipjuleit] *vt.* 操作(handle, operate)；操纵

【例】Bob *manipulates* his friends to get what he wants.

construct [kən'strʌkt] *vt.* 建造，构造

【记】con＋struct(结构)

【例】A famous architect *constructed* a model of a new cathedral.

convey [kən'vei] *vt.* 运输(transport, deliver)

【例】Trucks *conveyed* the goods from the distributor to the buyer.

fabricate ['fæbrikeit] *vt.* 制造(make)

【记】fabric(结构)＋ate→使出现结构→制造

【例】Jane *fabricated* the story that she was late because she was caught in traffic.

manufacture [ˌmænju'fæktʃə] *vt.* 制造

【记】manu(手)＋fact(做)＋ure→用手做→制造

【例】His books seem to have been *manufactured* rather than composed.

conserve [kən'sə:v] *vt.* 贮藏(preserve, store, retain)

【例】Turning off the lights as you leave a room *conserves* energy.

hoist [hɔist] *n.* 吊车(lift) *v.* 升起,提起

【例】He was *hoisted* up to the top of the building by a *hoist*.

concrete ['kɔnkri:t] *n.* 水泥

mill [mil] *n.* 压榨机，磨坊，磨粉机

生活

domestic [də'mestik] *adj.* 家内的(household)

【例】The police called the fight between the husband and wife a *domestic* matter.

idyllic [ai'dilik] *adj.* 田园诗的(pastoral, rustic)

scale [skeil] *n.* 秤

【例】I'll be glad when I tip the *scales* at a few pounds less.

furniture ['fə:nitʃə] *n.* 家具(furnishing)

rubbish ['rʌbiʃ] *n.* 垃圾（refuse, trash, waste）

trash [træʃ] *n.* 垃圾（rubbish, garbage, refuse, waste）

hurdle ['hɜːdl] *n.* 篱笆

sustenance ['sʌstənəns] *n.* 生计

【例】For *sustenance*, the vegetarian ate fruits, nuts, and vegetables.

nostalgia [nɔs'tældʒiə] *n.* 思乡，怀旧

【记】nost(家)＋alg(痛)＋ia(病)→思乡

【例】The old man remembered his college days with *nostalgia*.

singe [sindʒ] *n.* 微烧；烫焦（burn, scorch）

baggage ['bægidʒ] *n.* 行李（luggage, packing）

【记】参考luggage(行李)

【例】How much *baggage* can we take on the plane?

outing ['autiŋ] *n.* 郊游；远足（trip, excursion）

regimen ['redʒimen] *n.* 养生法

【记】regi(统治)＋men(人)→统治人身的法则→养生之道

slag [slæg] *n.* 渣滓（refuse, waste）

sojourn ['sɔdʒɜːn] *vi.* 逗留；寄居（stay）

【例】The explorers *sojourned* at the old castle expecting for a new find.

dwell [dwel] *vi.* 居住（reside, inhabit, live）

【例】Birds normally *dwell* on trees.

baby-sit ['beibisit] *vi.* 看管（婴孩）（take charge of）

【例】Children aren't invited to the weddings, so we'll need someone to *baby-sit*.

tease [tiːz] *vt.* 逗乐，戏弄（taunt, jeer）

【例】The girl was *teasing* their mother for more candy.

inhabit [in'hæbit] *vt.* 居住于，栖息于（reside, dwell, occupy, live in）

【记】in(里面)＋habit(住)→住里面→居住

【例】They decided to *inhabit* the dwelling and live in China.

scorch [skɔːtʃ] *vt.* 烤焦（burn）

【例】Do not leave the iron on that delicate fabric or the heat will *scorch* it.

nurture ['nɜːtʃə] *vt.* 养育（feed, nourish）

【例】Born in a rich family, Anne was delicately *nurtured*.

reside [riˈzaid] *vi.* 居住（dwell, live）

【例】My boss *resides* in a very fancy apartment building.

resident [ˈrezidənt] *adj.* 居住的，常驻的（inhabiting）

【例】The population of *resident* bacteria in a clean square centimeter on human skin exceeds a million.

土 地

deserted [diˈzɔːtid] *adj.* 荒废的

【例】He find no prosperity in town but *deserted* street and shabby buildings.

desolate [ˈdesəlit] *adj.* 荒凉的（deserted, bleak, barren）

【记】de（加强）+sol（单独）+ate

【例】The *desolate* mining town was once a booming center of activity.

bleak [bliːk] *adj.* 荒凉的（desolate, gloomy）

【例】High Andes are *bleak*, treeless regions.

sterile [ˈsterail] *adj.* 贫瘠的；不育的（barren, arid, infertile）

【例】The "Great American Desert" was once assumed as a *sterile* region.

barren [ˈbærən] *adj.* 贫瘠的；不孕的（infertile, arid）*n.* 荒地

【记】bar=bare（空的）+ren

【例】Many people think of deserts as *barren* regions, but many species of plants and animals have adapted to life there.

agrarian [əˈɡrɛəriən] *adj.* 有关土地的，耕地的

clay [klei] *n.* 粘土，泥土

clod [klɔd] *n.* 土块

外 表

stodgy [ˈstɔdʒi] *adj.* 躯体笨重的

stout [staut] *adj.* 矮胖的

【例】A *stout* passenger took up two seats on the bus.

obese [əuˈbiːs] *adj.* 肥胖的，肥大的（overweight）

corpulent [ˈkɔːpjulənt] *adj.* 肥胖的

【记】corp（身体）+ulent→体胖的

【例】Overeating has made her *corpulent*.

shabby [ˈʃæbi] *adj.* 褴褛的，破旧的

【例】The *shabby* old man asked me for a dollar.

ragged ['rægid] *adj.* 褴褛的，破烂的（tattered, scruffy）

【记】rag(破布)＋ged→破烂的

bald [bɔːld] *adj.* 秃头的，光秃的（hairless）

【记】参考 bold(大胆的)

【例】The *bald* man wore a hat to protect his head from the sun.

aspect ['æspekt] *n.* 样子，外表

【记】a＋spect(看)→看上去的样子→外观

【例】He was serious of *aspect* but wholly undistinguished.

costume ['kɔstjuːm] *n.* 服装（attire, dress）

【记】比较custom(习俗)

【例】The actors in the play had beautiful *costumes*.

attire [ə'taiə] *n.* 服装（clothing, dress）

outfit ['autfit] *n.* 服装（costume, suit）

【记】来自 fit out(装备)

garb [gɑːb] *n.* 服装，装束（uniform, outfit）

strap [stræp] *n.* 皮带（fastening, band）

guise [gaiz] *n.* 外观；装束（appearance）

【例】The thief robbed houses in the *guise* of a mailman.

clothing ['kləuðiŋ] *n.* 衣服（apparel, attire）

array [ə'rei] *vt.* 装扮

【例】The colorful *array* of candy made the children's eyes bulge.

cosmetics [kɔz'metiks] *n.* 化妆品

suit [sjuːt] *n.* 套装

sole [səul] *n.* 鞋底（bottom）

休　息

drowsy ['drauzi] *adj.* 昏昏欲睡的（sleepy）

【例】The heat made us all *drowsy*.

nap [næp] *n./v.* 小睡，打盹（doze）

recreation [ˌrekri'eiʃən] *n.* 消遣（pastime, amusement）

【例】For *recreation*, I like to go hiking and camping.

lull [lʌl] *n.* 歇息

beguile [bi'gail] *vi.* 消遣

【记】be＋guile(欺诈)

【例】Our journey was *beguiled* with spirited talk.

doze ［dəuz］*vi.* 瞌睡(与off连用)(nap, drowse)

【例】Mary *dozed* peacefully after a long day at work.

bask ［bɑːsk］*vt.* 取暖；曝日

【例】Tom enjoys sitting in the garden, *basking* in the sunshine.

预 知

fateful ［'feitful］*adj.* 预言性的

【例】Gates made a *fateful* decision to quit Harvard.

imminent ［'iminənt］*adj.* 即将来临的(impending, approaching)

【记】im(进)＋min(伸)＋ent→伸进来→来临的

【例】The *imminent* storm gives us a sign that the day is turning bad.

estimable ［'estiməbl］*adj.* 可估计的

apt ［æpt］*adj.* 有…倾向的(prone, likely)

【例】Bill is *apt* to forget half of the groceries if he doesn't take a list.

promising ［'prɔmisiŋ］*adj.* 有前途的，有希望的(prospective)

provident ［'prɔvidənt］*adj.* 有远见的(forward-looking)

【记】pro(前)＋vid=vis(看见)＋ent→有远见的

prospect ［'prɔspekt］*n.* 前景，期望(outlook, likelihood, possibility)

【记】pro(向前)＋spect(看)→向前看

【例】Older people are always concerned by the *prospect* that an unpreceding depression would bring chaos again.

prospective ［prɔs'pektiv］*adj.* 预期的(forward-looking, forthcoming)

perspective ［pə'spektiv］*n.* 远景(view, outlook)

【记】per(全部)＋spect(看)＋ive→远景

【例】Her ability to use *perspective* gives the appearance of depth to her art.

auspice ［'ɔːspis］*n.* 前兆

【记】au＋spic(看)＋e→提前看到的→前兆

tendency ［'tendənsi］*n.* 趋势(inclination, trend)

precursor ［priː'kɜːsə］*n.* 先兆；先驱(sign; forerunner, pioneer, ancestor)

【记】pre(提前)＋curs(跑)＋or→先兆

【例】Dark clouds are often treated as *precursor* of a storm.

prediction ［pri'dikʃən］*n.* 预言，预报(forecast, prophecy)

surmise [sə'maiz] *vt.* 臆测(guess, speculate)

【记】sur(下面)＋mise(说)→在下面说出的话→猜测

【例】With no news from the explorers we can only *surmise* their present position.

foretell [fɔː'tel] *vt.* 预言(predict)

【记】fore＋tell(告诉)

【例】No one could have *foretold* such strange events.

foresee [fɔː'siː] *vt.* 预知(foreshadow, predict)

【记】fore(前)＋see(看)→预先看到

【例】Those who can *foresee* difficulties on their way to success may keep calm when they really appear.

foresight ['fɔːsait] *n.* 预见，远见

【记】sight(视力)

current ['kʌrənt] *n.* 趋势(trend)

【例】He reads the newspaper every day to know the *current* of events.

forecast ['fɔːkɑːst] *n.* 先见，预见，预测，预报

灾难与不幸

disaster [di'zɑːstə] *n.* 灾难(catastrophe, calamity)

【例】The month-long period of rain was a *disaster* for the farmer.

helpless ['helplis] *adj.* 无助的(powerless)

disastrous [di'zɑːstrəs] *adj.* 灾难性的；悲惨的(catastrophic)

【例】A few *disastrous* investments ruined the company.

unfortunately [ʌn'fɔːtʃənətli] *adv.* 不幸地

【记】un(不)＋fortunately(幸运地)

calamity [kə'læmiti] *n.* 不幸之事，灾难(catastrophe, mishap)

【例】The Red Cross provides relief in case of *calamities* such as floods, earthquakes and hurricanes.

holocaust ['hɔləkɔːst] *n.* 大屠杀(slaughter)

【记】holo(全部)＋caust(烧)→全部烧死→大屠杀

carnage ['kɑːnidʒ] *n.* 大屠杀，残杀(massacre, slaughter)

【记】carn(肉)＋age

cataclysm ['kætəklizəm] *n.* 洪水，大灾难

【记】cata（下面）+clysm（洗）→洗掉→洪水

【例】The eruption of the volcano was an unexpected *cataclysm*.

avalanche [ˈævəlɑːntʃ] *n.* 雪崩

【例】Tons of snow rushed down the mountain in the *avalanche*.

catastrophe [kəˈtæstrəfi] *n.* 异常的灾祸（disaster）*v.* 使得灾祸

【例】The crash of the stock market was a financial *catastrophe*.

plague [pleig] *n.* 疫病，灾祸（disease）*v.* 折磨，使苦恼

【例】The ceaseless war posed a big *plague* for those innocent. / Runaway inflation further *plagued* the salary-earner.

casualty [ˈkæʒuəlti] *n.* 意外伤亡，事故

【例】Jane saw a *casualty* on the highway and phoned the police.

mishap [ˈmishæp] *n.* 灾祸，不幸（mischance, accident）

【记】mis（坏）+hap（运气）→不幸

【例】The fisherman drowned in a boating *mishap*.

adversity [ədˈvəːsiti] *n.* 不幸，逆境（misfortune）

【记】ad+vers（转）+ity→转错方向→不幸

【例】The *adversity* of losing one's job is difficult to bear.

afflict [əˈflikt] *vt.* 使痛苦，折磨（torture）

【记】af（一再）+flict（打击）→一再打击→折磨

【例】He was *afflicted* with arthritis.

致 命

defunct [diˈfʌŋkt] *adj.* 死的（dead, demised）

【记】de（分离）+funct（功能）

【例】Those rules of etiquette have been *defunct* for years.

lethal [ˈliːθəl] *adj.* 致命的（fatal, deadly）

【记】leth（死）+al

deadly [ˈdedli] *adj.* 致命的（fatal, lethal）

【例】Don't be scared; it's not a *deadly* wound.

demise [diˈmaiz] *n.* 死亡（death, end）

【例】The country mourned the president's

demise.

choke ［tʃəuk］ *n.* 窒息 *v.*（使）窒息（suffocate, block）

【例】My lawn mover has a *choke* that I have to adjust frequently.

smother ［'smʌðə］ *v.*（使）窒息；闷死（stifle, suffocate）

【例】The murderer *smothered* his victims with a pillow.

expire ［iks'paiə］ *vi.* 断气（perish）

【记】ex(出，离开)＋pire(呼吸)→离开呼吸→断气

【例】John's driver's license *expired* last week.

mortal ［'mɔːtl］ *adj.* 终有一死的 *n.* 凡人

【记】mort(死)＋al

【例】All *mortals,* however outstanding, are to die one day.

Anything one man can imagine, other men can make real.

—*Jules Verne*

但凡人能想像到的事物,必定有人能将它实现。

——凡尔纳

连 线 题

左列单词在右列中有一个或多个同义词,请画线连接。

(一)

baggage

calamity

conserve

deadly

demise

expire

obese

perspective

recreation

sojourn

amusement

catastrophe

death

fatal

luggage

mishap

outlook

overweight

pastime

perish

preserve

retain

stay

view

(二)

embrace

haul

instrument

outfit

plunge

posture

pratical

slap

trample

trudge

bearing

clap

cuddle

device

dive

equipment

hug

plod

pragmatic

transport

tread

(三)

aura

decorum

extol

fashionable

grandeur

laborious

laud

legendary

preeminent

refuge

arduous

atmosphere

ceremony

compliment

exalt

magnificence

popular

prominent

protection

renowned

shelter

(四)

affinity

chop

cleanse

consensus

deceitful

delude

fortunate

grant

homicide

impact

log

maintain

mutual

provide

award

beguile

collision

furnish

hew

journal

liking

lucky

purify

reciprocal

repair

slaughter

sly

unanimity

连线题答案

（一）

baggage	luggage
calamity	catastrophe
calamity	mishap
conserve	preserve
conserve	retain
deadly	fatal
demise	death
expire	perish
obese	overweight
perspective	view
perspective	outlook
recreation	pastime
recreation	amusement
sojourn	stay

（二）

embrace	hug
embrace	cuddle
haul	transport
instrument	device
outfit	equipment
plunge	dive
posture	bearing
pratical	pragmatic
slap	clap
trample	tread
trudge	plod

（三）

aura	atmosphere
decorum	ceremony
extol	exalt
fashionable	popular
grandeur	magnificence
laborious	arduous
laud	compliment
legendary	renowned
preeminent	prominent
refuge	shelter
refuge	protection

（四）

affinity	liking
chop	hew
cleanse	purify
consensus	unanimity
deceitful	sly
delude	beguile
fortunate	lucky
grant	award
homicide	slaughter
impact	collision
log	journal
maintain	repair
mutual	reciprocal
provide	furnish

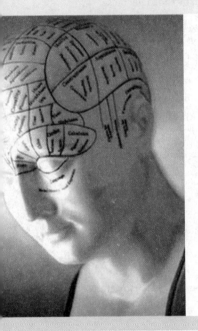

心　理

记忆小贴士：情感对应记忆法

　　人在特定的心理状态下对与之情绪、情感相符的事物会给予极大的关注。在悲伤的情绪下看那些表示悲伤的单词，记忆效果会比高兴时好。

傲 慢

partial ['pɑ:ʃəl] *adj.* 偏袒的

【记】part(部分)+ial

overbearing [ˌəuvə'bɛəriŋ] *adj.* 傲慢的(arrogant, haughty)

【记】over(过分)+bearing(忍受)→让别人过分忍受→傲慢的

arrogant ['ærəgənt] *adj.* 傲慢的(haughty, disdainful)

【例】The tennis player's *arrogant* reaction offended the fans.

haughty ['hɔːti] *adj.* 傲慢的，轻蔑的(disdainful, arrogant)

insolent ['insələnt] *adj.* 傲慢的；无礼的(haughty, arrogant; impudent)

【例】The *insolent* student yelled at his teacher.

fussy ['fʌsi] *adj.* 过分挑剔的(finicky, fastidious)

【例】If you weren't too *fussy*, we could have finished shopping an hour ago.

contemptuous [kən'temptjuəs] *adj.* 藐视的；傲慢的(arrogant, haughty)

【记】con+tempt(轻视，鄙视)+uous

【例】The *contemptuous* crowd heckled the speaker at the political rally.

domineering [ˌdɔmi'niəriŋ] *adj.* 盛气凌人的

【记】domin(统治)+eering→统治者的→盛气凌人的

【例】The *domineering* father made every decision in his children's lives.

presumptuous [pri'zʌmptʃuəs] *adj.* 专横的(self-conceited, audacious)

arrogance ['ærəgəns] *n.* 傲慢

【记】ar+rog(要求)+ance→一再要求→傲慢

【例】We didn't tip the waiter because of his *arrogance* toward us.

preference ['prefərəns] *n.* 偏爱

【记】prefer(喜欢)+ence

【例】The king showed *preference* to his eldest son.

bias ['baiəs] *n.* 偏见(prejudice, partiality)

【例】The classical music reviewer had a *bias* against rock music.

悲 伤

doleful ['dəulful] *adj.* 悲哀的(mournful, sorrowful)

【记】dole(悲哀)

upset [ʌp'set] *adj.* 难过的(disturbed, distressed)

trying ['traiiŋ] *adj.* 难堪的，痛苦的(difficult, grueling)

【例】It really was a *trying* day for him with no water and no electricity.

sentimental [ˌsentiˈmentl] *adj.* 伤感的，多愁善感的（emotional）

【例】Mary felt *sentimental* about life each autumn.

grieve [griːv] *vi.* 悲伤（sorrow）

【例】She *grieved* over her father's sudden death.

grieved [griːvd] *adj.* 伤心的

gloom [gluːm] *n.* 忧愁（sadness, depression）

torturous [ˈtɔːtʃərəs] *adj.* 痛苦的（tormenting）*v.* 折磨

【记】tort(扭)+urous→扭曲的→痛苦的

misery [ˈmizəri] *n.* 痛苦，苦恼

miserable [ˈmizərəbl] *adj.* 痛苦的；可怜的

distressed [diˈstrest] *adj.* 痛苦的

【记】dis+stress(压力，紧张)+ed

pensive [ˈpensiv] *adj.* 忧愁的，哀思的（thoughtful, contemplative）

【记】pens(挂)+ive→心思挂在脸上→忧愁的

lament [ləˈment] *n.* 悲伤 *vt.* 痛惜（mourn, grieve over）

【记】联想lame(跛足的)加上"nt"

torment [ˈtɔːment] *n.* 痛苦（anguish, agony）*v.* 折磨

【例】The murderer was *tormented* by guilt.

deplore [diˈplɔː] *vt.* 悲痛；深悔（grieve, mourn）

【例】They *deplore* the use of force as a solution to this problem.

吃 惊

inconceivable [ˌinkənˈsiːvəbl] *adj.* 不可思议的（unimaginable, unthinkable）

【记】in(不)+conceivable(可以想像的)

uncanny [ʌnˈkæni] *adj.* 不可思议的，离奇的（odd, strange）

【记】un(不)+canny(安静的，温和的)

marvelous [ˈmɑːviləs] *adj.* 不可思议的；了不起的

breathtaking [ˈbreθˌteikiŋ] *adj.* 惊人的，惊险的（stunning, exciting）

astound [əsˈtaund] *vt.* 使惊异（surprise, astonish）

【例】The daredevil *astounded* the audience with a dangerous feat.

astonish [əsˈtɔniʃ] *vt.* 使惊讶（amaze, astound, surprise）

【例】The magician *astonished* the children.

astonished [əˈstɔniʃt] *adj.* 惊讶的

【例】A hush fell over the *astonished* crowds as the governor announced his resignation.

incredible [inˈkredəbl] *adj.* 难以相信的(unbelievable, improbable)

【记】in(不)＋cred(相信)＋ible

striking [ˈstraikiŋ] *adj.* 显著的，惊人的(prominent, outstanding, impressive)

【例】His black skin and white teeth consist a *striking* contrast.

tremor [ˈtremə] *n.* 颤抖，战栗(tremble, shake)

trepidation [ˌtrepiˈdeiʃən] *n.* 惊恐，战栗(apprehension, alarm)

petrify [ˈpetrifai] *vt.* 使发呆(stupefy, terrify)

【记】petr(石头)＋ify

【例】I was totally *petrified* with fear.

scare [skɛə] *vt.* 惊吓，使受惊(terrify)

【例】The dogs *scared* the thief away.

startle [ˈstɑːtl] *vt.* 使大吃一惊(amaze, surprise) *n.* 吃惊

【例】The official hinted at *startling* new developments that would soon be made public.

stun [stʌn] *vt.* 使昏晕，使目瞪口呆 (astonish, daze, amaze)

【例】He was *stunned* when he knew he failed the exam, which he had been prepared for months.

dismay [disˈmei] *vt.* 使惊愕；使沮丧(disconcert, alarm)

【例】The loss *dismayed* the team members, who had practiced so hard.

动 机

impetuous [imˈpetjuəs] *adj.* 冲动的(impulsive)

impulse [ˈimpʌls] *n.* 冲动，刺激

【记】比较pulse(脉搏，跳动)

impulsive [imˈpʌlsiv] *adj.* 易冲动的

【例】On seeing the poor little girl, he has an *impulse* to adopt her.

urge [əːdʒ] *n.* 冲动

【例】The girl suppressed an *urge* to laugh.

incentive [inˈsentiv] *n.* 刺激；动机(motivation)

【例】People doubt about her *incentive* to marry that rich old fellow.

motivation [ˌməutiˈveiʃən] *n.* 动机(motive, incentive)

【记】比较motive(动机)

【例】Unfortunately his salary is his only *motivation* for working.

objective [əbˈdʒektiv] *n.* 目标(aim, goal)

【记】object(客观)＋ive

恶 意

grim [grim] *adj.* 不吉祥的

【例】Each day, the chance for peace became more *grim*.

sinister [ˈsinistə] *adj.* 不祥的；邪恶的(wicked, evil)

cruel [ˈkruəl] *adj.* 残忍的(ferocious, ruthless)

【例】The *cruel* ruler allowed the peasants to starve.

malevolent [məˈlevələnt] *adj.* 恶意的(malicious, spiteful)

【记】male(坏)＋vol(意念)＋ent→恶意的

malice [ˈmælis] *n.* 恶意(ill will, spite)

malicious [məˈliʃəs] *adj.* 心毒的，怀恶意的(vicious, spiteful)

【例】Don't listen to those *malicious* rumors; he is a good man.

ferocious [fəˈrəuʃəs] *adj.* 凶猛的(fierce, savage, bestial)

【记】feroc(凶猛)＋ious

【例】The *ferocious* winter storm buried the roads in a foot of snow.

烦 躁

gloomy [ˈgluːmi] *adj.* 忧闷的

【例】The streets were filled with *gloomy* faces after the earthquake.

impatient [imˈpeiʃənt] *adj.* 不耐烦的

【记】im(不)＋patient(耐心的)

【例】Susan is *impatient* and refuses to wait in line for anything.

stodgy [ˈstɔdʒi] *adj.* 枯燥乏味的(dull, boring)

boring [ˈbɔːriŋ] *adj.* 令人厌烦的

【例】Since it rained, the children spent a *boring* afternoon cleaning the basement.

bothersome [ˈbɔðəsəm] *adj.* 令人厌烦的，令人烦恼的(irritating, annoying)

boredom [ˈbɔːdəm] *n.* 烦恼，无聊（vexation, annoyance）

【记】bore（厌烦）＋dom

【例】The exciting novel chased away Jane's *boredom*.

tedious [ˈtiːdiəs] *adj.* 冗长乏味的，沉闷的（tiresome, boring）

【例】John's job at the factory is trivial and *tedious*.

sicken [ˈsikən] *adj.* 使厌倦；使作呕

uproar [ˈʌprɔː] *n.* 扰乱，喧嚣（disturbance, commotion）

【记】up（上）＋roar（吼叫）

intrude [inˈtruːd] *v.* 侵扰（encroach, infringe）

【记】in（进入）＋trude（突出）→突进入→侵扰

【例】I don't mean to *intrude*, but you have a telephone call.

chafe [tʃeif] *vt.* 烦扰（irritate）

【例】Coarse fabric will *chafe* your skin.

distract [diˈstrækt] *vt.* 分散（心思），打扰（abstract, divert）

【记】dis＋tract（拉）→心被拉开→分散

【例】The school students were *distracted* by the noise outside the class-room.

harass [həˈræs] *vt.* 侵扰（bother）

【记】参考ass（驴子）

【例】Don't *harass* me; I am working.

disarrange [ˌdisəˈreindʒ] *vt.* 扰乱（disturb）

【记】dis（不再）＋arrange（排列）

【例】Her sudden departure has *disarranged* my plan.

derange [diˈreindʒ] *vt.* 扰乱

【记】de（坏）＋range（排列）

【例】She is completely *deranged*.

vex [veks] *vt.* 使烦恼（annoy, irritate）

【例】He was greatly *vexed* by the new and unexpected development.

愤 怒

grouchy [ˈgrautʃi] *adj.* 不悦的，愠怒的（bad-tempered, petulant）

【例】"I don't like these homework," he said in a *grouchy* tone of voice.

indignant [inˈdignənt] *adj.* 愤慨的，义愤的（outraged）

【记】in（不）＋dign（礼貌）＋ant→不礼貌→愤慨的

furious ['fjuəriəs] *adj.* 狂怒的；狂暴的(frenzied, enraged)

nervous ['nə:vəs] *adj.* 易激动的

【记】nerv(神经)+ous

passionate ['pæʃənit] *adj.* 易怒的

【记】passion(激情)+ate

touchy ['tʌtʃi] *adj.* 易怒的；棘手的(annoyed, offended)

fury ['fjuəri] *n.* 勃然大怒(rage, wrath)

rage [reidʒ] *n.* 激怒，愤怒(fury, anger)

enrage [in'reidʒ] *vt.* 激怒(infuriate, aggravate)

【记】en+rage(暴怒)

【例】John's insolence *enraged* his supervisor.

outrage ['autreidʒ] *vt.* 激怒；侵犯(anger; offend)

【记】out(出)+rage(愤怒)→出离愤怒

【例】The mayor's cruel remarks *outraged* the citizens.

exasperate [ig'zæspəreit] *vt.* 激怒(annoy, irritate)

【记】ex+asper(粗鲁)+ate→表现的粗鲁→发怒

【例】The traffic jam *exasperated* the motorists who were caught in it.

fret [fret] *vt.* 激怒(annoy, worry)

【例】That noise *frets* me.

provoke [prə'vəuk] *vt.* 激怒，煽动 (incite, stir up, cause, elicit)

【例】The bear *provoked* the bees by disturbing their hive.

incense ['insens] *vt.* 激怒

【记】in(进入)+cense(光)→使怒火中烧

【例】The decision to reduce the pay levels *incensed* the work-force.

感 觉

indefatigable [ˌindi'fætigəbl] *adj.* 不疲倦的(tireless, dogged)

【记】in(不)+de(表强调)+fatig(疲倦)+able

sensuous ['senʃuəs] *adj.* 感觉的，美感的

【例】Advertisements use *sensuous* colors to appeal to the audience.

faint [feint] *adj.* 昏晕的

【例】He felt *faint* for a moment.

ravenous ['rævinəs] *adj.* 极饿的（famished, starving）

listless ['listlis] *adj.* 倦怠的，没精打采的（sluggish, lifeless）

【记】list（渴望）＋less→倦怠的

【例】I feel so *listless*; I think I need a nap.

beat [biːt] *adj.* 疲倦的（exhausted, tired, worn out）

【例】I can't move a bit. I am *beat*.

downhearted [daun'hɑːtid] *adj.* 无精打采的（depressed, downcast）

【例】We were all *downhearted* at the death of our friend.

daze ['deiz] *n.* 昏晕 *vt.* 使发昏，茫然（dazzle, confusion）

【例】The driver recovered slowly from her *daze* after the accident.

intuition [ˌintjuː'iʃən] *n.* 直觉

starve [stɑːv] *v.*（使）挨饿

【例】Come on, where is the food? I am *starving*.

hunger ['hʌŋgə] *v./n.* 饥饿

【例】She *hungers* for his love.

famish ['fæmiʃ] *vt.* 使挨饿

【例】When's lunch? I am *famished*.

exhaust [ig'zɔːst] *vt.* 使疲倦（use up, drain）

【记】ex＋haust（拉）→（用力）拉出→疲惫

【例】The children thoroughly *exhausted* their mother's patience.

gorge [gɔːdʒ] *vt.* 塞饱

【例】Boys *gorged* themselves with candy.

高 兴

hilarious [hi'lɛəriəs] *adj.* 高兴的（delightful）

exultant [ig'zʌltənt] *adj.* 欢腾的；狂欢的（happy; jubilant）

【记】ex＋（s）ult（激动）＋ant→出现激动→欢腾的

brisk [brisk] *adj.* 活泼的，轻快的（swift, energetic）

【例】A *brisk* walk before breakfast is a good way to start the day.

gleeful ['gliːful] *adj.* 极高兴的，兴奋的（delightful, exultant）

joyous ['dʒɔiəs] *adj.* 快乐的，高兴的

【记】joy（高兴）＋ous

exalted [ig'zɔːltid] *adj.* 兴奋的（exited）

【例】 The *exalted* prince entered the hall and everyone stood up.

blessed [blesid] *adj.* 愉快的（amused, blithe）

【例】 They enjoyed a few moments of *blessed* silence after the whole day's noise.

pleasing [ˈpliːziŋ] *adj.* 愉快的（blithe, amusing）

【例】 Because the meal was so *pleasing*, I left a large tip for the server.

pleasure [ˈpleʒə] *n.* 快乐（enjoyment）

elation [iˈleiʃən] *n.* 得意洋洋

【记】 elate＋ion

【例】 John's *elation* is apparent from the huge smile on his face.

ecstasy [ˈekstəsi] *n.* 恍惚；狂喜

【例】 Mary was in *ecstasy* when she won the piano competition.

excitement [ikˈsaitmənt] *n.* 激动，兴奋；刺激

【例】 *Excitement* flowed through the crowd when the famous athlete entered the room.

bliss [blis] *n.* 狂喜（ecstasy）

【例】 Jane was in a state of *bliss* after getting her degree.

rapture [ˈræptʃə] *n.* 狂喜（ecstasy, delight）

【记】 rapt(着迷)＋ure

tingle [ˈtiŋgl] *vi.*（因兴奋）激动

【例】 The uncertainty of national events made his blood *tingle*.

brighten [ˈbraitn] *vt.* 使快活

【记】 bright(光亮)＋en

【例】 His face *brightened* up.

enrapture [inˈræptʃə] *vt.* 使狂喜（delight; exult）

【记】 en＋rapture(狂喜)

【例】 Her smile *enraptured* him so he would not move his eyes.

ravish [ˈræviʃ] *vt.* 使陶醉；使狂喜

【例】 He was *ravished* by her beauty, and forgot that she was ravishing his fortune.

好 奇

curious [ˈkjuəriəs] *adj.* 好奇的（acquisitive）

【例】The family had a few *curious* traditions.

curiosity [ˌkjuəriˈɔsiti] *n.* 好奇心

【例】Just out of *curiosity,* I wonder how much this apartment costs.

inquisitive [inˈkwizitiv] *adj.* 好奇的（nosy, curious）

【记】in(进入)＋quisit(询问)＋ive→喜欢询问的→好奇的

【例】I was mad at the *inquisitive* kid, who kept on asking me silly questions.

焦 急

concerned [kənˈsəːnd] *adj.* 焦虑的

【例】Mary is *concerned* with finishing her work before 12:00.

intense [inˈtens] *adj.* 紧张的

【例】Under years of *intense* pressure, he finally gave up hope and commited suicide.

suspense [səˈspens] *n.* 焦虑（anticipation, uncertainty）

【记】sus＋pense(挂)→挂念→焦虑

strain [strein] *n.* 紧张（stress, tension）

【例】Insurance costs are a big *strain* on our budget.

fluster [ˈflʌstə] *vt.* 使慌乱（confuse, disconcert）

【例】Don't get *flustered*!

tense [tens] *adj.* 紧张的（nervous, strained）

【例】The bath relaxed Mary's *tense* muscles.

abashed [əˈbæʃt] *adj.* 羞愧的，局促不安的（uneasy）

【记】abash(羞愧)＋ed；比较blush(脸红)

沮 丧

languid [ˈlæŋgwid] *adj.* 精神不振的（sluggish, listless）

【记】langu(松弛)＋id→精神不振的

downcast [ˈdaunkɑːst] *adj.* 沮丧的（depressed, dejected）

【例】The *downcast* student couldn't believe that he'd failed the test.

dismal [ˈdizml] *adj.* 沮丧的（gloomy, somber）

【例】Mary cried during the *dismal* movie.

dejected [di'dʒektid] *adj.* 失望的，沮丧的(depressed, dispirited)

【记】deject(失望)＋ed

depress [di'pres] *vt.* 使沮丧(deject, dispirit)

【记】de(加强)＋press(压)

【例】He was *depressed* because he had not passed his examinations.

depression [di'preʃən] *n.* 沮丧

【例】He committed suicide during a fit of *depression*.

dampen ['dæmpən] *vt.* 使沮丧(dismay, depress)

【例】I don't want to *dampen* your enthusiasm, but take it easy!

cheerless ['tʃiəlis] *adj.* 不愉快的；阴郁的

恐　惧

formidable ['fɔ:midəbl] *adj.* 可畏惧的，可怕的(dreadful, frightening)

【例】He is kind, but unfortunately with a *formidable* face.

fright [frait] *n.* 惊吓，恐怖

terror ['terə] *n.* 恐怖

terrify ['terəfai] *vt.* 使恐怖，使惊吓

【例】The animals were *terrified* by the storm.

panic ['pænik] *n.* 恐慌(fear, scare)

【例】The rumor that we are having an earthquake arouse a *panic*.

horror ['hɔːrə] *n.* 恐惧

dread [dred] *n.* 畏惧，恐怖 *v.* 畏惧(fear)

【例】John *dreads* calculating his taxes.

cower ['kauə] *vi.* 畏缩(recoil)

【例】The children *cowered* each time they heard the thunder.

intimidate [in'timideit] *vt.* 恐吓(frighten, threaten)

【记】in(进入)＋timid(害怕)＋ate→使害怕→恐吓

【例】I don't want to *intimidate* you, but very few people pass this exam.

menace ['menəs] *vt.* 威吓(threaten, intimidate)；胁迫

【记】men(人)＋ace(王牌)→用手中的一张王牌→胁迫

【例】The people are being *menaced* by the threat of war.

狂　热

insane [in'sein] *adj.* 发狂，精神错乱的(crazy)

【记】in(不)＋sane(清醒的)

【例】The murderer was judged to be *insane* and was then released.

crazy ['kreizi] *adj.* 狂热的

【例】The *crazy* defendant was declared unfit to stand trial.

radical ['rædikl] *adj.* 激进的(severe, extreme)

【例】The American Revolution is not a *radical* one, but a gradual evolution.

radically ['rædikəli] *adv.* 激进地(drastically)

mania ['meinjə] *n.* 癫狂，狂热

【记】man(疯狂)＋ia(病)

frenzy ['frenzi] *n.* 狂热(great excitement)

【记】参考frantic(疯狂的)

fanatic [fə'nætik] *adj.* 狂热的，狂热者的(frantic, fervent)

【记】fan(迷)＋atic→着迷的人→盲信者

fanaticism [fə'nætisizəm] *n.* 狂热；盲从

满 意

relieved [ri'li:vd] *adj.* 放心的

【记】名词relief(宽慰)

satisfactory [ˌsætis'fæktəri] *adj.* 令人满意的(appealing)

content [kən'tent] *adj.* 满足的(satisfied, complacent)

【例】After a good meal and good conversation, we were all *content*.

satiate ['seiʃieit] *vt.* 使饱享；使满足

【记】sat(满)＋iate

【例】Some cold lemonade *satiated* my thirst.

gratify ['grætifai] *vt.* 使满意(satisfy)

【记】grat(满意)＋ify→满足，高兴

【例】Anne was *gratified* by the manager's efforts to help her.

梦 想

solicitous [sə'lisitəs] *adj.* 渴望的；焦虑的(avid; concerned)

【例】The parents are *solicitous* about their son's health.

desire [di'zaiə] *vt.* 想要 *n.* 欲望

【例】His excellence at work leaves nothing to be *desired*.

desirous [di'zaiərəs] *adj.* 渴望的

【例】I am *desirous* of a good job and a healthy family.

desirable [di'zaiərəbl] *adj.* 理想的，如意的

【例】I envy Jane because her job is so *desirable*.

aspire [əs'paiə] *vi.* 热望（crave, yearn）

【例】I *aspire* to being the president of a bank.

aspiration [ˌæspə'reiʃən] *n.* 热望，渴望（avidity）

【记】a＋spir(呼吸)＋ation

【例】Children often have big *aspirations*.

hunger ['hʌŋgə] *v./n.* 渴望

【例】She *hungers* for his love.

long [lɔŋ] *vi.* 渴望（crave, yearn）

【例】People in the war *longed* for peace day and night.

crave [kreiv] *vt.* 渴求（desire, yearn）

【例】Anne *craved* unusual food when she was pregnant.

realize ['riəlaiz] *vt.* 实现（implement, carry out）

【例】He finally *realized* his lifelong ambition to learn how to play the violin.

mean [miːn] *vt.* 意欲（intend）

【例】I didn't *mean* to hurt you; I am sorry.

yen [jen] *n.* 热望，渴望 *v.* 热望，渴望（yearn）

【例】Jane has a *yen* to go climbing in the Rockies.

court [kɔːt] *v.* 追求（pursue）

【例】He is *courting* wealth and fame all his life.

情　感

touching ['tʌtʃiŋ] *adj.* 动人的，令人感伤的（moving, impressive）

【记】touch(感动)＋ing

impassive [im'pæsiv] *adj.* 无感情的（apathetic, indifferent）

【记】im(不)＋pass(感情)＋ive

【例】The nurse's *impassive* attitude annoyed me.

cherish ['tʃeriʃ] *vt.* 珍爱（care for）

【例】Mary *cherished* the idea of touring the castles of Europe.

affection [ə'fekʃən] *n.* 友爱；爱情

affectionate [ə'fekʃənit] *adj.* 挚爱的，亲切的（kind, genial）

【记】affection(感情)＋ate

【例】Jane gave her mother an *affectionate* hug.

emotional [i'məuʃnl] *adj.* 情绪的，情感的

nostalgia [nɔs'tældʒiə] *n.* 思家病，乡愁，向往过去，怀旧之情

sentimental [ˌsenti'mentl] *adj.* 感伤性的，感情脆弱的

emotive [i'məutiv] *adj.* 使感动的，感情的，动感情的

lovelorn ['lʌvlɔːn] *a.* 失恋的

passionate ['pæʃənit] *adj.* 多情的，热情的(impassioned, fervent)

【记】passion(激情)＋ate

【例】Mary is very *passionate* about gardening.

热 情

vigorous ['vigərəs] *adj.* 朝气蓬勃的

【例】Mary stretched her muscles before an hour of *vigorous* exercise.

hospitable ['hɔspitəbl] *adj.* 好客的(sociable, companionable)

positive ['pɔzitiv] *adj.* 积极的(active)

【记】比较passive(消极的)

energetic [ˌenə'dʒetik] *adj.* 积极的，精力旺盛的(active)

【记】energy(精力)

【例】The boss appreciated the *energetic* workers.

ardor ['ɑːdə] *n.* 热心(enthusiasm)

【例】The teacher was impressed by Bill's *ardor* for learning.

ardent ['ɑːdənt] *adj.* 极热心的，热情的 (passionate, enthusiastic, fervent, zealous)

【例】Jane's *ardent* admirer sent her flowers everyday.

eager ['iːgə] *adj.* 渴望的；热心的

【例】Bill was *eager* to go fishing for the weekend.

impassioned [im'pæʃənd] *adj.* 热烈的(emotional, ardent)

【记】im(不)＋passion(激情)＋ed

avid ['ævid] *adj.* 热切的(eager)

【例】The *avid* tennis fans cheered for their favorite tennis player.

devoted [di'vəutid] *adj.* 热心的(enthusiastic)

【例】Mary is a *devoted* member of her

church.

readily [ˈredili] *adv.* 愿意地(eagerly, willingly)

enthusiasm [inˈθjuːziæzəm] *n.* 热情(passion)

【例】Jane's *enthusiasm* for gardening is evident by all of these beautiful flowers.

zeal [ziːl] *n.* 热心，热情，热忱(zest, enthusiasm)

zealous [ˈzeləs] *adj.* 热心的(enthusiastic, fervent)

【例】The *zealous* soldier hoped to be sent into battle.

zest [zest] *n.* 浓烈的兴趣；热心(enthusiasm, interest)

hail [heil] *vt.* 欢呼，欢迎(acclaim, applaud)

【例】Birds are singing, *hailing* the coming of the spring.

态 度

jealous [ˈdʒeləs] *adj.* 妒忌的(envious, resentful)；猜疑的

indifferent [inˈdifərənt] *adj.* 冷漠的；不积极的(uninterested, nonchalant)

【记】in(不)＋different(不同的)

【例】People were annoyed at the boss's *indifferent* attitude toward those who died in the accident.

profane [prəˈfein] *vt./adj.* 亵渎(的)(humiliate; disrespectful)

【记】比较fane(神庙)

【例】Please don't *profane* things that are sacred to other people.

flatter [ˈflætə] *vt.* 奉承，阿谀，谄媚

【例】He was good at *flattering* others.

begrudge [biˈɡrʌdʒ] *vt.* 羡慕；嫉妒(grudge, stint, envy, admire)

【记】be＋grudge(怨恨，吝啬)

【例】She *begrudged* his youth.

desperate [ˈdespərit] *adj.* 不顾一切的；绝望的(extremely serious)

【例】Mary was *desperate* for a raise because her bills were mounting.

contrite [kənˈtrait] *adj.* 悔悟的(repentant, remorseful)

【记】con＋trite(摩擦)→(心灵)摩擦→悔悟的

【例】The driver who caused the car accident was very *contrite* over it.

forlorn [fəˈlɔːn] *adj.* 绝望的；被遗弃的(wretched, lonely)

【记】for(出去)＋lorn(被弃的)

犹 豫

dubious ['djuːbjəs] *adj.* 怀疑的(doubtful)

【例】The *dubious* employees shook their heads as they carried out the order.

skeptical ['skeptikl] *adj.* 怀疑的(dubious, incredulous)

【例】The *skeptical* student refused to accept the theory of evolution.

suspicion [sə'spiʃən] *n.* 怀疑(doubt, distrust)

【记】sus=sub(下)+spic(看)+ion→从下面看→怀疑

suspicious [sə'spiʃəs] *adj.* 可疑的,猜疑的(dubious, fishy)

【例】Aunt Jane was *suspicious* of everyone who came to her front door.

fishy ['fiʃi] *adj.* 值得怀疑的(suspicious, dubious)

【例】Are you telling the truth? Your story sounds *fishy* to me.

incredulity [ˌinkri'djuːliti] *n.* 怀疑(suspicion, disbelief)

misgiving [mis'giviŋ] *n.* 疑惧,疑虑

poise [pɔiz] *n.* 犹疑

halt [hɔːlt] *v.* 踌躇;停止

【例】The police ordered the thief to *halt*.

scruple ['skruːpl] *v./n.* 踌躇;顾忌(hesitaion, scrupulousness)

【例】She wouldn't *scruple* to tell a lie if she thought it would be useful.

flounder ['flaundə] *vi.* 踌躇

【记】另一个意思是"比目鱼"

demur [di'məː] *vi.* 踌躇

【例】Anne *demurred* at the statement that she assigned too much homework.

hesitate ['heziteit] *vi.* 犹豫,踌躇;含糊(falter, vacillate)

【例】John *hesitated* when I asked him to help me move some furniture.

doubt [daut] *vt./n.* 怀疑(suspect)

【例】After he lost the game, Bill had *doubts* about his athletic ability.

suspect [sə'spekt] *vt.* 怀疑

【例】I *suspect* his motives.

憎 恨

loath [ləuθ] *adj.* 不喜欢的，不情愿的（reluctant, unwilling）

loathe [ləuð] *vt.* 厌恶（hate, dislike）

【例】I just *loathe* my neighbor's dog because it barks all the time.

hideous ['hidiəs] *adj.* 骇人听闻的；丑恶的（ugly, ill-looking）

【例】Despite its low price, no one would buy the *hideous* tie.

sick [sik] *adj.* 厌恶的

complaint [kəm'pleint] *n.* 抱怨，怨言

【例】The boss had a *complaint* about Bill's tardiness.

grievance ['gri:vəns] *n.* 不满（dissatisfaction）

【记】griev(悲伤)＋ance→说悲伤的话→牢骚

【例】The committee has many *grievances* against the school board.

aversion [ə'və:ʃən] *n.* 厌恶（dislike, distaste）

【记】a＋vers(转)＋ion→转开→厌恶

【例】Her *aversion* to buses makes it necessary for her to own a car.

hatred ['heitrid] *n.* 憎恶，憎恨（abomination）

disgust [dis'gʌst] *vt.* 厌恶

【例】The raw fish *disgusted* me, so I left the table.

grudge [grʌdʒ] *vt.* 怨恨；妒忌；勉强给予

【例】He *grudges* her earning more money than he does.

detest [di'test] *vt.* 憎恶（abhor, hate, loathe）

【例】My children *detest* onions.

resent [ri'zent] *vt.* 憎恨（loathe, hate, detest）

【记】re(反)＋sent(感情)→相反的感情→憎恨

【例】I bitterly *resent* your critism.

abhor [æb'hɔ:] *vt.* 憎恶（detest, despise, loathe）

【记】ab＋hor(恨，怕)；比较horrible(可怕的)

【例】People from all around the world *abhor* terrorism.

abhorrent [æb'hɔrənt] *adj.* 可恶的，可恨的（detestable）

连 线 题

左列单词在右列中有一个或多个同义词,请画线连接。

(一)

	acquisitive
bias	anger
bliss	care for
cherish	crave
	disbelief
curious	dislike
deplore	disturbance
incredulity	drastically
	eagerly
loathe	ecstasy
long	grieve
outrage	hate
	partiality
radically	prejudice
readily	suspicion
uproar	willingly
	yearn

(二)

bothersome	abstract
chafe	agony
dismay	anguish
distract	annoy
doleful	arrogant
fussy	astonish
impetuous	disconcert
incentive	finicky
overbearing	impulsive
	irritate
stun	irritating
torment	motivation
torturous	mournful
uncanny	strange
vex	tormenting

（一）

bias	prejudice
bias	partiality
bliss	ecstasy
cherish	care for
curious	acquisitive
deplore	grieve
incredulity	suspicion
incredulity	disbelief
loathe	hate
loathe	dislike
long	crave
long	yearn
outrage	anger
radically	drastically
readily	eagerly
readily	willingly
uproar	disturbance

（二）

bothersome	irritating
chafe	irritate
dismay	disconcert
distract	abstract
doleful	mournful
fussy	finicky
impetuous	impulsive
incentive	motivation
overbearing	arrogant
stun	astonish
torment	anguish
torment	agony
torturous	tormenting
uncanny	strange
vex	annoy

行　为

记忆小贴士:情景记忆法

　　情景记忆是对个人亲身经历过的、在一定时间和地点发生的事件或情景的记忆。在学习本章表示行为的单词时,回忆自己过去的相关经历,会起到事半功倍的效果。

帮 助

benevolent [bi'nevələnt] *adj.* 慈善的(charitable, generous)

【记】bene(好)+vol(心意)+ent

【例】Some *benevolent* soul donated clothes to the orphanage.

munificent [mjuː'nifisnt] *adj.* 慷慨的(generous, liberal)

【记】muni(礼物)+fic(做)+ent→做出来给大家→慷慨的

charity ['tʃæriti] *n.* 施舍(benevolence, altruism);慈善事业

【例】The *charity*'s goal is to help people help themselves.

charitable ['tʃæritəbl] *adj.* 慷慨的,慈善的(generous, benevolent)

【例】Because it was Susan's first offense, the judge was *charitable* and gave her probation.

generous ['dʒenərəs] *adj.* 慷慨的,大方的(lavish, handsome)

【记】gener(产生)+ous→(不断)产生,丰富的→慷慨的

generously ['dʒenərəsli] *adv.* 宽大地

obliging [ə'blaidʒiŋ] *adj.* 施恩的;愿帮忙的(helpful)

【例】He was so thankful for the *obliging* hostess who took care of him when he was ill.

sympathetic [ˌsimpə'θetik] *adj.* 同情的;和谐的

liberal ['libərəl] *adj.* 心胸宽大的(lenient, broad-minded);慷慨的

【记】liber(自由)+al→心胸自由

instrumental [ˌinstru'mentl] *adj.* 有帮助的(significant, useful)

gainful ['geinful] *adj.* 有利的,有报酬的(profitable, lucrative)

【记】gain(获得)+ful→有利的

【例】He kept on teaching in a small college, though he knows this job is not *gainful*.

benefit ['benifit] *vt.* 对…有益处

【例】Volunteer work *benefits* society.

beneficial [ˌbeni'fiʃəl] *adj.* 有益的(profitable, lucrative)

【例】Mary's college classes were *beneficial* to her career path.

prop [prɔp] *n./vt.* 支持(support, mainstay)

【例】Her daughter was the only *prop* to the old lady during her illness.

redress [ri'dres] *n.* 救济

compassion [kəm'pæʃn] *n.* 怜悯,同情(sympathy)

【记】com+pass(感情)+ion

【例】Everyone felt *compassion* for the mourning family.

assist [əˈsist] *vt.* 辅助(aid, help)

【例】A nurse a*ssisted* the surgeon during the operation.

extricate [ˈekstrikeit] *vt.* 救出；使解脱(release; liberate)

【记】ex＋tric(复杂)＋ate→从复杂中走出→解脱

【例】Jane *extricated* herself from an unhappy relationship with her boyfriend.

donate [ˈdəuneit] *vt.* 捐赠(contribute, present)

【例】Steve *donated* the old couch to charity.

raise [reiz] *vt.* 募捐

【例】He *raised* one million to help the orphan.

bestow [biˈstəu] *vt.* 赠予

【记】be＋stow(地方)→给予地方

【例】He was *bestowed* the honor of "hero citizen."

rescue [ˈreskjuː] *vt.* 拯救(save)

【例】The firefighter *rescued* six people from the burning building.

champion [ˈtʃæmpjən] *vt.* 支持(support)

【例】Bill *championed* the party's nominee for president.

salvage [ˈsælvidʒ] *vt.*(海上)救护，抢救(recover, rescue)

【例】I was able to *salvage* some data from the ruined computer file.

save [seiv] *v.* 拯救(rescue)

adopt [əˈdɔpt] *vt.* 收养(introduce)

【例】Because the Johnsons couldn't have children, they *adopted* an orphan.

保 护

assert [əˈsəːt] *vt.* 维护

【例】Employees should learn to *assert* their rights.

preserve [priˈzəːv] *vt.* 保存(keep, save, maintain)

【记】pre(预先)＋serve(保存)

【例】Max eats only good things hoping to *preserve* his health.

retain [riˈtein] *vt.* 保留(hold, reserve, withhold, keep)

【例】We *retained* the original fireplace when we redecorated the room.

shield [ʃild] *vt.* 庇护，保护（protect）

【例】He *shielded* me by claiming that he broke the window.

defend [di'fend] *vt.* 防护

【例】Mary *defended* her actions when she was accused of cheating.

escort [es'kɔːt] *vt.* 护送（accompany）

【例】A bodyguard *escorted* the celebrity around town.

convoy ['kɔnvɔi] *vt.* 护送（accompany, escort）

【记】con＋voy(路，看)→照看一路→护送

【例】The army *convoyed* the supply trucks to the center of the battle.

safeguard ['seifˌgɑːd] *vt.* 维护，保卫（protect）

【记】联想"舒肤佳"香皂

【例】We have found a way of *safeguarding* our money.

抽象行为

behave [bi'heiv] *v.* 举止端正，表现

【例】"*Behave* yourself", the mother warned her child.

behavior [bi'heivjə] *n.* 行为（conduct, deed）

conduct [kən'dʌkt] *v.* 行为（behave）

【例】She *conducted* herself stoically in her time of grief.

deport [di'pɔːt] *vt.* 举止

【例】She *deported* herself well.

abstract [æb'strækt] *adj.* 抽象的（theoretical, conceptual）

【例】Professor Brewer's books are very *abstract* and hard to read.

abstraction [æb'strækʃən] *n.* 抽象概念

【例】By looking at what happened in many similar cases, we were able to create an *abstraction* that also covered other instances.

action ['ækʃən] *n.* 行动（activity）

【例】The continuous *action* of the sewing machine shook the table.

处　理

shift　〔ʃift〕*n./v.* 转移；替换（change, alteration）

【例】Workers in this factory work on 3 *shifts*.

dissipate　〔ˈdisipeit〕*v.* 驱散，消散（disappear）

【例】The fog is *dissipating*.

deal　〔diːl〕*vi.* 处理

【例】You need to learn how to *deal* with problems like this.

dispose　〔disˈpəuz〕*vi.* 处理；丢掉（deal with; get rid of）

【例】Man proposes, God *disposes*.

bestow　〔biˈstəu〕*vt.* 应用，使用

【记】be＋stow（地方）→给予地方

【例】On this interesting story I *bestowed* much thought.

exert　〔igˈzəːt〕*vt.* 施加

【记】ex＋ert（力）→出力→施加

【例】He *exerted* more influence on the committee than anyone else.

displace　〔disˈpleis〕*vt.* 转移

【记】dis＋place（位置）→取代（位置）→转移

【例】My computer has *displaced* my old typewriter.

tackle　〔ˈtækl〕*vt.* 处理（deal, handle）

【例】Susan *tackled* the problem and solved it easily.

transact　〔trænˈzækt〕*vt.* 处理（deal, manage）

【例】These two companies often *transact* business over the phone.

discard　〔disˈkɑːd〕*vt.* 丢弃（reject）

【例】I tried to *discard* the old toys, but the children found them and put them back in the toy box.

utilize　〔ˈjuːtilaiz〕*vt.* 利用（use, make use of）

【例】Efficient workers *utilize* time wisely.

harness　〔ˈhɑːnis〕*vt.* 利用（utilize）

【例】Before steam engine was *harnessed* in the large machinery, the efficiency was very low.

arrange　〔əˈreindʒ〕*vt.* 排列（put together, plan）

【记】ar＋range（列）

【例】The florist *arranged* the roses in the vase.

reject　〔riˈdʒekt〕*vt.* 抛弃

【记】re(回)＋ject(扔)→扔回来，拒绝

cancel ['kænsl] *vt.* 取消(call off, nullify)

【例】The boss *canceled* the meeting.

undo [ʌn'duː] *vt.* 取消(cancel, annul)

【记】un(不)＋do(做)→取消

【例】What is done cannot be *undone*.

delete [di'liːt] *vt.* 删除(erase, remove from)

【例】References to places of battle were *deleted* from soldiers' letters during the war.

contrive [kən'traiv] *vt.* 设计(plan)

【例】Baby-sitters *contrive* ways to amuse the children.

implement ['impliment] *vt.* 实现(carry out, fulfil, execute)

【记】im(进入)＋ple(满)＋ment→使圆满→实现

【例】Once we made a plan, the remaining task would be to *implement* it.

effectuate [i'fektʃueit] *vt.* 使实现

【记】effect(效果)＋uate(表示动词)

【例】The scientists *effectuated* a shockwave.

glean [gliːn] *vt.* 收集(collect, gather)

【例】The scientists were delighted at these information *gleaned* from the investigation.

purge [pəːdʒ] *vt.* 消除(clear, purify)

【记】比较pure(纯的)

【例】The old tycoon did a lot of good deeds to *purge* away his sins.

erase [i'reiz] *vt.* 消除(eliminate)

【记】e＋rase(擦)

【例】Bill *erased* his mistake before turning in his assignment.

eradicate [i'rædikeit] *vt.* 根除(eliminate, get rid of, remove)

【例】One of the major goals of the government is to *eradicate* poverty in poor areas of China.

efface [i'feis] *vt.* 消除(erase)

【记】ef＋face(脸)→去掉表面→消除

【例】Weathering has *effaced* the inscription on the tombstone so that people cannot read it.

despatch [dis'pætʃ] *vt.* 迅速处理(dispose)

【例】The chairman *despatched* the meeting in 20 minutes.

forsake [fə'seik] *vt.* 遗弃，抛弃，摒绝（abandon, desert）
【记】for(god's)sake看在上帝的份儿上，不要抛弃我。
【例】I had to *forsake* my smoking habit because I was having trouble breathing.

adopt [ə'dɔpt] *vt.* 采用（foster）
【记】ad＋opt(选择)→采用
【例】Susan *adopted* a strict diet when she learned she was sick.

process [prɔ'ses] *vt.* 处理（treat）
【例】These materials are to be *processed* before they can be used.

scrap [skræp] *vt.* 废弃

abandon [ə'bændən] *vt.* 抛弃，放弃（discard, give up）
【记】a(没)＋bandon(权力)→不再有权力→抛弃
【例】He *abandoned* his wife and went away with all their money.

jettison ['dʒetisn] *vt.* 抛弃，丢弃（discard）
【例】The manager *jettisoned* the whole marketing plan.

促 进

impulsive [im'pʌlsiv] *adj.* 推动的（propelling, driving）

hasten ['heisn] *v.* 催促；赶紧（hurry; quicken）
【例】She *hastened* her to go to work.

urge [ə:dʒ] *v.* 推进；催促（advocate, encourage, impel, press）
【例】The teacher *urged* on the necessity of sufficient practice to achieve a high score.

prod [prɔd] *vt.* 刺激（poke, spur）
【例】Bob is lazy; he won't do any work if he's not *prodded* into it.

stimulate ['stimjuleit] *vt.* 刺激，激励，激发（motivate, encourage, incite, actuate）
【记】stimul(刺激)＋ate
【例】The mass was *stimulated* by his words and burned Caesar's house.

promote [prə'məut] *vt.* 促进
【记】pro(前)＋mote(动)→促进
【例】The go-between tried to *promote* relationship between the boy and the girl.

further [ˈfəːðə] *vt.* 促进，增进(advance, promote)

【例】He wants to *further* his education in China.

elicit [iˈlisit] *vt.* 得出，引出(provoke)

【例】After much questioning among the people concerned, the head-master at last *elicited* the truth about the incident.

instigate [ˈinstigeit] *vt.* 鼓动(prompt)

【记】in(进入)＋stig(刺激)＋ate→进入刺激→鼓动

【例】He *instigated* the ending of a free working lunch in the company.

encourage [inˈkʌridʒ] *vt.* 鼓励(urge)

【例】The coach *encouraged* Jimmy to practise more often.

inspire [inˈspaiə] *vt.* 鼓舞，激发(fire the imagination, encourage)

【例】I was *inspired* to work harder than ever before.

evoke [iˈvəuk] *vt.* 唤起(arouse, produce)

【记】e＋voke(喊)→喊出→唤起

【例】Bill's soft voice *evoked* a feeling of peace and calmness.

arouse [əˈrauz] *vt.* 唤起(awake, evoke)

【记】a＋rouse(唤起)

【例】A book with a very colorful cover *aroused* Bill's interest.

kindle [ˈkindl] *vt.* 激起

【记】比较candle(蜡烛)

【例】Her cruelty *kindled* hatred in my heart.

intensify [inˈtensifai] *vt.* 加强(enhance, strengthen)

【例】The general *intensified* the defense of the northern border by sending more troops there.

fortify [ˈfɔːtifai] *vt.* 加强(strengthen, reinforce)

【记】fort(强)＋ify→力量化→加强

【例】We *fortified* the bridge with extra supports.

propel [prəˈpel] *vt.* 推进，促进(drive, push forward)

【记】pro(前)＋pel(推)→推进

【例】The football player *propelled* the ball forward with a good kick.

foment [fəuˈment] *vt.* 引发(incite, stir up)

【记】比较ferment(酶，酝酿)

【例】The event *fomented* widespread public opinion.

incite [inˈsait] *vt.* 引起；激动；煽动(arouse, provoke; stir)

【记】in(进入)＋cite(唤起)→激起

【例】Troublemakers who *incite* riots are under arrest.

impulse [ˈimpʌls] *v.* 推动(urge, momentum)

【记】比较pulse(脉搏，跳动)

spur [spə:] *vt.* 刺激，鞭策(stimulate, provoke, urge)

【例】*Spurred* by his encouraging students, the teacher started to talk about his first love.

prompt [prɔmpt] *vt.* 鼓动(stimulate, motivate)

【例】The man confessed that poverty *prompted* him to steal.

得 到

due [dju:] *adj.* 应得的 *n.* 应得物

【例】You finally received your *due*.

attainment [əˈteinmənt] *n.* 成就(accomplishment, achievement)

【记】at＋tain(拿住)＋ment→得到的→成就

【例】*Attainment* of the Olympic gold medal thrilled the athlete.

gain [gein] *v.* 得到，赚到(acquire, benefit, earn, profit, win)

【例】The Smiths *gained* a small fortune in real estate.

obtain [əbˈtein] *vt.* 得到(acquire, attain, gain)

【例】His intelligent work has *obtained* him great fame.

seize [si:z] *vt.* 夺取，捕获(capture)

【例】The airfield was *seized* by enemy troops.

redeem [riˈdi:m] *vt.* 取回；赎回(rescue, save)

【记】re(重新)＋deem(买)→赎回

【例】I *redeemed* the watch that I had pawned at the pawn shop.

procure [prəˈkjuə] *vt.* 获得，取得(acquire, obtain)

【例】He swears he will *procure* a solution to this difficult problem.

acquire [əˈkwaiə] *vt.* 获得(obtain, attain)

【例】Susan *acquired* an appreciation of classical music.

acquisitive [əˈkwizitiv] *adj.* 可获得的

【记】ac＋quisit(得到)＋ive→一再得到→可获得的

【例】She boasts an *acquisitive* mind.

躲 避

elude [iˈluːd] *vt.* 躲避(escape, evade)
【记】e(出)＋lude(玩)→玩出去→躲出去
【例】The gangster *eluded* the police.

elusive [iˈluːsiv] *adj.* 躲避的
【记】e(出)＋lus(玩)＋ive
【例】We got a glimpse of the *elusive* movie star as he entered his private car.

sly [slai] *adj.* 躲躲闪闪的(secret, furtive)
【例】The *sly* spy managed to trap those loyal people.

evade [iˈveid] *vt.* 逃避，回避(dodge, avoid)
【记】e＋vade(走)→逃跑
【例】Jane *evaded* doing her chores at home by pretending to be sick.

evasive [iˈveisiv] *adj.* 逃避的，推诿的(elusive, equivocating)
【例】Anne's *evasive* manner caused me to doubt everything she said.

evasion [iˈveiʒən] *n.* 逃避
【例】John's *evasion* of questions about where he was last night alarmed his parents.

escape [isˈkeip] *v.* 避免；逃避
【例】My birds *escaped* when I accidentally left their cage open.

shun [ʃʌn] *vt.* 避开(avoid, eschew)
【例】John *shuns* businesses that don't employ union labor.

eschew [isˈtʃuː] *vt.* 避开；远离(avoid; shun)
【例】Jane *eschews* both alcohol and tobacco.

✓ **avoid** [əˈvɔid] *vt.* 避免，回避，躲开(shun, escape)
【例】I drove carefully to *avoid* an accident.

dodge [dɔdʒ] *vt.* 躲开；逃避责任(avoid; evade)
【例】The politician *dodged* many controversial issues in her speech.

avert [əˈvəːt] *vt.* 转移；避免，防止(shift; prevent, avoid)
【记】a＋vert(转)→转开→避免
【例】She *averted* her eyes from the dying child.

反　抗

insubordinate [ˌinsəˈbɔːdənit] *adj.* 不服从的（disobedient, rebellious）
【记】in(不)＋subordinate(服从的)

defiant [diˈfaiənt] *adj.* 大胆反抗的（hostile, rebellious）
【例】The *defiant* teenager frequently skipped school.

opposed [əˈpəuzd] *adj.* 反对的
【记】oppose(反对)＋d

rebellion [riˈbeljən] *n.* 反抗（revolt, opposition）
【记】re(反)＋bell(打斗)＋ion→反抗

resist [riˈzist] *v.* 抵抗（oppose）
【记】re(始终)＋sist(坐)→始终以静坐抵抗
【例】They found a bacterium that *resisted* the antibiotic.

demur [diˈməː] *vi.* 抗议（protest, object）
【例】The workers *demur* at working on Sundays.

traverse [trəˈvəːs] *vt.* 反对
【记】tra(横)＋verse(转)→横过

defy [diˈfai] *vt.* 蔑视，反抗
【例】If you *defy* the law, you'll be sent to prison.

反　叛

outrageous [autˈreidʒəs] *adj.* 暴乱的（offensive, disgraceful）

turbulent [ˈtəːbjulənt] *adj.* 骚动的，骚乱的（violent）

riot [ˈraiət] *n.* 暴乱，骚动（disturbance, disorder, chaos）

defection [diˈfekʃən] *n.* 背叛，缺陷
【记】de(坏)＋fect(做)＋ion→做坏事→背叛

uprising [ˈʌpraiziŋ] *n.* 叛乱
【记】来自rise up(起义)

uproar [ˈʌprɔː] *n.* 骚动，
【记】up(上)＋roar(吼叫)

turmoil [ˈtəːmɔil] *n.* 骚动；混乱（disorder, chaos）
【记】tur＋moil(喧闹)→混乱
【例】The *turmoil* of exams made the students very irritable.

treason [ˈtriːzn] *n.* 通敌，叛国罪（treachery）

rebel [re'bel] *vi.* 谋反

【例】 The students *rebelled* against their government.

rebellion [ri'beljən] *n.* 造反，叛乱

【记】 re(反)＋bell(打斗)＋ion→反抗

betray [bi'trei] *vt.* 背叛

【记】 be＋tray(盘子)→和盘托出→背叛

【例】 The soldier *betrayed* his country and gave top secret to the enemy.

subvert [səb'vəːt] *vt.* 颠覆，推翻(destroy, undermine)

【记】 sub(下面)＋vert(转)→下面转变→颠覆

【例】 Writings that *subvent* the Christianity are forbidden.

plot [plɔt] *vt.* 密谋，策划(plan, map out, outline)

【例】 They are *plotting* to rob a bank.

overturn [ˌəuvə'təːn] *v.* 推翻，颠倒

否 定

exclusion [iks'kluːʒən] *n.* 拒绝(rejection)

【例】 The *exclusion* of women from the temple made them feel sad.

decline [di'klain] *v.* 拒绝(refuse)

【例】 I *declined* their offer of help.

relinquish [ri'liŋkwiʃ] *vt.* 放弃(abandon, give up, quit)

【记】 re(再次)＋linqu(离开)＋ish→再次离开→放弃

【例】 The soldiers had to *relinquish* some unwieldy equipment to their enemies during their retreat.

renounce [ri'nauns] *vt.* 放弃，否认(abandon, reject)

【记】 re(反)＋nounce(说)→否认

【例】 She *renounced* the position when she got pregnant.

gainsay ['geinsei] *vt.* 否认(deny)

【记】 gain=against(反对)＋say(说)→否认

【例】 He is a good man; there is no *gainsaying* his innocence.

deny [di'nai] *vt.* 否认

【例】 They *denied* the fact by making a fake story.

disclaim [dis'kleim] *vt.* 拒绝承认，否认(refuse)

【记】 dis＋claim(喊)

【例】 Each employee *disclaimed* responsibility for the mistake.

reject ［ri'dʒekt］ *vt.* 拒收(refuse, turn down)

【记】re(回)+ject(扔)→扔回来→拒收

【例】He *rejected* their invitation point-blank.

服　从

submit ［səb'mit］ *vi.* 服从(give in, yield)

【例】Christians *submit* themselves to God's will.

submissive ［səb'misiv］ *adj.* 顺从的(obedient, meek)

submission ［səb'miʃən］ *n.* 屈服；服从

【记】sub(下面)+miss(放)+ion→放在下面→屈服

subjection ［səb'dʒekʃən］ *n.* 服从(subjugation, subduing)

obedience ［ə'biːdjəns］ *n.* 服从，顺从(deference, submission)

【记】动词obey(服从)

【例】I was pleased by my dog's *obedience* to my commands.

succumb ［sə'kʌm］ *vi.* 屈服(submit, yield)

【例】The country *succumbed* after only a short siege.

enthrall ［in'θrɔːl］ *vt.* 使服从

【记】en+thrall(奴隶)→使服从

【例】The magician *enthralled* us with fascinating tricks.

defer ［di'fəː］ *vi.* 服从，屈从(yield)

【记】de(坏)+fer(带来)

【例】He *defferred* to Tim's superior knowledge.

负面效果行为

lash ［læʃ］ *v.* 鞭打(whip, flog)

【例】The horse was *lashed* because it lagged.

sustain ［sə'stein］ *vt.* 遭受(suffer)

【例】He *sustained* a fatal injury in the accident.

pervert ［pəː'vəːt］ *vt.* 导入邪途；曲解(deviate, distort)

【记】per(全部)+vert(转)→全都转到邪道

【例】The analysis *perverts* the meaning of the poem.

coddle ［'kɔdl］ *vt.* 娇养，溺爱

【例】You *coddle* your children too much. They are getting spoiled.

entail ［in'teil］ *vt.* 惹起；使负担(require; involve)

【例】The task *entailed* strict attention to procedure.

inflict [in'flikt] *vt.* 使遭受(损伤、苦痛等)(incur, impose)

【记】in(进入)+flict(打斗)→导致痛苦

【例】The economic depression has *inflicted* hundreds of millions of loss in Asia.

distort [dis'tɔːt] *vt.* 歪曲(misrepresent, twist)

【例】An electrical disturbance *distorted* the picture on the television set.

abuse [ə'bjuːz] *vt.* 滥用

【记】ab(不)+use(使用)→不正当使用→滥用

【例】Rulers who *abuse* their power should be removed from office.

改 良

correct [kə'rekt] *adj.* 正确的 *vt.* 纠正(ratify)

【记】cor+rect(直，正)

【例】The answers have been *corrected* at the back of the workbook.

innovation [ˌinəu'veiʃən] *n.* 改革，革新(reformation)

【记】innovate(革新)+ion

【例】Susan's design *innovations* saved the company a great deal of money.

modify ['mɔdifai] *vt.* 修改(change, adapt)

【记】mod(方式，规范)+ify→规范化→修改

【例】I *modified* my travel plans by staying an extra night in Rome.

modification [ˌmɔdifi'keiʃən] *n.* 更改，修改(change)

ornament ['ɔːnəmənt] *n.* 装饰物；装修(decoration, embellishment)

【记】orn(装饰)+ament

coax [kəuks] *vt.* 耐心调理

【例】Jane *coaxed* her little baby to sleep.

gild [gild] *vt.* 虚饰(embellish)

【例】She was *gilding* the lily by attaching something unnecessary to the new car.

modulate ['mɔdjuleit] *vt.* 调整(change, modify)

【记】mod(方式，模式)+ulate→对模式进行调整→调整

【例】The opera singer *modulated* her voice skillfully.

mend [mend] *vt.* 改正，修正(revise, correct)；改进

【例】We must do something to *mend* his reputation.

renovate ['renəuveit] *vt.* 革新(renew, restore)

【记】re(重新)+nov(新)+ate→重新翻新→革新

【例】The school is closed for *renovation*.

substantiate [səbs'tænʃieit] *vt.* 加强(corroborate, verify)

【例】Evidences *substantiated* that he was the murderer.

strengthen ['streŋθən] *v.* 加强, 巩固(reinforce)

【例】Our enemy has greatly *strengthened* during the truce talks.

reinforce [,ri:in'fɔ:s] *vt.* 加强, 加固(increase, strengthen)

【记】re(再次)+in+force(力量)→再次增加力量

【例】The Congress passed a bill on *reinforcing* information technology in the coming decade.

garnish ['gɑ:niʃ] *vt.* 加装饰(adorn, decorate)

【记】garn=gar(花)+ish→用花来装饰

【例】The cool drink was *garnished* with a slice of lemon.

embellish [em'beliʃ] *vt.* 装饰, 修饰(decorate, adorn)

【记】em+bell(美)+ish→使美

【例】Anne *embellished* the shirt collar with lace.

embroider [im'brɔidə] *vt.* 装饰

【记】em+broider(刺绣)→用刺绣来装饰

【例】Susan *embroidered* the edges of all her pillowcases.

temper ['tempə] *v.* 缓和, 调节(modify, modulate)

【例】He *tempered* his doctrinaire logic with a little practical wisdom.

adjust [ə'dʒʌst] *vt.* 调节; 使适于(adapt)

【记】ad+just(合适的)

【例】Mary *adjusted* the TV to get a clearer picture.

refine [ri'fain] *vt.* 精炼, 精制

【例】He needs to *refine* his style of writing.

干 涉

conciliatory [kən'siliətəri] *adj.* 善于调解的(reconciling)

【记】concil(协商)+iatory

【例】One of the diplomats made a few *conciliatory* suggestions that helped bring about a truce.

hurdle [ˈhəːdl] *n.* 障碍(barrier, obstacle)

barrier [ˈbæriə] *n.* 栅栏，屏障，障碍(obstacle, block, barricade)

【例】 The *barrier* between the desks gave both workers some privacy.

barricade [ˈbærikeid] *n.* 障碍物(barrier, impediment)

【记】 barric(阻止)＋ade

【例】 The students erected a *barricade* on campus as a protest.

obstacle [ˈɔbstəkl] *n.* 障碍(barrier, impediment)

snag [snæg] *n.* 障碍(disadvantage, obstacle)

【例】 The ship stroke a *snag* near the bank of the river.

forestall [fɔːˈstɔːl] *v.* 预先阻止(prevent, preempt)

【例】 Bill *forestalled* a major crisis by taking care of small problems before they became worse.

intercede [intəˈsiːd] *vi.* 调停，求情(intervene, mediate)

【记】 inter(中间)＋cede(走)→在中间奔走→调停

【例】 Whenever I argued with my brother, my parents would *intercede*.

intercept [intəˈsept] *vt.* 中途拦截；阻止(hold back, stop)

【记】 inter(中间)＋cept(拿)→拦截

【例】 John threw the football to Susan, but Bob *intercepted it*.

intervene [ˌintəˈviːn] *vi.* 干涉(interfere, influence)

【记】 inter(中间)＋vene(来)→来到中间→干涉

【例】 The brothers wouldn't stop arguing until their mother *intervened*.

interfere [ˌintəˈfiə] *vi.* 干涉，干预(intervene, meddle)；妨碍

【例】 Please stop *interfering*. This is none of your business.

meddle [ˈmedl] *vi.* 干预(interfere, intervene)

【例】 Few people like someone who *meddles* in the affairs of others.

tamper [ˈtæmpə] *vi.* 干预(interfere, intervene)

【例】 The secretary *tampered* with the prime minister's schedule.

mediate [ˈmiːdieit] *vt.* 调停(intercede, intervene)

【记】 medi(中间)＋ate→在中间(走)→调停

【例】 The UN is reponsible for *mediating* between two countries which are at war.

balk [bɔːk] *vt.* 妨碍(block, hinder, stall)

【例】 His plan was *balked*.

hinder [ˈhində] *vt.* 妨碍(hamper, impede, retard)

【例】The tall fence *hindered* the children from going to the lake.

hamper ['hæmpə] *vt.* 妨碍(hinder, impede, handicap)

【例】The fierce storm *hampered* our efforts to get to town by sunset.

handicap ['hændikæp] *vt.* 妨碍; 使不利(hamper, impede, obstruct)

【例】A sore throat *handicapped* the singer.

incapacitate [ˌinkə'pæsiteit] *vt.* 使不能(disable, handicap)

【记】比较capacity(能力)

【例】Poor health *incapacitated* him from work all his life.

prevent [pri'vent] *vt.* 阻碍(block, cumber, hinder, obstruct)

【例】His laziness *prevented* his career.

clog [klɔg] *vt.* 阻碍(block, jam)

【记】分割记忆c＋log(圆木头)

【例】The accident *clogged* the highway and caused a traffic jam.

stunt [stʌnt] *vt.* 阻碍(hinder, impede)

【例】The barren environment *stunt* the tree from developing into a big one.

encumber [in'kʌmbə] *vt.* 阻碍, 妨碍(burden, hamper)

【记】en＋cumber(躺)→躺着不动→阻碍

【例】there is a hiker who was *encumbered* with a heavy pack.

obstruct [əb'strʌkt] *vt.* 阻碍, 妨碍(hinder, impede)

【记】ob(反)＋struct(建造)→违规建造→妨碍

【例】Some paper got in the sink and *obstructed* the drain.

foil [fɔil] *vt.* 阻止(defeat, frustrate)

【例】What ultimately *foiled* his victory was his flawed character.

block [blɔk] *vt.* 阻碍(hinder, obstruct)

【例】The tree *blocked* our view.

跟 踪

trace [treis] *n.* 痕迹(remnant, residue) *vt.* 跟踪, 追溯(detect)

【例】The cunning fox leaves no *traces* for the hunters. / Trapper who *traced* the fox for five consecutive weeks finally captured it.

vestige ['vestidʒ] *n.* 痕迹, 遗迹(remnant, trace)

stalk [stɔːk] *v.* 跟踪(猎物)(trace)

【例】The hunter carefully *stalked* the deer.

entrap [in'træp] *vt.* 以网或陷阱捕捉(trick, entice)

【记】en+trap(陷阱)

【例】The hounds *entrapped* the fox.

固 定

stationary ['steiʃənəri] *adj.* 固定的(fixed, immobile, static)

【例】I think your arm is broken. Try to keep it *stationary* until we get to the hospital.

immobile [i'məubail] *adj.* 固定的(fixed, stationary)

【记】im(不)+mobile(能动的); 比较mobile phone(移动电话)

fix [fiks] *v.* 固定(set, determine)

【例】He *fixed* a picture to the wall.

fixed [fikst] *adj.* 固定的(stationary)

【记】fix(固定)+ed

【例】Since this is a new company, there are no *fixed* rules.

solidly ['sɔlidli] *adv.* 牢固地(squarely, firmly)

【例】He bases his hypothesis *solidly* on Newton's theory.

locate ['ləukeit] *vt.* 设置, 使位于(situate, set)

【记】loc(地方)+ate→(找出)地方所在→使位于

【例】The new building will be *located* in the center of town.

bear [bɛə] *vt.* 支撑(support, stand)

【例】Can the ice *bear* my weight?

install [in'stɔ:l] *vt.* 安装, 设置(set up, equip)

【记】in(进入)+stall(停止)→停放在里面→安装

【例】In order to make the computer operate better, they need to *install* the new software.

set [set] *vt.* 放置(situate) *adj.* 固定的(prescribed, fixed)

【例】The movie was *set* in the platform of the railway station.

sustain [sə'stein] *vt.* 支撑, 维持(stand, keep, prolong)

【例】Mary *sustained* her plants with plenty of water and sunshine.

brace [breis] *vt.* 支持, 使固定(strengthen, support) *n.* 支撑物

【例】The rope acted as a *brace* to hold the tree upright.

观　察

perceive [pəˈsiːv] *vt.* 察觉到，看见(discern, see)
【记】per(全部)＋ceive(拿到)→觉察
【例】The world we *perceived* is only a small part of the real world.

perceptive [pəˈseptiv] *adj.* 感觉敏锐的，观察入微的(discerning, penetrating)
【记】per(全部)＋cept(知道)＋ive
【例】A *perceptive* scholar questioned the professor's theory.

detect [diˈtekt] *vt.* 探测，发觉(explore, discover)
【例】I *detected* Bob's lie because he wouldn't look at me directly.

detectable [diˈtektəbl] *adj.* 可发觉的，可看穿的(apparent, measurable)

discernible [diˈsɜːnəbl] *adj.* 可觉察的

inquiry [ˈinkwaiəri] *n.* 调查研究(investigation, quest)

observe [əbˈzɜːv] *vt.* 看到(watch)
【记】TOEFL常考词义为"遵守"

observation [ˌɔbzəˈveiʃən] *n.* 观察
【记】动词observe(观，看)

perspective [pəˈspektiv] *n.* 透视；观点(view, outlook)
【记】per(全部)＋spect(看)＋ive→远景
【例】Her ability to use *perspective* gives the appearance of depth to her art.

insight [ˈinsait] *n.* 洞察力，见识(understanding)

investigate [inˈvestigeit] *v.* 调查，研究(research, survey)
【例】The police would *investigate* this accident.

pierce [piəs] *vt.* 洞察
【例】Large glowing yellow eyes *pierced* the darkness.

survey [səˈvei] *vt.* 调查(review, research)；遵守
【例】Two women were *surveying* the other people on the platform.

scan [skæn] *vt.* 浏览，扫描(browse)
【例】They *scanned* the picture and stored it on the disk.

skim [skim] *vt.* 略读(scan)
【例】He *skims* the book and says it has no use.

spot [spɔt] *vt.* 认出(notice, see, sight)

【例】The amateur *spotted* the comet before the pros.

identify [aiˈdentifai] *vt.* 认出(recognize)

【记】iden(相同)+tify→和(记忆中)相同→认出

【例】The doctor *identified* the disease that made me sick.

realize [ˈriəlaiz] *vt.* 认识到

【例】The man laughed when he *realized* what had happened.

scrutinize [ˈskruːtinaiz] *vt.* 细察(examine, inspect)

【记】scrutin(检查)+ize

【例】The lawyer had *scrutinized* all the documents related to this case.

locate [ˈləukeit] *vt.* 找出(find)

【记】loc(地方)+ate→找出地方所在

【例】They tried to *locate* the source of error.

坚 持

irreconcilable [iˈrekənsailəbl] *adj.* 不能妥协的(unconformable, incompatible)

【记】ir(不)+reconcilable(可以和解的)

indomitable [inˈdɔmitəbl] *adj.* 不屈不挠的(invincible, relentless)

【记】in(不)+domit(支配，统治)+able→不可支配的

sturdy [ˈstəːdi] *adj.* 不屈的, 顽强的(strong, stout)

【例】The *sturdy* bridge withstood the shaking of the earthquake.

obstinate [ˈɔbstinit] *adj.* 固执的(stubborn)

【记】ob+stin(站)+ate→坚决站着→固执的

bigoted [ˈbigətid] *adj.* 固执己见的(narrow-minded, intolerant)

【例】The *bigoted* manager refused to hire minority workers.

persistent [pəˈsistənt] *adj.* 坚持不懈的(dogged)

【记】per(始终)+sist(坐)+ent→始终坐着→坚持不懈地(背单词)

【例】I told the *persistent* salesman to leave me alone.

inflexible [inˈfleksəbl] *adj.* 坚定的(rigid, unbending)

【记】in(不)+flexible(灵活的)

steadfast [ˈstedfæst] *adj.* 坚决, 坚定, 不变的(firm, unchanging)

unshaken [ʌnˈʃeikən] *adj.* 坚决的, 不动摇的

【记】un(不)+shaken(动摇)

durable [ˈdjuərəbl] *adj.* 耐久的, 耐用的(lasting, enduring)

【记】dur(持续)+able

【例】This very *durable* watch is both waterproof and shatterproof.

tough [tʌf] *adj.* 强硬的，坚韧的，粗暴的(strong, hard)

【例】That cop is really *tough;* she never let any burglar go away out of her hand.

headstrong ['hedstrɔːŋ] *adj.* 顽固的(obstinate, stubborn)

stubborn ['stʌbən] *adj.* 顽固的

tenacious [tə'neiʃəs] *adj.* 抓住不放的，顽强的(stubborn, resolute)

【记】ten(拿)+acious

【例】The *tenacious* applicant soon got the job.

resolute ['rezəluːt] *adj.* 坚决的 (firm, determined, steadfast)

hardheaded [hɑːd'hedid] *adj.* 顽固的(stubborn, obstinate)

【记】hard(硬的)+head(想法)+ed→铁石心肠的

stoically ['stəuikli] *adv.* 坚韧地

fortitude ['fɔːtitjuːd] *n.* 坚忍，刚毅(endurance, courage)

【记】fort(强)+itude表示状态→强的状态

【例】The soldiers were given a medal for their *fortitude* during the battle.

resist [ri'zist] *v.* 坚持(withstand)

【记】re(始终)+sist(坐)→始终坐着→坚持

【例】He could *resist* no longer.

remain [ri'mein] *vi.* 保持，逗留(stay)

【例】He *remained* at home for the whole day waiting for his lovely girlfriend to come.

persevere [ˌpəːsi'viə] *vi.* 坚持，不屈不挠

【记】比较severe(严重)

【例】You will need to *persevere* if you want the business to succeed.

perseverance [ˌpəːsi'viərəns] *n.* 坚定不移(persistance, endurance)

maintain [mein'tein] *vt.* 坚持(认为)(keep, sustain, persist, insist)

【记】main=man(手)+tain(拿)→用手拿住→保持

【例】No matter how hard we tried to persuade him, he *maitained* his wrong idea.

insist [in'sist] *vt.* 主张；坚持说(claim; adhere)

【例】She *insisted* that she never wanted to play hero in the battle.

揭 示

implicit [im'plisit] *adj.* 暗示的(inferred, implied)
【记】im(进入)+plic(重叠)+it→重叠状态→含蓄的

reflection [ri'flekʃən] *n.* 反映(indication, revelation)
【例】Your tone of voice is a *reflection* of your attitude.

expose [iks'pəuz] *vt.* 使暴露，受到，揭露(uncover, subject to)
【例】The ocean bottom is *exposed* to a pressure hundreds of times bigger than that of the surface of the earth.

exposure [iks'pəuʒə] *n.* 曝光(disclosure, uncovering)
【例】Because of the reporter's *exposure* of fraud, the bank president was sentenced to prison.

reveal [ri'vi:l] *vt.* 展现；揭露(exhibit, expose, disclose)
【例】The doctor didn't *reveal* the truth to him.

revelation [ˌrevə'leiʃən] *n.* 显示；揭露(disclosure)

unveil [ʌn'veil] *v.* 揭露，显露(disclose, reveal)
【记】un(不)+veil(罩面纱)→揭开
【例】Anne *unveiled* her painting at the opening of the art exhibit.

show [ʃəu] *v.* 展示(demonstrate)
【例】The jeweler *showed* the necklace to the customer.

transpire [træn'spaiə] *vt.* 泄露
【例】It was *transpired* that the king was already dead.

profess [prə'fes] *vt.* 表示(allege, claim, state)
【例】Don't ask me. I didn't *profess* I was an expert.

signify ['signifai] *vt.* 表示，意味着(indicate, mean)
【例】Dark clouds *signify* that it will rain soon.

bare [bɛə] *vt.* 露出(expose)
【例】The dog *bared* its teeth and growled.

exhibit [ig'zibit] *vt.* 显示(show)
【记】ex(出)+hibit(拿)→拿出→展览
【例】Jane *exhibited* her sculptures at the art museum.

leak [li:k] *vt.* 泄漏(seep, escape)
【例】A spy is expected never to *leak* anything to the opponent, while at the same time get as much information as possible.

divulge [dai'vʌldʒ] *vt.* 泄露(disclose; reveal)

【例】The president asked the managers not to *divulge* the news of the merger.

denote [di'nəut] *vt.* 指示；表示(indicate, show)

【记】de(加强)＋note(注意)→加强注意→指示

【例】The mark'∧'*denotes* a place of omission.

indicate ['indikeit] *vt.* 指示；表示(show, suggest, hint)

【记】in＋dic(言, 说)＋ate→表示

【例】The smile on the old man's face *indicates* that he appreciated my help very much.

betray [bi'trei] *vt.* 泄漏(expose)

【记】be＋tray(盘子)→和盘托出→泄漏

【例】His accent *betrayed* him a southerner.

控 制

irrepressible [,iri'presəbl] *adj.* 不可压制的；难以征服的 (insuppressible, uncontrolled)

【记】ir(不)＋repressible(可以压制的)；比较press(压, 按)

unruly [ʌn'ru:li] *adj.* 难控制的(uncontrollable)

【记】un(不)＋rul(e)(法)＋y

operate ['ɔpəreit] *vt.* 操纵(manipulate, navigate, steer)

【例】He who doesn't know how to *oprerate* a computer will be left behind the information age.

handle ['hændl] *vt.* 操纵

【记】hand(手)＋le→操纵

【例】I'm under so much pressure that I can't *handle* it anymore.

理 解

intelligible [in'telidʒəbl] *adj.* 可理解的(apprehensible)

evident ['evidənt] *adj.* 明白的(obvious, manifest)

【记】e＋vid=vis(看)＋ent

【例】The happy couple's love for each other is *evident*.

explicit [iks'plisit] *adj.* 明确的；清楚的(straightforward)

【例】The new tax law is *explicit;* that type of certificate is tax exempt.

elusive [i'lu:siv] *adj.* 难懂的(elusory, intangible)

【记】e(出)＋lus(玩)＋ive→耍人→让人难懂的

【例】The boy was annoyed by the *elusive* words while reading the story.

mysterious [mis'tiəriəs] *adj.* 神秘的；难以理解的(cryptic; undecipherable)

ignorant ['ignərənt] *adj.* 无知的，不了解的(unaware)

【例】He who is *ignorant* of the situation can't really understand me.

ignorance ['ignərəns] *n.* 无知

【记】ig(不)＋nor(知道)＋ance

grasp [græsp] *n./v.* 领会，理解(understanding, comprehension)

【例】It is said that you do not need to have a *grasp* of English language to test well.

comprehend [,kɔmpri'hend] *vt.* 理解(understand)

【例】I could not *comprehend* the instructions for operating the computer.

comprehensive [,kɔmpri'hensiv] *adj.* 综合的；有理解力的

【例】A *comprehensive* survey was used to determine public opinion.

掠 夺

rapacious [rə'peiʃəs] *adj.* 强夺的

【记】rap(抓，夺)＋acious

strip [strip] *vt.* 剥，夺去(deprive, take off)

【例】He *stripped* the paper off the wall.

bereave [bi'ri:v] *vt.* 剥夺(deprive, be devoid of)

【记】be＋reave(抢夺)

【例】He was *bereaved* of his wife last year.

loot [lu:t] *vt.* 掠夺(plunder, seize)

【例】Following the explosions in the town centre, groups of robbers *looted* the shops.

harry ['hæri] *vt.* 掠夺；折磨(harass, pester)

【例】We have to *harry* him for money.

ravage ['rævidʒ] *vt.* 掠夺

【例】A tornado *ravaged* the countryside.

grind [graind] *vt.* 折磨；压榨(crush, mill)

【例】Laws *grind* the poor, and rich men rule the law.

torment ['tɔ:ment] *vt.* 折磨(anguish, agony)

【例】The murderer was *tormented* by guilt.

迷　惑

equivocal [i'kwivəkəl] *adj.* 模棱两可的，意义不清的（ambiguous）

【记】equi(平的)＋voc(声音)＋al→用平平的声音→意义不清的

enigma [i'nigmə] *n.* 谜（mystery）

【例】The *enigma* surrounding the murder perplexed the detective.

enigmatic [ˌenig'mætik] *adj.* 像谜般的，神秘的（mysterious, secretive）

【例】The Egyptian pyramids seem quite *enigmatic* to the people of modern times.

maze [meiz] *n.* 迷宫；迷惑（complexity, labyrinth）

【记】比较maize(玉米)

labyrinth ['læbərinθ] *n.* 迷宫；错综复杂之事件

riddle ['ridl] *n.* 谜（puzzle, mystery）

puzzle ['pʌzl] *n.* 难题，谜（mystery）*v.*(使)迷惑

elude [i'luːd] *vt.* 困惑

【记】e(出)＋lude(玩)→玩出去→躲出去

【例】The gangster *eluded* the police.

captivate ['kæptiveit] *vt.* 迷惑（attract, fascinate, enamour）

【例】The entertaining game *captivated* the children.

enthrall [in'θrɔːl] *vt.* 迷惑（captivate）

【记】en＋thrall(奴隶)

【例】The magician *enthralled* us with fascinating tricks.

bewilder [bi'wildə] *vt.* 迷惑，把…弄糊涂（befuddle, confuse）

【例】Jimmy's strange behavior *bewildered* his parents.

perplex [pə'pleks] *vt.* 迷惑，困惑，难住（puzzle, confuse）

【记】per(全部)＋plex(交错重叠)→困惑

【例】The question *perplexed* me.

tangle ['tæŋgl] *vt.* 使缠结，使纠缠（knot, snarl）

【例】Her hair got all *tangled* up in the fence.

confound [kən'faund] *vt.* 使糊涂，迷惑（confuse, puzzle）

【例】My computer *confounds* and annoys me daily.

entangle [in'tæŋgl] *vt.* 使纠缠；使迷惑（embroil; involve）

【记】en＋tangle(纠缠)

【例】The fishing line became *entangled* in the weeds.

fascinate ['fæsineit] *vt.* 使迷惑（enchant, enthrall, intrigue）

【例】He's *fascinated* with Buddhist ceremonies.

blur [blə:] *vt.* 使模糊(become indistinct)

【例】His eyes were *blurred* with tears.

dazzle [ˈdæzl] *vt.* 使目眩；使迷惑(blind, bewilder)

【例】The excellent performance *dazzled* the audience.

判 断

dogmatic [dɔgˈmætik] *adj.* 教条的；武断的(opinionated; arbitrary)

【例】The book explained the *dogmatic* principles of the religion.

illegible [iˈledʒəbl] *adj.* 难辨认的(unreadable)

【记】il(不)+legible(可读的)→不能读的

【例】Parts of the document are faded and *illegible*.

pending [ˈpendiŋ] *adj.* 未决的(suspending)

【记】pend(挂)+ing

【例】The date of our next meeting is still *pending*.

resolve [riˈzɔlv] *vt.* 决定(determine)

【例】He *resolved* on going out.

resolved [riˈzɔlvd] *adj.* 下定决心的

determine [diˈtə:min] *vt.* 决定(fix, calculate, evaluate)

【例】Anne has *determined* that she will win the election.

determination [diˌtə:miˈneiʃən] *n.* 决定，决心

【例】Jane's *determination* to overcome her handicap was an inspiration to everyone.

discretion [disˈkreʃən] *n.* 判断力

【例】The decorator showed no *discretion* in her purchases for our new house, everything costing too much money.

decide [diˈsaid] *v.* 决定(determine)

【例】I could not *decide* on what to order from the menu.

deem [di:m] *v.* 认为(think, consider)

【例】He *deems* highly of this plan.

vindicate [ˈvindikeit] *vt.* 辨明

【例】I consider that I have been completely *vindicated*.

discern [dɪˈsɜːn] vt. 辨明(detect, distinguish)
【例】I can't *discern* the difference between the twins.

assert [əˈsɜːt] vt. 断言, 宣称(declare)
【例】The lawyer *asserted* that his client was innocent.

conclude [kənˈkluːd] vt. 推断出, 断定
【例】The scientist examined the data and *concluded* that the theory was invalid.

affirm [əˈfɜːm] vt. 断言
【记】af(一再)+firm(肯定)→断言
【例】The court *affirmed* the accused to be innocent.

破　坏

breakdown [ˈbreɪkdaʊn] n. 崩溃, 倒塌; 失败
【例】After his father's death, Tom was on the verge of a *breakdown*.

collapse [kəˈlæps] n./v. 倒塌, 崩溃(crash)
【记】col(共同)+lapse(滑下)→倒塌
【例】Jane's marriage *collapsed* after only three years. / The *collapse* of the stock market in 1929 signaled the beginning of the Depression.

breach [briːtʃ] n. 破裂(opening, break)
【例】The flood was caused by a small *breach* in the dam.

shatter [ˈʃætə] n. 碎片(fragment) v. 粉碎(break)
【例】The explosion *shattered* every window in the house.

scrap [skræp] n. 碎片, 废料

fragment [ˈfrægmənt] n. 碎片, 破片(piece, scrap)
【记】frag(随)+ment

fracture [ˈfræktʃə] n./v. 断裂(break)
【记】fract(碎裂)+ure→碎的状态→骨折

rupture [ˈrʌptʃə] n./v. 破裂, 决裂(burst, breach)
【记】rupt(断)+ure
【例】Water streamed from the *rupture* in the pipe.

crumble [ˈkrʌmbl] v. 粉碎, 崩溃(collapse, crash)
【记】比较crumb(面包屑, 小量)
【例】His last hope *crumbled* to nothing.

squash [skwɒʃ] v. 压碎(flatten, squeeze)

【例】The ripe tomato *squashed* when it fell to the floor.

crash [kræʃ] *v.* 撞碎(crumble, shatter)

【例】The vase *crashed* when it fell off the bookcase.

ravage ['rævidʒ] *vt.* 破坏(devastate, ruin)

【例】A tornado *ravaged* the countryside.

raze [reiz] *vt.* 摧毁(damage, bulldoze, demolish)

【例】The old school was *razed* to ground and a new one was built.

demolish [di'mɔliʃ] *vt.* 破坏(destroy, raze)

【记】demol(破坏)+ish

【例】The car was *demolished* in the accident.

disfigure [dis'figə] *vt.* 破坏(destroy, wreck)

【记】dis+figure(形象)→破坏(形象)

【例】The forest fire *disfigured* the landscape.

frustrate ['frʌstreit] *vt.* 破坏；挫败(baffle, thwart)

【例】The failure in the first battle *frustrated* the soldiers.

smash [smæʃ] *vt.* 破碎(shatter, destroy)

【例】I accidentally *smashed* the window with a baseball.

devastate ['devəsteit] *vt.* 使荒废；破坏(destroy, demolish)

【记】de+vast(大量)+ate→大量弄坏

【例】Hurricanes often *devastate* the coffee crop.

devastation [ˌdevəs'teiʃən] *n.* 毁坏

disrupt [dis'rʌpt] *vt.* 使中断，使分裂(disturb, disorder)

【记】比较rupture(破裂)

【例】An emergency announcement *disrupted* the TV show.

mangle ['mæŋgl] *vt.* 撕裂，毁坏(mutilate)

【记】比较mingle(混合)

【例】The symphony was dreadfully *mangled*.

spoil [spɔil] *vt.* 损坏，糟蹋(decay, ruin, rot, go bad)；宠坏

【例】Mary *spoiled* her children with expensive toys.

engulf [in'gʌlf] *vt.* 吞没，吞食(devour, swallow)

【记】en+gulf(沟)→使入沟→吞没

【例】Huge waves *engulfed* the small boat.

devour [di'vauə] *vt.* 吞食，吞没；毁灭(eat up, consume)

【记】de+vour(吞食)

【例】 Halfway up the mountain, the hungry hikers *devoured* their food.

crumple ['krʌmpl] *vt.* 压皱(rumple, wrinkle)

【例】 Anne *crumpled* the letter and threw it away.

crush [krʌʃ] *vt.* 榨，挤，压碎(crunch)

【例】 The huge machine *crushed* the rocks into small stones.

disintegration [dis,inti'greiʃən] *n.* 瓦解

rift [rift] *n.* 裂缝，裂口，断裂

ruins [ruinz] *n.* 毁灭，崩溃，废墟，遗迹

强 迫

compulsive [kəm'pʌlsiv] *adj.* 强迫的(irresistible, obsessive, obsessed)

【例】 Bill is *compulsive* about saving everything. He can't throw anything away.

pressure ['preʃə] *n.* 压迫(tension)

【记】 press(压)＋ure

【例】 He feels the *pressure* soon after he takes up the job.

tease [tiːz] *vt.* 强求

【例】 The girl was *teasing* their mother for more candy.

compel [kəm'pel] *vt.* 强迫(coerce, force)

【例】 The boss *compelled* us to work over the weekend.

constrain [kən'strein] *vt.* 强迫(compel)

【例】 Hunger *constrained* the orphan to beg for food.

accelerate [æk'seləreit] *vt.* 迫使

【记】 ac＋celer(速度)＋ate→加速

勤 奋

laborious [lə'bɔːriəs] *adj.* 勤劳的

【记】 labor(劳动)＋ious→劳动的，勤劳的

【例】 Anne received a raise for her *laborious* efforts.

industrious [in'dʌstriəs] *adj.* 勤勉的(assiduous, diligent, sedulous)

assiduous [ə'sidjuəs] *adj.* 勤勉的(diligent, industrious)

【记】 as＋sid(坐)＋uous→一直坐着(工作)→勤勉的

【例】 The *assiduous* student worked hard to earn her degree.

diligent ['dilidʒənt] *adj.* 勤勉的，勤奋的(industrious, assidous)

【例】The *diligent* workers finished the project on time.

serious ['siəriəs] *adj.* 认真的(careful)

【例】The girl carried on *serious* study of Italian.

cordial ['kɔːdjəl] *adj.* 真诚的，诚恳的(friendly)

【记】cord(心)＋ial→以心相对→真诚的

【例】Our *cordial* hostess offered to hang up our coats.

deliberate [di'libərit] *adj.* 认真的，故意的(careful; intentional, purposive)

【记】de＋liber(自由)＋ate

【例】It's a *deliberate* decision by the school board.

attempt [ə'tempt] *n.* 努力，尝试(effort) *vt.* 尝试(try, endeavor)

effort ['efət] *n.* 努力，成就(attempt, exertion, endeavor)

endeavor [in'devə] *vi.* 努力(strive, struggle, try)

【例】Tom *endeavored* to get better grades in college.

strive [straiv] *vi.* 努力，奋斗；力求(endeavor, struggle)

【例】The poor family *strived* to pay the rent each month.

忍 受

reluctant [ri'lʌktənt] *adj.* 不情愿的，勉强的(unwilling)

【例】Jane seems *reluctant* to marry Jim.

tolerate ['tɔləreit] *vt.* 忍受，容忍；宽恕(bear, put up with)

【例】I could not *tolerate* my neighbor's loud stereo any longer.

tolerable ['tɔlərəbl] *adj.* 可容忍的(bearable, endurable)

insufferable [in'sʌfərəbl] *adj.* 难以忍受的(unbearable)

【记】in(不)＋sufferable(忍受的)

undergo [ˌʌndə'gəu] *vt.* 经历，忍受(experience)

【例】The family *underwent* the great hardship in the past 10 years.

stand [stænd] *vt.* 忍受(bear, tolerate)

【例】Birds with feathers could easily *stand* the cold winter here; they still migrate in winter.

endure [in'djuə] *vt.* 忍受，容忍(bear, tolerate)

【例】I hope your house will *endure* the coming hurricane.

abide [ə'baid] *vt.* 忍受

【记】abide by(遵守)

【例】His boss couldn't *abide* his incompetence any more and fired him.

认　可

permit [pə'mit] *vt.* 允许(allow, consent)
【例】 Do you *permit* your children to smoke?

permissible [pə'misəbl] *adj.* 可容许的
【记】 per(全部)＋miss(放开)＋ible→容许的

permissive [pə'misiv] *adj.* 许可的(allowable)
【例】 His *permissive* answer cheered the students up.

tacit ['tæsit] *adj.* 心照不宣的，默许的(unspoken, implicit)
【例】 What is *tacit* in her obscure refusal is that you still have hope.

reception [ri'sepʃən] *n.* 接受(acceptance, admission)

connive [kə'naiv] *vi.* 纵容，默许
【例】 The guards were suspected of *conniving* at the prisoner's escape.

connivance [kə'naivəns] *n.* 默许

concede [kən'siːd] *vi.* 让步；承认(admit, accept)
【记】 con＋cede(让)
【例】 I *conceded* and admitted I was wrong.

concession [kən'seʃən] *n.* 让步，迁就(compromise, bargain)
【记】 concede(让步)的名词
【例】 The governor would make no *concessions* on the issue of crime.

recognize ['rekəgnaiz] *vt.* 认识；认出；承认(acknowledge)
【例】 I *recognized* Peter although I hadn't seen him for 10 years.

recognition [ˌrekəg'niʃən] *n.* 认识；承认(realization)

nod [nɔd] *n./vi.* 点头，首肯(consent, approve)

confess [kən'fes] *v.* 忏悔，坦白(confide, disclose)
【例】 John *confessed* that he broke the window.

approve [ə'pruːv] *v.* 赞成，称许；批准(agree, assent)
【记】 ap＋prove(证明)
【例】 My parents *approved* of my date.

comply [kəm'plai] *vi.* 顺从(obey)，应允
【例】 A good citizen *complies* with the laws of the country.

concur [kən'kəː] *vi.* 同意(consent)
【例】 After hearing my point, Bill *concurred* with me.

avow [ə'vau] *vt.* 公开承认(acknowledge, declare, admit)
【记】 a＋vow(誓言)

【例】He *avowed* that he would never cooperate with them again.

ratify [ˈrætifai] *vt.* 批准（approve, endorse）

【例】The government *ratified* the treaty.

guarantee [ˌɡærənˈtiː] *vt.* 确保（secure, assure）

【例】No one can *guarantee* that you will pass the exam if you don't work hard.

endorse [inˈdɔːs] *vt.* 确认；赞同，支持（support, ratify, certify）

【例】The labor union *endorsed* the democratic candidate for president.

corroborate [kəˈrɔbəreit] *vt.* 确证（confirm, substantiate）

【记】cor+robor(力量)+ate→强化

【例】These data *corroborate* the hypothesis of the experiment.

grant [ɡrɑːnt] *vt.* 准予

【例】The governor *granted* the petitioner's request.

admit [ədˈmit] *vt.* 承认（acknowledge, accept）

【例】You should *admit* the truth.

acknowledge [əkˈnɔlidʒ] *vt.* 承认（admit, accept）

【例】Bill *acknowledged* his failure to complete the job.

affirm [əˈfəːm] *vt.* 批准

【记】af(一再)+firm(肯定)→断言

pardon [ˈpɑːdn] *vt.* 原谅，宽恕

【例】*Pardon*, I didn't quite catch your meaning.

失 误

innocent [ˈinəsnt] *adj.* 幼稚的

【记】in(无)+noc(害)+ent→无害的

【例】The bad guy introduced *innocent* children to drugs, which caused a bad influence on the society.

regardless [riˈɡɑːdlis] *adj.* 不管，不顾（despite, whatever, notwithstanding）

heedless [ˈhiːdlis] *adj.* 不留心的

erroneous [iˈrəunjəs] *adj.* 错误的（incorrect, mistaken）

【例】The so-called facts you gave me were totally *erroneous*.

neglect [nigˈlekt] *vt.* 疏忽（ignore, overlook）；忘记

【记】neg(不)+lect(选择)→不选择→忽视

【例】If you *neglect* this property, it will depreciate.

negligent [ˈneglidʒənt] *adj.* 忽略的

negligence [ˈneglidʒəns] *n.* 过失；疏忽

ridiculous [riˈdikjuləs] *adj.* 荒谬的

【例】It is *ridiculous* to become angry about such an insignificant matter.

slovenly [ˈslʌvənli] *adj.* 马虎的

credulous [ˈkredjuləs] *adj.* 轻信的

【记】cred(相信)＋ulous

useless [ˈjuːslis] *adj.* 无效的(invalid, futile)

futile [ˈfjuːtl] *adj.* 无益的；徒劳的(useless; vain)

【例】It would be *futile* for you to explain it again. I just don't understand algebra.

offhand [ɔfˈhænd] *adj.* 无准备的(unprepared, impromptu)

【例】I gave an *offhand* guess that it's about three o'clock.

fallible [ˈfæləbl] *adj.* 易错的

【记】fall(错误)＋ible→犯错误的

【例】He knows every rule in the factory, but still *fallible*.

defect [ˈdiːfekt] *n.* 缺陷(fault, shortcomings, imperfection)

【记】de(坏)＋fect(做)→做坏了→缺陷

【例】The manufacturer didn't sell the car due to a *defect* in the engine.

defective [diˈfektiv] *adj.* 有缺陷的

【例】His *defective* hearing has affected his pronunciation.

drawback [ˈdrɔːbæk] *n.* 弊端(disadvantage, defect, demerit)

【例】The *drawback* to working the morning shift is having to get up early.

flaw [flɔː] *n.* 缺点，瑕疵(fault, defect)

【例】The *flaw* in your theory is that you didn't account for gravity.

oblivion [əˈbliviən] *n.* 忘却，遗忘

【记】ob(离开)＋liv(活)＋ion→忘却

【例】The once popular writer's works were consigned to *oblivion* after he died.

blunder [ˈblʌndə] *v.* 犯大错(make foolish mistakes, bungle)

【例】I really *blundered* when I forgot to introduce my friends.

expire [iksˈpaiə] *vi.* 失效(terminate)

【记】ex＋pire(呼吸)→离开呼吸→断气

【例】John's driver's license *expired* last week.

overlook [ˌəuvəˈluk] *vt.* 忽略(ignore, neglect)；疏忽

【记】来自 look over(忽视)

【例】You have *overlooked* several of the mistakes in this work.

ignore [ig'nɔː] *vt.* 忽视(disregard, neglect)

【记】i(不)＋gnore(知道)→不知道→不理睬

【例】*Ignoring* something will not make it go away.

omit [əu'mit] *vt.* 省略，省去；遗漏(exclude, leave out)

【例】He is a celebrity; don't *omit* his name in the list.

absurd [əb'səːd] *adj.* 荒谬的(ridiculous)

【记】ab(离开)＋surd(合理的)→不合理的→荒谬的

【例】Wearing a swimming suit during a snowstorm is *absurd*.

abortive [ə'bɔːtiv] *adj.* 失败的(unsuccessful)

【记】abort(放弃)＋ive→失败的

err [əːr] *vi.* 犯错(mistake)

【例】Bill *erred* when he said Detroit is the capital of Michigan.

思 考

consider [kən'sidə] *vt.* 考虑

【例】Mary *considered* each option before making a decision.

considerate [kən'sidərit] *adj.* 考虑周到的(thoughtful)

【例】Jane is so *considerate*. She's always doing favors for people.

meditative ['mediteitiv] *adj.* 深思的(thoughtful)

【记】动词meditate(思考)

【例】Once again Newton sat under the apple tree with a *meditative* appearance.

tender ['tendə] *adj.* 细心的；考虑周到的

conscious ['kɔnʃəs] *adj.* 有意识的

【例】I fainted briefly but was *conscious* again in a few seconds.

recollection [ˌrekə'lekʃən] *n.* 记起，回想(remembrance, memory)

ruminate ['ruːmineit] *v.* 沉思(meditate)

【例】I *ruminated* a while before answering the question.

speculate ['spekjuleit] *v.* 推测；沉思(hypothesize, conjecture)

【例】He *speculated* there will be a comet visiting the earth this May, but failed.

ponder ['pɔndə] *vt.* 考虑 *vi.* 沉思(meditate)

【记】pond(重量)＋er→掂重量→考虑

【例】He and the council had already *pondered* the list of members who returned to the parliament.

embalm [im'bɑːm] *vt.* 铭记

【例】Ancient Egyptians used oils and natural substances to *embalm* the dead.

contemplate ['kɔntempleit] *vt.* 凝视；沉思(muse, ponder)

【例】Philosophers *contemplate* the existence of humankind.

elevate ['eliveit] *vt.* 提高(思想)

【记】e(出)+lev(举)+ate→举出→升高

【例】A child should be given books which *elevate* his mind.

recall [ri'kɔːl] *vt.* 忆起，记忆(recollect, remember)

【例】The victim was asked to *recall* what happend to him the day when he was robbed.

haunt [hɔːnt] *vt.* 萦绕于心

【例】Memories *haunt* him like ghosts.

探　索

venture ['ventʃə] *n./vi.* 冒险(risk)，冒昧

【例】May I *venture* to ask you a question, sir?

risk [risk] *n./vt.* 冒险

【例】You should not have *risked* the confrontation with the government.

probe [prəub] *v.* 探查(investigation, inspection)

【例】The detective *probed* into the circumstances of the murder.

explore [iks'plɔː] *v.* 探险，探索(search)

【记】ex+plore(大喊)→喊出来→探索

【例】The adventurer *explored* a dangerous underground cave.

seek [siːk] *v.* 寻找，探求(endeavor, try, campaign for, search for)

【例】We *sought* an answer to the question, but couldn't find one.

grope [grəup] *vi.* 摸索(fumble, search)

【例】Tom *groped* around in the dark until he found the light switch.

ferret ['ferit] *vt.* 搜索(search)

【例】The detective finally *ferreted* out the criminal.

拖　延

tardy ['tɑːdi] *adj.* 延迟的(late, slow)

【记】tard(迟缓)+y

【例】The *tardy* student tried to sneak into class.

perpetuate [pə'petʃueit] *vt.* 使⋯永恒，使⋯延续

【例】Every kind of plant has its own way to *perpetuate* itself.

detain [di'tein] *vt.* 使延迟(delay, retard)

【记】de＋tain(拿，抓)→拘留

【例】Please do not *detain* me; I am in a hurry.

delay [di'lei] *vt.* 推迟，耽搁，延误(detain, postpone)

【例】Today I will *delay* this matter till I can decide what I should do.

prolong [prə'lɔŋ] *vt.* 拖长，延长(extend, lengthen)

【记】pro(向前)＋long(长)→延长

【例】His journey to China was *prolonged* because there is too much to see.

protract [prəu'trækt] *vt.* 延长(lengthen, prolong)

【记】pro(前)＋tract(拉)→延长

【例】Let's not *protract* the debate any longer.

retard [ri'tɑːd] *vt.* 延迟(detain)

【记】re(使)＋tard(迟缓)→延迟

【例】The heavy winds *retarded* the plane's speed.

postpone [ˌpəust'pəun] *vt.* 延搁(delay, put off)

【记】post(后)＋pone→推后

【例】The meeting was *postponed* by one day because my boss was sick.

defer [di'fəː] *vt.* 延期(delay, postpone)

【记】de(坏)＋fer(带来)

【例】Mike *deferred* his judgment until he heard more explanation.

adjourn [ə'dʒəːn] *vt.* 延期(defer, delay)

【例】The meeting was *adjourned* until four o'clock.

习　惯

inclined [in'klaind] *adj.* 倾向⋯的(liable)

【记】in(内)＋clin(倾斜)＋ed→内心的倾向

【例】The weak girl is *inclined* to get tired easily.

prone [prəun] *adj.* 倾向于(liable)

【例】The lazy man is *prone* to idleness.

habitually [hə'bitjuəli] *adv.* 习惯地

【记】habit(习惯)＋ually

bent [bent] *n.* 爱好；倾向

【例】Jimmy showed a *bent* for music so his parents let him take piano lessons.

aptitude [ˈæptitjuːd] n. 自然倾向

【记】apti(能力)+tude

【例】I have no musical *aptitude* and I can't even sing a simple tune.

propensity [prəˈpensiti] n. 倾向(inclination)

【例】Anne has a *propensity* for eating when she's nervous.

trend [trend] n. 倾向，趋势(tendency, propensity)

penchant [ˈpentʃənt] n. 倾向；爱好(inclination; preference)

【记】pen(笔)+chant(咏唱)→用笔"歌唱"→爱好

custom [ˈkʌstəm] n. 习惯

【例】Carving pumpkins into grotesque heads is a Halloween *custom* in the United States.

accustomed [əˈkʌstəmd] adj. 习惯的(habitual, conventional)

【记】be accustomed to 习惯于

【例】The recent immigrants have not yet become *accustomed* to American food.

interest [ˈintrist] n. 兴趣

tend [tend] vi. 趋向，往往是(care for, prone)

【例】Female drivers *tend* to drive slower than male ones, which resulted in less accidents.

inure [iˈnjuə] vt. 使习惯(accustom)

【例】The doctors were *inured* to such injuries.

限　制

temperance [ˈtempərəns] n. 节制，自制(self-control, moderation)；戒酒

【例】His *temperance* couldn't be counted on, otherwise he would not have become addicted.

bondage [ˈbɔndidʒ] n. 束缚

【例】Lincoln emancipated the slaves from their *bondage*.

deterrent [diˈterənt] n. 制止物，威慑物

【记】de+ter(吓唬)+rent

【例】Thoughts of his parents' anger served as a strong *deterrent* when Mike considered misbehaving.

neutralize [ˈnjuːtrəlaiz] v. 压制

【例】Alkalis *neutralize* acids.

check [tʃek] *v.* 抑制（restrain, stop）

【例】Raising interest rate is commonly used as a tool to *check* inflation.

circumscribe [ˈsəːkəmskraib] *vt.* 划界限；限制（encompass, encircle）

【记】circum（绕圈）＋scribe（画）→画圈

【例】The moves you can make in a chess game are *circumscribed* by the rules of the game.

shackle [ˈʃækl] *vt.* 加桎梏，束缚（chain, fetter）

【例】Women in the past were *shackled* by outdated attitudes.

fetter [ˈfetə] *vt.* 束缚，羁绊（restrict, inhibit）

【例】I hate to be *fettered* by rules and regulations.

restrict [risˈtrikt] *vt.* 限制（restrain, limit）

【例】He *restricted* himself to two cigarettes a day.

restrain [risˈtrein] *vt.* 限制（restrict, limit）

【记】re＋stain（拉紧）→限制

【例】The alcoholist tried his best to *restrain* himself from alcohol.

confine [kənˈfain] *vt.* 限制

【记】con（全部）＋fine（限制）→全限制

【例】Bill *confined* his dog to the house all day.

quell [kwel] *vt.* 压制（quash, suppress）

【例】The army *quelled* the rebellion.

curb [kəːb] *vt.* 抑制（check, control）

【例】In the 1970's, many governments' efforts to *curb* inflation were unsuccessful.

bound [baund] *n.* 限制

leash [liːʃ] *n./v.* 束缚

【例】I managed to hold my anger in *leash*.

学 习

literate [ˈlitərit] *adj.* 有文化的，能读写的

【记】liter（文学）＋ate

chalk [tʃɔːk] *n.* 白垩，粉笔 *vt.* 用粉笔写

【例】The kids *chalked* pictures onto the sidewalk.

transcript [ˈtrænskript] *n.* 成绩单

scholarship [ˈskɔləʃip] *n.* 奖学金

article ［ˈɑːtikl］*n.* 论文，文章

【例】The last *article* in the publisher's contract explained the author's rights.

ken ［ken］*n.* 视野；知识(knowledge)

【记】比较kin(亲戚)

stationery ［ˈsteiʃənəri］*n.* 文具

brochure ［brəuˈʃjuə］*n.* 小册子(pamphlet)

pamphlet ［ˈpæmflit］*n.* 小册子

credit ［ˈkredit］*n.* 学分

【例】This college course is worth three *credits*.

semester ［səˈmestə］*n.* 学期(term)

thesis ［ˈθiːsis］*n.* 学位论文

discourse ［disˈkɔːs］*n.* 演讲(lecture)；论文(disquisition)

【例】Eventually the *discourse* at the party came around to politics.

margin ［ˈmɑːdʒin］*n.* 页边的空白(edge, rim)，栏外

term ［təːm］*n.* 学期；专用名词

【例】Knowing more technical *terms* gives a translator more advantages.

discipline ［ˈdisiplin］*v.* 训练(manage)；学科，纪律

【例】The five little kids stand in a line, showing that they are well *disciplined*.

commence ［kəˈmens］*vi.* 获得学位

cram ［kræm］*vt.* 仓促用功

【例】He was up all night *cramming* for the history midterm.

academic ［ˌækəˈdemik］*adj.* 学院的(collegiate)；理论的

【例】John was invited to give an *academic* address at a conference.

遗　留

heredity ［hiˈrediti］*n.* 遗传

【例】Both a person's *heredity* and environment help to shape his character.

heritage ［ˈheritidʒ］*n.* 遗产(legacy, bequest)

bequest ［biˈkwest］*n.* 遗产(legacy, heritage)，遗传

【例】The *bequest* was subject to heavy taxes.

legacy ［ˈlegəsi］*n.* 遗产(bequest, heritage)，遗物

【例】My farm is a *legacy* from my grandfather.

relic [ˈrelik] *n.* 遗物，遗迹，废墟，纪念物

remains [riˈmeins] *n.* 残余，遗迹，遗体

运 动

stray [strei] *adj.* 漂泊的（wandering, random）; 走失的

【例】 The *stray* dog was picked up by the dogcatcher because he had no collar.

roam [rəum] *n./v.* 漫步（wander）

【例】 Visitors *roamed* around the town.

stalk [stɔːk] *v.* 阔步

【例】 The man *stalked* off in a huff.

rumble [ˈrʌmbl] *v.* 隆隆行驶（grumble, roar）

【例】 The truck *rumbled* along the road.

scale [skeil] *n./v.* 攀登（climb, raise）

【例】 The athletes *scaled* the peak.

ascend [əˈsend] *v.* 攀登，登高（climb）

【记】 a＋scend(爬)→爬上→攀登

【例】 The businessman steadily *ascended* in the ranks of his company. / As Jane *ascended* the mountain, Bill took pictures.

budge [bʌdʒ] *v.* 移动（move）

【例】 The lid of the jar was stuck tight and would not *budge*.

locomote [ˌləukəˈməut] *vi.* 移动，行动（move）

traverse [trəˈvəːs] *vt.* 走过（span, stretch across）

【记】 tra(横)＋verse(转)→横过

【例】 The road *traverses* a wild and mountainous region.

stroll [strəul] *vt.* 漫步（walk, ramble）

【例】 We *strolled* through the park.

insinuate [inˈsinjueit] *vt.* 迂回进入

【记】 in(进入)＋sinu(弯曲)＋ate→绕着弯进入→迂回进入

【例】 The ivy *insinuates* itself into every crevice.

zigzag [ˈzigzæg] *n.* Z字形，锯齿形，蜿蜒曲折

motion [ˈməuʃən] *n.* 运动，动作 *v.* 运动

【记】 mot(动)＋ion

战 胜

unquenchable [ʌnˈkwentʃəbl] *adj.* 不可熄灭的，不能遏制的（insatiable）

lag [læg] *n./vi.* 落后（drag, trail）

subjection [səbˈdʒekʃən] *n.* 征服

overcome [ˌəuvəˈkʌm] *v.* 战胜，胜过（defeat, surmount）

【例】He *overcame* a strong temptation to run away.

surpass [səˈpɑːs] *vt.* 超过，超越，胜过（exceed, surmount）

【记】比较pass（通过）

【例】The excellent runner *surpassed* all previous records.

transcend [trænˈsend] *vt.* 超越（surpass, go beyond）

【记】tran（超过）＋scend（爬）

【例】The genius of Shakespeare *transcended* that of all other English poets.

surmount [səːˈmaunt] *vt.* 克服；登上；越过（conquer, overcome, exceed, surpass）

【记】sur（超过）＋mount（山）→登上（山顶）→超越困难

【例】Mary *surmounted* the problems caused by her handicap and finished college.

precede [priːˈsiːd] *vt.* 先于 *vi.* 领先（come before）

【记】pre（前）＋cede（走）→领先

【例】An informal meeting will *precede* the conference.

vanquish [ˈvæŋkwiʃ] *vt.* 征服，克服（conquer, overcome）

【例】They successfully *vanquished* the enemy.

All human wisdom is summed up in two words—wait and hope.
—*Alexandre Dumas Pére*
人类所有的智慧可以归结为两个词——等待和希望。
——大仲马

连 线 题

左列单词在右列中有一个或多个同义词，请画线连接。

（一）

check	across
	bequest
drawback	care for
	conquer
err	defect
	demerit
explore	disadvantage
	heritage
ken	knowledge
	lengthen
legacy	meditate
	mistake
protract	overcome
	prolong
ruminate	prone
	restrain
tend	search
	span
traverse	stop
	stretch
vanquish	

（二）

blur	allow
	allowable
collapse	careful
	consent
elusive	crash
	decay
enigma	elusory
	harass
exhibit	indistinct
	intangible
harry	mystery
	pester
permissive	rot
	ruin
permit	show
serious	
spoil	

（三）

elude	chaos
	disorder
forestall	dogged
	escape
observe	evade
	fixed
obstinate	give in
	immobile
persistent	preempt
	prevent
renovate	renew
	restore
resist	static
	stubborn
stationary	watch
	withstand
submit	yield
turmoil	

（四）

abandon	accompany
	annul
behavior	arouse
	cancel
benevolent	charitable
	conduct
efface	deed
	discard
escort	erase
	generous
evoke	give up
	momentum
impulse	opposition
	produce
process	revolt
	treat
rebellion	urge
undo	

连线题答案

（一）

check	restrain
check	stop
drawback	disadvantage
drawback	defect
drawback	demerit
err	mistake
explore	search
ken	knowledge
legacy	bequest
legacy	heritage
protract	lengthen
protract	prolong
ruminate	meditate
tend	care for
tend	prone
traverse	span
traverse	stretch
traverse	across
vanquish	conquer
vanquish	overcome

（二）

blur	indistinct
collapse	crash
elusive	elusory
elusive	intangible
enigma	mystery
exhibit	show
harry	harass
harry	pester
permissive	allowable
permit	allow
permit	consent
serious	careful
spoil	decay
spoil	ruin
spoil	rot

（三）

elude	escape
elude	evade
forestall	prevent
forestall	preempt
observe	watch
obstinate	stubborn
persistent	dogged
renovate	renew
renovate	restore
resist	withstand
stationary	fixed
stationary	immobile
stationary	static
submit	give in
submit	yield
turmoil	disorder
turmoil	chaos

（四）

abandon	discard
abandon	give up
behavior	conduct
behavior	deed
benevolent	charitable
benevolent	generous
efface	erase
escort	accompany
evoke	arouse
evoke	produce
impulse	urge
impulse	momentum
process	treat
rebellion	revolt
rebellion	opposition
undo	cancel
undo	annul

语　言

记忆小贴士：循环记忆法

　　人脑有一个特点，对某个信息要反复刺激才能记住。循环记忆法，就是基于此点。它的诀窍在不断的快速循环记忆中记牢单词。

诽 谤

injurious [in'dʒuriəs] *adj.* 侮辱，诽谤的；有害的（harmful, deleterious）

【记】injury＋ous

asperse [əs'pəːs] *vt.* 诽谤（slander）

【记】a＋sperse(散开)→散布坏东西→诽谤

【例】Don't *asperse* my reputation.

aspersion [əs'pəːʃən] *n.* 诽谤

【例】I resent your casting *aspersions* on my brother and his ability.

indignity [in'digniti] *n.* 侮辱

malign [mə'lain] *vt.* 诋毁，诽谤（defame, slander）

【例】"Have I not taken your part when you were *maligned*?"

defame [di'feim] *vt.* 诽谤，损毁名誉（slander, malign）

【记】de＋fame(名声)

【例】The politician *defamed* his opponent in his speech.

disparage [dis'pæridʒ] *vt.* 轻视；毁谤（denigrate, depreciate）

【记】dis＋par(平等)＋age→不平等→贬低

【例】Before you *disparage* this idea, give us a better one.

humiliate [hjuː'milieit] *vt.* 屈辱；贬抑（shame, humble, insult）

【记】hum(地)＋iliate→使人想找地缝→羞辱别人

【例】Dave's cruel jokes *humiliated* me.

slander ['slændə] *n./vt.* 造谣，诽谤（defame, malign）

【例】To utter or spread *slander* is against the law.

insult ['insʌlt] *n./vt.* 侮辱，凌辱

【例】He *insulted* her by calling her a stupid fool.

讽 刺

satirical [sə'tirəkl] *adj.* 讽刺的（acid, sardonic）

sardonic [saː'dɔnik] *adj.* 讽刺的，嘲笑的（sarcastic, derisive）

【例】Bill's *sardonic* sense of humor is often misunderstood.

sarcastic [saː'kæstik] *adj.* 讽刺的，挖苦的

【例】I was being *sarcastic* when I said this movie was thrilling. It's really bad.

sarcasm ['saːkæzəm] *n.* 讽刺，挖苦（irony, scorn）

cynical 　［ˈsinikəl］ *adj.* 讥讽的，冷嘲热讽的（contemptuous, sarcastic）

　　【例】His *cynical* remarks simply show how uninformed he is.

mock 　［mɔk］ *n.* 嘲弄 *vt.* 嘲弄，挖苦（mimic, ridicule）

taunt 　［tɔ:nt］ *n./vt.* 嘲笑（tease, insult）

　　【记】比较daunt（恐吓）

　　【例】They *taunted* Tom into losing his temper.

jeer 　［dʒiə］ *vi.* 揶揄，嘲笑（deride, gibe）

　　【例】Don't *jeer* at the person who came last in the race—it's very unkind.

flout 　［flaut］ *vt.* 嘲弄（scoff, despise）

　　【例】He *flouted* his mother's advice.

sneer 　［sniə］ *vt.* 嘲笑（scoff, scorn）

　　【例】James *sneered* at my old bicycle. He has a new one.

deride 　［diˈraid］ *vt.* 嘲笑，愚弄（ridicule, mock, gibe）

　　【记】de（坏）＋ride（笑）

　　【例】The politician *derided* his opponents at every opportunity.

gibe 　［dʒaib］ *n./vt.* 讥笑（deride, ridicule, mock, make fun of）

　　【例】Don't make *gibes* about her behavior.

呼　喊

clamor 　［ˈklæmə］ *n.* 叫嚣（uproar, hubbub）

　　【记】clam（喊）＋or

　　【例】The *clamor* from the backyard drew us out of the house.

exclaim 　［iksˈkleim］ *v.* 呼喊；惊叫（shout; ejaculate）

　　【例】Mary *exclaimed* that someone forgot to turn the water off in the bathroom.

exhale 　［eksˈheil］ *vt.* 呼出（breathe out, respire）；发出；散发

　　【记】ex＋hale（气）→呼出气

　　【例】Bill inhaled the cigarette smoke and then *exhaled* deeply.

howl 　［haul］ *vt.* 咆哮（wail, bawl）

　　【例】The wolf *howled* in the moonless night.

acclaim 　［əˈkleim］ *v.* 喝彩，欢呼；称赞（applaud, approve, praise）

　　【记】ac＋claim（喊）

　　【例】The crowd *acclaimed* the hero as he rode through the town. /The ballerina was *acclaimed* for her wonderful performances.

建 议

counsel [ˈkaunsəl] v. 劝告(advise) n. 商议，忠告

【例】Mary *counseled* her daughter about good study habits.

propose [prəˈpəuz] v. 提出，提议(advance, suggest)

【例】Man *proposes*, God disposes.

proposal [prəˈpəuzl] n. 提案；建议(advice)

offer [ˈɔfə] n. 提议(proposal) vt. 提出，提议(suggest, propose)

【记】of(一再)＋fer(带来)→一再带来→提供

recommend [ˌrekəˈmend] vt. 劝告；推荐(suggest)

【例】She *recommended* the book to her students.

remind [riˈmaind] vt. 提醒(awake)

【记】re(再次)＋mind=ment(思考)→提醒(自己)

【例】Satire tends to *remind* people that what they see, read and hear is partially true.

suggest [səˈdʒest] vt. 提议；暗示(hint, insinuate)

【例】I *suggested* that it would be quicker to travel by train.

mention [ˈmenʃən] vt. 主张；提及

【记】ment(思考)＋ion→思考想到→提到

【例】I hope you didn't *mention* my name to her.

advice [ədˈvais] n. 建议，忠告(suggestion)

【例】In times of trouble, people ask friends for *advice*.

advise [ədˈvaiz] vt. 告知；劝告(suggest)

【例】The weather report *advised* carrying an umbrella today.

advance [ədˈvɑːns] vt. 提出

【例】Tom *advanced* his idea at the beginning of the meeting.

submit [səbˈmit] vt. 提交(propose)

【例】Christians *submit* themselves to God's will.

交 流

reciprocal [riˈsiprəkl] adj. 相互的；交往的(mutual, exchanged)

【例】The treaty should be signed on the basis of *reciprocal* benefits.

correspondence [ˌkɔriˈspɔndəns] *n.* 通信
　【记】 cor＋respond(反应)＋ence
　【例】 Jane saved all of her grandmother's *correspondence*.

liaison [liːˈeizən] *n.* 联络(contact, connection)

propagate [ˈprɔpəgeit] *vt.* 宣传
　【例】 Missionaries went far afield to *propagate* their faith.

communicate [kəˈmjuːnikeit] *vt.* 传达 *vi.* 通信；交流
　【记】 commune (交谈)＋ic＋ate→大家交
谈→交流
　【例】 Mary *communicated* the news as tactfully
as she could.

impart [imˈpɑːt] *vt.* 给予；传递；告诉(inform,
disseminate)
　【记】 im(进入)＋part(部分)→成为(信息的)一部分→传递
　【例】 A teacher's job is mainly *imparting* knowledge to students.

remit [riˈmit] *vt.* 汇寄
　【记】 re(再)＋mit(送)→再送出去→汇款
　【例】 Please kindly *remit* us the money without delay.

consort [kənˈsɔːt] *vt.* 结交(associate, connect)
　【例】 The father is annoyed that his daughter *consorts* with all kinds of
strange people.

disseminate [diˈsemineit] *vt.* 散布，传播(disperse, distribute, spread, impart)
　【记】 dis＋semin(种子)＋ate→散布(种子)
　【例】 The Public Relations Department *disseminates* information.

tip [tip] *vt.* 接触(contact)

夸 大

bombastic [bɔmˈbæstik] *adj.* 夸大的(boastful)
　【记】 比较bomb(炸弹)

pretentious [priˈtenʃəs] *adj.* 装腔作势的(showy, ostentatious)

boast [bəust] *vi.* 自夸 *vt.* 吹嘘(brag, self-praise)
　【例】 He *boasted* about the big fish he had caught.

boastful [ˈbəustful] *adj.* 自夸的(bragging, conceited)
　【例】 When telling of her success, Mary tried not to be *boastful*.

vanity ['væniti] *n.* 虚荣心(self-conceit, pride)

【记】van(空)+ity→虚荣心

conceit [kən'si:t] *n.* 自负,自高自大(vanity, arrogance)

【例】The popular athlete was known for *conceit* and arrogance.

exaggerate [ig'zædʒəreit] *v.* 夸大,夸张(overstate, overemphasize)

【例】Bill *exaggerates* every story he tells his friends.

brag [bræg] *vt.* 夸张(boast, talk big)

【例】Sue *bragged* that she could eat an entire pie in two minutes.

命 令

imperative [im'perətiv] *adj.* 命令的

【记】imper(命令)+ative

【例】Don't talk in an *imperative* tone of voice.

bidding ['bidiŋ] *n.* 命令,要求

【例】The servant grumbled but did his employer's *bidding*.

prescription [pris'kripʃən] *n.* 指示(instruction, direction)

【例】The general demanded that his men act strictly to his *prescription*.

rally ['ræli] *n./v.* 召集(gathering, assemblage)

【记】比较ally(联盟)

【例】We *rallied* together to save our leader from prison.

disband [dis'bænd] *v.* 解散(dismiss, split up)

【记】dis+band(队)

【例】The rock group *disbanded* after its first concert.

distribute [di'stribjut] *vt.* 分发,分送(allocate, allot)

【例】Someone dressed in a rabbit costume *distributed* leaflets to passersby.

assign [ə'sain] *vt.* 分配,指派(allot, distribute)

【例】The manager *assigned* Bill to the Jones project.

instruct [in'strʌkt] *vt.* 命令(direct, inculcate)

expedite ['ekspidait] *vt.* 派出

【记】ex+ped(脚)+ite→脚跨出去→加速

【例】The person I talked to on the phone promised to *expedite* the shipment of the book I ordered.

dispatch [dis'pætʃ] *vt.* 派遣(send)；分配(allocate, allot)

【例】The teacher *dispatched* the student to the principal's office.

nominate ['nɔmineit] *vt.* 任命(appoint, name)

【记】nomin(名称)+ate→任命

【例】I *nominate* Mary for the office of treasurer.

evacuate [i'vækjueit] *vt.* 疏散

【记】e+vacu(空)+ate→使空→疏散

【例】The Civil Defense *evacuated* all inhabitants from the area where the storm was predicted to strike.

summon ['sʌmən] *vt.* 召唤(call)

【记】sum(下面)+mon→从下面把人命令上来→召唤

【例】The shareholders are *summoned* to hold a general meeting.

destine ['destin] *vt.* 指定(designate)

【例】Lisa is *destined* for the presidency.

designate ['dezigneit] *vt.* 指定；指派(assign, nominate, specify)

【例】The team *designated* Sally as the captain.

monitor ['mɔnitə] *v.* 监控(inspect, control)

【记】另一个词义是"班长"

【例】The president can *monitor* the whole campus through advanced computer system.

accredit [ə'kredit] *v.* 委任；任命

【例】The president will *accredit* you as his assistant.

批 评

culpable ['kʌlpəbl] *adj.* 该受谴责的(guilty, blameworthy)

【记】culp(罪行)+able

critical ['kritikl] *adj.* 评论的，批评的

【例】The movie review was *critical* of the director's casting choices.

censure ['senʃə] *n./vt.* 责难(disapproval)

【例】Bill received a *censure* from his boss for the failure of the project. / The warden *censured* the guard for letting the prisoner escape.

reproach [ri'prəutʃ] *v.* 责备

【记】比较approach(接近)

【例】Do not *reproach* yourself. It was not your fault.

chide ['tʃaid] *vt.* 斥责(blame, rebuke)

【例】 My mother *chided* me for eating junk food.

decry [di'krai] *vt.* 非难，谴责（condemn, denounce）

【记】 de＋cry（喊）

【例】 A staunch materialist, he *decries* economy.

deprecate ['deprikeit] *vt.* 抗议，抨击（fustigate, attack）

【例】 Lovers of peace *deprecate* war.

castigate ['kæstigeit] *vt.* 谴责（condemn, denounce）

【例】 It is not good to *castigate* children too harshly.

denounce [di'nauns] *vt.* 谴责，声讨（censure, condemn）

【记】 de（坏）＋nounce（讲话）→讲坏话→抨击

【例】 Jane loudly *denounces* anyone who litters.

condemn [kən'dem] *vt.* 谴责

【记】 联想damn（咒骂）

【例】 The newspaper editorial *condemned* the court's decision.

berate [bi'reit] *vt.* 痛骂（scold, reproach）

【记】 be＋rate（骂）

【例】 Don't congratulate yourself too much, or *berate* yourself either.

rap [ræp] *vt.* 责难

rebuke [ri'bjuːk] *vt./n.* 斥责（censure, reprove）

【记】 re（反）＋buke（打）→反打→斥责

【例】 My efforts were met with *rebukes* and insults!

blame [bleim] *vt./n.* 谴责

【例】 Who took the *blame* for the failure of the project?

repudiate [ri'pjuːdieit] *vt.* 批判（reject, renounce）

【例】 The scientist *repudiated* the results of the shoddy experiment.

说 话

hoarse [hɔːs] *adj.*（声音）嘶哑的（husky, rough）

【例】 Bob's *hoarse* voice sounded as if his throat really hurt.

colloquial [kə'ləukwiəl] *adj.* 会话的，口语的（oral）

【记】 col（共同）＋loqu（说）＋ial

【例】 Bob deletes *colloquial* expressions from his formal writing.

dumb [dʌm] *adj.* 哑的，无言的

【例】 Mike keeps *dumb* when he doesn't know the answer.

hubbub ['hʌbʌb] *n.* 嘈杂（uproar）

dialogue [ˈdaiəlɔg] *n.* 对话（conversation）

【记】dia（对着）＋logue（说）→对着说

【例】The entire play consisted of *dialogue* and no movement.

nonsense [ˈnɔnsens] *n.* 胡说，废话

excuse [iksˈkjuːz] *n.* 借口（reason）

compliment [ˈkɔmplimənt] *n.* 问候

【例】Carry my *compliments* to your kinsmen.

gossip [ˈgɔsip] *n.* 闲话

oration [ɔˈreiʃən] *n.* 演说（speech, address）

hearsay [ˈhiəsei] *n.* 谣传，风闻（rumor, gossip）

【记】hear（听）＋say（说）→道听途说

【例】It's just *hearsay*, but it's rumored that John is going to quit.

interrupt [ˌintəˈrʌpt] *v.* 打断，插嘴（intermit, halt）

【例】It's impolite to *interrupt* while others are talking.

rumble [ˈrʌmbl] *v.* 低沉地说

【例】He *rumbled* a command to the soldiers.

gabble [ˈgæbl] *v.* 急促而不清楚地说出

【记】比较gobble（贪婪地大吃）

【例】"Articulate your words, don't *gabble*."said the mother.

solicit [səˈlisit] *v.* 恳求（request, demand）

【例】Bob was almost arrested for *soliciting* in an apartment building.

declaim [diˈkleim] *v.* 朗诵；演讲

【记】de＋claim（宣称）

【例】A preacher stood *declaiming* in the town center.

confide [kənˈfaid] *v.* 倾诉（confess, disclose）

【记】con（全部）＋fide（相信）→吐露（真情）

【例】Mary *confided* in John that she had lost her job.

refer [riˈfəː] *v.* 言及，提到（mention）

【记】re（再次）＋fer（带来）→再次带来→提到

【例】The president *refered* several times to the Paris Treaty during his address at the summit meeting.

chat [tʃæt] *v./n.* 闲谈

【例】Dave *chatted* on the telephone all evening.

grumble ['grʌmbl] *vi.* 喃喃诉苦(complain, grunt)

【例】That student is discourteous; he *grumbles* no matter how one tries to please him.

equivocate [i'kwivəkeit] *vi.* 说模棱两可的话，支吾

【例】If you *equivocate* on the witness stand, you might be charged with perjury.

coax [kəuks] *vt.* 哄

【例】Jane *coaxed* her little baby to sleep.

outwit [aut'wit] *vt.* 哄骗

【记】out(出)＋wit(机智)→用计谋去→哄骗

【例】The fox *outwitted* the farmer and stole a chicken.

effuse [i'fju:z] *vt.* 流出；散布

【记】ef(出)＋fuse(流)

【例】I can't believe that kind of words *effuse* from her mouth.

accost [ə'kɔst] *vt.* 向人搭话(address, speak to)

【例】She was often *accosted* by complete strangers.

说 明

account [ə'kaunt] *n.* 描述

【例】When you return, please give an *account* of your trip.

exposition [ˌekspə'ziʃən] *n.* 展览(exhibition)；说明，阐明(description)

enunciate [i'nʌnsieit] *v.* 阐明；清晰发音(articulate)

【记】e(出)＋nunci(清楚)＋ate→讲出来→清楚表达

【例】You must *enunciate* your lines, or the audience will never understand you.

narrate [nə'reit] *v.* 叙述(describe, recount)

【例】The story is *narrated* by its hero.

insinuate [in'sinjueit] *vt.* 暗示(allude, hint, imply)

【记】in(进入)＋sinu(弯曲)＋ate→绕着弯进入→迂回进入

【例】Are you *insinuating* that I am responsible for the accident?

cover ['kʌvə] *vt.* 报道

【例】Channel 4 is *covering* the match.

convey [kən'vei] *vt.* 表达(communicate)

【例】If you leave a message, I'll *convey* it to him.

illuminate [iˈljuːmineit] *vt.* 说明（clarify）

【例】Cleverly made attacks can often serve to *illuminate* important differences between candidates, as well as entertain the voters.

render [ˈrendə] *vt.* 表达（deliver, perform, express）

【例】The jury's finding amounted to the clearest verdict yet *rendered* upon the scandal.

elucidate [iˈljuːsideit] *vt.* 阐明，说明（clarify, explain）

【记】e(出)＋lucid(清楚)＋ate→弄清楚→阐明

【例】Lisea cannot simply *elucidate* her ideas well enough to carry on a reasonable conversation!

clarify [ˈklærifai] *vt.* 澄清，阐明

【记】clar(清楚)＋ify

【例】The explanation *clarified* the details of the plan.

expound [iksˈpaund] *vt.* 解释（explain, interpret）

【例】The priest *expounded* his religion.

construe [kənˈstruː] *vt.* 解释；翻译（expound; translate, interpret）

【例】The offended customer had *construed* my words to mean something I didn't mean at all!

delineate [diˈlinieit] *vt.* 刻画；记述（depict, portray）

【记】de(加强)＋line(线)＋ate→用力画线→描画

【例】He *delineated* his plan in this notebook.

exemplify [igˈzemplifai] *vt.* 例证，例示（illustrate）

【例】Your diligence *exemplifies* the characteristics of a good employee.

depict [diˈpikt] *vt.* 描写，叙述（delineate, describe, portray）

【例】The poet tried to *depict* the splendor of the setting sun in his poem.

emphasize [ˈemfəsaiz] *vt.* 强调，着重（underscore, underline, highlight, stress, accentuate）

【例】The speaker will *emphasize* team work and patience in her speech.

illustrate [ˈiləstreit] *vt.* 说明（exemplify, explain）

【记】il(不断)＋lustr(光明)＋ate→不断给光明→说明

【例】I *illustrated* my point about politics with examples from a book.

highlight [ˈhailait] *vt.* 突出显示；强调（climax, underline, underscore, stress）

【例】A beam of light was cast onto the dancer, *highlighting* her vivid imitation action of a peacock.

specify [ˈspesifai] *vt.* 详述（define）

【例】The student *specified* several reasons for his being late.

elaborate [iˈlæbəreit] *vt.* 详细阐述(explain, embellish)

【例】We ask Mary to *elaborate* her trip to Tibet.

divulge [daiˈvʌldʒ] *vt.* 宣布(reveal)

【例】The president asked the managers not to *divulge* the news of the merger.

proclaim [prəˈkleim] *vt.* 宣布,声明(announce, declare)

【记】pro(前)+claim(喊)→宣布

【例】The ringing bells *proclaimed* the news of the birth of the prince.

cite [sait] *vt.* 引用;举例(mention, quote, refer to)

【例】When writing research papers, writers must *cite* the sources they use. / The critic *cited* Mary's outstanding performance.

reiterate [riːˈitəreit] *vt.* 重述(restate)

【记】re(反复)+iterate(重申)

【例】The spokesman *reiterated* the policy of the government.

accentuate [ækˈsentʃueit] *vt.* 重读;强调(emphasize, underline, highlight, rscore)

【记】ac+cent=cant(唱,说)+uate→不断说→强调

【例】The tall girl wore short skirts that *accentuated* her height, making her look even taller.

协 商

uniform [ˈjuːnifɔːm] *adj.* 统一的,一致的(alike, consistent)

unanimity [ˌjuːnəˈnimiti] *n.* 全体一致(harmony, accord)

unanimous [juˈnæniməs] *adj.* 意见一致的(uniform)

【例】My friends and I made a *unanimous* decision to order pizza.

reconcile [ˈrekənsail] *vt.* 和解(conform, harmonize)

【例】Anne *reconciled* her disagreement with Mary.

reconciliation [ˌrekənsiliˈeiʃn] *n.* 和解(compromise, pacification)

convention [kənˈvenʃn] *n.* 协定;会议 (conference)

【例】Any country who fails to conform to international *convention* will be condemned.

pact [pækt] *n.* 协定(treaty, agreement)

consult [kənˈsʌlt] *v.* 商量;请教(ask for)

【例】I *consulted* the weather report before planning the picnic.

negotiate [ni'gəuʃieit] *v.* 谈判，交涉（discuss）；议定

【例】The two parties are *negotiating* about the contract.

confer [kən'fə:] *v.* 协商（discuss）

【记】con（共同）＋fer→共同带来观点→协商

【例】I *conferred* with my friends about what we should eat for dinner.

placate ['plækeit] *vt.* 安抚

【记】plac（平静）＋ate

【例】To *placate* an infant, a mom has to offer vocal reassurance.

争　论

eloquent ['eləkwənt] *adj.* 雄辩的，有口才的（persuasive, fluent）

【例】The *eloquent* lecture was interesting to listen to.

eloquence ['eləkwəns] *n.* 雄辩

【记】e（出）＋loqu（说）＋ence→总能说出→雄辩

【例】Because of her *eloquence*, Anne made an excellent lobbyist.

debate [di'beit] *n./v.* 争论，辩论（discussion, argument）

debatable [di'beitəbl] *adj.* 争论中的，未决定的（controversial, unsettled）

【记】来自debate（争论）

【例】It is *debatable* as to which football team is the best.

squabble ['skwɔbl] *n.* 口角，争论（quarrel, argument）

dispute [dis'pju:t] *n./v.* 争论，辩论（disagreement, argument, question）

【例】A territorial *dispute* between the two countries occurred.

retort [ri'tɔ:t] *v.* 反驳（refute, reply）

【记】re（反）＋tort（歪曲）→反驳

【例】"It was no business of yours", he *retorted*.

brawl [brɔ:l] *n./vi.* 争吵（bicker, quarrel）

【例】The disagreement soon erupted into a *brawl*.

bicker ['bikə] *vi.* 争吵（brawl, quarrel）

【例】The couple *bickered* over little things.

haggle ['hægl] *vi.* 争论（argue, bargain）

【例】The housewife *haggled* about the price with the vendor for half an hour.

gainsay ['geinsei] *vt.* 反驳(oppose)
【记】gain=against(反对)+say(说)
【例】He is a good man; there is no *gainsaying* his innocence.

refute [ri'fju:t] *vt.* 驳斥，反驳，驳倒(disprove, rebut)
【记】re(反)+fute=fuse(流)→反流→反驳
【例】I *refuted* him easily.

disprove [dis'pru:v] *vt.* 反驳，证明…有误
【记】dis+prove(证明)
【例】The research *disproved* information I had taken for granted.

controvert ['kɔntrəvə:t] *vt.* 反驳；辩论(deny, contradict)
【记】contro(反)+vert(转)
【例】what he said is a fact that can't be *controverted*.

controversy ['kɔntrəvə:si] *n.* 争论
【例】I am really tired of public *controversy* concerning the morals of the president.

controversial [ˌkɔntrə'və:ʃəl] *adj.* 引起争论的
【例】Mike wrote a very *controversial* book about the weakness of our political leaders.

contradict [ˌkɔntrə'dikt] *vt.* 反驳；抵触(counteract, oppose)
【记】contra(相反)+dic(言)→相反之言
【例】I hate to *contradict* your statement, but there are many snakes in Australia.

contradictory [ˌkɔntrə'diktəri] *adj.* 矛盾的，反驳的(opposing)

contravene [ˌkɔntrə'vi:n] *vt.* 反对；违反(contradict, oppose)
【记】contra(相反)+vene(走)→违背
【例】Don't do whatever may *contravene* the law of the country.

连 线 题

左列单词在右列中有一个或多个同义词，请画线连接。

（一）

confer	accord
	allocate
contravene	allot
	clarify
decry	complain
	condemn
dialogue	contradict
	conversation
dispatch	denounce
	discuss
elucidate	explain
	grunt
grumble	harmony
	oppose
reiterate	refute
	reply
retort	restate
unanimity	

（二）

	advise
	connection
asperse	contact
	deleterious
counsel	derisive
exclaim	designate
impart	direction
	disseminate
injurious	ejaculate
liaison	harmful
	inform
mock	instruction
prescription	mimic
	ridicule
sardonic	sarcastic
specify	shout
	slander

连线题答案

（一）

confer	discuss
contravene	contradict
contravene	oppose
decry	condemn
decry	denounce
dialogue	conversation
dispatch	allocate
dispatch	allot
elucidate	clarify
elucidate	explain
grumble	complain
grumble	grunt
reiterate	restate
retort	refute
retort	reply
unanimity	harmony
unanimity	accord

（二）

asperse	slander
counsel	advise
exclaim	shout
exclaim	ejaculate
impart	inform
impart	disseminate
injurious	harmful
injurious	deleterious
liaison	contact
liaison	connection
mock	mimic
mock	ridicule
prescription	instruction
prescription	direction
sardonic	sarcastic
sardonic	derisive
specify	designate

属　性

记忆小贴士：无意识记忆法

无意识记忆并不是无注意力记忆，而是时间分散记忆。首先准备一个袖珍笔记本，将要记忆的单词写在笔记本上。只要有时间就拿出来读读。每读记一遍，就在你的大脑中加深一层印象。

安 静

sedate [si'deit] *adj.* 安静的（calm, composed）
【记】sed=sid（坐）＋ate→安静地坐着

tranquil ['træŋkwil] *adj.* 安静的（serene, quiet, peaceful）
【例】It is not easy to remain *tranquil* when events suddenly change your life.

placid ['plæsid] *adj.* 安静的（tranquil, serene）
【例】The baby looks so *placid* and content after she has been fed.

static ['stætik] *adj.* 静的，静态的（changeless, stagnant）
【例】*Static* air pressure indicates that the weather will not change soon.

serene [sə'riːn] *adj.* 平静的；沉静的（calm, tranquil）
【记】seren（安静）＋e
【例】Tired of noisy city life, he went to the countryside for a *serene* life.

serenity [sə'reniti] *n.* 安静；从容（calmness, tranquility）

still [stil] *adj.* 静止的（motionless, stationary, fixed）
【例】The restaurant was as *still* as a library.

lull [lʌl] *vt.* 使平静（calm down, soothe）
【例】The mother *lulled* her baby to sleep.

肮 脏

disgraced [dis'greist] *a.* 不光彩的，丢脸的（humiliating）
【记】dis＋graced（体面的）→不体面的
【例】The boy felt *disgraced* because he knew that he had been wrong to steal.

dingy ['dindʒi] *adj.* 肮脏的（dirty, shabby）

messy ['mesi] *adj.* 肮脏的，凌乱的（untidy, dirty）
【记】mess（凌乱）＋y

slovenly ['slʌvənli] *adj.* 不洁的（untidy）

frowzy ['frauzi] *adj.* 不整洁的；臭的（filthy）

obscene [ɔb'siːn] *adj.* 猥亵的（indecent, filthy）
【记】ob（不）＋scene（场景）→不堪入目的

indecent [in'diːsənt] *adj.* 淫猥的(improper, unacceptable)
【记】in(不)＋decent(正派的)

impure [im'pjuə] *adj.* 脏的，不纯洁的(adulterated, unrefined)
【记】im(不)＋pure(纯洁的)

blemish ['blemiʃ] *n./vt.* 玷污(defect, flaw)
【记】blem(弄伤)＋ish
【例】One illness will *blemish* your perfect attendance record.

smear [smiə] *vt.* 弄脏(smudge, stain)
【例】The vast spill *smeared* the once beautiful coast.

defile [di'fail] *vt.* 弄污(contaminate)
【记】de＋file=vile(卑鄙)
【例】Watching too many violent TV shows *defiled* the child's mind.

spot [spɔt] *vt.* 玷污 *n.* 污点(stain)
【例】The amateur *spotted* the comet before the pros.

不 合 适

incompetent [in'kɔmpitənt] *adj.* 不称职的
【记】in(不)＋competent(能干的)

unbecoming [ˌʌnbi'kʌmiŋ] *adj.* 不配的，不适当的
【例】The careless woman often wore *unbecoming* clothes to work.

inept [i'nept] *adj.* 不适宜的(incompetent, inefficient)
【记】in(不)＋ept(熟练的)

unseemly [ʌn'siːmli] *adj.* 不适宜的(unsuited, incongruous)
【例】Jane was regretful for her *unseemly* behavior at the grand party.

ineligible [in'elidʒəbl] *adj.* 无资格的；不适当的(disqualified, unsuitable)
【记】in(无)＋eligible(有资格的)

impropriety [ˌimprə'praiəti] *n.* 不适当
【记】im(不)＋propriety(得体)

程 度

fervent ['fəːvənt] *adj.* 白热的；强烈的(ardent)
【记】ferv(热)＋ent
【例】Jenny is a *fervent* supporter of the feminist movement.

rough [rʌf] *adj.* 大致的（approximate, about）

【例】I got a *rough* idea that he is a tall man.

roughly [ˈrʌfli] *adv.* 概略地，粗糙地（approximately, nearly, more or less）

intense [inˈtens] *adj.* 强烈的（severe）

【例】Under years of *intense* pressure, he finally gave up hope and committed suicide.

intensive [inˈtensiv] *adj.* 密集的，加强的（concentrated）

intensely [inˈtensli] *adv.* 激烈地，热情地（extremely）

exorbitant [igˈzɔːbitənt] *adj.* 过分的，过度的（excessive, unreasonable）

【例】I will not pay such an *exorbitant* price for these shoes!

probable [ˈprɔbəbl] *adj.* 很可能的，大概（likely）

violent [ˈvaiələnt] *adj.* 激烈的（vehement, radical, sudden）

drastic [ˈdræstik] *adj.* 激烈的（violent）

【例】The principal felt that the cheater's punishment should be *drastic*. / The emergency called for *drastic* measure.

dead [ded] *adv.* 完全地（completely）

【例】You are *dead* right on this point.

deadly [ˈdedli] *adj.* 极度的（extremey）

【例】They sat in *deadly* silence.

sharp [ʃɑːp] *adj.* 急剧的（sudden）

【例】There is a *sharp* rise on crime, as the result of the starvation.

categorical [ˌkætiˈgɔrikəl] *adj.* 绝对的，无条件的 （definite, positive, absolute, unconditional）

【例】The Japanese made a *categorical* surrendering to China in 1945 after 8 years of invasion.

impetuous [imˈpetjuəs] *adj.* 猛烈的

vehement [ˈviːimənt] *adj.* 猛烈的，激烈的（passionate, ardent）

vehemence [ˈviːiməns] *n.* 热切，激烈（passion, ferocity）

burning [ˈbəːniŋ] *adj.* 强烈的

complete [kəmˈpliːt] *adj.* 完全的 *vt.* 完成

【例】Bill told us the *complete* story over coffee.

completely [kəmˈpliːtli] *adv.* 十分，完全地（entirely, wholly）

inordinate ［i'nɔ:dinit］*adj.* 无节制的；过度的（excessive, immoderate）

【记】in(不)＋ordin(正常)＋ate→过度的

considerable ［kən'sidərəbl］*adj.* 相当的（a great deal, large, much, substantial）

substantial ［səb'stænʃəl］*adj.* 相当的（plentiful, considerable）

【例】Mary has a *substantial* amount of money in the bank.

grossly ［'grəusli］*adv.* 非常（greatly）

extremely ［iks'tri:mli］*adv.* 极端地，非常地（exceptionally, intensely）

nearly ［'niəli］*adv.* 几乎（almost）

virtually ［'və:tjuəli］*adv.* 几乎（almost, practically, actually）

hardly ［'hɑ:dli］*adv.* 几乎不（scarcely, barely）

barely ［'bɛəli］*adv.* 仅仅（merely）

【例】There was *barely* enough food to go around.

profoundly ［prə'faundli］*adv.* 深刻地，深度地（deeply, greatly）

【记】profound(深刻的)＋ly

【例】Television programs with written subtitles help those *profoundly* deaf people to understand the world.

clean ［kli:n］*adv.* 完全地（totally, completely）

【例】I *clean* forgot about it.

entirely ［in'taiəli］*adv.* 完全地，全然地（totally, solely）

utterly ［'ʌtəli］*adv.* 完全地，彻底地（completely, absolutely）

somewhat ［'sʌm(h)wɔt］*adv.* 有点（rather, to some degree）

【例】He is a clever boy, though *somewhat* slow.

fairly ［'fɛəli］*adv.* 相当地（relatively, somewhat）

absolute ［ˌæbsə'lu:t］*adj.* 绝对的（sheer）

【记】比较solute(化学溶质)

【例】The prime minister had *absolute* control of his cabinet.

radical ［'rædikəl］*adj.* 根本的，基本的，激进的

纯

sheer ［ʃiə］*adj.* 纯粹的；全然的（pure, total）

【例】Don't believe him; his words are *sheer* nonsense.

pure ［pjuə］*adj.* 纯的，纯洁的（clean, unadulterated）

unblemished ［ʌn'blemiʃt］*adj.* 洁白的，无瑕的（flawless, perfect）

innocent ［'inəsnt］*adj.* 清白的（guiltless, faultless）

【记】in(无)＋noc(害)＋ent→无害的

【例】Anne was found *innocent* of the crime.

impeccable [im'pekəbl] *adj.* 无瑕的(faultless, stainless)

【记】im(无)＋pecc(斑点)＋able→无瑕的

perfect ['pəːfikt] *adj.* 无瑕的，完好无损的(intact, untouched)

【记】per(全部)＋fect(做)→全部做完→完美的

【例】Thousands of years past, still we found those mummies staying *perfect* in their coffins.

virtuous ['vəːtjuəs] *adj.* 贞洁的(moral, righteous)

chaste [tʃeist] *adj.* 贞洁的；纯正的(pure, virtuous)

【例】The students were advised to remain *chaste* until marriage.

大

colossal [kə'lɔsl] *adj.* 巨大的(immense, huge)

【记】源自希腊神话中名为Colossus的大力神

【例】Bill made a *colossal* mistake when he bought that used car.

spacious ['speiʃəs] *adj.* 广大的，宽敞的(roomy, capacious)

【记】spac(地方)＋ious→地方大的

【例】Working in a *spacious* room contributes to one's working efficiency.

expansive [iks'pænsiv] *adj.* 广阔的；可扩张的，可膨胀的(extensive, large)

【例】The book's *expansive* index listed hundreds of important items.

prodigious [prə'didʒəs] *adj.* 巨大的(colossal, enormous)

【记】prodig(巨大)＋ious

【例】I have a *prodigious* amount of work to do before I leave.

massive ['mæsiv] *adj.* 巨大的(heavy, huge, enormous)

【例】Doctors prescribe *massive* doses of penicillin for patients with pneumonia.

enormous [i'nɔːməs] *adj.* 巨大的(huge, vast, immense, tremendous)

【记】e(出)＋norm(正常)＋ous→超出了正常状态→巨大的

【例】We prepared an *enormous* dinner because we were very hungry.

mighty ['maiti] *adj.* 巨大的(powerful, strong)

【记】might(巨大)＋y

vast [vɑːst] *adj.* 巨大的，大量的 (gigantic, huge, immense, tremendous, broad, enormous）

tremendous ［triˈmendəs］*adj.* 巨大的，惊人的（huge, great）

immense ［iˈmens］*adj.* 巨大的；无限的

【记】im(不)＋mense(测量)→不能测量→无限的

titanic ［taiˈtænik］*adj.* 巨大有力的（huge, immense）

【记】美国影片《泰坦尼克号》的英文

【例】The politician tried to reduce the *titanic* deficit.

commodious ［kəˈməudjəs］*adj.* 宽敞的（spacious, capacious, roomy）

【记】com(共同)＋mod(范围)＋ious→大家都有范围→宽敞的

broad ［brɔːd］*adj.* 宽的，广泛的（wide, general）

loose ［luːs］*adj.* 宽松的

bulky ［ˈbʌlki］*adj.* 庞大的；笨重的（cumbersome）

【例】The *bulky* boxes won't fit in the trunk of the car.

capacious ［kəˈpeiʃəs］*adj.* 容量大的；宽敞的（spacious）

方 位

forth ［fɔːθ］*adv.* 向前（ahead）

entry ［ˈentri］*n.* 入口；进入

【例】There is a back *entry* into the house.

exit ［ˈeksit］*n.* 出口（outlet, way-out）

【记】ex(出)＋it(走)→走出→出口

【例】The actress exited secretly from an unseen *exit*.

outlet ［ˈautlet］*n.* 出路，出口（socker, access）

【例】There is no *outlet* to the sea in Chongqing.

site ［sait］*n.* 地点（location, position）

destination ［ˌdestiˈneiʃən］*n.* 目的地

【例】Our vacation *destination* is Phoenix.

veer ［viə］*v.* 改变方向（turn, swerve）

【例】The car *veered* to the left toward ours and we were scared.

spot ［spɔt］*n.* 地点（location）

head ［hed］*vi.* 向某处走去（set out for, make for）

【例】Where are you *heading* for?

公 正

valid [ˈvælid] *adj.* 正当的

【例】I have the *valid* excuse for arriving late at work.

upright [ˈʌprait] *adj.* 正直的

【记】up(上)＋right(正的)

【例】The *upright* witness told the truth at the trial.

unfair [ʌnˈfɛə] *adj.* 不公平的(unjust, partial)

【记】un(不)＋fair(公正的)

fairly [ˈfɛəli] *adv.* 公正地

guileless [ˈgaillis] *adj.* 不狡猾的，诚实的(frank, honest)

【例】His *guileless* smile disarmed us; we began to believe him.

equitable [ˈekwitəbl] *adj.* 公平的，公正的(fair, just)

【例】Twenty dollars is an *equitable* price for this lamp.

detached [diˈtætʃt] *adj.* 公正的

disinterested [disˈintristid] *adj.* 公正的(impartial, unbiased)

【例】Mary is completely *disinterested* in the matter and can judge fairly.

unbiased [ʌnˈbaiəst] *adj.* 公正的(neutral, impartial)

partially [ˈpɑːʃəli] *adv.* 不公平地

impartial [imˈpɑːʃəl] *adj.* 公正的，无偏见的(fair, unbiased)

【例】The judge should make his appraisal *impartial*.

conscience [ˈkɔnʃəns] *n.* 良心，良知

conscientious [ˌkɔnʃiˈenʃəs] *adj.* 尽职的；正直的(diligent)

incorruptible [ˌinkəˈrʌptəbl] *adj.* 廉洁的

【记】in(不)＋corruptible(易收买的)

decent [ˈdiːsnt] *adj.* 正派的；体面的(reasonable, proper)

【例】Don't walk around in your underwear. Go put on some *decent* clothes! / The house was in *decent* shape when we bought it.

faithful [ˈfeiθful] *adj.* 忠实的(loyal)

【记】faith(忠诚)＋ful

【例】In Amish tribe, the *faithful* are not allowed to own automobiles.

justly [ˈdʒʌstli] *adv.* 公正地

devotion [diˈvəuʃən] *n.* 献身；忠诚；专心（loyalty, dedication）

【例】Is it true that dogs show strong *devotion* to their masters?

integrity [inˈtegriti] *n.* 正直（honesty）

probity [ˈprəubiti] *n.* 正直（integrity, honesty）

fidelity [fiˈdeliti] *n.* 忠诚（loyalty, faithfulness）

【记】fid（相信）＋elity→相信→坚贞

dedicate [ˈdedikeit] *vt.* 奉献，致力于

【例】This room is *dedicated* to food preparation.

合　适

sober [ˈsəubə] *adj.* 适度的

qualified [ˈkwɔlifaid] *adj.* 合格的

rational [ˈræʃənl] *adj.* 合理的（reasonable）

becoming [biˈkʌmiŋ] *adj.* 合适的，相称的（fitting, suitable）

【例】John's new haircut is very *becoming*.

reliable [riˈlaiəbl] *adj.* 可靠的，可信赖的（dependable）

【记】动词rely（依靠）

【例】The subway is the most *reliable* way of getting to the airport during rush hours.

preferable [ˈprefərəbl] *adj.* 可取的（advisable）

【记】prefer（喜欢）＋able

【例】A *preferable* option is to store the food in a refrigerator rather than throw them away.

available [əˈveiləbl] *adj.* 可用的（obtainable, accessible）

【例】The hotel is *available* for the wedding reception next week.

competent [ˈkɔmpitənt] *adj.* 能胜任的（capable, qualified）

【例】Mike did a *competent* job fixing my car.

fit [fit] *adj.* 适合的（suitable）

【例】This violent movie is not *fit* for children.

fitting [ˈfitiŋ] *adj.* 恰当的，得体的（proper, appropriate）

【记】fit（合适）＋ting

【例】It is a *fitting* gesture to offer a reward to someone who returns something you have lost.

feasible [ˈfiːzəbl] *adj.* 切实可行的（practical, possible, viable）

【记】feas（做）＋ible→能够做的→可行的

【例】Before you carry out the plan, make sure it is *feasible*.

expedient [iksˈpiːdjənt] *adj.* 权宜的；方便的（suitable, convenient）

【例】*Expedient* solutions rarely solve long-term problems.

pertinent [ˈpəːtinənt] *adj.* 适当的；切题的（relevant）

temperate [ˈtemprit] *adj.* 适度的，有节制的（appropriate, reasonable, self-controlled）

【例】A *temperate* answer to a rude question is difficult to give.

suitable [ˈsjuːtəbl] *adj.* 适合的

plausible [ˈplɔːzəbl] *adj.* 似合理的（reasonable）

【例】Susie's story about how she lost her books sounded *plausible,* but it wasn't actually true.

methodical [məˈθɔdikl] *adj.* 有条理的（systematic）

【记】method（方法）＋ical→有方法的→有条理的

entitled [inˈtaitld] *adj.* 有资格的（eligible, qualified）

correspondence [ˌkɔriˈspɔndəns] *n.* 对应；符合

【记】cor＋respond（反应）＋ence

【例】There is close *correspondence* between my handwriting and yours.

propriety [prəˈpraiəti] *n.* 适当（correctness）

tally [ˈtæli] *vi.* 符合（accord, agree）

【例】The report *tallies* with your description of the accident.

coincide [ˌkəuinˈsaid] *vi.* 相符合，相巧合

【记】co（共同）＋in＋cide（落下）→共同落下→巧合

【例】Our vacations *coincided,* so we traveled together.

suit [sjuːt] *vt.* 合适，适应（accommodate, fit, adapt）

【例】This candidate does not *suit* our qualifications.

advisable [ədˈvaizəbl] *adj.* 合理的（rational, sound）

【例】It is *advisable* to save part of your paycheck each month.

adapt [əˈdæpt] *v.* (使)适应（adjust, accommodate）

【例】Jane *adapted* quickly to the new procedures.

adaptable [əˈdæptəbl] *adj.* 能适应的

【例】 If you are not *adaptable,* you will feel uncomfortable in college.

adaptation [ˌædæpˈteiʃn] *n.* 适应(accomodation)

【例】 The movie was an *adaptation* of a classic novel.

conformity [kənˈfɔːmiti] *n.* 一致,符合

尖 刻

incisive [inˈsaisiv] *adj.* 尖锐的

【例】 His *incisive* criticism gave us a thorough understanding of Dicken's writings.

caustic [ˈkɔːstik] *adj.* 刻薄的

【例】 The *caustic* remark caused the candidate to lose the election.

acid [ˈæsid] *adj.* 尖酸的

【例】 The critic's *acid* remarks hurt the director's feelings.

acrimonious [ˌækriˈməunjəs] *adj.* 尖酸的(bitter, spiteful)

【例】 The *acrimonious* debate resulted in much resentment.

acrid [ˈækrid] *adj.* 辛辣的(pungent, bitter, acrimonious, trenchant)

【例】 Burning rubber produces an *acrid* smoke.

acrimony [ˈækriməni] *n.* 刻薄

【记】 acri(尖,酸)+mony→尖刻

【例】 They were able to reach a decision without *acrimony*.

精 巧

cunning [ˈkʌniŋ] *adj.* 可爱的(cute, clever)

【例】 What a *cunning* kitten!

elegant [ˈeligənt] *adj.* (举止、服饰)雅致的(refined, exquisite, elaborate)

【记】 e(出)+leg=lig(选)+ant→选出的→好的

【例】 Successful women on political stage often have an *elegant* manner.

handy [ˈhændi] *adj.* 方便的;灵巧的(convenient; skilful)

ingenious [inˈdʒiːnjəs] *adj.* 机灵的(clever, intelligent);精巧制成的

【记】 in(内)+geni(产生)+ous→自内心产生→聪明的

【例】 By such *ingenious* adaptations, orchids can attract insects from afar to fertilize them.

exquisite [ˈekskwizit] *adj.* 精美的(delicate, fine, elaborate)

【记】 ex+quisite(要求)→按要求做出来→精美的

【例】Tom was so absorbed by the *exquisite* vase at the museum.

delicate ['delikit] *adj.* 精巧的(dainty, elegant)

【例】Roses have a *delicate* beauty.

refined [ri'faind] *adj.* 精致的；文雅的(elegant, well-mannered)

【例】The reproduction of the masterpiece is less *refined* than the original one.

dexterous ['dekstərəs] *adj.* 灵巧的(adroit, skillful)

【记】dexter(右边的)＋ous

crafty ['kræfti] *adj.* 灵巧的，巧妙的(cunning, sneaky)

【例】The spy thought of a *crafty* plan to steal the documents.

elaborate [i'læbəreit] *vt.* 精心制作(或计划) *adj.* 精心构思的(careful)

【例】We ask Mary to *elaborate* her trip to Tibet.

距 离

remote [ri'məut] *adj.* 遥远的，远程的(distant, inaccessible)

distant ['distənt] *adj.* 远的(remote)

【例】My parents live in a *distant* state, and I rarely see them.

gap [gæp] *n.* 差距(distance)

【例】A generation *gap* lies between parents and children.

proximity [prɔk'simiti] *n.* 临近(nearness)

【记】proxim(接近)＋ity

【例】He look around the *proximity* for his lost dog.

distribute [di'stribjut] *vt.* 分布

【例】180 pounds of muscles are well *distributed* over his 6-foot frame.

adjacent [ə'dʒeisənt] *adj.* 邻近的(adjoining, neighboring)

【例】Tom's house is *adjacent* to the park.

access ['ækses] *vt.* 接近

【记】ac＋cess(走)→走过去→通道

【例】Bill could not *access* any information from the computer.

adjoin [ə'dʒɔin] *vt.* 贴近，毗连，靠近(abut)

【记】ad(一再)＋join(连)→一再连上→毗连

【例】The living room *adjoins* the dining room.

adjoining ［ə'dʒɔiniŋ］*adj.* 接近的，邻接的（adjacent, neighboring）

【记】adjoin＋ing

【例】We requested *adjoining* rooms at the hotel.

肯　定

infallible ［in'fæləbl］*adj.* 必然的；不会错的

【记】in(无)＋fallible(错误的)

inevitable ［in'evitəbl］*adj.* 不可避免的，必然的（unavoidable, certain）

【例】Death is the *inevitable* ending of life.

definite ［'definit］*adj.* 明确的；肯定的（specific, straightforward）

【例】She made him no *definite* answer.

confident ［'kɔnfidənt］*adj.* 确信的，自信的

【记】con＋fid(相信)＋ent

【例】I am *confident* that he will pay his bills.

undoubtedly ［ʌn'dautidli］*adv.* 勿庸置疑地，的确（unquestionably, surely）

ascertain ［,æsə'tein］*vt.* 确定；探知（determine, make sure）

【记】as＋certain(确信)

【例】Did the doctor *ascertain* the cause of your sickness?

空

null ［nʌl］*adj.* 空的

empty ［'empti］*adj.* 空的（vacant, void）

【例】The room is *empty*. All the furniture has been removed.

vacant ［'veikənt］*adj.* 空的；未被占用的（unoccupied, empty）

【记】vac(空)＋ant

void ［vɔid］*n.* 空间(space) *adj.* 空的（invalid, null）

【例】His wife's death left a painful *void* in his life.

vacuum ［'vækjuəm］*n.* 真空（gap, void）

evacuate ［i'vækjueit］*vt.* 使…空（remove）

【记】e＋vacu(空)＋ate→使空

【例】The Civil Defense *evacuated* all inhabitants from the area where the storm was predicted to strike.

bare [bɛə] *adj.* 空的

【例】*Bare* words, no bargain.

明 显

sensible ['sensəbl] *adj.* 明显的，感觉得到的（discernible）

【记】sens（感觉）＋ible

【例】I am *sensible* that a good deal more is still to be done.

imposing [im'pəuziŋ] *adj.* 令人难忘的（impressive）

【例】The pyramids of Egypt are *imposing* structure.

obvious ['ɔbviəs] *adj.* 明显的（distinct, evident）

pronounced [prə'naunst] *adj.* 明显的（notable, prominent）

【记】pronounce（发音）＋ed→（人人都能）发的音→著名的

【例】The result will become *pronounced* after two weeks' medication.

sharp [ʃɑːp] *adj.* 明显的，清晰的（clear）

【例】High quality cameras deliver *sharp* images.

outstanding [aut'stændiŋ] *adj.* 显著的（notable, remarkable）

【记】来自stand out（醒目，突出）

emphatic [im'fætik] *adj.* 显著的；强调的；有力的（powerful）

【例】The supervisor's *emphatic* speech on worker productivity produced amazing results.

remarkable [ri'mɑːkəbl] *adj.* 值得注意的（striking, considerable）

impressively [im'presivli] *adv.* 令人难忘地

markedly ['mɑːkidli] *adv.* 显著地，明显地（significantly, substantially, noticeably）

【例】By driving a cheap car, the billionaire clearly intended not to show his wealth *markedly*.

especially [is'peʃəli] *adv.* 尤其（notably, particularly）

普 遍

routine [ruː'tiːn] *adj.* 常规的（regular, conventional, usual）

【例】Anne took a *routine* coffee break at 2:30 PM.

extensive [iks'tensiv] *adj.* 大量的；广泛的（comprehensive; thorough）

【例】The editor made *extensive* changes in the article.

mediocre [ˈmiːdiəukə] *adj.* 平常的；普通的(ordinary, average)

【记】medi(中间)＋ocre→平庸的

【例】I got *mediocre* grades last semester.

hackneyed [ˈhæknid] *adj.* 平凡的

【记】参考hack(陈腐的)，Internet用语hacker(黑客)

【例】The old professor's *hackneyed* style of coaching arouses complaints from among students.

universal [ˌjuːniˈvəːsl] *adj.* 普遍的(general, absolute)

catholic [ˈkæθəlik] *adj.* 普遍的，广泛的(universal)

【例】Her musical tastes were *catholic* and ranged from classics to jazz.

general [ˈdʒenərəl] *adj.* 普通的(ordinary)

generally [ˈdʒenərəli] *adv.* 广泛地，一般地(widely, usually, broadly)

exhaustive [igˈzɔːstiv] *adj.* 无遗漏的，彻底的，广泛的(comprehensive, thorough)

【例】The real-estate agent gave the prospective buyers an *exhaustive* tour of the new house.

average [ˈævəridʒ] *adj.* 一般的(normal)

mostly [ˈməustli] *adv.* 多半地；通常

【记】most(主要的)＋ly

usually [ˈjuːʒuəli] *adv.* 通常，大抵(customarily, commonly)

commonplace [ˈkɔmənˌpleis] *n.* 平凡事，平凡话 *adj.* 平凡的(average, ordinary)

事物属性

tender [ˈtendə] *adj.* 嫩的(soft)

concrete [ˈkɔnkriːt] *adj.* 具体的

【例】Bill prefers *concrete* facts to abstract ideas.

portable [ˈpɔːtəbl] *adj.* 可携带的(movable, transportable)

【记】port(拿)＋able→可拿的

【例】A *portable* PC now became necessary in many MBA programs.

sloppy [ˈslɔpi] *adj.* 泥泞的(muddled, semi-liquid)

【记】slop(溅，弄脏)＋py

congested [kənˈdʒestid] *adj.* 拥挤的(overcrowded)

【记】con(共同)＋gest(管道)＋ed→共同在一个管道→拥挤的

【例】The *congested* highway made many commuters late for work.

数 量

fraught [frɔːt] *adj.* 充满的（full of）

【记】比较 freight（装运的货物）

【例】It was clearly not a job *fraught* with hope, but I have to take it for a living.

sole [səul] *adj.* 惟一的（only, mere, exclusive）

【例】His *sole* purpose when playing cards is to relax.

solitary [ˈsɔlitəri] *adj.* 单一的（lonesome, isolated）

【记】solit（单独）＋ary

【例】He has taken a *solitary* approach to his pursuit of another basketball gold medal.

quantity [ˈkwɔntiti] *n.* 量，数量（amount）

quantitative [ˈkwɔntitətiv] *adj.* 定量的

【记】quant（数量）＋itative→定量的

【例】A *quantitative* analysis showed that he has grown 10 pounds fatter.

excess [ˈekses] *n./adj.* 过度（的）（surplus）

【记】ex＋cess（走）→走出格→过分

【例】Don't bring any *excess* baggage on this trip.

excessive [ikˈsesiv] *adj.* 过多的，极度的（overabundant, inordinate）

【例】You must curb your *excessive* spending, or you will become penniless.

redundant [riˈdʌndənt] *adj.* 过多的，冗长的（unnecessary, superfluous）

sporadic [spəˈrædik] *adj.* 零星的（irregular, intermittent）

【例】The gunfire was *sporadic* until midnight.

numerous [ˈnjuːmərəs] *adj.* 众多的

【记】numer（数字）＋ous

innumerable [iˈnjuːmərəbl] *adj.* 无数的（countless, numerous）

【记】in（不）＋numer（数）＋able→数不过来→无数的

countless [ˈkauntlis] *adj.* 无数的（innumerable, many）

【记】count（数）＋less

sufficient [səˈfiʃənt] *adj.* 足够的，充分的（enough, adequate）

【记】其动词形式为 suffice

skimpy ['skimpi] *adj.* 太少的（scant, inadequate）

sparsely ['spɑːsli] *adv.* 稀少地，稀疏地（thinly, scarcely）

bulk [bʌlk] *n.* 大批（mass, volume, most majority）

majority [mə'dʒɔriti] *n.* 多数，大多数

block [blɔk] *n.* 一块（木或石等）

【例】The floor was made of wooden *blocks.*

multitude ['mʌltitjuːd] *n.* 众多（host, mass）

【记】multi(多)＋tude

sum [sʌm] *n.* 总数

teem [tiːm] *vi.* 充满（abound, be full of）

【例】The stream *teemed* with fish.

pervade [pə'veid] *vt.* 遍布；弥漫（permeate）

【记】per(全部，遍)＋vade(走)→遍布

【例】The spicy smell *pervaded* the kitchen.

suffuse [sə'fjuːz] *vt.* 充满（fill）

【记】suf(到处)＋fuse(流)→到处流→充满

【例】His eyes were *suffused* with tears.

abundant [ə'bʌndənt] *adj.* 充裕的（sufficient）

【记】a＋bun(小圆面包)＋d＋ant(蚂蚁)→蚂蚁有充裕的小圆面包

【例】The *abundant* crops would feed the village throughout the winter.

further ['fəːðə] *adj.* 更多的（additional）

【例】He wants to receive *further* education in China.

adequate ['ædikwit] *adj.* 足够的（sufficient）

【例】What you have given us is not *adequate*; you must find more.

spare [spɛə] *adj.* 多余的，剩下的

times [taimz] *n.* 时期，次

total ['təutl] *n.* 总数，合计

volume ['vɔljuːm] *n.* 量，大量

特 殊

original [ə'ridʒənl] *adj.* 独创的

【记】origin(起源)＋al

【例】His idea is not *original*; many pioneers had the same thought.

unique [juː'niːk] *adj.* 独一无二的（unrivaled, matchless）

【例】The sales clerk showed me a most *unique* necklace.

extraordinary [iks'trɔːdinəri] *adj.* 非凡的，特别的（remarkable, outstanding）

erratic [i'rætik] *adj.* 古怪的（odd, eccentric）

【例】Bill's *erratic* moods upset everyone in our office.

eccentric [ik'sentrik] *adj.* 古怪的（odd, erratic, bizarre）

【记】ec＋centr(中心)＋ic→非中心→异常的

【例】My neighbor's *eccentric* behavior is sometimes frightening.

bizarre [bi'zɑː] *adj.* 古怪的（odd, erratic, eccentric）

queer [kwiə] *adj.* 奇怪的，古怪的（strange, fishy）

【记】比较queen(皇后)

quaint [kweint] *adj.* 奇异的，不凡的（queer, odd）

given ['givn] *adj.* 特定的（specified）

particularly [pə'tikjuləli] *adv.* 独特地，显著地（especially）

abnormal [æb'nɔːməl] *adj.* 异常的（exceptional）

【记】ab(离开)＋normal(正常的)→异常的

odd [ɔd] *adj.* 古怪的

weird [wiəd] *adj.* 怪异的，超自然的

sensitive ['sensitiv] *adj.* 敏感的

idiosyncrasy [idiə'siŋkrəsi] *n.* 个人特性

【例】Tom has an *idiosycracy* of playing football all by himself.

trait [treit] *n.* 特点，特性（characteristic, attribute）

character ['kæriktə] *n.* 性格

【例】He has a changeable *character*.

characteristic [ˌkæriktə'ristik] *n.* 特性，特征 *adj.* 特有的，典型的（distinctive, distingui-shing）

bear [bɛə] *vt.* 具有，带有（carry）

【例】The comet will *bear* the name of the finder.

危　险

destructive [di'strʌktiv] *adj.* 破坏(性)的，危害的

【记】de(坏)＋struct(结构)＋ive→破坏结构

【例】The *destructive* winds carried away the roof of the house.

critical ['kritikl] *adj.* 危急的；临界的

【例】You must calm down in this *critical* moment.

perilous ['periləs] *adj.* 危险的（dangerous, hazardous）

hazard [ˈhæzəd] *n.* 危险(risk, danger); 公害

hazardous [ˈhæzədəs] *adj.* 危险的(dangerous, perilous)

【例】People hesitated whether to begin the *hazardous* journey to the unknown west or not.

dangerous [ˈdeindʒərəs] *adj.* 危险的(hazardous, risky)

【例】The *dangerous* road had several sharp turns.

endanger [inˈdeindʒə] *vt.* 危害(harm)

【记】en+danger(危险)

【例】The animals that lived in the marsh were *endangered* by the drought.

harmful [ˈhɑːmful] *adj.* 有害的(dangerous, detrimental)

deleterious [ˌdiliˈtiəriəs] *adj.* 有害的(harmful, detrimental)

detriment [ˈdetrimənt] *n.* 损害

【记】de+trim(修剪)+ent→剪坏→损害

【例】The *detriment* caused by your thoughtless remark will never be forgotten.

detrimental [ˌdetriˈmentl] *adj.* 有害的, 有损的

【例】The *detrimental* newspaper article may lead to a lawsuit.

peril [ˈperil] *n.* 危机; 危险的事物

jeopardy [ˈdʒepədi] *n.* 危险(danger, risk)

injure [ˈindʒə] *vt.* 伤害, 损害, 损伤(hurt, wound)

【例】There were two people *injured* in the car accident.

maim [meim] *vt.* 使残废(disable, mutilate); 损伤

【记】比较main(主要的)

【例】He was seriously *maimed* in a car accident.

impair [imˈpɛə] *vt.* 损害(harm, damage)

【记】im(进入)+pair(坏)→使…坏→损害

【例】His misdeeds greatly *impaired* our friendship.

threaten [ˈθretn] *v.* 威胁(menace, terrify)

【例】They *threaten* to kill all the people without receiving the ransom.

味 道

balmy	['bɑːmi] *adj.* 芳香的
	【记】balm(香气)+y
delicious	[di'liʃəs] *adj.* 美味的, 怡人的
palatable	['pælətəbl] *adj.* 味美的(savory, flavorous)
	【记】palate(上颚)+able
fragrant	['freigrənt] *adj.* 香的, 芬芳的(aromatic)
pungent	['pʌndʒənt] *adj.* 辛辣的(acrid, penetrating)
	【记】pung(刺)+ent→刺激的
	【例】The aged cheese had a *pungent* taste.

odor ['əudə] *n.* 臭气(smell, scent; fame)
【例】The *odor* of the gabbage can irritate the inhabitants.

taste [teist] *n.* 品味; 味道(flavor, savor; appreciation)
【例】The theatre ceased to cater to the audience's low *taste* by showing erotic movies.

aura ['ɔːrə] *n.* 气味

flavor ['fleivə] *n.* 味, 风味
【例】This yogurt has the *flavor* of strawberries.

aroma [ə'rəumə] *n.* 香气, 芬芳, 芳香(fragrance, scent, perfume)
【例】The roses gave the room a pleasant *aroma*.

smell [smel] *v.* 发出气味
【例】The fish *smells* bad in three days.

stink [stiŋk] *vi.* 发出臭味(smell bad)
【例】The garbage *stinks* up the yard.

savor ['seivə] *vt.* 尝味(taste, relish)
【例】I want to *savor* this great moment of accomplishment.

acid ['æsid] *adj.* 酸的(sour, tart) *n.* 酸
【例】Strong *acid* corrodes metal.

物理属性

hectic ['hektik] *adj.* 发热的(feverish)
【记】hect(许多)+ic→许多事要做→紧张兴奋的

impervious [im'pəːvjəs] *adj.* 不能渗透的(impenetrable, impermeable)

【记】im(不)＋pervious(渗透的)

【例】Since my watch is *impervious* to water, I wear it while I swim.

ponderous [ˈpɒndərəs] *adj.* 沉重的，笨重的(heavy)

crisp [krisp] *adj.* 脆的；卷曲的(crunchy, brittle)

【例】The autumn leaves were dry and *crisp*.

lofty [ˈlɔfti] *adj.* 高耸的(high, towering)

【记】loft(阁楼，顶楼)＋y

【例】The *lofty* mountains towered over the village.

slippery [ˈslipəri] *adj.* 滑的，使人滑跤的(slick, smooth)

dense [dens] *adj.* 密集的(thick, close)

【例】The airport was closed because of the *dense* fog.

crooked [ˈkrukid] *adj.* 扭曲的(bent, twisted)

【记】crook(弯曲)＋ed→拐弯抹角的

【例】The electrician straightened the *crooked* wires.

shallow [ˈʃæləu] *adj.* 浅的(superficial)

【例】It is possible to drown even in *shallow* water.

ethereal [əˈθiəriəl] *adj.* 轻的，天上的(light, delicate)

lithe [laið] *adj.* 柔软的；易弯的(flexible, supple)

sloppy [ˈslɔpi] *adj.* 稀薄的

【记】slop(溅，弄脏)＋py

slim [slim] *adj.* 细长的，苗条的(slender, thin)

tenuous [ˈtenjuəs] *adj.* 细的；稀薄的(thin, weak)

【记】ten(细，薄)＋uous

【例】The precious jewel is hung only with a *tenuous* thread that appeared very fragile.

compact [kəmˈpækt] *adj.* 压缩的；密集的(packed)

【记】com＋pact(打包，压紧)

【例】Jane has a *compact* kitchen with room for only one person.

supple [ˈsʌpl] *adj.* 柔软的，易曲的(flexible, lithe)

malleable [ˈmæliəbl] *adj.* 有延展性的(pliable)；可锻的

【记】malle(锤子)＋able→可锻的

depression [diˈpreʃən] *n.* 凹陷

小

| faint | [feint] *adj.* 微弱的(feeble, unsteady) |

【例】 I stayed up until I saw *faint* rays of light from the rising sun.

| ignoble | [ig'nəubl] *adj.* 卑微的(despicable, dishonorable) |

【记】 ig(不)＋noble(高贵)

minuscule	[mi'nʌskju:l] *adj.* 极小的(tiny)
negligible	['neglidʒəbl] *adj.* 可以忽略的，不予重视的(insignificant, minimal)
slight	[slait] *adj.* 轻微的，微小的(tiny, microscopic)
trivial	['triviəl] *adj.* 微不足道的(unimportant, trifling)

【例】 I didn't bother Bob with my *trivial* concerns because he was busy.

feeble	['fi:bl] *adj.* 微弱的(weak, infirm)
trifling	['traifliŋ] *adj.* 微小的(insignificant, trivial)
minute	[mai'nju:t] *adj.* 微小的(tiny, minuscule)

【记】 min(小)＋ute

| insular | ['insjulə] *adj.* 狭隘的(isolated; narrow-minded) |

【记】 insul(岛)＋ar

【例】 The head of the tribe has an *insular* prejudice over those strangers.

| diminutive | [di'minjutiv] *adj.* 小的(small, tiny) |

【例】 The child placed the cute, *diminutive* furniture in a dollhouse.

| tiny | ['taini] *adj.* 小的，极小的(microscopic, minute, little, minuscule) |
| fine | [fain] *adj.* 细微的(thin, small) |

虚 幻

| mythical | ['miθikəl] *adj.* 神话的，虚构的(legendary, fictious) |
| fictitious | [fik'tiʃəs] *adj.* 虚构的(invented, imaginary) |

【记】 fict(做，造)＋itious→造出的→虚构的

imaginary	[i'mædʒinəri] *adj.* 虚构的
imaginative	[i'mædʒinətiv] *adj.* 富于想像的
illusion	[i'lju:ʒən] *n.* 幻觉(hallucination)
fantasy	['fæntəsi] *n.* 幻想，空想；怪念头(dream; fancy)
superstition	[ˌsju:pə'stiʃən] *n.* 迷信

【例】 Fear of the number 13 is an old *superstition*.

| panacea | [ˌpænə'siə] *n.* 万灵药(cure-all) |

【记】pan(全部)＋acea(治疗)

figment ['figmənt] *n.* 虚构之事

【记】fig(做)＋ment→做出的东西→虚构

conceive [kən'siːv] *v.* 想像(devise, visualize)

【例】The inventor *conceived* a new gadget.

occult [ɔ'kʌlt] *adj.* 神秘的,不可思议的(supernatural)

需 要

gratuitous [grə'tjuitəs] *adj.* 不需要的(unwanted)

【例】Her *gratuitous* performance is not expected by the producer.

indispensable [,indis'pensəbl] *adj.* 不可缺少的,绝对必要的(essential, vital)

imperative [im'perətiv] *adj.* 急需的(necessary, urgent)

【记】imper(命令)＋ative

【例】The man is dying; an immediate operation is *imperative*.

真 实

tangible ['tændʒəbl] *adj.* 可见的,确实的(touchable, substantial)

【记】tang(接触)＋ible→确实(存在)的

【例】One *tangible* benefit of my new job is a company car.

authentic [ɔː'θentik] *adj.* 可靠,有根据的,真实的(genuine, real)

【记】aut(自己)＋hent(得到)＋ic→亲自得到→真实的

【例】Is your diamond ring *authentic*?

genuine ['dʒenjuin] *adj.* 真实的,真正的(authentic, real)

【例】My necklace is made with *genuine* pearls.

truly ['truːli] *adv.* 真实地,不假(genuinely, actually)

actual ['æktʃuəl] *adj.* 实际的,现行的,真实的(practical, real)

【例】Is this vase an *actual* antique or a copy?

重 要

superb [sjuː'pəːb] *adj.* 超级的

pivot ['pivət] *n.* 转折点,关键

pivotal ['pivətl] *adj.* 关键的;枢纽的

【例】Chairman of the board is the *pivotal* figure among the managing board.

foremost [ˈfɔːməust] *adj.* 第一流的(prime)

【记】fore(前)+most(最)→最先的

【例】He is one of the *foremost* atom scientists in China.

elementary [ˌeləˈmentəri] *adj.* 基本的，初级的

【例】I took a course in *elementary* chemistry.

fundamental [ˌfʌndəˈmentl] *adj.* 基础的，基本的(essential, elementary)

【例】The refugees were too poor to meet their *fundamental* needs of life.

momentous [məuˈmentəs] *adj.* 极重要的(important, critical)

【记】moment(时刻)+ous→刻不容缓的→重要的

vital [ˈvaitl] *adj.* 极重要的(important, crucial, essential)

【例】It is absolutely *vital* that food supplies should be maintained at any cost.

cardinal [ˈkɑːdinl] *adj.* 首要的，基本的(essential)

【记】cardi(铰链，要点)+nal

【例】To study hard is our *cardinal* thing to do.

crucial [ˈkruːʃəl] *adj.* 严重的；极重要的(decisive, critical)

【例】Knowing first aid is *crucial* for saving lives.

significant [sigˈnifikənt] *adj.* 有意义的；重要的(important, telling)

dominant [ˈdɔminənt] *adj.* 占优势的，主导的(predominant, prevalent)

【例】The *dominant* color in the design is red.

predominate [priˈdɔmineit] *vt.* 占优势，支配(prevail)

【记】pre+domin(统治)+ate

【例】Cheap and inferior commodities often *predominate* the morning market.

predominantly [priˈdɔminəntli] *adv.* 占主导地位地，显著地(primarily, chiefy, principally)

【例】In this company, employees are *predominantly* white, which is a sign of racial discrimination against the colored people.

fateful [ˈfeitful] *adj.* 重大的

【例】Gates made a *fateful* decision to quit Harvard.

primary [ˈpraiməri] *adj.* 重要的(crucial, vital)

【记】prim(最初的)+ary

primarily [praiˈmərili] *adv.* 首先，主要地(chiefly, mainly, principally)

essential [iˈsenʃəl] *adj.* 重要的；基本的；必需的(crucial; fundamental; necessary, vital)

【例】Cells are an *essential* structure in living organisms.

key [ki:] *adj.* 主要的，关键的（dominant, primary）

optimum [ˈɔptiməm] *adj.* 最优的（best）

【记】optim(最好)+um

【例】Under *optimum* conditions, these cultivated grass grow best.

leading [ˈliːdiŋ] *adj.* 最主要的（principal, chief）

chiefly [ˈtʃiːfli] *adv.* 主要地，多半地（mainly, principally）

【记】chief(主要)+ly

largely [ˈlɑːdʒli] *adv.* 主要地，很大程度上（mainly, for the most part）

sum [sʌm] *n.* 要点

preference [ˈprefərəns] *n.* 优先；优先权（inclination, privilege）

【记】prefer(喜欢)+ence

【例】The king showed *preference* to his eldest son.

forte [ˈfɔːtei] *n.* 长处（strong point）

【记】fort(强)+e→强大→长处

elite [iˈliːt] *n.* 精华，中坚（best）

【记】e(出)+lite=lig(选)→选出的(人物)→精英人物

【例】The movie star felt like one of the *elite*.

gist [dʒist] *n.* 要旨（theme）

merit [ˈmerit] *n.* 优点（advantage）

【记】比较demerit(缺点)

motif [məuˈtiːf] *n.* 主题（theme, subject）；主旨

【例】The composer's symphony had an obvious waltz *motif*.

tenor [ˈtenə] *n.* 要旨，要义（nature）

【例】The *tenor* of this speech is to pursue a noble life.

principal [ˈprinsəpl] *adj.* 重要的（main, chief, central）

major [ˈmeidʒə] *adj.* 主要的

sole [səul] *adj.* 惟一的

【例】His *sole* purpose when playing cards is to relax.

壮 丽

glorious [ˈglɔːriəs] *adj.* 壮丽的

splendid [ˈsplendid] *adj.* 灿烂的，辉煌的（magnificent）

【记】splend(明亮)+id→灿烂的

【例】Thank you for cooking a most *splendid* meal tonight!

splendor ['splendə] *n.* 光彩，壮丽（grandeur, magnificence）

grand [grænd] *adj.* 盛大的，壮丽的（splendid, magnificent）

【例】We held a *grand* celebration party for her success.

gorgeous ['gɔːdʒəs] *adj.* 绚丽的（beautiful, admirable, very colorful）

【记】参考gorge（峡谷）

【例】The flower appears a *gorgeous* shape under the sun.

radiant ['reidjənt] *adj.* 绚丽的；容光焕发的（joyous, beaming）

【记】radi（光，线）＋ant→绚丽的

【例】Dozens of *radiant* candle flames lit the room.

spectacular [spek'tækjulə] *adj.* 引人入胜的，壮观的（breathtaking, impressive, striking）

【例】The most *spectacular* thing that ever happened this century would be the introduction of computer.

solemn ['sɔləm] *adj.* 庄严的；隆重的（grave, somber）

superb [sjuː'pəːb] *adj.* 壮丽的（excellent, first-rate）

magnificent [mæg'nifisnt] *n.* 壮丽的，华丽的（gallant, splendid）

【记】magni（大）＋ficent→壮丽的

Everybody is ignorant, only on different subjects.
所有的人都是无知的，只是对不同的题材无知而已。

—*W.Rogers* 罗杰斯

连 线 题

左列单词在右列中有一个或多个同义词,请画线连接。

(一)

endanger	acrid
gist	feverish
hectic	gallant
magnificent	harm
malleable	important
momentous	microscopic
predominate	minute
pungent	penetrating
tangible	pliable
tiny	prevail
	splendid
	substantial
	theme
	touchable

(二)

adjacent	additional
cunning	adjoining
erratic	attribute
extensive	characteristic
fit	clever
further	comprehensive
multitude	cute
portable	eccentric
trait	empty
vacant	host
	mass
	movable
	neighboring
	odd
	suitable
	thorough
	transportable
	unoccupied

(三)

becoming	accord
chaste	agree
congested	almost
emphatic	excessive
entirely	fitting
fraught	full of
inordinate	immoderate
nearly	incongruous
tally	overcrowded
unseemly	powerful
	pure
	solely
	suitable
	totally
	unsuited
	virtuous

(四)

bulky	ardent
extremely	cumbersome
fidelity	enormous
innocent	exceptionally
massive	faithfulness
obscene	faultless
tranquil	filthy
unbiased	guiltless
vehement	impartial
	indecent
	intensely
	loyalty
	neutral
	passionate
	peaceful
	quiet
	serene

连线题答案

(一)

endanger	harm
gist	theme
hectic	feverish
magnificent	gallant
magnificent	splendid
malleable	pliable
momentous	important
predominate	prevail
pungent	acrid
pungent	penetrating
tangible	touchable
tangible	substantial
tiny	microscopic
tiny	minute

(二)

adjacent	adjoining
adjacent	neighboring
cunning	cute
cunning	clever
erratic	odd
erratic	eccentric
extensive	comprehensive
extensive	thorough
fit	suitable
further	additional
multitude	host
multitude	mass
portable	movable
portable	transportable
trait	characteristic
trait	attribute
vacant	unoccupied
vacant	empty

(三)

becoming	fitting
becoming	suitable
chaste	pure
chaste	virtuous
congested	overcrowded
emphatic	powerful
entirely	totally
entirely	solely
fraught	full of
inordinate	excessive
inordinate	immoderate
nearly	almost
tally	accord
tally	agree
unseemly	unsuited
unseemly	incongruous

(四)

bulky	cumbersome
extremely	exceptionally
extremely	intensely
fidelity	loyalty
fidelity	faithfulness
innocent	guiltless
innocent	faultless
massive	enormous
obscene	indecent
obscene	filthy
tranquil	serene
tranquil	quiet
tranquil	peaceful
unbiased	neutral
unbiased	impartial
vehement	passionate
vehement	ardent

状　态

记忆小贴士：全身心记忆法

　　根据测试，参与记忆单词的器官和身体部位越多，单词在大脑中的印象就越深刻，记忆的时间也就越长。边读边写边记，来一个全身总动员吧。

变 化

diverse [dai'vəːs] *adj.* 不同的(different, various)

【例】Jane made a pretty bouquet of *diverse* flowers.

diversify [dai'vəːsifai] *vt.* 使多样化(vary)

【例】That factory has *diversified* its products.

fickle ['fikl] *adj.* 多变的(changeable, capricious)

【例】The weather in this area is *fickle,* and you can never foretell.

manifold ['mænifəuld] *adj.* 多样的(various, many);多方面的

【记】mani(许多)+fold(层次)→繁多的

【例】The newlywed couple received the *manifold* blessings of their friends and relatives.

lavish ['læviʃ] *adj.* 丰富的(liberal)

【记】lav(洗)+ish→冲掉→浪费的

【例】My neighbors spoiled their children with *lavish* gifts.

profuse [prə'fjuːs] *adj.* 极其丰富的(abundant, exuberant)

【记】pro(向前)+fuse(流)→表示充足,丰富的

vary ['vɛəri] *vt.* 改变(differ, deviate from, range)

【例】He *varies* his writing style according to his readers.

various ['vɛəriəs] *adj.* 各种的(diversified)

variation [ˌvɛəri'eiʃən] *n.* 变化(alteration, change)

【记】vari(变化)+ation

【例】The global warming trend has made considerable *variation* of temperature.

variant ['vɛəriənt] *adj.* 不同的(different)

【记】vari(变化)+ant

mutation [mjuː'teiʃən] *n.* 变化(transformation)

【记】mut(变)+ation

【例】A little frog was transformed into a monster due to a *mutation* aroused by nuclear emission.

transition [træn'ziʃən] *n.* 转变,变迁;过渡(change, shift)

【记】trans(交换)+it(走)+ion→转变

【例】Spring is a *transition* from winter into summer.

transform [træns'fɔːm] *vt.* 变换(change, transmute)

【记】trans(变)+form(形)→变形

【例】A fresh coat of paint can *transform* a room.

enrich [in'ritʃ] *vt.* 丰富(make rich, enhance)

【记】en+rich(富)

【例】I *enriched* my coffee with cream and sugar.

convert [kən'vəːt] *vt.* 转换(change, transform)

【记】con+vert(转)

【例】I *converted* the spare bedroom into a reading room.

copious ['kəupjəs] *adj.* 丰富的(plentiful)

冲 突

hostile ['hɔstail] *adj.* 敌对的，不友好的(antagonistic, unfriendly)

【例】The *hostile* cat hissed whenever I came near.

diverge [dai'vəːdʒ] *vt.* 分歧，差异(differ, deviate)

【记】di+verge(转)→转开→分歧

【例】I'm afraid our opinions *diverge* from each other on the direction of investment.

divergent [dai'vəːdʒənt] *adj.* 分叉的；分歧的(different)

【例】Thousands of *divergent* tree branches made a thick canopy overhead.

belligerent [bi'lidʒərənt] *adj.* 好战的；交战的(hostile, aggressive)

【例】It is unwise to take a *belligerent* attitude.

repulsive [ri'pʌlsiv] *adj.* 排斥的(revolting, disgusting)

offensive [ə'fensiv] *adj.* 无礼的；攻击性的(aggressive)

【记】动词offend(进攻，冒犯)

【例】I would take it as an *offensive* action if you don't stop making those terrible noises.

strife [straif] *n.* 冲突；竞争(squabble, conflict)

feud [fjuːd] *n.* 世仇 *vi.* 不合

【例】The *feud* between our families has lasted for generations.

struggle ['strʌgl] *n./vi.* 竞争，奋斗(fight)

【例】The human being *struggles* with his environment.

strike [straik] *v.* 打击(hit)

【例】In France, going on strike is frequently being utilised by the union in fighting for the workers' interest, which *strikes* the nation's economy heavily.

contend [kən'tend] *v.* 争斗 (compete, rival)

【例】The armies are *contending* for control of strategic territory.

compete [kəm'pi:t] *vi.* 竞争

【例】Children sometimes *compete* for their parents' attention.

frown [fraun] *vi.* 皱眉; 反对

【例】My father *frowned* when I came home late last night.

parallel ['pærəlel] *vt.* 匹敌 (match, rival)

【例】His paintings *parallels* that of Qi Baishi.

tantalize ['tæntəlaiz] *vt.* 逗惹, 使…着急 (provoke, tease)

【例】Everytime I reached for the bird, it disppeared. I withdrew, it reappeared. It posed a *tantalizing* question for me.

rival ['raivəl] *vt.* 竞争, 匹敌 (compete, match)

【例】Edison is a genius who can't be *rivaled* by ordinary mortals though advancedly educated.

assail [ə'seil] *vt.* 猛击; 决然面对 (attack, assault)

【记】as+sail(跳上去)→跳上去打→猛打

【例】A police officer *assailed* the crook with a baton.

fulminate ['fulmincit] *vi.* 猛烈爆发 (explode)

【记】fulmin(闪电, 雷声)+ate→像雷声一般发作→猛烈爆发

【例】The government has determined to *fulminate* against the crime wave.

baste [beist] *vt.* 殴打; 公开责骂 (lash, beat)

【例】The man was *basted* for his crime.

repulse [ri'pʌls] *vt.* 排斥

【记】re(反)+pulse(推)→排斥

【例】Tom *repulsed* the attacker by punching him in the stomach.

repel [ri'pel] *vt.* 排斥 (resist, reject)

【记】re(反)+pel(推)→排斥

【例】The soldiers *repelled* the enemy.

emulate ['emjuleit] *vt.* 努力赶上或超过

【例】I tried to *emulate* Mary's skill at playing the piano.

punch [pʌntʃ] *vt.* 重击 (blow, hit)

【例】Plain Indians *punched* their hand-held drums while dancing.

thump ［θʌmp］ *vt.* 重击（strike, pound）

【例】The salesman *thumped* the door knocker.

adverse ［'ædvə:s］ *adj.* 敌对的；不利的（hostile, unfavorable, negative）

【例】The *adverse* weather conditions made travel difficult.

impact ［'impækt］ *v.* 冲击（affect, influence）

【例】The Cultural Revolution greatly *impacted* many Chinese families.

admonish ［əd'mɔniʃ］ *vt.* 警告（warn）

【记】ad（加强）＋mon（警告）＋ish→加强警告

【例】Mary *admonished* the children not to talk to strangers.

穿 透

stab ［stæb］ *v./n.* 刺，戳（jab, injure）

【例】He *stabbed* the woman with a knife and she died.

sheathe ［ʃi:ð］ *vt.*（将刀剑）入鞘（cover, encase）

【例】He *sheathes* his sword.

insert ［in'sə:t］ *vt.* 插入（put in, add）

【记】in（进入）＋sert（插）

【例】He *inserted* the key in the lock but could not open the door.

pierce ［piəs］ *vt.* 穿透，戳穿（penetrate, puncture）

【例】I *pierced* the paper with my pencil.

transfix ［træns'fiks］ *vt.* 刺穿（pierce, impale）

【例】The fisherman *transfixed* the shark with a harpoon.

impale ［im'peil］ *vt.* 刺穿，刺住（pierce, penetrate）

【记】im（进入）＋pale（尖木）→刺穿

【例】She had the butterflies *impaled* on small pins.

penetrate ［'penitreit］ *vt.* 刺穿，进入（pierce）

【记】pen（全部）＋etr（进入）＋ate

【例】The knife *penetrated* her finger and made it bleed.

interject ［ˌintə'dʒekt］ *vt.* 突然插入

【例】May I *interject* a note of caution?

punch ［pʌntʃ］ *vt.* 打孔

【例】Workers have to *punch* holes in the mountain to get the road through.

发 展

successful [sək'sesful] *adj.* 成功的(fruitful)

incipient [in'sipiənt] *adj.* 初期的
【记】in(进入)+cip(掉)+ient→掉进来→刚开始的

initiate [i'niʃieit] *vt.* 开始,创始(start, begin, commence)
【例】Mary *initiated* a conversation with the man sitting next to her.

initial [i'niʃəl] *adj.* 初始的(original, beginning, early, oldest)
【记】in(进入)+it(走)+ial→走进→开始的
【例】His *initial* step to start a small business is to do a market research.

foremost ['fɔːməust] *adj.* 最初的(prime)
【记】fore(前)+most(最)→最先的
【例】He is one of the *foremost* atom scientists in China.

original [ə'ridʒənl] *adj.* 最初的(earliest, initial)
【记】origin(起源)+al
【例】His idea is not *original*. Many pioneers had the same thought.

originally [ə'ridʒənəli] *adv.* 本来;最初

primary ['praiməri] *adj.* 最初的(foremost, initial)
【记】prim(最初的)+ary

eventual [i'ventʃuəl] *adj.* 最后的(final, ultimate)
【记】比较event(事件)
【例】Owning a restaurant is Bill's *eventual* goal, but now he is just an assistant chef.

ultimate ['ʌltimit] *adj.* 最后的(final, eventual)
【记】ultim(最远)+ate
【例】*Ultimate* success can be only achieved by those who hang on.

final ['fainl] *adj.* 最后的(ultimate)
【例】After the *final* contest has completed, the judges will decide who wins.

progress ['prɔgres] *n./v.* 前进,发展
【记】pro(向前)+gress(走)→前进
【例】The year is *progressing*; it will soon be winter again.

triumph ['traiəmf] *n.* 成功(victory)
【例】In our moment of *triumph*, let's not forget those who made it all possible.

culmination　[ˌkʌlmiˈneiʃən] *n.* 顶点(climax, summit)

【例】At the *culmination* of her career, Mary gave a final concert.

peak　[piːk] *n.* 高峰；尖端(mountain top; summit, top)

【例】At the *peak* of their labor, they could lay five miles of rails a day.

process　[ˈprɔses] *n.* 过程(procedure) *vt.* 加工，处理

【例】These materials are to be *processed* before they can be used.

phase　[feiz] *n.* 阶段，态(stage, period)

【例】The three *phases* of matter are solid, liquid and gas.

condition　[kənˈdiʃən] *n.* 条件；状况

【例】My shoes are in bad *condition* and need to be replaced.

status　[ˈsteitəs] *n.* 状况

【例】The *status* of colonial women had been well studied.

result　[riˈzʌlt] *n.* 结果(outcome)

headway　[ˈhedwei] *n.* 进展(progress)

onset　[ˈɔnset] *n.* 开始(beginning)

【记】来自set on(攻击)

【例】He had a sudden *onset* of conscious loss and then fell down in the supermarket.

halt　[hɔːlt] *v.* 停止(stop, cease)

【例】The police ordered the thief to *halt*.

develop　[diˈveləp] *v.* 发展；产生；成长

【例】I will *develop* a headache if it gets too hot.

resume　[riˈzjuːm] *v.* 继续(continue, take up)

【记】re(重新)＋sume(拿)→继续

【例】We *resumed* our work after a rest.

exit　[ˈeksit] *v.* 退出

【记】ex(出)＋it(走)→走出→出口

【例】The actress *exited* secretly from an unseen exit.

climax　[ˈklaimæks] *v.*(使)达到高潮 *n.* 高峰，顶点(peak, culmination)

【例】The movie *climaxed* with Tom's revealing that he was really the child's father.

emerge　[iˈməːdʒ] *vi.* 出现(appear, come into prominence)

【记】e(出)＋merge(沉)→沉的东西出现→浮现

【例】The divers *emerged* from the water.

proceed　[prəˈsiːd] *vi.* 进行(carry on, go on)

【记】pro(向前)＋ceed(走)→进行

【例】Business *proceeded* as usual.

commence [kə'mens] *vi.* 开始(begin)

【例】The second term *commences* in March.

vanish ['væniʃ] *vi.* 消失(disappear, fade)

【记】van(空)＋ish→变空→消失

【例】The magician made the flowers *vanish* with a wave of his hand.

launch [lɔ:ntʃ] *vt.* 发动(start, begin)

【例】My company *launched* a new insurance plan.

engender [in'dʒendə] *vt.* 产生(generate, produce)

【记】en(使)＋gender(产生)→使产生

【例】John's kind acts *engendered* my friendship.

beget [bi'get] *vt.* 引起;产生(arise, bring)

【例】Hunger *begets* crime.

generate ['dʒenəreit] *vt.* 造成(produce, give rise to)

【记】gener(产生)＋ate

【例】His improper behavior *generates* a good deal of suspicion.

terminate ['tə:mineit] *vt.* 终止(end, finish, conclude, stop)

【记】termin(结束)＋ate

【例】The author *terminated* his contract with the publisher.

accomplished [ə'kɔmpliʃt] *adj.* 完成的

【例】The prediction was literally *accomplished*.

conclude [kən'klu:d] *vi.* 结束

【例】The movie *concludes* at ten o'clock.

conclusive [kən'klu:siv] *adj.* 决定性的;最后的(decisive, definitive, final)

【例】The committee didn't reach any *conclusive* decision.

advance [əd'va:ns] *vt.* 使前进(proceed);提出(propose)

【例】The date of the meeting has been *advanced* from Friday to Monday.

achieve [ə'tʃi:v] *vt.* 完成;实现;达到(accomplish, fulfil)

【例】Bill could not *achieve* his schooling because he is too lazy.

分 离

detach [di'tætʃ] *vt.* 分开;分离(remove, separate)

【例】Sally *detached* the spray nozzle from the hose.

detached [di'tætʃt] *adj.* 分离的(separated, disconnected)

【例】The house has a *detached* garage rather than an adjoining one.

solitude ['sɔlitjuːd] *n.* 与外界隔绝(isolation, loneliness)

sever ['sevə] *vt.* 分开，断绝(separate)

【例】The road was *severed* at several places.

rend [rend] *vt.* 分离(apart, seperate)

【例】The cruel enemies *rent* the child away from his mother.

segregate ['segrigeit] *vt.* 隔离，分离(alienate, separate)

【记】se(分开)＋greg(群体)＋ate→和群体分开→隔离

【例】Solid and liquid are *segregated* and then mixed again in the experiment.

disunite [ˌdisjuː'nait] *vt.* 使分离

【记】dis(不)＋unite(统一)→不统一→分离

【例】He managed to *disunite* the links of a chain.

scatter ['skætə] *vt.* 使分散(disperse, spread)

【例】The farmer *scattered* the corn in the yard for the hens.

缓 和

cushion ['kuʃən] *n.* 垫层 *vt.* 缓解

【例】The sofa *cushions* have new upholstery.

soothe [suːð] *v.* 安慰；缓和；减轻(appease, relieve)

【例】Kind words can *soothe* when someone is upset.

relax [ri'læks] *v.* (使)松弛，放松(ease)

【例】Don't worry about it; just try to *relax*.

placate ['plækeit] *vt.* 安抚(appease, pacify)

【记】plac(平静)＋ate

【例】To *placate* an infant, a mom has to offer vocal reassurance.

console [kən'səul] *vt.* 安慰(conciliate, comfort)

【例】The physician *consoled* the parents of the accident victim.

assuage [ə'sweidʒ] *vt.* 缓和 (alleviate, mitigate, soothe)

【记】as＋suage(甜)→变甜→缓和

【例】I pray that our Heavenly Father may *assuage* the anguish of your bereavement.

mollify [ˈmɔlifai] vt. 缓和 (appease, assuage)
【记】moll(软)+ify→软化→缓和
【例】He tries to find ways of *mollifying* her.

mitigate [ˈmitigeit] vt. 缓和；减轻 (alleviate, relieve)
【记】miti(小)+gate(做)→缓减
【例】Nothing could *mitigate* the cruelty with which she had treated him.

slacken [ˈslækən] vt. 使松弛 (loosen, slow down)
【记】slack(松弛)+en
【例】I *slackened* the line to let the fish swim.

pacify [ˈpæsifai] vt. 镇定；抚慰 (appease, placate)
【记】pac(和平, 平静)+ify
【例】Even a written apology failed to *pacify* the indignant hostess.

恢 复

rally [ˈræli] n./v. 恢复
【记】比较ally(联盟)
【例】They paused to fresh themselves and *rally* their strength.

revive [riˈvaiv] v. 复兴；复苏 (revitalize)
【记】re(重新)+vive(活)→复苏
【例】The fresh air soon *revived* him.

revert [riˈvəːt] v. 回复 (come back, return)
【例】After her divorce she *reverted* to using her maiden name.

retract [riˈtrækt] v. 收回, 撤回 (take back, withdraw)
【记】re(回)+tract(拉)→拉回→收回
【例】The company *retracted* its offer of a free ham, because it ran out of hams.

retrieve [riˈtriːv] v. 重新找回 (recover, save)
【记】re(重新)+trieve(找到)→重新找到
【例】Jane *retrieved* the lost document from the garbage can.

energize [ˈenədʒaiz] vt. 供给能量；使活跃
【例】I *energized* the motor when I turned on the electric switch.

restore [risˈtɔː] vt. 恢复 (recover, bring back)
【记】re(回)+store(储存)→返回储存→恢复
【例】The people are eager to *restore* law and order after long time chaos.

rehabilitate [ˌriːhə'biliteit] *vt.* 恢复(restore)

【记】reh(重新)＋abili(能力)＋tate→重新获得能力→恢复

【例】After World War II, many factories were *rehabilitated* rather than bulldozed.

recover [ri'kʌvə] *vt.* 恢复(resume)

【例】The patient did not *recover* himself since he was knocked down in a car accident.

revoke [ri'vəuk] *vt.* 取消，撤回(cancel, repeal)

【记】re(反)＋voke(喊)→喊反话→取消

【例】The drunk driver had his driving licence *revoked.*

refresh [ri'freʃ] *vt.* 使清新 *vi.* 恢复精神(renew, revive)

【记】re(重新)＋fresh(新鲜的)

【例】She felt *refreshed* after her sleep.

混 乱

intricate ['intrikit] *adj.* 错综复杂的(complicated, entangled)；难懂的

【记】in(进入)＋tric(复杂)＋ate

complex [kəm'pleks] *adj.* 复杂的(complicated, tangled) *n.* 综合体

【记】com＋plex(交叉重叠)→复杂的

【例】The student thought the algebraic formula was *complex.*

disarray [disə'rei] *n./vt.* 杂乱；混乱

【记】dis＋array(排列)

【例】I couldn't find the papers in all the *disarray* on my desk.

confuse [kən'fjuːz] *vt.* 混淆

【记】con(共同)＋fuse(流)→流到一起→混合

【例】Please don't *confuse* Australia with Austria.

jumble ['dʒʌmbl] *v.* 混杂(muddle, mix)

【例】The papers in the office were all *jumbled* up.

shuffle ['ʃʌfl] *vt.* 搅乱，混合(mix, blend)

【例】He *shuffled* the cards before each new round.

complicate ['kɔmplikeit] *vt.* 使复杂；使陷入

【例】Getting angry with each other will only *complicate* the matter.

befuddle [bi'fʌdl] *vt.* 使混乱(confuse)

【例】The *befuddled* deer could not move out of the path of the car.

muddle ['mʌdl] *vt.* 使混乱（confuse, make into a mess）

【记】mud(泥)＋dle→混入泥→混乱

【例】The lesson was not clear and it has *muddled* me.

聚　集

assemble [ə'sembl] *vt.* 聚集（gather, congregate）

【例】After *assembling* the things he needed, Bob baked a beautiful cake.

assembly [ə'sembli] *n.* 集会

【例】An *assembly* was called so that everyone could vote on the issue.

party ['pɑːti] *n.* 团体；一伙

association [əˌsəuʃi'eiʃən] *n.* 协会（society）

【例】Translators *Association* of China was founded in 1982.

gather ['ɡæðə] *v.* 聚集，集合（compile, collect）

【例】Children, *gather* round, and Miss Alice will tell you a fable.

attend [ə'tend] *vt.* 参加（join）

【例】Bob didn't *attended* school until he was 17.

convene [kən'viːn] *vt.* 集合（assemble, gather）

【记】con(共同)＋vene(走)→走到一起

【例】Party congresses at all levels are *convened* by Party committees at their respective levels.

congregate ['kɔŋɡriɡeit] *vt.* 聚集（assemble, gather）

【记】con(共同)＋greg(集会)＋ate

【例】Each morning people at work *congregate* around the coffee pot.

accompany [ə'kʌmpəni] *vt.* 伴随（travel with）

【记】ac＋company(伴侣)

【例】If you go to the opera, I will *accompany* you.

扩　大

sprawl [sprɔːl] *n.* 扩展 *v.* 蔓延（spread）

【记】比较crawl(爬)

【例】Suburban *sprawl* caused really bad traffic jams.

broaden ['brɔːdn] *v.* 放宽，变阔

【记】broad(宽)+en

【例】The city *broadened* the road at the dangerous turn.

swell [swel] *v.* 膨胀(expand, inflate)

【例】My ankle began to *swell* when I injured it.

expand [iks'pænd] *vi.* 扩张(outspread)

【记】ex+pand(分散)→分散出去→扩张

【例】The balloon *expanded* slowly.

dilate [dai'leit] *vt.* 使膨胀，使扩大(expand, widen)

【记】di(分开)+late→扩大

【例】I *dilated* the opening in the turkey and pushed the stuffing in.

augment [ɔːg'ment] *vt.* 增大，增加(enlarge, increase)

【记】aug(提高)+ment→增大

【例】The addition to the house greatly *augmented* its value.

粘 附

stick [stik] *v.* 粘住，粘贴(cling, attach)

【例】The stamp is not sticky enough to *stick* on the envelope.

sticky ['stiki] *adj.* 粘连的(adhesive)

attachment [ə'tætʃmənt] *n.* 连接物，附件

【例】The vacuum cleaner has six different *attachments*.

cohere [kəu'hiə] *vi.* 附着(connect, fit)

【记】co(共同)+here(粘)→共同粘→连贯

【例】The sushi rice grains *cohere*.

cling [kliŋ] *vi.* 黏附(adhere, stick)

【例】The child *clung* to his mother, begging her not to leave.

adhere [əd'hiə] *vi.* 黏着，坚持(stick, hold, cling)

【例】There is a piece of lettuce *adhering* to the side of your plate.

adherent [əd'hiərənt] *adj.* 依附的(adhesive, sticky) *n.* 追随者，信徒

【例】The political party's loyal *adherents* contributed a lot of money.

频 率

constant ['kɔnstənt] *adj.* 不变的，持续的(invariable, continous)

【例】 The *constant* noise from the road crew gave Bill a headache.

incessant [in'sesnt] *adj.* 不断的 (ceaseless, continual)

【记】 in(不)+cess(停止)+ant

coherent [kəu'hiərənt] *adj.* 连贯的 (logical, unified)

【例】 The student had a *coherent* explanation for being late.

incoherent [ˌinkəu'hiərənt] *adj.* 不连贯的 (disconnected)

【记】 in(不)+coherent(连贯的)

ceaseless ['si:slis] *adj.* 不停的 (incessant, endless)

【记】 cease(停)+less(否定后缀)

【例】 The *ceaseless* noise of the dripping faucet drove us crazy.

speedy ['spi:di] *adj.* 快的，迅速的

swift [swift] *adj.* 快速的 (quick)

【例】 The *swift* current carried the raft downstream.

successive [sək'sesiv] *adj.* 连续的 (consecutive)

【例】 The baseball player hit four *successive* home runs.

consecutive [kən'sekjutiv] *adj.* 连续的 (successive)

【例】 In his speech the president said that agricultural exports went up for twelve *consecutive* years.

prompt [prɔmpt] *adj.* 迅速的 (quick)

fitful ['fitfəl] *adj.* 一阵阵的；断续的

【记】 fit(一阵)+ful

【例】 Please sit. Your *fitful* pacing is bothering me.

continually [kən'tinjuəli] *adv.* 不断地 (constantly, ceaselessly)

gradually ['grædjuəli] *adv.* 逐渐地 (slowly, by degree, little by little)

haunt [hɔ:nt] *vt.* 常到 (frequent)

【例】 Do you *haunt* the movie theaters?

frequency ['fri:kwənsi] *n.* 频率，周率，发生次数

缺 乏

insufficient [ˌinsə'fiʃənt] *adj.* 不足的，不够的 (inadaquate)

scanty ['skænti] *adj.* 贫乏的 (sparse, meager)

【记】 scant(不足的)+y

【例】 The *scanty* resources defines this area as barren.

meager ['mi:gə] *adj.* 贫乏的，不足的 (scanty)

needy [ˈniːdi] *adj.* 贫穷的(poor)

【记】need(需要)＋y→急需的→贫穷的

【例】Those *needy* children had to work for their keep.

stingy [ˈstindʒi] *adj.* 缺乏的

devoid [diˈvoid] *adj.* 缺乏的(empty, lacking)

【记】de＋void(空)→缺乏的

【例】The hot air was *devoid* of even the slightest amount of moisture.

scarce [skɛəs] *adj.* 缺乏的，不足的(sparse)

forfeit [ˈfɔːfit] *vt.* 丧失(sacrifice) *adj.* 丧失了的(lost)

【例】His lands were *forfeit*.

衰 弱

degenerate [diˈdʒenəreit] *adj.* 堕落的 *vi.* 退步(degrade, deteriorate)

【记】de(坏)＋gener(产生)＋ate→往坏产生→堕落

【例】I was shocked by the lack of morals in this *degenerate* book.

decadence [ˈdekədəns] *n.* 衰落，颓废

【记】de＋cad(落下)＋ence

【例】The mayor criticized the teenagers for their *decadence*.

decline [diˈklain] *v.* 衰落(go down, drop)

【例】As the dog grew older, its health *declined*.

languish [ˈlæŋgwiʃ] *vi.* 变衰弱(wither, fade)

【例】The prisoners have been *languishing* for years in the dungeon.

ebb [eb] *vi.* 衰退(decay)

【例】The water washed up on the shore, then slowly *ebbed* away.

flag [flæg] *vi.* 衰退，减弱(decline)

【例】His interest in this topic is *flagging* as shown in his dull eyes.

deplete [diˈpliːt] *vt.* 耗尽，使衰竭(exhaust)

【例】I always replenish my food supply before it is *depleted*.

degrade [diˈgreid] *vt.* 使降级；使堕落(degenerate, lower)

【记】de(向下)＋grade(级)→向下降级

【例】He *degraded* himself by cheating and telling lies.

enervate [ˈenəveit] *vt.* 使衰弱(enfeeble, weaken)

【例】 The dullness of the lecture as well as the heat of the day *enervated* the students, who were all too tired.

随 机

informal [inˈfɔːml] *adj.* 不拘礼节的，随便的

indefinite [inˈdefinit] *adj.* 不明确的；不定的（infinite, unlimited）

【记】 in(不)+definite(确定的)

【例】 Don't expect too much; it is still *indefinite* that your favorite star will come.

casual [ˈkæʒuəl] *adj.* 非正式的，随便的（informal）

【例】 The picnic was *casual*, so we all wore shirts.

potential [pəˈtenʃəl] *adj.* 可能的；潜在的（possible, conceivable）

【例】 The inventor determined *potential* markets for the new product.

contingent [kənˈtindʒənt] *adj.* 可能发生的（accidental, unforeseen）

【例】 Mary's offer to buy the house was *contingent* upon her getting a mortgage.

dispensable [disˈpensəbl] *adj.* 可有可无的（unnecessary, unimportant）

【例】 This magazine is *dispensable,* so let's discontinue our subscription.

occasional [əˈkeiʒənəl] *adj.* 偶然的（accidental, haphazard）

【例】 The silence was broken by an *occasional* scream.

fortuitously [fɔːˈtjuːitəsli] *adv.* 偶然地，意外地（accidentally, coincidentally）

【例】 He is not a good swimmer; he just won the game *fortuitously*.

haphazard [hæpˈhæzəd] *adj.* 偶然的；随便的（casual, random, indiscriminate）

【记】 hap+hazard(偶然, 运气)→偶然的

【例】 I didn't mean to meet my old friend at the airport; it is just a *haphazard* meeting.

random [ˈrændəm] *adj.* 任意的，随意的（patternless, unplanned）

doubtful [ˈdautful] *adj.* 未确定的；不可靠的（treacherous）

【例】 John felt *doubtful* about getting married.

lottery [ˈlɔtəri] *n.* 碰巧之事

【例】 "Marriage is just a *lottery*; don't believe in love." said the old man.

accidental [ˌæksiˈdentl] *adj.* 偶然的（occasional）

【记】 ac+cid(落下)+ental→意外的

【例】 I made an *accidental* error on my exam.

缩 减

constrict ［kən'strikt］ *v.* (使)收紧，压缩(reduce, compress)

【记】strict(严格的，精密的)

【例】The snake *constricted* its body around its prey and killed it.

dwindle ['dwindl] *vi.* 减少(diminish, decrease)

【例】The stream will continue to *dwindle* if it doesn't rain.

detract ［di'trækt］ *vi.* 去掉；减损(lessen, derogate)

【记】de＋tract(拉)

【例】Their argument *detracted* from the otherwise pleasant conversation.

contract ［'kɔntrækt］ *vi.* 收缩(shrink, reduce)

【记】con＋tract(拉)→拉到一起→收缩

【例】Plastic bags *contract* when being heated.

reduce ［ri'djuːs］ *vt.* 减少，简化(simplify)

【例】Statistics helps to *reduce* unwieldy data to comprehensible form.

diminish ［di'miniʃ］ *vt.* 减少；缩小(decrease, dwindle)

【记】di(向下)＋mini(小)＋ish→小下去→缩小

【例】Unexpected expenses *diminished* the size of my bank account.

curtail ［kəː'teil］ *vt.* 缩减(cut back, reduce)

【记】cur＋tail(尾巴)→尾巴短了→减缩

【例】The discussions were *curtailed* when the fire alarm went off.

indent ［in'dent］ *vt.* 缩排，缩进

【例】Remember to *indent* the first line of every paragraph.

subtraction ［səb'trækʃən］ *n.* 减少

稳 定 性

erratic ［i'rætik］ *adj.* 不稳定的(unpredictable)

【例】Bill's *erratic* moods upset everyone in our office.

stable ［'steibl］ *adj.* 稳定的(immobile, steady)

【例】Don't lean on my desk! It's not *stable*.

unstable ［ʌn'steibl］ *adj.* 不稳定的，不牢固的(variable, troubled, inconstant)

steady ［'stedi］ *adj.* 稳固的 *vt.* 使稳定

steadily ［'stedili］ *adv.* 稳定地，有规则地(consistently)

poise ［pɔiz］ *n.* 平衡；稳定(balance)

物理属性变化

ascent [ə'sent] *n.* 上升

【例】The rock climbers made their *ascent* slowly.

descent [di'sent] *n.* 下降

extend [iks'tend] *v.* 扩充，延伸（stretch, increase）

【例】The headmaster *extended* our holiday by four days.

extension [iks'tenʃən] *n.* 延伸

【例】The handle isn't long enough, so I need an *extension.*

hike [haik] *v.* 上升

【例】My coat had *hiked* up in the back.

hoist [hɔist] *v.* 升起（raise）*n.* 起重机

【例】He was *hoisted* up to the top of the building by a hoist.

stretch [stretʃ] *v.* 伸展，伸长（pull taut, expand）

【例】She *stretched* herself out on the couch and fell asleep.

transform [træns'fɔ:m] *vt.* 明显地改变…外观或形状

【记】trans(变)＋form(形)→变形

【例】A fresh coat of paint can *transform* a room.

deform [di'fɔ:m] *vt.* 使变形（disfigure, distort）

【记】de(坏)＋form(形状)→使变形

【例】A constant wind *deformed* the tree.

elevate ['eliveit] *vt.* 抬高

【记】e(出)＋lev(举)＋ate→举出→升高

【例】The marchers *elevated* the flag as they passed the president.

sharpen ['ʃɑ:pn] *vt.* 削尖

【例】The boy *sharpened* the pencil with a knife.

enhance [in'hæns] *vt.* 增加（raise, improve, heighten）

【例】You can *enhance* your appearance with makeup.

abate [ə'beit] *v.* 减少（lessen, diminish, dwindle, subside）

【例】It is reported that flu has been *abating* due to a warm winter.

accumulate [ə'kju:mjuleit] *vt.* 积聚（aggregate, amass, accrue）

【记】ac＋cumul(堆积)＋ate→积累

【例】The television screen *accumulates* dust.

amplify [ˈæmplifai] *vt.* 放大，增强

【例】We need to *amplify* the electric current .

amplification [ˌæmplifiˈkeiʃən] *n.* 扩大

物理状态

stuffy [ˈstʌfi] *adj.* 闷热的，不通风的(airless, stale)

tilted [ˈtiltid] *adj.* 倾斜的(slanted)

regularly [ˈreɡjuləli] *adv.* 有规律地，整齐地(routinely)

【例】Take the medicine *regularly* three times a day.

coil [kɔil] *n.* 盘绕 *v.* 卷(curl, wind)

【例】The snake *coiled* itself around its prey.

slope [sləup] *n.* 倾斜，斜面 *v.* 倾斜(slant, tilt, incline)

slant [slænt] *n.* 斜面 *vt.* 使倾斜(tilt, slope)

【例】The roof was built at a *slant* so rain would run off it.

protrude [prəuˈtruːd] *v.* (使)突出(project, stick out)

【记】pro(前)＋trude(伸出)→突出

【例】John's teeth *protrude* from his gums at an odd angle.

rotate [ˈrəuteit] *v.* (使)旋转(turn, alternate)

【例】The coach *rotates* her players frequently near the end of the game.

roll [rəul] *v.* 滚动(scroll)

【例】If you *roll* my log, I will *roll* yours.

dangle [ˈdæŋɡl] *v.* 悬摆(suspend, hang)

【例】The monkey loved to *dangle* from the branch and eat bananas.

project [prəˈdʒekt] *v.* 凸出，投射(protrude)

【例】His eyebrows *project* noticeably.

encompass [inˈkʌmpəs] *vt.* 包围，环绕(encircle, cover)；包含

【记】en＋compass(包围)

【例】A thick fog *encompassed* the village.

active [ˈæktiv] *adj.* 活动的，活跃的

【例】Susan's personal life is very *active*.

hump [hʌmp] *vi.* 隆起

【例】The land here *humped* into a hummock.

tower [ˈtauə] *vi.* 屹立，高耸

【例】The skyscraper *towered* among the city.

spin ['spin] v. 旋转

【例】The wheels of the car were *spinning*.

concave ['kɔn'keiv] adj. 凹的，凹入的 n. 凹，凹面

convex ['kɔnveks] adj. 表面弯曲如球的外侧的，凸起的

pitch [pitʃ] n. 程度，斜度

吸 引

glamor ['glæmə] n. 魅力（attraction, charm）

glamorous ['glæmərəs] adj. 富有魅力的（fascinating, charming）

【记】参考 glamour（魔力）

【例】The young president ceased to be *glamorous* when he announced a higher tax rate.

catching ['kætʃiŋ] adj. 迷人的（charming）

【记】catch（抓）+ing→心被抓住→迷人的

【例】Mary is quite *catching* on campus.

engross [in'grəus] vt. 使全神贯注于；吸引（absorb, preoccupy）

【例】The football game *engrossed* Tom completely.

engrossed [in'grəust] adj. 全神贯注的（absorbed）

attractive [ə'træktiv] adj. 吸引人的，有魅力的（pretty, appealing）

conspicuous [kən'spikjuəs] adj. 引人注目的（noticeable, obvious）

【记】con+spic（看）+uous→大家都看→引人注目的

【例】The crack in the ceiling was very *conspicuous*.

inviting [in'vaitiŋ] adj. 诱人的（attractive）；引人注目的

【例】The restaurant appeared to be cozy and *inviting,* so we ate there.

bait [beit] n. 饵，引诱物（lure）

【例】Cheese is good *bait* for catfish.

charisma [kə'rizmə] n. 魅力，感召力

【例】The performer's *charisma* kept our attention and caused us to listen to everything she said.

draw [drɔː] v. 吸引，拉（attact）

【例】The great parade of overseas Chinese on the main street of Paris *drew* a crowd of twenty thousand.

enrapture [in'ræptʃə] vt. 使出神

【记】en＋rapture(狂喜)

【例】Her smile *enraptured* him so he would not move his eyes.

induce [in'dju:s] *vt.* 导致，诱使(cause, produce)

【记】in(进入)＋duce(引导)

【例】The careless worker *induced* the fire with a cigarette butt.

intoxicate [in'tɔksikeit] *vt.* 使陶醉

【记】in(进入)＋toxic(毒)＋ate→进入毒→使迷醉

【例】He was *intoxicated* by many awards he received and ceased his step toward the peak of his career.

lure [ljuə] *vt.* 诱惑(entice, tempt)

【记】比较allure(引诱)

【例】Many young Japanese engineers have been *lured* to the Middle East by the promise of high wages.

entice [in'tais] *vt.* 诱惑(lure, tempt)

【例】I *enticed* Mary to dinner by offering to pay for her meal.

tempt [tempt] *vt.* 诱使(lure, entice)

【例】We refused the offer even though it *tempted* us.

addict [ə'dikt] *vt.* 对…有瘾

【例】Alcohol may *addict* you.

addicted [ə'diktid] *adj.* 沉溺的，上瘾的

【例】Max smokes but he is not *addicted.*

absorb [əb'zɔ:b] *vt.* 吸收，吸引(attract, allure)

【记】ab＋sorb(吸)

【例】I used a sponge to *absorb* the spilled milk.

absorbing [əb'zɔ:biŋ] *adj.* 引人入胜的(enchanting, fascinating)

虚 弱

delicate ['delikit] *adj.* 脆弱的

pitiful ['pitiful] *adj.* 可怜的

【记】名词pity(可怜)

fragile ['frædʒail] *adj.* 脆的(breakable, brittle)

【记】frag(碎)＋ile→易碎的

【例】You must cushion *fragile* objects carefully when you pack them.

emaciate [i'meiʃieit] *vt.* 使瘦弱

【记】e＋maci(瘦)＋ate

【例】A long illness had *emaciated* my father.

emaciated [i'meiʃieitid] *adj.* 瘦弱的; 憔悴的(skinny; haggard)

【例】A bus transported the *emaciated* refugees to the camp.

flimsy ['flimzi] *adj.* 脆弱的; 薄弱的(thin)

【记】比较film(胶片).

fragmentary ['frægməntəri] *adj.* 碎片的; 不连续的(discontinuous)

frail [freil] *adj.* 虚弱的, 脆弱的(fragile, flimsy)

【记】frail=fract(打碎的)→脆弱的

【例】My grandmother is *frail*, but she's still very alert.

brittle ['britl] *adj.* 易碎的(fragile)

【例】Steel is not as *brittle* as cast iron; it doesn't break as easily.

slender ['slendə] *adj.* 苗条的, 微弱的(slim)

impotence ['impətəns] *n.* 无力; 虚弱(powerlessness)

【记】im(无)＋potence(能力)→无能

limp [limp] *adj.* 柔软的, 无力的

【记】比较limb(四肢)

隐 藏

cryptic ['kriptik] *adj.* 神秘的, 隐藏的(mysterious)

【记】crypt(神秘)＋ic

【例】I do not understand your *cryptic* remarks!

secluded [si'klu:did] *adj.* 隐蔽的, 隐退的(remote, isolated)

【例】To find the true self, one is suggested to live a *secluded* life for a while.

seclusion [si'klu:ʒən] *n.* 归隐; 隔离(solitude, isolation)

【记】se(分开)＋clus=clude(关闭)＋ion→隔离

【例】Emily Dickinson's *seclusion* made her life a mystery to the public.

dissemble [di'sembl] *v.* 隐藏; 伪装(disguise, dissimulate)

【记】dis＋semble(相似)→隐藏

【例】The criminal suspect was *dissembling* when he said he was asleep in bed at the time of the crime.

lurk [lə:k] *vi.* 躲藏(prowl, slink)

【例】The villagers reported that the lion from the zoo was still *lurking* close to.

sneak [sni:k] *vi.* 潜行（lurk, skulk）

【记】比较 snake（蛇）

【例】The man *sneaked* about the place watching for a chance to steal something.

conceal [kən'si:l] *vt.* 把…隐藏起来（disguise, hide）

【例】The criminal *concealed* the knife in his boot.

feign [fein] *vt.* 假装（simulate, sham）

【记】比较 feint（佯攻）

【例】The hunter had to *feign* death when he suddenly found out that a bear was coming toward him.

pretend [pri'tend] *vt.* 伪装（camouflage, disguise）

【例】He *pretended* not to know the facts.

simulate ['simjuleit] *vt.* 伪装，扮演（feign, fake）

【例】The computer program *simulated* the effects of aging.

hide [haid] *v.* 隐藏（conceal）

【例】The gangsters *hid* out in a remote cabin until it was safe to return to the city.

obscure [əb'skjuə] *vt.* 掩盖（hide, cloud）

【记】ob（离开）＋scure（跑）→跑开→掩盖

【例】The darkness of the night *obscured* the burglar's figure.

screen [skri:n] *vt.* 遮蔽（veil, conceal）

【例】The moon was *screened* by clouds.

Fear not that thy life shall come to an end, but rather fear that it shall never have a beginning.

不要害怕你的生活将要结束，应该担心你的生活永远不曾真正开始。

——J. H. Newman（纽曼）

连 线 题

左列单词在右列中有一个或多个同义词,请画线连接。

(一)

brittle	veil
curtail	attraction
dangle	charm
enhance	conceal
erratic	cut back
glamor	entice
impotence	fragile
lurk	hang
screen	heighten
tempt	improve
	lure
	powerlessness
	prowl
	reduce
	slink
	suspend
	unpredictable

(二)

consecutive	adhesive
convene	assemble
expand	come back
haunt	conceivable
languish	ease
potential	fade
relax	frequent
revert	gather
scarce	outspread
sticky	possible
	return
	sparse
	successive
	wither

(三)

commence	abundant
diversify	begin
fickle	blow
foremost	capricious
impale	changeable
profuse	continue
punch	exuberant
resume	hit
	penetrate
	pierce
	prime
	vary

（一）

brittle	fragile
curtail	reduce
curtail	cut back
dangle	suspend
dangle	hang
enhance	improve
enhance	heighten
erratic	unpredictable
glamor	attraction
glamor	charm
impotence	powerlessness
lurk	prowl
lurk	slink
screen	veil
screen	conceal
tempt	lure
tempt	entice

（二）

consecutive	successive
convene	assemble
convene	gather
expand	outspread
haunt	frequent
languish	wither
languish	fade
potential	possible
potential	conceivable
relax	ease
revert	come back
revert	return
scarce	sparse
sticky	adhesive

（三）

commence	begin
diversify	vary
fickle	changeable
fickle	capricious
foremost	prime
impale	pierce
impale	penetrate
profuse	abundant
profuse	exuberant
punch	blow
punch	hit
resume	continue

附录一 索引

austerity ······ 138	ban ············ 21	beforehand ··· 164	bidding ······ 274
austerity ······ 143	band ········· 100	befuddle ······ 323	bidding ········· 36
authentic ······ 307	band ········· 168	beget ········· 320	bigoted ······ 244
authoritative ··· 106	band ········· 182	begrudge ······ 219	bill ············ 15
authority ······ 106	band ········· 88	beguile ······ 174	bill ············ 24
authorize ······ 20	bandit ········· 64	beguile ······ 198	bill ············ 38
autocrat ······ 66	banish ········· 109	behave ········· 194	biochemistry ··· 27
autonomy ··· 107	bankruptcy ··· 38	behave ········· 228	biographer ··· 61
available ······ 293	banquet ······ 190	behavior ······ 228	bird ············ 12
avalanche ··· 201	bar ············ 20	belie ········· 175	bizarre ········· 302
avant-garde ··· 65	barbarian ······ 64	believer ········· 63	blackmail ··· 175
avarice ········· 142	bare ········· 246	belittle ········· 132	blame ········· 276
avaricious ··· 142	bare ········· 298	belligerent ··· 315	bland ········· 150
average ······ 299	barely ········· 289	benefactor ······ 63	blast ············ 28
aversion ······ 221	bark ········· 112	beneficial ··· 226	blast ············ 55
avert ········· 234	barley ········· 151	beneficiary ··· 64	bleach ········· 27
aviator ········· 60	barn ············ 51	benefit ······ 226	bleak ········· 197
avid ············ 142	barometer ······ 55	benefit ········· 39	bleed ········· 93
avid ············ 218	barren ········· 197	benevolent ··· 226	blemish ········· 287
avoid ········· 234	barricade ······ 240	benign ········· 136	blend ········· 27
avow ········· 255	barrier ········· 240	bent ········· 260	blessed ········· 118
awe ············ 188	barter ········· 40	bequest ······ 263	blessed ········· 213
awkward ······ 133	bashful ······ 136	berate ········· 276	blessing ······ 176
axis ············ 194	basin ············ 6	bereave ······ 248	blink ········· 191
baboon ········· 14	bask ········· 199	beset ············ 44	bliss ········· 213
baboon ········· 14	bask ········· 199	besides ········· 156	blizzard ······ 55
baby-sit ······ 196	baste ········· 316	besiege ········· 44	block ········· 184
bachelor ······ 63	bat ············ 14	bestow ········· 227	block ········· 241
backward ······ 154	battery ········· 88	bestow ········· 229	block ········· 301
baggage ······ 196	beak ········· 15	betray ········· 236	blunder ········· 257
bait ············ 332	bear ········· 242	betray ········· 247	blunt ········· 133
balance ······ 32	bear ········· 302	beverage ······ 151	blunt ········· 134
bald ············ 198	beast ········· 13	bewilder ······ 249	blur ············ 250
balk ············ 240	beat ········· 212	bias ········· 157	board ········· 106
ballot ········· 107	beaver ········· 15	bias ········· 206	board ········· 167
balmy ········· 304	becoming ··· 293	bicker ········· 281	boast ········· 273
balmy ········· 54	beet ········· 151	bidding ······ 190	boastful ······ 273

catharsis

garlic 51	given 302	granite 8	habitat 32
garner 38	glacial 8	grant 183	habitually 260
garnish 239	glacier 8	grant 256	hackneyed 26
gash 93	glamor 332	grasp 191	hackneyed 299
gasoline 26	glamorous 332	grasp 248	haggle 281
gasp 13	glaring 159	grateful 176	hail 219
gather 324	glaring 190	gratify 216	hail 55
gauche 135	glaze 159	gratitude 176	halt 220
gauge 161	glaze 177	gratuitous 169	halt 319
gaze 192	gleam 159	gratuitous 307	hamper 241
gear 194	glean 230	gravitation 88	handicap 241
gem 8	gleeful 212	gravity 84	handle 247
general 299	glide 192	graze 13	handy 295
generalize 161	gloom 207	graze 50	haphazard 328
generally 299	gloomy 158	grease 15	harass 210
generate 320	gloomy 209	greasy 15	hardheaded 139
generous 226	glorious 186	greedy 142	hardheaded 245
generously 226	glorious 309	greenhouse 51	hardly 289
genial 136	glossary 102	gregarious 12	hardy 140
genre 102	glossy 159	gregarious 137	harmful 303
genteel 68	glucose 71	grievance 221	harness 229
gentility 137	gnaw 192	grieved 207	harrow 179
gentry 66	goods 39	grim 143	harry 248
genuine 307	gorge 116	grim 209	harsh 100
genus 14	gorge 212	grind 248	harsh 143
geographer 60	gorgeous 186	grip 190	harvest 50
geography 5	gorgeous 310	grope 259	hasten 231
geologist 60	gorilla 14	grossly 289	hasty 162
geology 8	gossip 277	grouchy 210	hatch 13
geometry 76	govern 107	grudge 221	hatchet 42
geothermy 6	grab 192	grumble 278	hatred 221
germinate 112	gracious 137	grumpy 135	haughty 206
gibe 271	gradually 326	guarantee 256	haul 193
gild 178	grain 150	guileless 292	haunt 259
gild 238	granary 51	guise 198	haunt 326
girdle 167	grand 310	gush 166	haven 184
gist 309	grandeur 188	habitat 14	hay 51

cling to	遵守;坚持
cope with	处理(take care of, deal with, handle)
correspond to	与…相应
dedicate oneself to	致力于
deprive of	剥夺
dispose of	处理,处置
every walk of life	各行各业
fall into	陷入,进入
first rank	一流的
follow one's lead	听某人的话,效法某人
from one's standpoint	从某人的立场
from one's point of view	从某人的观点
get rid of	消除
get...in tune	使…和谐
give way to	让步于
graze on	(牛羊等)吃(草)
have...in common	有共性,有共同点
hold back	阻止
in addition to	除…外
in advance	预先
in favor of	倾向于
in harmony with	与…协调一致
in high gear	高速地
in one's own right	by oneself
in significant measure	在很大程度上
in so far as	在…的范围内;就…而言
in the strictest sense	在最严格的意义上
jibe with	与…一致
keep abreast with	跟上(keep up with)
make a tribute to	对…做贡献,对…有意义
make an impact on	对…产生影响

make one's way to	转向
make way for	让步于
notwithstanding	虽然,尽管(however)
on the whole	总体上
only that...	因为(because)
per capita	人均
pick up	拣起;沿着…
play a part in	在…中扮演角色;在…中起作用
preside over	管理,监控
prior to	在…前
provided with	提供…
put an end to	结束
regardless of	不管,不顾
short of	1.差点,几乎 2. prep. 除了(except)
shoot up	迅速成长,增长
subject to	取决于…;受…控制
subsist on	依靠
take advantage of	利用
take on	呈现(例) The city takes on a new look.
	承担(例) He has to take on extra work.
take sth.for granted	想当然认为…
tip the scale at	称重…,体重…
to the extreme	达到极点
to the point of	到…的程度
to the extent of	到…的程度
up to	达到(as many as)
usher in	带来,开始
wipe out	消除
with respect to	考虑到

第二部　TOEFL 阅读部分考核词组

account for	explain
ahead of	in front of, preceding
as a result of	because of
as a substitute for	in place of
as well as	in addition of
attribute to	testify as
be fraught with	full of, charge with
break apart	split
break out	begin
break up	separate
bring about	produce, cause, introduce
by-product	derivative
call for	require
call off	cancel
cling to	persist to, stick to
come down with	
come through	survive(特定上下文中有此含义)
come to	regain consciousness
come up with	produce
count on	rely on, count
couple with	in addition
deal with	concern
devote to	dedicate, specialize in
dispose of	get rid of
dissent from	disagree
do away with	get rid of
draw from	take from
drive out of	force out of
dwindle away	eventually disappear

easily moved	portable
excel in	be outstanding in
extract from	remove from
feed up	disgust; eat
figure out	solve
from time to time	occasionally
get along	manage
get over	recover from
get rid of	discard, eliminate
give in	yield to
give out	announce
hand in	submit
hand out	distribute
hold up	withstand
look after	care for
look over	inspect
make do with	replace(特定上下文中有此含义)
make up	constitute
make up for	compensate for
on the outskirts	at the edges
on the wane	dwindling
on the whole	generally
outlet for	release from
pertain to	associate with,relate to
plague with	afflict by
put up with	tolerate
rather than	instead of
put off	postpone
put up	supply
run out	become depleted
set off	begin

set up	arrange,establish
sit on	serve on
stand against	defiance of
stretch across	span
subterranean	underground
take down	record
take after	resemble
take for	confuse sb with
take in	deceive
take into account	consider
take off	depart
take on	assume
turn down	reject
turn into	become
up to	a maximum of, as many as
wear away	erode
wear out	no longer usable
with respect to	with regard to

附录三 托福经典 400 题

1. Honey guides, or indicator birds, <u>collaborate</u> with honey badgers in seeking out bee colonies.
   (A) work together   (B) travel north   (C) live   (D) compete

2. Diffusion is the spontaneous spreading of matter caused by the <u>random</u> movement of molecules.
   (A) patternless   (B) whirling   (C) constant   (D) rampant

3. The attack on Fort Sumter near Charleston <u>provoked</u> a sharp response from the North, which led to the American Civil War.
   (A) demanded   (B) elicited   (C) expedited   (D) defied

4. The <u>amenities</u> of civilization are left behind when an individual embarks on a camping trip in a remote area.
   (A) activities   (B) rules   (C) comforts   (D) signs

5. Parsley is <u>cultivated</u> throughout much of the world.
   (A) seen   (B) grown   (C) dried   (D) cooked

6. A ford is a place where it is possible to cross a <u>creek</u> or river.
   (A) trench   (B) gorge   (C) ravine   (D) stream

7. Grandma Moses, a popular painter, spent her life in a <u>tranquil</u> little farming community.
   (A) lovely   (B) serene   (C) isolated   (D) snobbish

8. The works of novelist Joyce Carol Oates are moving chronicles of <u>contemporary</u> life in the United States.
   (A) simultaneous   (B) controversial   (C) modern   (D) temperate

9. The tendency of the human body to reject foreign matter is the main <u>obstacle</u> to successful tissue transplantation.
   (A) factor in   (B) impediment to   (C) occurrence in   (D) phenomenon of

10. Hypnotized individuals can be induced to act <u>bizarrely</u>.
    (A) in harmful ways   (B) against their wills
    (C) oddly   (D) emotionally

11. When telephone calls are tansmitted by satellite, a <u>dim</u> echo can often be heard on the line.

　（A）weak　　　　（B）static　　　　（C）harsh　　　　（D）deep

12. In North America, the first canoes were constructed from logs and <u>propelled</u> by means of wooden paddles.

　（A）carved　　　　（B）docked　　　　（C）driven forward　（D）carried upright

13. W.C. Handy, the <u>renowned</u> composer and musician, was known as the "father of the blues."

　（A）kindly　　　　（B）noble　　　　（C）famous　　　　（D）dashing

14. It is now common for physically disabled individuals to receive the <u>bulk</u> of their education in regular school programs.

　（A）majority　　　　（B）assignments　（C）texts　　　　（D）rest

15. The nests of most finches are constructed <u>sloppily</u>.

　（A）elaborately　　（B）messily　　　　（C）characteristically（D）annually

16. Large areas of Alaskan land remain <u>desolate</u> due to harsh climate.

　（A）inaccessible　　（B）immature　　　（C）parched　　　　（D）barren

17. The comic routines of Stan Laurel and Oliver Hardy involved pantomime and <u>a novel</u> use of props.

　（A）an original　　（B）an appropriate　（C）a literal　　　（D）a funny

18. <u>Subterranean</u> streams have cut through limestone to form miles of passage and caves, such as Kentucky's Mammoth Cave.

　（A）Secondary　　（B）Underground　（C）Unharnessed　（D）Miniscule

19. Salesmanship is the ability to <u>sway</u> people to willingly buy products or support new ideas.

　（A）educate　　　　（B）expect　　　　（C）allow　　　　（D）persuade

20. The fire dance is the <u>climax</u> of the ceremony of the Navajo night chants.

　（A）addition to　　（B）high point in　（C）substitute for　（D）beginning of

21. A fossil is a <u>remnant</u> of a once-living organism.

　（A）bone　　　　（B）solvent　　　　（C）picture　　　　（D）vestige

22. If stored while wet, hay may build up heat and <u>ignite</u> spontaneously.

　（A）sprout　　　　（B）catch fire　　　（C）release gases　（D）spoil

23. It was not <u>poverty</u>, but rather a concern for simplicity that kept Puritan churches unadorned.

　（A）theology　　　　　　　　　（B）hunger for power

　（C）frontier conditions　　　　（D）lack of money

24. Strict sanitary procedures help to <u>forestall</u> outbreaks of disease.

(A) prevent   (B) control   (C) minimize   (D) preview

25. <u>Deceptive</u> labeling of certain types of merchandise is not all owed under the Pure Food and Drug Act of 1906.

(A) Alarming   (B) Misleading   (C) Extravagant   (D) Tasteless

26. When planting shrubbery, it is advisable to <u>tamp</u> the dirt around the roots after covering them.

(A) water   (B) fertilize   (C) pack down   (D) tamper with

27. Alexander Woollcott's <u>flamboyant</u> personality combined sharpness of wit with sentimentality.

(A) devious   (B) humorous   (C) singular   (D) showy

28. In terms of precipitation, ten inches of snow is the <u>equivalent</u> of an inch of rain.

(A) the symbol of   (B) the same as

(C) the product of   (D) as thick as

29. After many years of unsuccessfully <u>endeavoring</u> to form his own orchestra, Glenn Miller finally achieved world fame in 1939 as a big band leader.

(A) requesting   (B) trying   (C) offering   (D) deciding

30. The manic-depressive usually <u>fluctuates</u> between great excitement and deep depression.

(A) recovers   (B) falls   (C) improves   (D) alternates

31. In the Navejob household, grandparents and other relatives play <u>indispensable</u> roles in raising children.

(A) dominant   (B) exemplary   (C) essential   (D) demanding

32. Laser beams can be used to <u>bore</u> metals and other hard materials.

(A) trim   (B) melt   (C) drill   (D) slice

33. The concept of upward social mobility has been an <u>abiding</u> feature of American life.

(A) enduring   (B) unaffected   (C) intriguing   (D) observable

34. When <u>squashed</u> the stem and leaves of the jewelweed exude a juice that will soothe some skin irritations.

(A) boiled   (B) aged   (C) crushed   (D) chopped

35. The Coriolis force causes all moving projectiles on Earth to be <u>deflected</u> from a straight line.

(A) sprung   (B) deviated   (C) be retracted   (D) be conceived

36. The legislative filibuster is a parliamentary <u>tactic</u> designed to delay or prevent action by the majority.

(A) tradition   (B) rule   (C) observance   (D) maneuver

37. Because of its old mannerisms, the praying mantis has always <u>intrigued</u> human beings.

（A）af scinated （B）aggravated （C）offended （D）terrified

38. Hundreds of years ago cloves were used to <u>remedy</u> headaches.

（A）disrupt （B）diagnose （C）evaporate （D）cure

39. Ocean waves can cut <u>imposing</u> cliffs along coastlines.

（A）immobile （B）impermeable

（C）impressive （D）imaginative

40. Neon light is utilized in airport beacons because it can <u>permeate</u> fog.

（A）pass through （B）transmit （C）suspend （D）break up

41. A computer will always follow the same <u>sequence</u> when solving a problem,no matter how complicated that problem may be.

（A）imprint （B）definition （C）progression （D）ordinance

42. Weight lifting is the gymnastic sport of lifting weights in a <u>prescribed</u> manner.

（A）vigorous （B）popular （C）certain （D）careful

43. A number of the Mikasuki Indians still <u>reside</u> on their reservation in northern Florida.

（A）work on （B）visit （C）live on （D）protect

44. The lilac flower has a unique <u>odor</u>.

（A）scent （B）tint （C）shape （D）size

45. An allergy is <u>an adverse</u> reaction of the body to certain substances.

（A）a natural （B）a negative （C）a routine （D）a selective

46. Tax <u>rebates</u> can have far reaching effects on the economy.

（A）accountants （B）laws （C）refunds （D）credits

47. Arizona's rapid population growth and wealth <u>spurred</u> the movement for statehood at the end of the nineteenth century.

（A）stimulated （B）financed （C）spanned （D）disrupted

48. Mergers may be effected to revive or rejuvenate failing businesses by the <u>infusion</u> of new management and personnel.

（A）inspection （B）introduction （C）evaluation （D）concentration

49. A fable is <u>a didactic</u> tale focused on a single character trait.

（A）an authentic （B）a muddled （C）an instructive （D）an old-fashioned

50. Biologists have <u>ascertained</u> that specialized cells convert chemical energy into mechanical energy.

（A）determined （B）argued （C）pretended （D）hypothesized

51. In mathematics the term "solid" describes a geometric <u>figure</u> with three dimensions.

（A）angle （B）shape （C）triangle （D）equation

52. Shellac varnish is purified lac that is secreted by scale insects.

　（A）refined　　　（B）starchy　　　（C）resilient　　　（D）virtuous

53. The role of the performing artist is to interpret, not alter, the notes on a printed sheet of music.

　（A）omit　　　（B）reproduce　　　（C）compose　　　（D）change

54. Modern printing equipment quickly turns out duplicate copies of textual and pictorial matter.

　（A）identical　　　（B）excessive　　　（C）illustrated　　　（D）legible

55. After reading Philip Morrison's paper on gamma-ray astronomy in 1959, a fellow physicist was prompted to ask, "Wouldn't using gamma rays be a good way to communicate across the galaxy?"

　（A）petitioned　　　（B）cautioned　　　（C）motivated　　　（D）requested

56. During the rainy season the Mississippi River may carry away hundreds of acres of valuable topsoil from one area and arbitrarily deposit it in another.

　（A）subsequently　　（B）lawfully　　　（C）mercilessly　　　（D）randomly

57. Teachers of young children should scrupulously avoid ridicule and sarcasm.

　（A）theoretically　　（B）naively　　　（C）diligently　　　（D）confidently

58. Ice can be used to keep food from spoiling.

　（A）rotting　　　（B）aging　　　（C）toughening　　　（D）evaporating

59. An expert in any field may be defined as a person who possesses specialized skills and is capable of rendering very competent services.

　（A）obtaining　　　（B）mastering　　　（C）providing　　　（D）financing

60. Plays that entail direct interaction between actor and audience present no unusual difficulties for actors.

　（A）advocate　　　（B）involve　　　（C）elicit　　　（D）exaggerate

61. The issue of loose construction versus strict construction of the United States Constitution contributed to the emergence of political parties.

　（A）joining　　　（B）urgency　　　（C）appearance　　　（D）activity

62. Some critics have praised James Michener's epic novels for their facts but deplored their characterization.

　（A）emulated　　　（B）ridiculed　　　（C）complimented　（D）lamented

63. Materials such as clay, wax, glass, and rubber are widely used in industry today because they are malleable.

　（A）easy to manufacture　　　　（B）readily available
　（C）pliable　　　　　　　　　　（D）buoyant

64. Starfish, five-armed sea creatures, <u>creep</u> across coral reefs by using suckers on the bottom of their arms.

（A）dig deeply　　（B）move slowly　　（C）dive　　　　（D）jump

65. Repeated burning of any vegetation cover alters its composition and <u>hence</u> its contribution to soil development.

（A）in conclusion　（B）as a result　　（C）otherwise　　（D）by comparison

66. Woodrow Wilson <u>endeavored</u> to preserve world peace by supporting the establishment of an organization to settle international disputes.

（A）tried　　　　（B）needed　　　（C）decided　　　（D）neglected

67. The Group of Seven, a clique of Canadian artists painting at the turn of the century, has been credited with <u>arousing</u> a widespread awareness of Canada's rugged landscape.

（A）stimulating　　（B）prolonging　　（C）glorifying　　（D）politicizing

68. Comets are still regarded with <u>awe</u> by some people.

（A）wonder　　　（B）concern　　　（C）resentment　　（D）detachment

69. The Badlands National Park was established in South Dakota to preserve this <u>weirdly</u> beautiful region.

（A）truly　　　　（B）strangely　　（C）exceedingly　　（D）impressively

70. In 1925 Clarence Darrow <u>competently</u> opposed William Jennings Bryan at the renowned Scopes "Monkey Trial."

（A）adeptly　　　（B）maliciously　　（C）privately　　（D）rashly

71. In the book Autobiography of Values, the aviation hero Charles Lindbergh reveals his <u>paradoxical</u> and often sobering thoughts on life.

（A）contradictory　（B）poignant　　（C）mystic　　　（D）paramount

72. Proteins are composed of more than twenty amino acids that are <u>liberated</u> during digestion.

（A）congregated　（B）multiplied　　（C）freed　　　（D）conscripted

73. An electric arc is a <u>luminous</u> current of electricity that leaps from one electrode to another.

（A）ludicrous　　（B）glowing　　　（C）magnetic　　（D）flickering

74. After its founding, the United States government followed a policy <u>explicitly</u> designed to aid national shipping.

（A）prematurely　（B）economically　（C）specifically　（D）proudly

75. In many societies the person who fails to conform to conventional behavior is likely to be <u>shunned</u> by others.

（A）preserved　　（B）instructed　　（C）avoided　　（D）selected

76. Accountants record all information <u>pertaining</u> to the economic aspects of an organization's activities.

(A) submitted to　(B) associated with　(C) limiting　(D) taxing

77. Willa Cather <u>procured</u> the inspiration for her fictional characters from the Nebraskan farmers among whom she was raised.

(A) endorsed　(B) deposed　(C) elevated　(D) obtained

78. The compact dictionaries published in recent years are not as <u>unwieldy</u> as some of the older editions.

(A) complete　(B) tiresome　(C) reliable　(D) cumbersome

79. Molly Brown was labeled "unsinkable" after she helped to <u>evacuate</u> passengers from the ill-fated ship the Titanic.

(A) anticipate　(B) comfort　(C) remove　(D) shelter

80. It is seldom acceptable to <u>abbreviate</u> words in formal writing.

(A) omit　(B) explain　(C) invent　(D) shorten

81. Ella Grasso, elected governor of Connecticut in 1974, supported the <u>enactment</u> of a freedom-of-information law.

(A) passing　(B) advocates　(C) drafting　(D) circulation

82. Eyespots, the most <u>rudimentary</u> eyes, are found in protozoan flagellates, flatworms, and segmented worms.

(A) hostile-looking　(B) perceptive　(C) primitive　(D) strangely formed

83. Some children display an <u>unquenchable</u> curiosity about every new thing they encounter.

(A) insatiable　(B) inherent　(C) indiscriminate　(D) incredible

84. In autumn chipmunks fill their expansive cheek pouches with food that they carry away to store for the <u>harsh</u> winter ahead.

(A) cozy　(B) severe　(C) lonely　(D) dry

85. Ocean-going vessels have often used flags to indicate their national <u>allegiance</u>.

(A) loyalty　(B) destination　(C) cargo　(D) allowance

86. The action in James Baldwin's novel Go Tell It on the Mountain <u>spans</u> two days in the lives of several members of a strict religious sect.

(A) comments on　(B) predicts　(C) begins with　(D) covers

87. Although many people had long regarded the "Star-Spangled Banner" as the national <u>anthem</u>, it was not officially designated as such until 1916.

(A) symbol　(B) hero　(C) motto　(D) song

88. Amrlia Earhart was the first woman to make a <u>solo</u> flight across the Atlantic.

(A) a noteworthy　(B) a speedy

(C) an unaccompanied　(D) an uninterrupted

89. The city of Winston-Salem, North Carolina, received its name in 1913, when the <u>adjoining</u> towns of Winston and Salem were combined.

    (A) separate   (B) neighboring   (C) colonial   (D) competing

90. The metric system did not develop haphazardly, but was <u>deliberately</u> constructed.

    (A) readily   (B) purposely   (C) correctly   (D) wholly

91. Because it symbolized strength, the oak was traditionally <u>worshiped</u> and had numerous mythological associations.

    (A) bought   (B) transported   (C) engraved   (D) revered

92. Modern nursing practices not only hasten the recovery of the sick but also <u>promote</u> better health through preventive medicine.

    (A) permit   (B) determine   (C) accelerate   (D) accompany

93. Ships passing on the high seas exchange <u>salutes</u> by lowering and raising their flags once.

    (A) information   (B) ceremonies   (C) greetings   (D) privileges

94. Diamonds that are <u>flawed</u> or are too small for jewelry are used to cut very hard metals.

    (A) tiny   (B) imperfect   (C) lustrous   (D) crude

95. Leaves are not distributed <u>haphazardly</u> on a plant stem, but are arranged in a very precise way that assures them the maximum light.

    (A) dangerously (B) densely   (C) randomly   (D) linearly

96. In the United States, the <u>provisions</u> of the constitution of any state may not conflict with those of the federal Constitution.

    (A) stipulations   (B) interrelations

    (C) jurisdictions   (D) interpretations

97. James Polk, the eleventh President of the United States, <u>resolutely</u> refused to be nominated for a second term.

    (A) surprisingly (B) firmly   (C) regrettably   (D) angrily

98. When <u>menaced</u> by a predator in close proximity, a snake may suddenly alter its behavior.

    (A) threatened   (B) bitten   (C) wounded   (D) trapped

99. In 1963 Maria Mayer was awarded the Nobel Prize in physics of her findings on the <u>constituents</u> of the atomic nucleus.

    (A) discovery   (B) dimensions   (C) components (D) connotations

100. One of the responsibilities of the Coast Guard is to make sure that all ships <u>obediently</u> follow traffic rules in busy harbors.

    (A) skillfully   (B) safely   (C) dutifully   (D) currently

101. Spearmint oil is distilled for flavoring chewing gum and candy and used as a disguise for <u>disagreeable</u> tastes in medicines.

　(A) unfortunate　　(B) distinctive　　(C) unpleasant　　(D) multiple

102. Ravaged by pollution and war, many famous monuments have become eroded and <u>stained</u>.

　(A) discolored　　(B) dismembered　　(C) discredited　　(D) displaced

103. When the United States stock market fell in 1929, many stockholders were forced to sell their shares at <u>ludicrously</u> low prices.

　(A) predictably　　(B) relatively　　(C) suspiciously　　(D) ridiculously

104. Plants without leaves, such as algae and fungi, are the first forms of life to grow back after a natural <u>catastrophe</u>.

　(A) disaster　　　(B) event　　　(C) phenomenon　　(D) explosion

105. North American fur trade waned in the early 1800's mainly due to the <u>diminishing</u> number of fur-bearing animals.

　(A) staggered　　(B) ceased　　　(C) declined　　　(D) collapsed

106. When required by their parents to eat spinach and other green vegetables, many children only do so <u>reluctantly</u>.

　(A) imitatively　　(B) impatiently　　(C) unwillingly　　(D) unknowingly

107. A goose hisses when it <u>charges</u> its adversaries.

　(A) comes across　　　　　　　　(B) communicates with

　(C) attacks　　　　　　　　　　(D) eats

108. Certain colors when incorporated into the decor of a room can produce a <u>cozy</u> atmosphere.

　(A) light　　　(B) roomy　　　(C) cluttered　　(D) comfortable

109. Apple trees need moisture in order to <u>thrive</u>.

　(A) flower　　(B) flourish　　(C) pollinate　　(D) bend

110. The first important <u>exposition</u> in the United States was held in Philadelphia in 1876.

　(A) exhibition　　(B) excursion　　(C) concert　　(D) contest

111. In Washington Irving's tale "Rip Van Winkle," the main character encounters some odd-looking people <u>dwelling</u> in the caves of the Catskill Mountains.

　(A) living　　(B) working　　(C) dancing　　(D) sleeping

112. While Billie Holiday did not invent the music called "the blues", she most <u>assuredly</u> helped popularize it.

　(A) finally　　　　　　　　　(B) certainly

　(C) earnestly　　　　　　　　(D) enthusiastically

113. In the northeastern United States, it rains <u>intermittently</u> throughout the spring.

（A）steadily 　　（B）abundantly 　　（C）periodically 　　（D）daily

114. One-room schoolhouses can still be found in <u>isolated</u> areas of North America where there are no other school for many miles.

（A）bare 　　（B）deprived 　　（C）remote 　　（D）developed

115. The use of barbed-wire fencing by farmers in the nineteenth century <u>infuriated</u> cattle ranchers, whose herds were often injured after becoming entangled in the sharp spikes.

（A）puzzled 　　（B）enraged 　　（C）concerned 　　（D）amazed

116. Most plants depend upon their roots to <u>anchor</u> themselves in the soil and to absorb water and inorganic chemicals.

（A）secure 　　（B）reproduce 　　（C）moisten 　　（D）distribute

117. In the United States there are more people who are <u>obese</u> today than twenty years ago.

（A）gainfully employed 　　（B）upwardly mobile

（C）excessively overweight 　　（D）privately educated

118. Anthropologist Barbara Myerhoff <u>furthered</u> her reputation as an authority on Native American culture with her study of the symbols, myths, and rituals of the Huichols.

（A）deserved 　　（B）retained 　　（C）renewed 　　（D）advanced

119. In 1795 John Jay <u>resigned</u> his position as the first chief justice of the United States and became a state governor.

（A）advertised 　　（B）gave up 　　（C）took over 　　（D）rearranged

120. Most tachometers measure the speed of rotation of a <u>spinning</u> shaft or wheel in terms of revolutions per minute.

（A）pumping 　　（B）wavering 　　（C）floating 　　（D）whirling

121. Almost insolvable in water, quinine dissolves <u>readily</u> in alcohol.

（A）easily 　　（B）partly 　　（C）frequently 　　（D）violently

122. The American Medical Association has called for the sport of boxing to be <u>banned</u>.

（A）forbidden 　　（B）regulated 　　（C）studied 　　（D）reorganized

123. Before the advent of <u>synthetic</u> fibers, people had to rely entirely on natural products for making fabrics.

（A）modern 　　（B）flexible 　　（C）colored 　　（D）artificial

124. The difference between the polar and equatorial diameters of Mars has not been <u>unequivocally</u> determined.

（A）easily 　　（B）definitely 　　（C）conventionally 　　（D）arithmetically

125. The western slopes of the mountains of the Sierra Nevada Range are deeply incised by numerous streams.

　　(A) fed　　　　(B) cut　　　　(C) flooded　　　(D) distended

126. As a result of his pioneering work with Louis Armstrong in the late 1920's Earl Hines has been called the father of modern jazz piano.

　　(A) professional　(B) artistic　　(C) excellent　　(D) original

127. The significance of magazines among contemporary media is sometimes grossly underestimated because of television's seeming dominance.

　　(A) greatly　　(B) easily　　(C) possibly　　(D) graphically

128. A former state senator who preached judicial restraint, Sandra Day O'Connor was expected to align herself with conservative when she was appointed to the United States Supreme Court.

　　(A) advocated　(B) questioned　(C) practiced　　(D) admired

129. Important features of dehydrated foods are their lightness in weight and their compactness.

　　(A) frozen　　(B) dried　　　(C) organic　　(D) healthful

130. Niagara Falls is a great tourist attractions, luring millions of visitors each year.

　　(A) serving　　(B) attracting　(C) entertaining　(D) receiving

131. For many adolescents, participation in sports is one way that they can feel true self esteem.

　　(A) loyalty　　(B) liberty　　(C) selfishness　(D) pride

132. In Mississippi many individuals of Acadian descent, called Cajuns, still maintain a separate folk culture.

　　(A) doctrine　　(B) language　　(C) ancestry　　(D) citizenship

133. Automatons are mechanical objects that become relatively self-operating once they have been actuated.

　　(A) timed　　(B) constructed　(C) cleaned up　(D) set in motion

134. South Carolina's mineral resources are abundant, but not all of them can be lucratively mined.

　　(A) profitably　(B) safely　　(C) easily　　(D) extensively

135. Within the bounds of given data, the biographer seeks to illuminate factual information about a person and transform it into insight.

　　(A) constraints　(B) archives　　(C) networks　　(D) goals

136. The most important crop in Alberta Canada is winter wheat which is planted in late summer and is ripe for harvesting by late spring.

　　(A) ready　　(B) intended　　(C) selected　　(D) sold

137. Records indicate that the tortoise can live longer than any other animal with a <u>spine</u>.

  (A) tail   (B) mouth   (C) shell   (D) backbone

138. Tennessee possesses many caverns with <u>gorgeous</u> rock formations.

  (A) beautiful   (B) large   (C) significant   (D) flat

139. Fossils are the <u>traces</u> of plants and animals of past geological ages that have been preserved in the Earth's crust.

  (A) registers   (B) residue   (C) profusion   (D) precursors

140. Louisa May Alcott's novel Little Women, which <u>recounts</u> the experiences of the four March sisters during the American Civil War, is largely autobiographical.

  (A) praises   (B) narrates   (C) exaggerates   (D) classifies

141. The Weddell seal of Antarctica can dive to a depth of about 1,000 feet and remain <u>submerged</u> for as long as an hour and ten minutes.

  (A) underwater   (B) fearless   (C) unconscious   (D) breathless

142. The disappearance of lichens from an area gives warning of an <u>endangered</u> environment.

  (A) an unusual   (B) a threatened   (C) a crowded   (D) an infertile

143. Bladder wrack, a tough, leathery brown seaweed, <u>clings to</u> rocks tenaciously.

  (A) grows under   (B) hides under   (C) sticks to   (D) yields to

144. In Ship of Fools, the vices and follies of a group of passengers are <u>ruthlessly</u> exposed as the narrative and the ship flow to their destination.

  (A) mercilessly   (B) clearly   (C) artfully   (D) gradually

145. Light from the Sun and distant stars <u>traverses</u> a vacuum in space.

  (A) fills   (B) creates   (C) surrounds   (D) crosses

146. Seminal contributions to science are those that change the <u>tenor</u> of the questions asked by succeeding generations.

  (A) nature   (B) results   (C) intonation   (D) punctuation

147. When natural gas burns, the hydrocarbon molecules <u>break up</u> into atoms of carbon and hydrogen.

  (A) contract   (B) vaporize   (C) collide   (D) separate

148. For one to two years before Election Day, a candidate for the presidency of the United States travels <u>extensively</u> around the country debating national and international issues.

  (A) widely   (B) energetically   (C) rapidly   (D) progressively

149. The initial appearance of the silver three-cent piece <u>coincided with</u> the first issue of three-cent stamps in 1851.

(A) occurred at the same time as　　(B) collided with

(C) was necessitated by　　(D) was similar to

150. Abrasives are sharp, hard materials used to <u>wear away</u> the surface of softer, less resistant materials.

  (A) add roughness to　　(B) fortify

  (C) erode　　(D) provide a gloss on

151. In Silent Spring, Rachel Carson forcefully decried the <u>indiscriminate</u> use of pesticides.

  (A) haphazard　　(B) unpleasant　　(C) regional　　(D) periodic.

152. Myths have <u>inspired</u> many of the world's greatest poets, artists, musicians, and scientists.

  (A) contradicted the ideas of　　(B) fired the imagination of

  (C) overwhelmed　　(D) comforted

153. Many farms in the southern United States <u>yield</u> hay and tobacco.

  (A) store　　(B) fertilize　　(C) sow　　(D) produce

154. John Adams, one of the American Revolution's most <u>devoted</u> patriots, was the lawyer who successfully defended the British soldiers charged with murder after the Boston Massacre.

  (A) daring　　(B) puzzling　　(C) dedicated　　(D) persuasive

155. The ruby is the hardest of all gems <u>save</u> the diamond.

  (A) connected to　　(B) like　　(C) superior to　　(D) except

156. Some cells, such as epithelia, <u>proliferate</u> more rapidly when the body is asleep than when it is awake.

  (A) cluster　　(B) multiply　　(C) adapt　　(D) heal

157. According to a United States law passed in 1986, states participating in daylight saving time <u>simultaneously</u> advance their clocks one hour in the last Sunday in April.

  (A) conceptually　　(B) systematically

  (C) at the same time　　(D) for a brief period

158. The octopus has three hearts that <u>pump</u> blood through its body.

  (A) drive　　(B) filter　　(C) dilute　　(D) aerate

159. The inhabitants of Jamestown, the first permanent English colony in America, nearly starved because they had <u>squandered</u> their provisions.

  (A) buried　　(B) wasted　　(C) lost　　(D) sold

160. For some animals, <u>locomotion</u> is accomplished by changes in body shape.

  (A) evolution　　(B) movement

  (C) survival　　(D) escape

161. Social reformer Jacob Riis's efforts to improve the rundown neighborhoods of New York City were aided by his <u>intimate</u> friend, Theodore Roosevelt.

(A) close   (B) wealthy   (C) influential   (D) charismatic

162. The skunk protects itself from enemies by spraying them with a substance that <u>stinks</u>.

(A) stings the eyes   (B) smells bad

(C) causes itching   (D) discolors the skin

163. Although <u>plagued with</u> injuries, Sabrina Mar won the All-Around Championship in Gymnastics at the 1987 Pan-American Games.

(A) recovering from   (B) afflicted by

(C) fighting off   (D) frightened of

164. The first water mill was horizontal and resembled a <u>rudimentary</u> turbine.

(A) a flat   (B) a rusty

(C) an unconventional   (D) an unsophisticated

165. The best olive oil is obtained from olives that are <u>harvested</u> just after they ripen and before they turn black.

(A) preserved   (B) squeezed   (C) gathered   (D) sorted

166. In astronomy, a scale of magnitude from one to six <u>denotes</u> brightness of a star.

(A) signifies   (B) predicts   (C) contrasts   (D) examines

167. Many people who want warm coats can buy <u>fake</u> furs.

(A) costly   (B) soft   (C) heavy   (D) imitation

168. Humus is <u>decayed</u> organic matter that is an important type of fertile soil.

(A) derived   (B) compacted   (C) decomposed   (D) liquefied

169. Forests are <u>delicate</u> systems that, if disturbed, can be permanently destroyed.

(A) fragile   (B) expansive   (C) complex   (D) unusual

170. In modern writing, the destination between literary expression and colloquial expression is often <u>blurred</u>.

(A) exaggerated   (B) reversed   (C) indistinct   (D) unintentional

171. Recent discoveries in Montana indicate that some dinosaurs may have <u>resided</u> in colonies.

(A) lived   (B) died   (C) hunted   (D) fed

172. Asbestos is a mineral fiber that can cause cancer if <u>inhaled</u>.

(A) picked up   (B) taken indoors   (C) breathed in   (D) eaten up

173. Logrolling is a sport in which contestants perform various <u>maneuvers</u> while treading on a floating log.

(A) speeches   (B) duties   (C) marches   (D) moves

174. H. L. Mencken's sardonic prose left an indelible mark on the English Language.
    (A) an unrivaled   (B) an unmistakable (C) a pretentious   (D) a permanent

175. The school of Abstract Expressionism, developed during the mid-1940's represented a distinct departure from artistic realism.
    (A) definite   (B) brief   (C) logical   (D) dangerous

176. By providing legal representations, the American Civil Liberties Union works to defend citizens against breaches of their civil rights.
    (A) branches   (B) exercises   (C) perusals   (D) violations

177. Colonists brought the game of bowling to North America and it became so popular that several towns still bear the name of Bowling Green.
    (A) suggest   (B) desire   (C) honor   (D) carry

178. The most typical feature of the Moon's surface is its profusion of craters the largest of which are more than one hundred miles in diameter.
    (A) abundance   (B) type   (C) tolerance   (D) circle

179. In the street portraits of photographer Diane Arbus, a seemingly straightforward investigation of the art became an intense, introspective analysis of both subject and viewer.
    (A) an apparently   (B) an obviously   (C) a relatively   (D) a mostly

180. The Mandan Indians lived beside the Missouri River where they cultivated fields of beans, corn, squash, sunflowers, and tobacco.
    (A) surveyed   (B) farmed   (C) irrigated   (D) discovered

181. George Gershwin was the first American musician whose jazz compositions were seriously appreciated by concert audiences.
    (A) heard   (B) sought   (C) admired   (D) reviewed

182. In his novella The Old Man and The Sea, Ernest Hemingway celebrates the indomitable courage of an elderly fisherman.
    (A) discusses   (B) investigates   (C) praises   (D) analyzes

183. New England town meetings, in their most highly developed form, are assemblies of the voters.
    (A) protests   (B) gatherings   (C) responsibilities (D) liabilities

184. Less successful artists are often obliged to turn to engraving, stonecutting, sign painting, and other artist's tasks to earn a living.
    (A) inspired   (B) asked   (C) forced   (D) tempted

185. Midway through its first century as a nation, the United States had expanded its population to roughly five times its initial size.
    (A) actually   (B) approximately   (C) periodically   (D) at least

186. Because it is so small and so close to the Sun, the planet Mercury has been extremely difficult to <u>observe</u>.

    (A) watch   (B) identify   (C) contact   (D) approach

187. To conceal itself, an octopus sensing danger will <u>squirt</u> a black fluid through an opening under its head.

    (A) strain   (B) swallow   (C) soak up   (D) spurt out

188. The Smithsonian institution <u>possesses</u> a player pipe organ that features a drum and triangle in addition to its 183 pipes.

    (A) runs   (B) has   (C) manufactures   (D) displays

189. More than 89 of the buildings in Annapolis, Maryland, were <u>erected</u> before the Revolutionary War.

    (A) planned   (B) leveled   (C) enlarged   (D) constructed

190. San Francisco, one of the most <u>appealing</u> cities in the United States, is built on many hills.

    (A) progressive   (B) attractive   (C) photographed   (D) lively

191. Companies in the United States usually <u>reimburse</u> employees's travel expenses incurred on business trips.

    (A) share   (B) pay back   (C) ask for   (D) charge

192. Long-horned grasshoppers have <u>auditory</u> organs on their forelegs.

    (A) jumping   (B) digestive   (C) hearing   (D) tactile

193. In the days leading up to the American Revolution, both the colonies and the British Crown were reluctant to take the final <u>irrevocable</u> step.

    (A) irrational   (B) irreversible   (C) irresponsible   (D) irresistible

194. The quality and number of a city's public roads offer an excellent means of <u>gauging</u> its prosperity.

    (A) protecting   (B) enriching   (C) tracing   (D) judging

195. Although it is commonly believed that an ostrich hides its head when confronted by danger, it actually runs away <u>swiftly</u>.

    (A) rapidly   (B) forcefully   (C) hysterically   (D) comically

196. The <u>demolition</u> of so many of Toronto's fine nineteenth-century buildings has meant an irreparable cultural loss.

    (A) destruction   (B) sale   (C) renovation   (D) demarcation

197. Youth hostels provide inexpensive <u>lodging</u> for young people throughout the United States and in other countries.

    (A) clothes   (B) entertainment (C) transportation (D) accommodations

198. When <u>submerged</u>, the duckbill platypus keeps its eyes and ears closed, using its bill to locate food.

(A) undernourished   (B) under water

(C) moving quickly   (D) feeding

199. Arna Wendell Bon temp's novel *God Sends Sunday* was adapted for the stage in 1946 as a musical play <u>entitled</u> St. Louis Woman.

(A) named   (B) chosen for   (C) including   (D) starring

200. By the 1880's, living conditions in the <u>congested</u> Eastern Seaboard cities of the United States had become local scandals.

(A) developing   (B) diverse   (C) crowded   (D) wealthy

201. <u>With respect to</u> maneuverability, few birds can equal the capabilities of the hummingbird, which hovers for long periods and even flies backward.

(A) With regard to   (B) With fondness for

(C) In appreciation of   (D) In favor of

202. After launching itself into flight, the flying squirrel is supported by a membrane of skin stretched <u>tautly</u> between its front and back legs.

(A) tightly   (B) carefully   (C) tidily   (D) comfortably

203. Early twentieth-century journalist H.L.Menchkin cheerfully <u>mocked</u> all that conventional people in the United States held dear.

(A) observed   (B) described   (C) accepted   (D) ridiculed

204. The Passamaquoddy and Penobscot people were <u>confederates</u> of the colonist in Maine at the time of the Revolutionary War.

(A) guardians   (B) teacher   (C) allies   (D) observers

205. The American painter Mary Cassatt lived mainly in France, where she <u>embraced</u> the study of impressionism.

(A) took up   (B) figured out   (C) came across   (D) ran into

206. The use of penicillin is limited by its tendency to <u>induce</u> allergic reactions.

(A) bring about   (B) stop   (C) interact with   (D) increase

207. Robert Frost's poetry is noted for its plain language, <u>conventional</u> poetic forms, and graceful style.

(A) unique   (B) traditional   (C) natural   (D) complex

208. Congressman Sam Rayburn's 25 <u>consecutive</u> terms in the House of representatives marked one of the longest tenures of any representative in United States history.

(A) successive   (B) prolonged

(C) elected   (D) limited

209. By 1930 two million women office workers, secretaries, typists, and flies clerks comprised one fifth of the female labor force.

(A) opposed　(B) made up　(C) took in　(D) followed

210. Fertilizer applied to soil can replace depleted nutrients.

(A) organic　(B) acidic　(C) exhausted　(D) desirable

211. Hailed as the "Queen of Soul", Aretha Franklin imparts a gospel sound to most of her music.

(A) Inaugurated　(B) Categorized　(C) Acclaimed　(D) Promoted

212. People have harnessed the Sun's energy since ancient times.

(A) acknowledged　(B) worshiped　(C) utilized　(D) polluted

213. Quebec's status as defined in the Canadian Constitution has been a recurring subject of debate in that province.

(A) realistic　(B) repeated　(C) renowned　(D) recent

214. In Arizona a small reduction in rainfall or temperature can drastically influence the growth of trees.

(A) virtually　(B) radically　(C) primarily　(D) conveniently

215. Scientists routinely deal with concepts such as uncertainty, probability, and hypothesis.

(A) reluctantly　(B) carefully　(C) commonly　(D) occasionally

216. Before the development of movable metal type in the mid-fifteenth century, news was disseminated by word of mouth, by letter, or by public notice.

(A) organized　(B) requested　(C) distributed　(D) limited

217. Although the study of politics dates back to Aristotle and Plato, political science only emerged as a separate discipline toward the end of the nineteenth century.

(A) law　(B) field　(C) belief　(D) reason

218. Lorraine Hansberry acquired a deep affection for Africa and its people from her Uncle William, a professor of African history at Howard University.

(A) respect　(B) concern　(C) longing　(D) fondness

219. The Sun Dance is considered by many to be the most spectacular ritual of the North American Plains Indians.

(A) ceremony　(B) ancestor　(C) scene　(D) costume

220. Choreographer Twyla Tharp uses familiar dance movements in original ways to create works filled with clever gestures and abrupt changes in motion and mood.

(A) graceful　(B) creative

(C) sudden　(D) dramatic

221. Under the rules of the International Olympic Committee, Jim Thorpe <u>forfeited</u> his amateur status when he played semiprofessional baseball in 1911.

    (A) tested   (B) exploited   (C) announce   (D) lost

222. In her compositions *Musical Theater*, Agnes De Mile uses many specifically American <u>motifs</u>.

    (A) steps   (B) themes   (C) instruments   (D) tunes

223. The <u>sparsely</u> populated northern region of the Canadian province of Manitoba is rich in copper, gold, nickel, and zinc.

    (A) evenly   (B) thinly   (C) diversely   (D) recently

224. The five classic foot positions in ballet are the basis for the <u>ethereal</u> grace of the ballet dancer's art.

    (A) balance   (B) traditional   (C) disciplined   (D) delicate

225. Even a <u>stern</u> judge will seldom impose maximum penalties on young offenders.

    (A) strict   (B) ruthless   (C) biased   (D) conservative

226. The witch hazel plants <u>tolerate</u> poor soil, dust and limited sun.

    (A) suffer from   (B) survive in   (C) thrive in   (D) die from

227. It is not easy for him to bear the <u>drudgery</u> of living in the woods.

    (A) violence   (B) interest   (C) training   (D) tedium

228. In chemical factories, employees sometimes receive extra pay for doing <u>hazardous</u> work.

    (A) unusual   (B) difficult   (C) dangerous   (D) unpleasant

229. Many news organizations feel a responsibility to <u>safeguard</u> the rights of citizens.

    (A) define   (B) protect   (C) examine   (D) challenge

230. Galena, the chief ore of lead, is a <u>brittle</u>, leadgray mineral with a metallic luster.

    (A) petrified   (B) dense   (C) breakable   (D) sparkling

231. Boy's Clubs do not <u>deprive</u> poor children of the opportunity to participate in sports.

    (A) deny   (B) retract   (C) improvise   (D) dilute

232. As a result of the accident, the police <u>revoked</u> his driver's license.

    (A) reconsidered   (B) exorcised

    (C) canceled   (D) investigated

233. While serving in the Senate in the early 1970's, Barbara Jordan supported legislation to ban discrimination and to <u>deal</u> with environmental problems.

    (A) list   (B) forbid   (C) handle   (D) investigate

234. In a bullfight, it is the movement, not the color, of objects that <u>arouses</u> the bull.

    (A) confuses   (B) excites   (C) scares   (D) diverts

235. By today's standards, early farmers were <u>imprudent</u> because they planted the same crop repeatedly, exhausting the soil after a few harvests.

(A) unwise　　(B) stubborn　　(C) tiresome　　(D) unscientific

236. If wool is submerged in hot water, it tends to <u>shrink</u>.

(A) smell fade　　(B) fade　　(C) unravel　　(D) contract

237. After 1850, various states in the United States began to pass <u>compulsory</u> school attendance laws.

(A) harsh　　(B) diversified　　(C) mandatory　　(D) complicated

238. Poor writing often <u>confounds</u> the reader.

(A) convinces　　(B) embarrasses　　(C) bewilders　　(D) insults

239. The geographical ranges of the apes have <u>dwindled</u>.

(A) disappeared　　(B) diminished

(C) become overcrowded　　(D) lost foliage

240. The rosemary plant is an emblem of <u>fidelity</u> and remembrance.

(A) thoughtfulness　　(B) tenderness

(C) faithfulness　　(D) happiness

241. There is always excitement at the Olympic Games when a previous record of performance is <u>surpassed</u>.

(A) exceeded　　(B) matched　　(C) maintained　　(D) announced

242. The number of United States citizens who are <u>eligible</u> to vote continues to increase.

(A) encouraged　　(B) enforced　　(C) expected　　(D) entitled

243. But not all animal parents, even those that <u>tend</u> their offspring to the point of hatching or birth, feed their young.

(A) sit on　　(B) move　　(C) notice　　(D) care for

244. Animals add it to their reproductive strategies to give them an <u>edge</u> in their lifelong quest for descendants.

(A) opportunity　　(B) advantage　　(C) purpose　　(D) rest

245. And in the meantime those young are <u>shielded</u> against the vagaries of fluctuating of difficult-to-find supplies.

(A) raised　　(B) protected　　(C) hatched　　(D) valued

246. Printmaking is the generic term for a number of processes, of which woodcut and engraving are two <u>prime</u> examples.

(A) principal　　(B) complex　　(C) general　　(D) recent

247. Both woodcut and engraving have <u>distinctive</u> characteristics.

(A) unique　　(B) accurate　　(C) irregular　　(D) similar

248. Its peoples became great traders, <u>bartering</u> jewellery, pottery, animal pelts, tools, and other goods along extensive trading networks that stretched up and down eastern North America and as far west as the Rocky Mountains.

(A) producing　　(B) exchanging　　(C) transporting　　(D) loading

249. Over the next centuries, it was <u>supplanted</u> by another culture, the Mississippian, named after the river along which many of its earliest villages were located.

(A) conquered　　(B) preceded　　(C) replaced　　　(D) imitated

250. Only priests and those <u>charged with</u> guarding the flame could enter the temples.

(A) passed on　　(B) experienced at　(C) interested in　　(D) assigned to

251. Overland transport in the United States was still extremely <u>primitive</u> in 1790.

(A) unsafe　　(B) unknown　　(C) inexpensive　　(D) undeveloped

252. The company built a gravel road within two years, and the success of the Lancaster Pike encouraged <u>imitation</u>.

(A) investment　　(B) suggestion　　(C) increasing　　(D) copying

253. Like tree roots breaking up a sidewalk, the growing crystals <u>exert</u> pressure on the rock and eventually pry the rock apart along planes of weakness, such as banding in metamorphic rocks, bedding in sedimentary rocks, or preexisting or incipient fractions, and along boundaries between individual mineral crystals or grains.

(A) put　　(B) reduce　　(C) replace　　(D) control

254. A rock <u>durable</u> enough to have withstood natural conditions for a very long time in other areas could probably be shattered into small pieces by salt weathering within a few generations.

(A) large　　(B) strong　　(C) flexible　　(D) pressured

255. A rock durable enough to have withstood natural conditions for a very long time in other areas could probably be <u>shattered</u> into small pieces by salt weathering within a few generations.

(A) arranged　　(B) dissolved　　(C) broken apart　　(D) gathered together

256. The dominant salt in Death Valley is halite, or sodium chloride, but other salts, mostly carbonates and sulfates, also cause prying and wedging, as does <u>ordinary</u> ice.

(A) most recent　　　　　　(B) most common
(C) least available　　　　　(D) least damaging

257. As Philadelphia grew from a small town into a city in the first half of the eighteenth century, it became an increasingly important marketing center for a vast and growing agricultural <u>hinterland</u>.

(A) tradition　　(B) association　　(C) produce　　(D) region

258. Along with market days, the institution of twice-yearly fairs <u>persisted</u> in Philadelphia even after similar trading days had been discontinued in other colonial cities.

    (A) returned   (B) started   (C) declined   (D) continued

259. Although governmental attempts to <u>eradicate</u> fairs and auctions were less than successful, the ordinary course of economic development was on the merchants' side, as increasing business specialization became the order of the day.

    (A) eliminate   (B) exploit   (C) organize   (D) operate

260. One of the reasons Philadelphia's merchants generally prospered was because the surrounding area was <u>undergoing</u> tremendous economic and demographic growth.

    (A) requesting   (B) experiencing   (C) repeating   (D) including

261. When incubators are not used, aviculturists sometimes <u>suspend</u> wooden boxes outdoors to use as nests in which to place eggs.

    (A) build   (B) paint   (C) hang   (D) move

262. Similarly, these boxes should be protected from direct sunlight to avoid high temperatures that are also <u>fatal</u> to the growing embryo.

    (A) close   (B) deadly   (C) natural   (D) hot

263. Nesting material should be added in sufficient amounts to avoid both extreme temperature situations mentioned above and assure that the eggs have a soft, <u>secure</u> place to rest.

    (A) fresh   (B) dry   (C) safe   (D) warm

264. To measure soil texture, the sand, silt, and clay particles are <u>sorted out</u> by size and weight.

    (A) mixed   (B) replaced   (C) carried   (D) separated

265. Clay particles are highly cohesive, and when <u>dampened</u>, behave as a plastic.

    (A) damaged   (B) stretched   (C) moistened   (D) examined

266. In addition, an interviewer can go beyond written questions and <u>probe</u> for a subject's underlying feelings and reasons.

    (A) explore   (B) influence   (C) analyze   (D) apply

267. Emotional health is <u>evidenced</u> in the voice by free and melodic sounds of the happy, by constricted and harsh sound of the angry, and by dull and lethargic qualities of the depressed.

    (A) questioned   (B) repeated   (C) indicated   (D) exaggerated

268. Increasingly, too, schools were viewed as the most important <u>means</u> of integrating immigrants into American society.

    (A) advantages   (B) probability   (C) method   (D) qualifications

269. Unlike those available for painting, the opportunities to exhibit sculpture in the United-States around the turn of the twentieth century were quite scarce.

 (A) exciting　　(B) expensive　　(C) uncommon　　(D) popular

270. As late as 1905, the Monumental News, a journal dedicated to the promotion of sculpture, lamented, "Exhibitions of sculptors' works are so comparatively rare."

 (A) declared　　(B) complained　　(C) revealed　　(D) described

271. He was a champion of the City Beautiful Movement- an effort to increase the presence of urban art-and defended the central role that sculpture played in its national program.

 (A) critic　　(B) founder　　(C) creator　　(D) supporter

272. Constructing the town, Pullman hoped to produce an ideal environment that would help attract workers of a superior type to the railway car industry and retain them.

 (A) house　　(B) train　　(C) keep　　(D) reward

273. However, after 1885, with the high gloss of the experiment dulled, it became clear that the residents of Pullman had honest grievances about the overcharging of rent and other services.

 (A) stories　　(B) opinions　　(C) findings　　(D) complaints

274. We now have some evidence that the symbolism used in masks is often universal.

 (A) concern　　(B) interest　　(C) roof　　(D) reference

275. Coding schemes were developed to enable researchers to compare the detailed facial positions of individual portions of die face （eyebrows, mouth, etc.） for different emotions.

 (A) systems　　(B) presentations　　(C) proposals　　(D) investigations

276. As suspected, the two sets of masks had significant differences in certain facial elements.

 (A) excellent　　(B) important　　(C) continuous　　(D) genuine

277. Natural selection has acted in a variety of ways in different species to enhance the efficacy of the behaviors, known as "flight behaviors" or escape behaviors that are used by prey in fleeing predators: Perhaps the most direct adaptation is enhanced flight speed and agility.

 (A) encourage　　(B) resist　　(C) increase　　(D) reveal

278. Many species, like ptarmigans, snipes, and various antelopes and gazelles, flee from predators in a characteristic zigzag fashion.

 (A) reliable　　(B) fast　　(C) constant　　(D) unpredictable

279. Here, the alarmed prey flees for a short distance and then "freezes."

 (A) moving　　(B) selected　　(C) frightened　　(D) exhausted

280. "Flash" behavior is used <u>in particular</u> by frogs and orthopteran insects, which make conspicuous jumps and then sit immobile.

(A) especially　　(B) with difficulty　(C) expertly　　　(D) frequently

281. For example, James Reonell provided the first <u>accurate</u> map of the currents in the Atlantic Ocean, and the United Slates Coast Survey made extensive studies of the Gulf Stream.

(A) correct　　(B) published　　(C) detailed　　　(D) accepted

282. The HMS Challenger <u>expedition</u> provided valuable information about the seabed, including the discovery of manganese nodules that are now being seen as a potentially valuable source of minerals.

(A) boat　　　(B) evidence　　(C) voyage　　　(D) route

283. He <u>devised</u> new techniques for measuring ocean depths, and his work proved of great value in laying the first transatlantic telegraph cables.

(A) tested　　(B) understood　(C) popularized　(D) developed

284. It was in the mining regions where engineers, who needed a better system for organizing the various types of rock scattered across Earth's surface, first <u>grappled</u> with scientific approaches to understanding the age of various rocks-and the age of Earth.

(A) competed　　(B) struggled　(C) agreed　　　(D) searched

285. Rock type, hardness, and size thus established mountain type, and rock type also became a <u>proxy</u> for age.

(A) substitute　(B) preparation　(C) product　　(D) choice

286. Organic fanning <u>essentially</u> refers to farming that does not depend on chemical fertilizers; rather, soils are invigorated by applying manure and by plowing in crop wastes, such as corn stalks and bean vines, and compost.

(A) probably　(B) biologically　(C) basically　(D) automatically

287. Any variety of plant will make the full <u>complement</u> of vitamins it needs, regardless of species.

(A) demand　(B) effect　　(C) replacement　(D) range

288. The frame buffer is <u>nothing more than a</u> giant image memory for viewing a single frame.

(A) increasingly　(B) simply　　(C) paiticularly　(D) instantly

289. The computer computes the positions and colors for ihe figures in the picture, and sends this information to the recorder, which <u>captures</u> it on film.

(A) separates　(B) registers　(C) describes　(D) numbers

290. <u>Once</u> this process is completed, it is repeated for the next frame.

 (A) before   (B) since   (C) after   (D) while

291. Often, computer-animation companies first do motion tests with simple computer-generated line drawings before selling their computers to the <u>task</u> of calculating the high-resolution, realistic-looking images.

 (A) possibility   (B) position   (C) time   (D) job

292. They came to the short-lived colony known as New Sweden, founded in 1638, loose organization and local autonomy <u>fostered</u> a cultural line fusion between native and settler cultures that proved one of the most notable-and least understood-developments of early North American history.

 (A) encouraged   (B) predated   (C) predicted   (D) rejected

293. They came to the short-lived colony known as New Sweden, founded in 1638, loose organization and local autonomy fostered a cultural line fusion between native and settler cultures that proved one of the most <u>notable</u>-and least understood-developments of early North American history.

 (A) social   (B) predictable   (C) remarkable   (D) early

294. But Scandinavian men were familiar with hunting and <u>receptive</u> to learning the hunting methods of the local Native Americans.

 (A) suspicious of   (B) ready for   (C) dependent on   (D) new to

295. The most common symbol of pioneer North America, the log cabin, <u>emerged</u> in the Delaware Valley, and ought to serve as a symbol of this composite culture.

 (A) enlarged   (B) disappeared

 (C) remained   (D) developed

296. Horse-drawn coaches were neither a competitive nor a comfortable alternative given the <u>deplorable</u> slate of the nation's highways; and though bicycles were popular in both town and country, they, too, were hampered by poor road surfaces.

 (A) unusable   (B) worn   (C) awful   (D) difficult

297. Horse-drawn coaches were neither a competitive nor a comfortable alternative given the deplorable slate of the nation's highways; and though bicycles were popular in both town and country, they, too, were <u>hampered</u> by poor road surfaces.

 (A) restrained   (B) supported   (C) favored   (D) damaged

298. However, yellow dyes—whether from weld or some other plant source such as saffron or turmeric, <u>invariably</u> fade or disappear.

 (A) without exception   (B) steadily

 (C) after some time   (D) noticeably

299. The range of natural colors was hugely expanded and, indeed, superseded by the chemical dyes developed during the eighteen hundreds.

(A) strengthened　(B) improved　　(C) replaced　　　(D) complemented

300. Only the relatively small Florida gar, seldom longer than two feet, lives in the Everglades.

(A) slightfy　　(B) similarly　　(C) rarely　　　(D) apparently

301. As with all gars, the Florida gar is predatory and is adept at catching smaller fish from schools by using a fast sideways snap of the jaws.

(A) skilled　　(B) unusual　　(C) alone　　　(D) observed

302. They also have the dual ability to breathe air and water and can be observed regularly rising to the surface of the water to renew the air in their swim bladders.

(A) complex　　(B) useful　　(C) deep　　　(D) double

303. In rougher parts of the inland valleys area and in eastern Oregon prior to the arrival of the horse (first introduced to the area some 300 years ago), it was the principal mode of long-distance travel.

(A) original　　(B) simple　　(C) main　　　(D) ordinary

304. In winter, snowshoes were used for hunting expeditions, ID the Klamath area, where lakes were well stocked with waterfowl and plant products, Native Americans used mudshoes (built similarly to snowshoes) to keep from sinking in the mud.

(A) utilized　　(B) endangered　(C) supplied　　(D) hunted

305. The canoes were expertly carved in a variety of shapes and sizes to ensure a smooth and quiet voyage even in rough waters.

(A) guarantee　(B) decrease　(C) convince　(D) continue

306. Throughout Earth's history, carbon dioxide on Earth has mixed with rain to dissolve rocks; the dissolved rock and carbon dioxide eventually flow into the oceans, where they precipitate to form new terrestrial rocks, often with the help of life-forms.

(A) in the past　(B) first　　(C) ultimately　(D) occasionally

307. If this carbon dioxide were released from the Earth's rocks, along with other carbon dioxide trapped in seawater, our atmosphere would become as dense and have as high a pressure as that of Venus.

(A) caught　　(B) transported　(C) lacking　　(D) involved

308. Sulfuric acid may sound strange as a cloud constituent, but the Earth too has a significant layer of sulfuric acid droplets in its stratosphere.

(A) type　　　　　　　　(B) alternative

(C) product　　　　　　　(D) component

309. In an era when the United States was shifting from an agricultural to an industrially based economy, artists turned to the vitality of the city for their themes, sometimes documenting the lives of the nation's urban inhabitants with a literalness that shocked viewers accustomed to the bland generalizations of academic art.

(A) thoughtless　(B) regulated　(C) false　(D) dull

310. The developments toward realism and new pictorial subject matter introduced by this revolution are explained in part by the fact that the academic spirit had become anathema to many young painters by the beginning of the twentieth century, when the professional survival of an artist was largely contingent on membership in the National Academy of Design, the American equivalent of the French Academy of Arts.

(A) unrelated to　(B) separate from　(C) expanded on　(D) dependent on

311. The National Academy of Design perpetuated the Traditions of the French Academy, such as annual juried exhibitions.

(A) started　(B) influenced　(C) continued　(D) changed

312. Also a fertile period for American photography, the era before the Second World War witnessed the development of photojournalism, as well as social documentary and advertising photography.

(A) opposed　(B) observed　(C) influenced　(D) resulted in

313. Fulfillment in life-as opposed to concern about an afterlife-became a desirable goal, and expressing the entire range of human emotions and enjoying the pleasures of the senses were no longer frowned on.

(A) given up　(B) forgotten about　(C) argued about　(D) disapproved of

314. These changes in outlook deeply affected the musical culture of the Renaissance period—how people thought about music as well as the way music was composed, experienced, discussed, and disseminated.

(A) played　(B) documented　(C) spread　(D) analyzed

315. The thick, woolly fleece of the domestic sheep is its distinguishing feature and the source of much of its economic importance.

(A) quantity　(B) result　(C) basis　(D) cost

316. Much of the selective breeding that led to the fleece types known today took place in prehistory, and even the later developments went largely unchronicled.

(A) unquestioned　(B) unexplained　(C) unnoticed　(D) unrecorded

317. Antique depictions of sheep in sculpture, relief, and painting give even earlier clues to the character of ancient fleeces.

(A) proofs　(B) indications　(C) colors　(D) variations

318. They retain the characteristics of ancient sheep, providing living snapshots of the process that <u>gave rise to</u> modern fleeces.

(A) replaced by　　(B) favored over　　(C) brought about　　(D) found out

319. The <u>strikingly</u> new forms of architecture that appeared in the late nineteenth and twentieth centuries were built to meet the needs of industry and of commerce based on industry, in a society whose essential character and internal relationships had been sharply transformed by the Industrial Revolution.

(A) aggressively　　(B) specifically　　(C) noticeably　　(D) occasionally

320. About the middle of the nineteenth century, mechanized industrial production began to demand large, well-lighted interiors in which manufacturing could be <u>carried on</u>.

(A) conducted　　(B) supervised　　(C) moved about　　(D) improved

321. The marketing of industrial products <u>necessitated</u> large-scale storage spaces, and enormous shops selling under one roof a wide variety of items.

(A) identified　　(B) replaced　　(C) required　　(D) supplied

322. <u>Hence</u>, the characteristic new architectural forms of the late nineteenth and twentieth centuries have been the factory, the multistory office building, the warehouse, the department store, the apartment house, the railway station, the large theater, and the gigantic sports stadium.

(A) moreover　　(B) nevertheless　　(C) in contrast　　(D) for these reasons

323. Famed for their high-elevation forests, the Appalachian Mountains <u>sweep</u> south from Quebec to Alabama.

(A) brush　　(B) extend　　(C) clear　　(D) hurry

324. The Blue Ridge <u>technically</u> includes among its major spurs the Great Smoky Mountains and the Black Mountains; Mount Mitchell, in the latter range, is at 6,684 feet the highest peak east of the Mississippi River.

(A) partially　　(B) similarly　　(C) likely　　(D) officially

325. A rapidly advancing <u>contemporary</u> science that is highly dependent on new tools is Earth system science.

(A) little-known　　(B) informative　　(C) current　　(D) exciting

326. Important new tools that <u>facilitate</u> Earth system science include satellite remote sensing, small deep-sea submarines, and geographic information systems.

(A) enable　　(B) require　　(C) organize　　(D) examine

327. Earth system science was born from the <u>realization</u> of that interdependence.

(A) observation　　(B) assumption

(C) explanation　　(D) recognition

328. New tools for exploring previously <u>inaccessible</u> areas of the Earth have also added greatly to our knowledge of the Earth system.

(A) unreachable　(B) undiscovered　(C) unexplored　(D) unpredictable

329. There they have discovered new species and ecosystems <u>thriving</u> near deep-sea vents that emit heat, sasses, and mineral-rich water.

(A) surviving　　(B) flourishing　　(C) feeding　　(D) competing

330. Often working with no staff at all, these editors wrote copy, set type, delivered papers, <u>oversaw</u> billing, and sold advertising.

(A) estimated　　(B) supervised　　(C) collected　　(D) provided

331. Often working with no staff at all, these editors wrote copy, set type, <u>delivered</u> papers, oversaw billing, and sold advertising.

(A) confirmed　　(B) compared　　(C) questioned　　(D) presented

332. By 1900, Washington <u>boasted</u> 19 daily and 176 weekly papers.

(A) planned　　　　　　　　(B) financed

(C) was forced to close　　　　(D) took pride in having

333. Then came the close-up images obtained by the exploratory spacecraft Voyager 2, and within days, Europa was transformed—in our perception, at least—into one of the solar system's most <u>intriguing</u> worlds.

(A) changing　　(B) perfect　　(C) visible　　(D) fascinating

334. The tides on Europa pull and relax in an <u>endless</u> cycle.

(A) new　　　(B) final　　(C) temporary　　(D) continuous

335. A print may exist in several <u>versions</u>.

(A) ideas　　(B) numbers　　(C) functions　　(D) forms

336. Prints made from linoleum, which wears readily, will be fewer than those made from a metal plate, which is capable of striking fine-quality prints in the thousands. It is <u>customary</u> to number prints as they come off the press, the earlier impressions being the finest and therefore the most desirable.

(A) necessary　　(B) attractive　　(C) legal　　　(D) usual

337. Line, shape, or texture may be the predominant element <u>according to</u> the printing technique used.

(A) in addition to　(B) in order to　　(C) regardless of　　(D) depending on

338. Two of these laws, the Tennessee Valley Authority Act of 1933 and the National Recovery Act of 1933 (NIRA), had particular <u>significance</u> for water resource development.

(A) difference　　(B) disturbance　　(C) importance　　(D) excellence

339. To counter these natural obstacles, the Tennessee Valley Authority Act of 1933 created the Tennessee Valley Authority (TVA), a public agency with broad powers to promote development in the region, including the authority to build dams and reservoirs and to generate and sell hydroelectric power.

(A) explain   (B) measure   (C) exploit   (D) overcome

340. The TVA used its authority to transform the Tennessee River into one of the most highly regulated rivers in the world within about two decades.

(A) clean   (B) change   (C) control   (D) widen

341. The NIRA also gave the United States President unprecedented powers to initiate public works, including water projects.

(A) not extensive   (B) not used often

(C) not existing before   (D) not needing money

342. Stones suitable for use as anvils are not easy to find, and often a chimpanzee may carry a haul of nuts more than 40 meters to find a suitable anvil.

(A) diet   (B) type   (C) load   (D) branch

343. To make a twig more effective for digging out termites, for example, a chimp may first strip it of its leaves.

(A) search   (B) eat   (C) carry   (D) remove

344. This development radically changed the types of sediments that accumulated on the seafloor, because, while the organic parts of the plankton decayed after the organisms died, their mineralized skeletons often survived and sank to the bottom.

(A) depended   (B) matured   (C) dissolved   (D) collected

345. Newbery notwithstanding, Americans still looked on children's books as vehicles for instruction, not amusement, though they would accept a moderate amount of fictional entertainment for the sake of more successful instruction.

(A) in spite of   (B) in addition to   (C) as a result of   (D) as a part o

346. As the children's book market expanded, then, what both public and publishers wanted was the kind of fiction Maria Edgeworth wrote: stories interesting enough to attract children and morally instructive enough to allay adult distrust of fiction.

(A) clarify   (B) attack   (C) reduce   (D) confirm

347. A wave of nationalism permeated everything, and the self-conscious new nation found foreign writings (particularly those from the British monarchy) unsuitable for the children of a democratic republic, a state of self-governing, equal citizens.

(A) opposed   (B) improved

(C) competed with   (D) spread through

348. The characters of children in this fiction were serious, conscientious, self-reflective, and independent <u>testimony to</u> the continuing influence of the earlier American moralistic tradition in children's books.

（A）inspiration for （B）evidence of   （C）requirement for （D）development of

349. The <u>framework</u> of a lichen is usually a network of minute hairlike fungus that anchors the plant.

（A）structure   （B）fragment   （C）condition   （D）environment

350. Lichens, probably the <u>hardiest</u> of all plants, live where virtually nothing else can—not just on rugged mountain peaks but also on sunbaked desert rocks.

（A）most unusual （B）most basic   （C）most abundant （D）most vigorous

351. When water is scarce（as is often the case on a mountain）, lichens may become dormant and remain in that condition for <u>prolonged</u> periods of time.

（A）precise   （B）extended   （C）approximate   （D）regular

352. For decades, scientists wondered how the offspring of an alga and a fungus got together to form a new lichen, it seemed unlikely that they would just happen to <u>encounter</u> one another.

（A）lose   （B）support   （C）meet   （D）create

353. Scholars have deciphered other ancient languages, such as Sumerian, Akkadian, and Babylonian, which used the cuneiform script, because of the <u>fortuitous</u> discovery of bilingual inscriptions.

（A）important   （B）sudden   （C）early   （D）lucky

354. The Rosetta stone <u>thwarted</u> scholars' efforts for several decades until the early nineteenth century when several key hieroglyphic phrases were decoded using the Greek inscriptions.

（A）continued   （B）influenced   （C）encouraged   （D）frustrated

355. Over 25,000 islands are <u>scattered</u> across the surface of the Pacific, more than in all the other oceans combined, but their land area adds up to little more than 125,000 square kilometers, about the size of New York State, and their inhabitants total less than two million people, about a quarter of the number that live in New York City.

（A）widely known   （B）usually estimated
（C）rarely inhabited   （D）irregularly distributed

356. Many are uninhabitable, <u>by virtue of</u> their small size and particular characteristics, but even the most favored are very isolated fragments of land, strictly circumscribed by the ocean, strictly limited in terms of the numbers of people they can support.

（A）regarding   （B）because of
（C）taking advantage of   （D）in place of

357. Many are uninhabitable, by virtue of their small size and particular characteristics, but even the most favored are very isolated fragments of land, strictly <u>circumscribed</u> by the ocean, strictly limited in terms of the numbers of people they can support.

(A) located   (B) flooded   (C) restricted   (D) pushed

358. Simply surviving those ocean crossings of <u>indeterminate</u> length, in open canoes, to arrive on the shores of uninhabited and hitherto unknown islands, was a formidable achievement.

(A) undecided   (B) uncertain   (C) unacceptable   (D) increasing

359. With much of the water vapor already condensed into water and the concentration of carbon dioxide dwindling, the atmosphere <u>gradually</u> became rich nitrogen.

(A) accidentally   (B) quickly   (C) in the end   (D) by degrees

360. A second, more dense atmosphere, however, gradually <u>enveloped</u> Earth as gasses from molten rocks within its hot interior escaped through volcanoes and steam vents.

(A) surrounded   (B) changed   (C) escaped   (D) characterized

361. <u>At any rate</u>, plant growth greatly enriched our atmosphere with oxygen.

(A) regardless   (B) in addition

(C) although unlikely   (D) fortunately

362. The tides on Europa pull and relax in an <u>endless</u> cycle.

(A) new   (B) final   (C) temporary   (D) continuous

363. Although population and sedentary living were increasing at the time, there is little evidence that people lacked <u>adequate</u> wild food resources; the newly domesticated foods supplemented a continuing mixed subsistence of hunting, fishing, and gathering wild plants.

(A) sufficient   (B) healthful   (C) varied   (D) dependable

364. It has been suggested that some early cultivation was for medicinal and ceremonial plants <u>rather than</u> for food.

(A) in addition to   (B) instead of

(C) as a replacement   (D) such as

365. Many ants <u>forage</u> across the countryside in large numbers and undertake mass migrations; these activities proceed because one ant lays a trail on the ground for the others to follow.

(A) look up   (B) walk toward

(C) revolve around   (D) search for food

366. As a worker ant returns home after finding a source of food, it marks the route by <u>intermittently</u> touching its stinger to the ground and depositing a tiny amount of trail

pheromone—a mixture of chemicals that delivers diverse messages as the context changes.

(A) periodically　　(B) incorrectly　　(C) rapidly　　　　(D) roughly

367. A trail pheromone will evaporate to furnish the highest concentration of vapor right over the trail, in what is called a vapor space.

(A) include　　　　(B) provide　　　　(C) cover　　　　(D) select

368. In following the trail, the ant moves to the right and left, oscillating from side to side across the line of the trail itself, bringing first one and then the other antenna into the vapor space.

(A) falling　　　　(B) depositing　　　　(C) swinging　　　　(D) starting

369. Ultimately, literature is aesthetically valued, regardless of language, culture, or mode of presentation, because some significant verbal achievement results from the struggle in words between tradition and talent.

(A) frequently　　　　　　　　(B) normally

(C) whenever possible　　　　　(D) in the end

370. Verbal art has the ability to shape out a compelling inner vision in some skillfully crafted public verbal form.

(A) joyous　　　　(B) intricate　　　　(C) competing　　　　(D) forceful

371. They have shown exceptional imagination in applying the diverse forms of contemporary art to a wide variety of purposes.

(A) remarkable　　(B) fearless　　　　(C) expert　　　　(D) visible

372. The specialized requirements of particular urban situations have further expanded the use of art in public places: in Memphis, sculptor Richard Hunt has created a monument to Martin Luther King, Jr., who was slain there; in New York, Dan Flavin and Bill Brand have contributed neon and animation works to the enhancement of mass transit facilities.

(A) replacement　　(B) design　　　　(C) improvement　　(D) decoration

373. And in numerous cities, art is being raised as a symbol of the commitment to revitalize urban areas.

(A) show the importance of　　　　(B) promise to enlarge

(C) bring new life to　　　　　　　(D) provide artworks for

374. Artists are recognizing the distinction between public and private spaces, and taking that into account when executing their public commissions.

(A) judging　　　　　　　　(B) selling

(C) explaining　　　　　　　(D) producing

375. When the putrefied material is examined microscopically, it is found to be <u>teeming with</u> bacteria.

  （A）full of   （B）developing into （C）resistant to   （D）hurt by

376. Pasteur showed that structures present in air closely <u>resemble</u> the microorganisms seen in putrefying materials.

  （A）benefit from   （B）appear similar to

  （C）join together with   （D）grow from

377. He <u>postulated</u> that these bodies are constantly being deposited on all objects.

  （A）analyzed   （B）doubted   （C）persuaded   （D）suggested

378. In the minds of agrarian thinkers and writers, the farmer was a person on whose well-being the health of the new country <u>depended</u>.

  （A）improved   （B）relied   （C）demanded   （D）explained

379. And virtually all policy makers, whether they <u>subscribed to</u> the tenets of the philosophy held by Jefferson or not, recognized agriculture as the key component of the American economy.

  （A）contributed to （B）agreed with   （C）thought about   （D）expanded on

380. Farmers streamed to the West, filling frontier lands with <u>stunning</u> rapidity.

  （A）predictable   （B）impressive   （C）famous   （D）gradual

381. The wide variety of climates in North America has helped <u>spawn</u> a complex pattern of soil regions.

  （A）distinguish   （B）eliminate   （C）protect   （D）create

382. In general, the realm's soils also reflect the broad environmental <u>partitioning</u> into "humid America" and "arid America."

  （A）division   （B）modification   （C）opening   （D）circulating

383. Glaciation also <u>enhanced</u> the rich legacy of fertile soils in the central United States, both from the deposition of mineral-rich glacial debris left by meltwater and from thick layers of fine wind-blown glacial material, called loess, in and around the middle Mississippi Valley.

  （A）implied   （B）increased   （C）indicated   （D）informed

384. The forests of North America tend to make a broad <u>transition</u> by latitude.

  （A）elevation   （B）change   （C）advantage   （D）condition

385. When the bag was <u>ignited</u>, the metal burned with an intense flash.

  （A）set on fire   （B）cut into   （C）opened   （D）shaken

386. The <u>evolution</u> of the photoflash was slow, flashbulbs, containing fine wire made of a metal, such as magnesium or aluminum, capable of being ignited in an atmosphere of

pure oxygen at low pressure, were introduced only in the 1920's.

(A) publicity   (B) adoption   (C) development   (D) manufacture

387. In each case enough energy is given out to heat the oxidizable metal <u>momentarily</u> to a white-hot emission of visible light.

(A) effortlessly   (B) briefly   (C) electronically   (D) gradually

388. The Impressionists wanted to <u>depict</u> what they saw in nature, but they were inspired to portray fragmentary moments by the increasingly fast pace of modern life.

(A) reorganize   (B) deform   (C) represent   (D) justify

389. For example, the shift from the studio to the open air was made possible in part by the <u>advent</u> of cheap rail travel, which permitted easy and quick access to the countryside or seashore, as well as by newly developed chemical dyes and oils that led to collapsible paint tubes, which enabled artists to finish their paintings on the spot.

(A) achievement   (B) acceptance   (C) arrival   (D) advantage

390. Among the 165 paintings exhibited was one called Impression: Sunrise, by Claude Monet（1840-1926),Viewed through hostile eyes, Monet's painting of a rising sun over a misty, watery scene seemed messy, slapdash, and an <u>affront</u> to good taste.

(A) insult   (B) encouragement   (C) return   (D) credit

391. By far the most important United States export product in the eighteenth and nineteenth centuries was cotton, <u>favored</u> by the European textile industry over flax or wool because it was easy to process and soft to tile touch.

(A) preferred   (B) recommended   (C) imported   (D) included

392. Cotton could be grown throughout the South, but separating the fiber—or lint—from the seed was a <u>laborious</u> process.

(A) unfamiliar   (B) primitive   (C) skilled   (D) difficult

393. The interaction of improved processing and high demand led to the rapid spread of the cultivation of cotton and to a <u>surge</u> in production.

(A) sharp increase   (B) sudden stop
(C) important change   (D) excess amount

394. The growing market for cotton and other American agricultural products led to an <u>unprecedented</u> expansion of agricultural settlement, mostly in the eastern half of the United States—west of the Appalachian Mountains and east of the Mississippi River.

(A) slow   (B) profitable   (C) not seen before   (D) never explained

395. The origins of nest-building remain <u>obscure</u>, but current observation of nest-building activities provide evidence of their evolution.

(A) interesting   (B) unclear   (C) imperfect   (D) complex

396. Birds also <u>display</u> remarkable behavior in collecting building materials.

(A) communicate　(B) imitate　　　(C) initiate　　　(D) exhibit

397. The carrying capacity of the eagles, however, is only relative to their size and most birds are able to carry an extra <u>load</u> of just over twenty percent of their body weight.

(A) weight　　(B) number　　(C) section　　　(D) level

398. A survey must be based on a <u>precise</u>, representative sampling if it is to genuinely reflect a broad range of the population.

(A) planned　　(B) rational　　(C) required　　(D) accurate

399. In preparing to conduct a survey, sociologists must <u>exercise</u> great care in the wording of questions.

(A) utilize　　(B) consider　　(C) design　　　(D) defend

400. Even questions that are less structured must be carefully phrased in order to <u>elicit</u> the type of information desired.

(A) compose　　(B) rule out　　(C) predict　　(D) bring out

答案

1~10	AABCB DBCBC	201~210	AADCA ABABC
11~20	ACCAB DABDB	211~220	CCBBC CBDAC
21~30	DBDAB CDBBD	221~230	DBBDA ADCBC
31~40	CCACB DADCA	231~240	BCCBA DCCBC
41~50	CCCAB CABCA	241~250	ADDBB AABCD
51~60	BADAC DCACB	251~260	DDABC BDDAB
61~70	CDCBB AAABA	261~270	CBCDC ACCCB
71~80	ACBCC BDDCD	271~280	DCDDA BCDCA
81~90	ACABA DDCBB	281~290	ACDBA CDBBC
91~100	DCCBC ABACC	291~300	DACBD CAACC
101~110	CADAC CCDBA	301~310	ADCCA CADDD
111~120	ABCCB ACDBD	311~320	CBDCC DACCA
121~130	AADBB DAABB	321~330	CDBDC ADABB
131~140	DCDAA ADABB	331~340	DDDDD DDCDB
141~150	ABCAD ADAAC	341~350	CCDDA CDBAD
151~160	ABDCD BCABB	351~360	BCDDD BCBDA
161~170	ABBDC ADCAC	361~370	ADABD ABCDD
171~180	ACDDA DDAAB	371~380	ACCDA BDBBB
181~190	CCBCB ADBDB	381~390	DABBA CBCCA
191~200	BCBDA ADBAC	391~400	ADACB DADAD